FREEDOM AND REFORM

Essays in Honor of
HENRY STEELE COMMAGER

FREEDOM

WITH CONTRIBUTIONS BY

RICHARD B. MORRIS

ALLAN NEVINS

LEONARD W. LEVY

MILTON CANTOR

WILSON SMITH

JOHN D. WRIGHT, JR.

AUGUST MEIER

HAROLD M. HYMAN

MARIAN McKENNA

ARTHUR W. THOMPSON

SAUL BENISON

CHARLES E. LARSEN

WILLIAM E. LEUCHTENBURG

AND REFORM

Essays in Honor of
Henry Steele Commager

EDITED BY

Harold M. Hyman and Leonard W. Levy

HARPER & ROW, PUBLISHERS

NEW YORK, EVANSTON, AND LONDON

FIRST EDITION

LIBRARY OF CONGRESS CATALOG CARD NUMBER: 67-22521

I-R

Contents

Preface

This volume of essays is a birthday present for Henry Steele Commager. His friends and former doctoral students, including those who were unable to offer contributions of their own within these covers, honor him by joining in this expression of our professional admiration, personal affection, and sheer gratitude for having had the opportunity of coming under his influence. He has been a vital force in all our lives. No one who knows him expects that his unremitting ardor will diminish now that he has reached his sixty-fifth birthday or when he eventually retires formally from campus weights. Instead, the prophecy comes easily that Professor Commager will remain a center of where action is, a happening, a phenomenon composed of impressive depths of knowledge, astonishing breadths of interests, and rich reserves of talent and energy.

When such an implacable rationalist as Henry Commager becomes the subject of prophecy, supporting evidence must be convincing and close at hand. After all, he is the first to rip and rend whatever lacks adequate proofs. Veterans of Professor Commager's seminars remember with visceral vividness both his magisterial criticism and his awesome familiarity with appropriate sources. Imagine the impact when, mentor and student disagreeing about point of fact or derivative conclusion, Professor Commager burrowed in one of the several layered sediments of books, articles, newspapers, and court reports that made up the interior decoration of his Fayerweather office-seminar room, and emerged with precisely relevant information with which to stun the student—but sometimes, also, to sustain him. Little wonder that recollection should be vivid!

Further to justify a prediction of continuing activity on the part of such a man, Professor Commager, the classroom teacher, requires consideration. During his years at Columbia, when most of the contributors to this volume first experienced him, Morningside Heights' lecture landscape was graced with the presence of a pride of outstanding teacher-scholars. Among these, Commager and his constitutional history course attained a formidable height. Over the years, thousands of undergraduates and graduate students climbed it. The ascent was never easy. But it was always worth the effort. Commager repaid their attention, reading, and thinking, with bold, provocative ideas. He excited students with his own excitement about the past. His lectures, so often compelling, had a distinctive style. There was a certain grandeur about them, and they left listeners with an awareness of significant questions as well as answers that were always suggestive and sometimes shaking. On campuses or off (and he maintained a busy schedule of off-campus lecturing) Professor Commager spoke down to no audience, and he accepted from no source constrictions on what he wished to say or to write. Taken together, Henry Commager the teacher-lecturer was a movable feast. He drew up a menu from America's rich constitutional-political history which he found so engaging, and of which he was so critical. Out of his warm fondness for America as promise, he sang praises of achievements; out of his disappointment with America's achievements, he damned its bigots, knaves, and villains, and rang out the perils and promises of freedom. He has done so with vividness, eloquence, and distinction, during a teaching career that has now covered more than four decades. From 1926 to 1938, he taught at New York University; from 1939 to 1956 at Columbia University; and since then at Amherst College. In addition, he has probably lectured in most states of the Union and has graced the foremost lectureships of several European countries as well as of Israel and Chile. He has also served as Pitt Professor of American History at Cambridge University and as Harmsworth Professor of American History at Oxford University.

Henry Commager's career as scholar-writer further buttresses the prediction that his retirement, when it comes, will be nominal only, a preparation for further impacts, a tactical movement rather than a halt. A list of Professor Commager's publications appears elsewhere in this volume. Suffice it to say here that these publications span more than three decades, include more than four hundred items,[1]* and have earned him election to the National Academy of Arts and Letters and the even more selective American Academy of Arts and Letters.

No less than his seminars and lectures, his writings speak to his concerns, to employ the marvelously appropriate Quaker phrase. Professor Commager's concerns were, are, and predictably will be, America's bedrock performance as a free society. "It is surprising, almost disconcerting," he wrote recently in a mood of candid self-evaluation, "to look back from the perspective of over thirty years and discover how early you entered on those paths which you have long trod so familiarly, how long you have been preoccupied with these problems which still, in one way or another, excite your interest and stir your imagination, and require your participation."

These paths now so familiar came always to crossroads, both past and present, where freedom and reform conflicted with standpat or retrograde individuals, institutions, and interests. "Freedom as a method"—his phrase—was, is, and will be Professor Commager's touchstone for the past, present, and future: his "can't help but believes." After a recent rereading of some of his topical essays preparatory to reprinting them, Commager remarked that he was ". . . struck anew with the way in which the old familiar problems emerge in new guise, in which old and new arguments are directed into new channels."[2] Loyalty-security programs, thrusts against academic freedom, censorship, and other egregious manifestations of paranoid politics, plague Americans in the mid-1960's as in the late 1940's and early '50's. To be sure, improvement is discernible; as Professor Commager agrees, the enhanced vigor of the Supreme Court and other libertarian guardians in matters of race, representation, and restrictions on free speech has helped to redress balances. But other forces apply negative tugs. Viet Nam has replaced Korea as a focus for passion. John Birchers fit footprints which the late Joe McCarthy left in the substrata of political immorality and popular ignorance about history. Once more the University of California endures external attack and suffers internal upsets. But analogous tensions plagued Americans in the 1790's, the 1860's, and other times of our history. Professor Commager's wide-ranging interests, unending concerns, and effective scholarship have helped to illuminate all these dark corners in the nation's past.

Predictably, he will continue to insist that men employ lessons from the past in the service of the present's wants and the future's aspirations. Therefore, the prophecy holds that the years will catch up with him in the spirit of Lincoln's order to a sluggard general to make "a good ready" for imminent offensives. As always, Henry Commager will tilt at politicians and professors, scholars and statesmen, who are guilty of foggy thinking, deficient techniques, and undemocratic values.

The essays which follow are, then, an expression of thanks to him, from persons who one way or another have benefited from connection with this engaging, significant man. Two contributors —Richard B. Morris and Allan Nevins—were for many years his faculty colleagues and were partners also in discrete literary enterprises. Two others—Saul Benison and Marian McKenna—took their degrees with mentors other than Professor Commager, but, because they had profited from his guidance and inspiration, they asked for places in this volume, symbols, as it were, of many others of like association. All the other contributions are by Professor Commager's former doctoral students. We remember sometimes wincingly that he never learned to suffer anything short of intellectual rectitude, of which he was a model. If he sometimes seemed irascible and cutting, it was because he always demanded the utmost of which we were capable and never confused impersonal professional standards with his personal feelings toward us. He was, we remember fondly, an avuncular friend and adviser— warm, exhilarating, gracious, and impetuously generous with his time, his influence on our behalf, his affection, and even, when necessary, his pocketbook. During our graduate-student days, we felt that we were privileged to work under his direction. Now we know that we were.

In words uncannily appropriate for this volume, Professor Commager noted in the preface to the recent retrospective of his own work, "Instead of saying that these papers have a 'philosophical' unity it might be better to say that they seem to express a pretty consistent point of view." Further, Professor Commager even supplied a statement for this volume of tributary essays, of the theme which undergirds his own work as it does ours. All of his essays, he wrote, ". . . are addressed to the overarching problem of the reconciliation of liberty and order in a world troubled, as ours is, by the eccentricities of both. They deal with the claims of freedom as a method of working out solutions to intractable problems, with political institutions and practices. . . . They concern themselves with the national character—if there is such a thing—as a product of historical and social experience."[3]

As is true of the mentor, Professor Commager's former students have wide-ranging scholarly interests. But, like him, the disciples have held to broad central concerns. Freedom is a recurring element in the essays which follow; reform—even reform in medical research—is the parallel avenue which freedom sometimes has allowed Americans to travel, and which, at other times, has been clogged dangerously with impediments, obfuscations, and pitfalls. The themes of freedom and reform, then, unify and inform the apparent diversity of our essays.

All who are represented here offer Henry Commager their appreciation for past associations and present inspirations. We offer also our cordial best wishes on his sixty-fifth birthday and for his subsequent career, easily foreseeable as the fruitful continuation of what has gone before.

HAROLD M. HYMAN
LEONARD W. LEVY

FREEDOM AND REFORM

RICHARD B. MORRIS

The View from the Top of Fayerweather

I SHALL NEVER FORGET THAT DAY. It was in the spring of '56.
My lecture over, I had returned to my office some time after 5 P.M.
The sixth floor of Fayerweather Hall was deserted. My eyes casually took in the unattractive heap of unanswered correspondence
strewn over my desk and picked out a small white envelope on
which were typed the letters "DICK." Casually, almost indiffer-
ently, I opened it. It was from Henry Commager informing me
that he had just notified the Trustees that he had resigned from
Columbia to accept a post at Amherst, and that his decision was
irrevocable.

My initial reaction was of shocked disbelief. Those were the days
when giants bestrode the sixth floor, and Henry Commager walked
with giant strides. On the Columbia campus Commager stood out
almost like a historic landmark. One might just as well imagine
Columbia without the Low Library or St. Paul's Chapel. For the
scholarly world of Morningside Heights Commager's going would
mean an intellectual loss, but for me the loss would be much more
personal. True, real friendships can survive distance, and this one
has, but it seemed to me to have been more than fortuitous that
Henry Commager and I occupied adjacent offices. Since my own
coming to the Columbia faculty a decade earlier we had shared
students, ideas, projects, and enthusiasms. Our doors were always
open to the other's students, and we offered such comfort and gave
such reassurance as we could to each other's Ph.D. candidates, rid-

1

dled with the special anxieties which each generation of graduate students bears, in their case accentuated by the weak market for college teachers in those days.

In my mind's eye that afternoon an assortment of scenes passed in kaleidoscopic array—Henry Commager entering a room, suit rumpled, locks tousled, a gently sardonic smile twisting his mouth to one side, one arm piled high with books, the other clutching an assortment of mail, *Congressional Records*, and at least one nice fat dissertation. What immediately struck the observer was not the juggling skills of which the entrant was past master, but that teeming energy and zest for life of which he seemed the very incarnation.

When the poet Wordsworth recounted that he had "felt a presence that disturbs me with the joy of elevated thoughts," he must have conjured up outside Tintern Abbey a presence like that of Henry Commager. Commager has always possessed a special talent for transmuting even a trivial or commonplace observation into a generalization of more universal application, of brightening the drabbest moment with both wit and witticisms, and of puncturing wordiness with deft and incisive characterization.

As an examiner on constitutional history, Commager's presence was indeed felt. His very sniff would send shivers up the spines of candidates so unfortunate as to be less than adequately prepared in that dread field. They knew that his sniff was a portent of some very searching questions to come. Indeed, it was common gossip in those days that students indicating their preference in day and hours for their orals would make a point of checking Commager's teaching schedule, and then pick a time when he was lecturing. Such ingenious detective work just to take their chances with a less fearsome inquisitor!

Like so much other academic gossip this piece must be taken *cum grano salis*, for it does little justice to the man. Fearsome though Henry Commager's exterior may have seemed to some Ph.D. candidates, his own students knew him to be the kindest of men, deeply concerned with their personal problems, inexorably fixed on having them write English prose and eschewing academic jabberwocky which too often serves as a cover-up for a paucity of ideas. Commager's students were constantly reminded by their master that history was a respectable branch of belles lettres, but that knowledge did not give them license to ignore rigorous scientific methodology.

Other scenes came to mind that afternoon: The History faculty crowded into Commager's office for the traditional glass of sherry before the more formal departmental dinner meeting at the Faculty Club—Henry with Evan and the children (I know this dates me!) in their sprawling but comfortable Rye home, listening to a new recording—Henry and Cass Canfield of Harper & Row, using all the rich resources of the Century Association bar, along with their own distinctive brand of charm, to induce me to come in as a co-editor of the multivolume *New American Nation* series—Henry and I completely filling my small crowded study in Mount Vernon, going through our early draft of the *Encyclopedia of American History*—Henry, in the old Bobbs-Merrill offices in Indianapolis, hammering out brilliant editorial notes for his sections of *The Spirit of '76*—Henry, after an editorial conference on a *New American Nation* proffered manuscript, turning to me and remarking, "I wonder who wrote his first book."

Most of these images centered on the room next door to mine— that long, rectangular office lined with books from floor to ceiling. Other books tumbled in unsightly piles on the floor, while alongside lay unopened cartons of more books ordered from enticing booksellers' catalogues from Copenhagen, Leipzig, and Cambridge. Near the single off-centered window stood a large oaken desk, letters and manuscript heaped in disarray. (Henry never lost a manuscript, but it once took two years to uncover from that pile the typescript of a *New American Nation* book sent on to him for approval by a distinguished contributor!)

Students barged in at all hours, but amid the scholarly confusion and academic disorder I still see Henry Commager, back to the window, punching away furiously on his antique portable the first and final draft of still another brilliant essay for the *Sunday Times*, noble prose, logically structured, persuasively argued, packing the wallop of a demolition bomb. For Henry Commager no elaborate note-card system, no key-sort or IBM cards. A fabulous memory drawing upon an enormous range of reading could be counted on to come up with apt quotations, pertinent historical allusions, and a veritable outpouring of choice morsels from the world of arts and letters.

All this furious but disciplined energy found outlets in brilliant lectures on Columbia's campus and on a hundred others, in peripatetic operations abroad, in luminous essays and perceptive book reviews, in studies in depth of the American mind and the American character, in illuminating anthologies and significant editorial contributions. Still, neither singly nor in combination did these scholarly activities add up to the end result, the image of Henry Commager on Morningside Heights. To the academic community Henry had by the mid-1950's become the personification of the American conscience. To understand the things that made him what he has become one has to understand the American Enlightenment, whose notable men hardly conformed to any criterion of the average. One has to appreciate that devotion to the classics and that special cast of political thinking which Commager shares with the men of Jefferson's generation. But to at least an equal extent his mind and outlook have been shaped by the examples of the men of conscience of the nineteenth century, by Emerson, Thoreau, Theodore Parker, and James Russell Lowell.

What gives Henry Commager his distinctive style is that he is an authentic Jeffersonian liberal whose passionate humanism has survived the onslaughts of totalitarian repression, governmental centralization, and technological revolution. Though a Jeffersonian, he concedes, maybe with some misgivings, the validity of Hamiltonian notions of the necessity of big government in our time. To maintain liberty in the Leviathan state requires eternal vigilance, he constantly reminds us, and in the post-World War II years Henry Commager kept the vigil for liberty.

Dedicated to the majority rule which is the basis of democratic society but no less concerned with minority rights, Henry Commager in the years when he was at Columbia hurled his barbed literary darts at the Smith and McCarran Acts, while he saved for the Loyalty Program and McCarthyism the full brunt of his attack. Since World War II he has insistently reminded us of the need to safeguard the freedom to inquire, to travel, to criticize, and to dissent and to be free from censorship. An academic generation which sheepishly conformed took heart from Commager's reiterated conviction that freedom was a method, "probably the only method, of avoiding error and arriving at truth." A new academic generation has embraced this doctrine and has been emboldened to speak out. Although the sounds emanating from the New Left may be inspired as much from self-centered nihilism as from moral conviction, it is a tribute to men like Henry Commager that once more young people can be aroused over moral issues. Assuredly Henry Commager must take comfort from the new fervor heating up our college campuses, because as an American historian he would be the first to remind us that we were once a young nation led by young Patriots who took us down the road of revolution, crowning the first successful feat of decolonization in modern times by framing a Constitution which has proven to be the most durable of all modern instruments of government.

Standing at my desk that spring afternoon a decade ago, I could appraise the dimension of the loss, but had no special qualifications to foretell the things to come. We at Columbia have always had a very special feeling about Henry as I know he still has about Columbia. He came back to us on frequent visits as an Adjunct Professor and Speranza Lecturer, and while the ties may be attenuated they will never be sundered. The new moral commitments which our students share with others on campuses throughout the length and breadth of the land owe more to Henry Commager than any computer could possibly measure.

Every morning when I enter my office I am reminded of Henry Commager. On one wall are three Daumier prints, satirical delineations of judges and lawyers as puffed-up guardians of the status quo. It is as though the face of Henry Commager were to grace the wall instead of these striking drawings, for Daumier, like Commager, had no truck with cant, and, were he alive today, would be as withering in portraying the moral hypocrisies of our time as he was of his own. Above all, Daumier shared with Commager the two great virtues of intellectual honesty and tolerance of change.

Yes, from the top of Fayerweather we look back in fond recollection as we recall the days when Commager dwelt among us.

ALLAN NEVINS

Henry S. Commager as Historian:
An Appreciation

IT IS IMPOSSIBLE TO UNDERSTAND Henry Steele Commager as a historian unless one knows something of the man: his kinetic moods, his rapid flow of thought, his effervescent ideas, his insights, and his strongly partisan feelings on many subjects historic and current. He is almost a modern Hazlitt. Like that great essayist, he has wide-ranging intellectual gifts, and like him he is essentially a romantic—although in some mundane affairs, like keeping an eye upon publishers and their accounts, he can be sternly realistic. Like Hazlitt again he is equally interested in the past and the present, and knows well how to make the one shed illumination upon the other. This knowledge is a prime requisite in the equipment of a journalist, and by no means unimportant in the arsenal of a historian. It should be added that, despite his quickness of mind and romantic mutability of mood, he is a man of principle. Readers feel a moral pulse beating beneath even his blandest prose, and in writing both of old issues and present-day enigmas he is impatient of expediency and scornful of casuistry.

Not that much scorn enters into his writings, for his primary trait of mind and temperament is his capacity for enthusiasm. This is where he most nearly touches Hazlitt, who had a tremendous gusto for books, men, and causes. Henry S. Commager has an unfailing enthusiasm for political leaders in the Jeffersonian tradition. He could never be enthusiastic for coon-skin Jacksonians past or present, and was tolerant rather than enthusiastic about the rootless

6

intellectualism of the Wilsonian school. For true Jeffersonians down to FDR and Harry Truman, however, he has the deep feeling that Vernon L. Parrington had. The same gusto is manifest in his allegiance to some select causes, like civil liberties at home and international peace abroad. All enthusiasts are subject to contradictions, and he has not escaped them. But the important fact is that he is no neutralist, no Laodicean. When he likes books, as he likes Francis Parkman and Jane Austen, he likes them enormously. When he likes the ideas of de Tocqueville, Joseph Story, and Felix Frankfurter, he enunciates a heady loyalty. When he takes up a cause like some phase of the dignity of man, it is with fervor almost volcanic.

From his steady flow of ideas, his enthusiasms, and his marked likes (including a strong Anglophilism in books, manners, and outlook) and dislikes (including the huge, tawdry side of our politics), has naturally gushed a stream of miscellaneous writings. Its volume, in book-reviews, newspaper articles, magazine essays, and lectures, is phenomenal; its quality is unvaryingly high. "You should keep your eye upon this young man," Jacob Zeitlin said to me early in the 1930's; "those reviews of his in *Herald-Tribune Books* are astonishingly good; he would grace Columbia"—Zeitlin little guessing how far I had anticipated this advice. It should be realized that his historical books are as closely allied with this general production as the great books of Macaulay, Bagehot, and Froude were allied with their incessant magazine contributions. Here again Henry S. Commager reminds us of Hazlitt, though he makes no pretension to the critical genius of Hazlitt. The value of his great body of book-reviewing (for years he was a main pillar of *Books*) lay beyond the moment. It gave him, as such work gave John Fiske and James Truslow Adams, familiarity with a tremendous number of books old and new, so that he became one of our best-read historians. At the same time it gave him the capacity to distill into a thousand words the essence of a thoughtful volume, just as his essays on current affairs helped him to an analytical mastery of complex political and social developments.

His historical writings do not fit into neat patterns, as the work of most of the industrious modern historians from Hume and Vico onward has fitted. His books, as his temperament dictates, have come from him by spurts, responding to isolated impulses. At one time he appeared likely to throw his talents into biography. A little later he seemed disposed to turn to legal and constitutional history, in which he taught one of the most valuable courses ever given in Columbia University—a course to which students in law, government, and history alike flocked. Still later it was the history of ideas that most attracted him. The result of this moving focus has been a happy variety of volumes. They reflect his many-sided interest in life. Once when, on my yielding to some government assignment, I remarked to him, "Life is more important than books," I was astonished by the energy of his response: "Hear! Hear!" As life changes and history moves into new areas his response to the mutation has a proper logic.

In dealing with his many books, one fact should be pointed out at the beginning, before considering their scholarship, solidity of judgment, and literary distinction. This is his instinct for the fundamentals of historical study. He has been co-author of much the ablest and most finished basic summation of our history yet written. He has also been the most expert compiler and editor of the essential documents of that history, and of the most illuminating descriptive and narrative papers upon its course, ever brought together. This is a much larger achievement than some people realize—the achievement of a historian-educator of the first rank. His handiwork has been part and parcel of the training of many millions in the meaning of the American past, and his influence will endure in this training for decades to come.

No American has ever written a work equal to John Richard Green's *Short History of the English People*, which had an unequalled international success from the moment it was published in 1874, and is still widely read as an assured classic. Its merit was that it brought every side of British life into a complete narrative, with the people as hero, and the progress of thought the cable binding all the chapters together. Various Americans from Woodrow Wilson to Charles A. Beard have attempted a similar feat. The one book that merits comparison with Green's is Morison and Commager's *Growth of the American Republic* as it appears in its latest editions, for it has been steadily improved in thought, factual accuracy, and style as it has been augmented in length and depth. The first single-volume edition in 1930 dealt with the years 1763–1917. The fifth edition in 1962 covered, in a total of some 1800 pages, our record from the appearance of man in North America to the first acts and policies of President Kennedy. The prefatory promise was fully redeemed: "We believe that history embraces the whole of a people's activity: economic and social, literary and spiritual, as well as political and military."

The sweep of the story is matched by the vigor and eloquence of the style. The authors have identified their respective contributions, Morison being responsible for nearly all the first volume and Commager for nearly all the second, though each does some war chapters of his own in the other's book. They have doubtless given one another many facts, ideas, and interpretive touches. It need not be said that Morison's style is as felicitous as his learning is capacious and his ideas original. He marches down from Leif to 1860 with sure tread. Who but he would be likely to adorn the tale with a sentence like this? "Jefferson and Hamilton typified Goethe's two eternal spirits that contend for the government of all that men do or say: the spirit that creates and the spirit that denies, the hope that man can raise himself through the ages a little nearer God, and the mocking doubt that human nature can ever change its ways."

As for Commager's volume, it is particularly good on social change and intellectual growth, though it loses none of the excitement of our political combats or the epic thrust of the industrialization of an agricultural country. The chapter on "The American Mind During Reconstruction," ranging from the Currier & Ives lithographs to Godkin's *Nation*, from the Tweed Ring to the Greek scholarship of Gildersleeve, from McGuffey's Readers to H. H. Richardson's architecture, evokes a wide scene in vivid colors. The chapter on "Philosophy, Art, and Letters" in the decades around the turn of the century is equally effective. Although treatment of recent years is especially difficult, the analysis of cultural tendencies since Hiroshima is thorough and stimulating, if perhaps too optimistic in its emphasis on various types of renaissance in the arts. Yet nothing is neglected. Was the dropping of the first atomic bomb justified? The affirmative answer (in this instance no doubt mainly delivered by Morison but stamped by Commager's approval) could not be better given in one page than here. Just who was responsible for the defeat of the League? What did the Armory Show in New York accomplish? Henry S. Commager is particularly skillful in importing quotations from the novelists and poets into the narrative, lending touches of opal and gold to what most writers paint grayly.

Not on the same level with this, but a chunk of solid granite shoved underneath it, is the indispensable *Documents of American History*, which when it first appeared in 1934 received a wide salvo of applause as by far the most ambitious effort yet made to bring into a single volume the essential written sources upon our political, legal, and economic past. This again showed the instinct of Henry S. Commager for the fundamentals of historical study. The work grew, taking in laws, treaties, judicial decisions, party platforms, and memorable speeches, until the second edition of nearly 1100 pages (1940) met still warmer commendation. It was an indispensable volume for all general libraries, schools, colleges, and editorial or professorial desks. The text was impeccable, the editorial apparatus just right.

And this volume of documents had greater significance in that it reflected an impulse that was to be richly expressed in book after book assembled by Henry S. Commager—and some of them assembled as no other man could have done it. This was the impulse to illustrate our history, in all its variety and color, by writings drawn from the most veracious sources bearing on the life of the people: the letters, the chronicles, the diaries, the novels, the verse, and the more authentic bits of folklore. Nobody else of the time, we repeat, could have done it so well, for no other man so combined the wide reading necessary with the skill in literary craftsmanship. When *The Heritage of America* appeared in 1939, a rich collection of selections upon our civilization from the beginnings to the present, Stephen Vincent Benét made a just comment upon its variety: "Here is the stream, with its eddies and its turbulence, with queer straws floating in it and a few lasting landmarks, the stream of American history." This, once more a work of collaboration, was but the first of a series of collections that no student would care to do without.

Some would say that the most stimulating of them is *America in Perspective*, which made a timely appearance just as the nation emerged from the Second World War. It was intended as a contribution to thought and analysis rather than knowledge, and its penetrating introduction offered the editor's own conclusions upon

America as a land of continuous and hopeful experimentation. The selections chosen ranged from Crèvecoeur to Denis Brogan, and perhaps gave too cheerful a set of commentaries on the republic, glossing over the poverty and violence though not the vulgarity; but this was the fault of the commentators. A companion volume, *Living Ideas in America*, which came out in the year of Adlai E. Stevenson's unsuccessful first run for the Presidency, might almost have been considered a contribution to his campaign, so strongly did its excerpts from essays, speeches, letters, memoirs, and other papers sound the Jeffersonian note. It had enduring value in its insistence upon the value of independent thought and liberal attitudes.

Very different and of much greater value to the conventional historian and all general students of history were two massive treasuries of historical material, much of it little known, which grew out of the deep interest of Henry S. Commager in wartime history, social as well as military. The first of these, *The Blue and the Gray: The Story of the Civil War as Told by Participants*, so completely met a great need that it had a sustained appeal. Douglas Freeman told audiences that it was the best introduction to the war that the general reader could find. The same view was expressed by Avery Craven, declaring that the 450-odd personal narratives by statesmen, generals, privates, nurses, home-front workers, war correspondents, and others "have the force of the immediate and the vividness of proximity." In a thoughtful introduction Henry S. Commager pointed out that the war was by no means all fighting. "It was public opinion, it was the draft, it was prison and hospital, it was ordnance and supplies, it was politics and elections, and even play." He preferred to quote people who had been in the thick of the struggle, who had felt what Holmes called "the crush of Arctic ice." So well are these 1100 pages knit together by the interesting commentary of Henry S. Commager and his notes, that although the work is simply materials for history, it has the coherence, emphasis, and force of history itself.

Not quite as much can be said for the sister volumes called *The Spirit of '76: The Story of the American Revolution as Told by Participants*, for the original narratives of the War for Independence are less numerous, comprehensive, and compelling. This work, however, can also be called indispensable for the earnest student of the period treated. It is almost a portable library, completely edited, and containing much that anybody without access to large city collections would miss. Published in two volumes in 1958, with the collaboration of Richard B. Morris, it was reissued in one volume in time for the beginning of the bicentennial commemorations of the Revolution.

But in listing all these books, some students would say, we have not really touched the best of Henry S. Commager the restless, hardworking historian, who can often be both thoughtful and sparkling. They would be correct in asserting that his most original work lies elsewhere. It lies in the three of his books best known to professional historians and the multitude of earnest students in our universities and colleges. The three titles are utterly different from each other in kind and aim, but alike in spirit, for each exhibits his characteristic *brio* and ardor, and each deals with a special side of our past with a full consciousness of the other sides.

The first to appear was his *Theodore Parker*, a biography so much alive when it came out in 1936 that anyone cutting into its compressed vitality would have drawn blood. It was Henry S. Commager's salute to Emersonian New England, a country in which he was as spiritually at home as in Jeffersonian Virginia. In addition, it was a salute to all the freedoms and insurgencies for which the eloquent preacher and fighter had stood; abolition, the purification of religion from superstition and cant, and the righting of many an antique wrong. Finally, it was a personal salute to the kind of man who was a very hardheaded thinker and precise scholar, and yet at the same time an eloquent idealist, full of fire and poetry. Its portrait of Parker, done in loving detail, was lifelike. Its narrative of struggle and conflict in the Avernus-bound America of the 1850's was exciting enough to stir the imagination and sympathy of every sensitive reader. Over the years it still holds its place.

The book drew an adventitious interest from the fact that it appeared on the heels of Santayana's *The Last Puritan*. It of course especially appealed to New Englanders and their far-scattered descendants, physical and moral. Yet it was the more esteemed because by implication it struck stern critical notes. "The author's intellectual integrity is worthy of his subject," remarked the Springfield *Republican.* We have to say "by implication" because Henry S. Commager deliberately avoided any explicit set of judgments either on the man or his *milieu,* letting his facts and implications speak for themselves. Hence it was that although M. A. De Wolfe Howe called the book highly provocative, though O. G. Villard termed it "a great and lasting contribution to the literature of the antislavery era," and everyone praised its vigorous portraiture, some readers thought it too aloof. Newton Arvin, declaring that Henry S. Commager had every qualification for writing admirably of the man and his era "except sympathy with Parker's strongest impulses," put this idea in exaggerated terms. The sympathy lay beneath the surface, in a narrative so energetic that the author's critical interpretations did not need to be stated in bald sentences.

The second title in our triad is Henry S. Commager's shortest and most Jeffersonian volume, his *Majority Rule and Minority Rights,* a reconsideration of one of our oldest political problems that, growing out of public lectures, was published in 1943. It is eloquent, it is polished and allusive, and it is partisan. With his usual warmth of conviction the author asserts a staunch acceptance of the majority principle as applied through democratic means. The close knowledge of American political history and constitutional development evident in the book is so brightly yet firmly displayed that not a page lacks force and interest. For this element students have found it worth study ever since it appeared. Coming before the public while echoes of Franklin D. Roosevelt's Supreme Court battle rumbled around the horizon, its emphatic refutation of the usual arguments against the majority principle naturally seemed to some less valid in logic than in historical exemplification. Its subtitle might well be "The Vindication of Felix Frankfurter," remarked the *Nation,* and no less an authority than Thomas Reed Powell of the Harvard Law School believed that more moderation would have improved the argument. Yet even today many would agree with Sidney Hook that it is an "eloquent, forthright, and cogent" book.

With this short book might well be mentioned another, *Freedom, Loyalty, Dissent,* which appeared in 1954. It presents the case for freedom of thought and speech, much assailed in the McCarthy delusion, with rare spirit and energy. It contains one sentence that sums up much of the writer's philosophy and that all can accept: "The greatest danger that threatens us is neither heterodox thought nor orthodox thought, but an absence of thought."

Of the most important book of Henry S. Commager to date, in my general estimation, his *The American Mind*, it can again be said that he makes vital and exciting a subject that in other hands might have been pallid and opaque. The four hundred pages are accurately subtitled, "An Interpretation of American Thought and Culture since the 1880's." He begins with *Ben Hur*, *Little Women*, and *Tom Sawyer*; he ends with Sinclair Lewis, Scott Fitzgerald, and John Steinbeck. Or, it would be more illuminating to say that he begins with the organizational revolution embodied in the great corporations of Rockefeller and Carnegie and closes with the technological revolution that ushered in the age of leisure. Like all his work, the book combines exhilarating gusto with keenly critical candor. The author is as fiercely corrosive in dealing with the seamy side of politics, business, and culture as he is enthusiastic in celebrating the finer aspects of our national life. His main theme is American thought, and well does he analyze the literature of revolt in the time of Bryan and Debs, the new economics of Veblen and John R. Commons, and the sweeping recent alterations in religious and sociological theory. He is perhaps at his best, however, in his study of shifting attitudes toward politics from the Populist era through the New Deal, and the evolution of law from the day of Chief Justice Salmon P. Chase to the time Justice Holmes swung a wide door open to the future by his historic announcement that the Fourteenth Amendment did not enact the *Social Statics* of Herbert Spencer.

The sanity and vigor of the synthesis was as clear as the richness of the material and the breadth of the scene. In this volume Henry S. Commager made the America of 1880–1950 as vibrant as he had made some of the chapters of his volume in *The Growth of the American Republic*; and he made it exciting by a vital and mature treatment of much that had theretofore lacked effective study and presentation—the writings of philosophers and poets, of theologians and scientists, of economists and journalists, of historians and novelists. All this was caught up and woven together with rare felicity of phrasing, and charm of comment. The treatise was exhilarating and yet full of moderation; it was stimulatingly critical in places and yet permeated by a calm sympathy with the general flow of ideas and aspirations. Few books of American history have contained more numerous insights, or in the term used by Dixon Wecter, "fine perceptions." Few books have done more to send students and general readers to shelves they have neglected, or to open fresh horizons to view.

The best writers of books are always larger than their creations. It is impossible for those who know Henry S. Commager to take down one of his titles without feeling that the best is yet to come; that we shall yet have a fuller expression of his learning, his stimulating flow of ideas, and his sympathy, sometimes too impetuous, with all the causes that he deems good. The gaiety that matches his erudition, the tolerance that mellows his critical outlook, the good sense that holds his ardent impulses in rein—this makes part of a personality that, his intimates feel, will yet find fuller voice.

LEONARD W. LEVY

Accusatorial and Inquisitorial Systems of Criminal Procedure: The Beginnings

IN 1537 JOHN LAMBERT WAS CHAINED to a Smithfield stake and roasted in the flames as an obdurate heretic. A priest and fellow of Queen's College, Cambridge, he had had a long record of trouble with the authorities. Five years before his death the Archbishop of Canterbury, instigated by Sir Thomas More, summoned Lambert to Lambeth Palace for an inquisition into his religious beliefs. Suspected of having become a convert to Protestantism, he had to answer by sworn affidavit to forty-five "articles" or charges. Framed in the form of questions, the articles were calculated to expose Lambert's doctrinal convictions. He responded with all the candor that was becoming a zealot destined for martyrdom, but refused to answer the first article demanding whether he had ever before been suspected of heresy. His memory was uncertain, he claimed, but "though I did remember . . . yet were I more than twice a fool to show you thereof; for it is written in your own law, 'No man is bound to bewray [accuse] himself' "—to which he appended the Latin expression of that maxim, "Nemo tenetur seipsum prodere."[1]

The suspicion that Lambert was a heretic was founded partly on his alleged belief—one of the charges against him—that ecclesiastical judges had no right to compel suspects to swear on the Bible an oath to tell the truth. Lambert replied that he was not opposed to oaths when they were "lawful." What grieved him was

16

the habitual practice by the ecclesiastical judges of forcing a man to swear

to make true relation of all that they shall demand him, he not knowing what they will demand, neither whether it be lawful to show them the truth of their demands, or no: for such things there be that are not lawful to be showed. . . . Yea, moreover, if such judges sometimes, not knowing by any due proof that such as have to do before them are culpable, will enforce them, by an oath, to detect themselves, in opening before them their hearts; in this so doing, I cannot see that men need to condescend to their requests. For it is in the law (but I wot not certainly the place) thus: 'No man is bound to bewray himself.' Also in another place of the law it is written, 'Cogitationis poenam nemo patiatur,' 'No man should suffer punishment of men for his thought.' To this agreeth the common proverb, that is thus: 'Thoughts be free, and need pay no toll.' So that, to conclude, I think it lawful, at the commandment of a judge, to make an oath to say the truth, especially if the judge requireth an oath duly, and in lawful wise . . . and that also for purgation of infamy, when any infamy is lawfully laid against him.[2]

Thus Lambert twice claimed a right not to disclose to ecclesiastical judges information that would place him in criminal jeopardy. He would take no oath that would force him to incriminate himself, because he had not been duly accused. The right against self-incrimination even after due accusation was still more than a century away, but it originated as a defensive claim by the Lamberts who were denied freedom of thought and were victims of the canon law's inquisitorial system.

Several centuries of English experience with an accusatorial system of criminal justice explain Lambert's defiance of his inquisitors. He echoed protests that had been leveled against canon law procedures ever since the Church had introduced them to England. His argument on the illegality of the proceedings against him was founded on a system of trial that was antithetical to the inquisitorial system and older than Magna Carta. Indeed, accusatorial procedure antedated the Norman Conquest. From the early Middle Ages, civil and ecclesiastical authorities throughout western Europe had employed substantially similar accusatorial procedures. The latter half of the twelfth and first half of the thirteenth centuries was a period of transition that witnessed profound transformations of procedure. Old forms of trial, once universal, broke down and newer ones emerged. In England, the new forms, presentment and trial by jury, preserved the accusatorial character of the old; on the Continent and in the ecclesiastical courts, inquisitorial procedures were triumphant. By no coincidence the liberties of the subject were to thrive in England and be throttled on the Continent.

Community courts and community justice prevailed in England at the time of the Norman Conquest. The legal system was ritualistic, dependent upon oaths at most stages of litigation, and permeated by both religious and superstitious notions. Legal concepts were so primitive that there was no distinction between civil and criminal cases, or between secular and ecclesiastical cases. The proceedings were oral, very personal, and highly confrontative. Juries were unknown. One party publicly "appealed" or accused the other before the community meeting at which the presence of both was obligatory. To be absent meant risking fines and outlawry. After the preliminary statements of the parties, the court rendered judgment, not on the merits of the issue nor the question of guilt or innocence, but on the manner by which it should be resolved. Judgment in other words preceded trial because it was a decision on what form the trial should take. It might be by compurgation, by ordeal, or, after the Norman Conquest, by battle. Excepting trial by battle, only one party was tried or, more accurately, was put to his "proof." Proof being regarded as an advantage it was usually awarded to the accused party; in effect he had the privilege of proving his own case.[3]

Trial by exculpatory oath and compurgation, also called canonical purgation, consisted of a sworn statement to the truth of one's claim or denial, supported by the oaths of a certain number of fellow swearers. Presumably they, no more than he, would endanger their immortal souls by the sacrilege of false swearing. Originally the oath-helpers swore from their own knowledge to the truth of the party's claim. Later they became little more than character witnesses, swearing only to their belief that his oath was trustworthy. If he rounded up the requisite number of compurgators and the cumbrous swearing in very exact form proceeded without a mistake, he won his case. A mistake "burst" the oath, proving guilt.[4]

Ordeals were usually reserved for more serious crimes, for persons of bad reputation, for peasants, or for those caught with stolen goods. As an invocation of immediate divine judgment, ordeals were consecrated by the Church and shrouded with solemn religious mystery. The accused underwent a physical trial in which he called upon God to witness his innocence by putting a miraculous sign upon his body. Cold water, boiling water, and hot iron were the principal ordeals, all of which the clergy administered. In the ordeal of cold water, the accused was trussed up and cast into a pool to see whether he would sink or float. On the theory that water which had been sanctified by a priest would receive an innocent person but reject the guilty, innocence was proved by sinking—and hopefully a quick retrieval—guilt by floating. In the other ordeals, one had to plunge his hand into a cauldron of boiling water or carry a red-hot piece of iron for a certain distance, in the hope that three days later, when the bandages were removed, the priest would find a "clean" wound, one that was healing free of infection. How deeply one plunged his arm into the water, how heavy the iron or great the distance it was carried, depended mainly on the gravity of the charge.[5]

The Normans brought to England still another ordeal, trial by battle, paradigm of the adversary system, which gave to the legal concept of "defense" or "defendant" a physical meaning. Trial by battle was a savage yet sacred method of proof which was also thought to involve divine intercession on behalf of the righteous. God, rather than let a wrongdoer triumph, would strengthen the arms of the party who had sworn truly to the justice of his cause. Right, not might, would therefore conquer. Trial by battle was originally available for the settlement of all disputes, from debt and ownership to robbery and rape, but eventually was restricted to cases of serious crime. In this particular form of proof there was a significant exception to the oral character of the old procedures. The accusation leading to battle, technically known as an "appeal of felony," had to be written, and nothing but the most exact form, giving full particulars of the alleged crime, would be accepted. The indictment or accusation by grand jury would later imitate the "appeal" in this respect.[6]

Whether one proved his case by compurgation, ordeal, or battle, the method was accusatory in character. There was always a definite and known accuser, some private person who brought formal suit and openly confronted his antagonist. There was never any secrecy in the proceedings which were the same for criminal as for civil litigation. The judges, who had no role whatever in the making of the verdict, decided only which party should be put to proof and what its form should be; thereafter the judges merely enforced an observance of the rules. The oaths that saturated the proceedings called upon God to witness to the truth of the respective claims of the parties, or the justice of their cause, or the reliability of their word. No one gave testimonial evidence nor was anyone questioned to test his veracity.

It was the inquest, a radically different proceeding, which eventually supplanted the old forms of proof while borrowing their accusatorial character. An extraordinarily fertile and versatile device, the inquest was the parent of our double jury system, the grand jury of accusation and the petty jury of trial. Fortunately for the history of freedom, the inquest, a Norman import, was also one of the principal means by which the monarchy developed a centralized government in England. The survival of the inquest was insured by its close ties to royal power and royal prosperity; its particular English form was founded on the old accusatorial procedures. The word "inquest" derives from the Latin *inquisitio* or inquisition, but beyond the similarity in name shared nothing in common with the canon law procedure which became, in fact, its opposite and great rival. The inquest was also known as the *recognitio* or recognition, which meant a solemn answer, or finding, or declaration of truth. The inquest was just that, an answer or declaration of truth—a *veri dictum* or verdict—by a body of men from the same neighborhood who were summoned by some official, on the authority of the crown, to reply under oath to any inquiries that might be addressed to them. Men of the same locality were chosen simply because they were most likely to know best the answers to questions relating to it—who had evaded taxes, who owned certain lands, who was suspected of crime, or who knew of misconduct among the king's officers?[7]

At first the inquest was used mainly in administrative and financial inquiries. The Domesday Book, for example, that enormously detailed description or census of landowners and their property down to the last calf and acre, including its cash value, was compiled, at least in part, by an elaborate inquest for tax assessment purposes. The king's representatives went into the counties in 1086, summoned men from each "hundred" or county subdivision —originally the "hundred" was a hundred households—put them under oath, and demanded their verdicts or truthful answers concerning who owned what and how much. After an abortive attempt by Henry I to establish a system of resident judges, royal commissioners, who in the passage of time undertook duties that became increasingly judicial, periodically went on circuit, or "eyre," throughout the country to transact the king's business. They inspected the provinces, gathered revenues and information, occasionally heard lawsuits, and superintended the local details of the king's government. They also aided the Exchequer's fiscal business by assessing taxes, holding sheriffs and other revenue collectors to account, and inquired into the proprietary rights of the crown. Financial and executive business was similarly conducted with the help of inquests which increasingly involved the itinerant royal judges in matters connected with the administration of justice. The king had a stake not only in suits which concerned his royal demesne and his own litigation; he looked to all fines, amercements, escheats and forfeitures of every sort that contributed to his royal revenues, including the profits that might accrue from purely private suits. He claimed, for example, the goods of felons: not only did he acquire the chattels of a condemned man who had been defeated in battle by private appeal of felony; the king had a right, too, to plunder his lands for a year or sell off that right to a local lord. As Stephen says, "The rigorous enforcement of all the proprietary and other profitable rights of the Crown which the articles of eyre confided to the justices was naturally associated with their duties as administrators of the criminal law, in which the king was deeply interested, not only because it protected the life and property of his subjects, but also because it contributed to his revenues." Thus the king's traveling justices were a major factor in the early centralization of England, and their most useful instrument became the inquest in matters both civil and criminal.[8]

What was long an irregular and in some respects an extraordinary procedure became under King Henry II (1154–1189) normal and systematic. A man of powerful will, administrative genius, and reformer's spirit, Henry II increased tremendously the jurisdiction of the royal courts, and wherever they traveled on eyre through the kingdom, the inquest followed. Henry II disliked and distrusted the traditional forms of proof. More boldly than his predecessors he regarded breaches of peace or threats to life and limb as offenses of a public nature, warranting more than merely private retribution. Crimes of a serious nature he took to be offenses against the king's peace, requiring settlement in the king's courts by the king's system of justice, whenever possible, rather than by the older proofs only, and the king's system was founded on the inquest, the representative verdict of the neighborhood. Under Henry II what was once only an administrative inquiry would become the foundation of the jury of accusation and the jury of trial in both civil and criminal matters.

Older forms of proof or trial were becoming corrupted, their irrationality apparent to the new, university-trained royal administrators. Compurgation, having hardly survived the Conquest in criminal matters, was the most untrustworthy of all. It had become too easy a proof, almost a certain success for the party, however culpable or liable, who was lucky enough to be awarded the right to resort to his oath with the support of oath-helpers. They swore only to their belief that his oath was reliable, no longer to their knowledge that it was in fact true. Compurgators who had become little more than character witnesses could no longer be punished for perjury, making the procedure pretty much a ritualistic farce. Moreover, the oaths of compurgators seemed inconsistent with the oaths of the sworn inquest, a much more impartial body. Henry II placed little more trust in ordeals than he did in compurgation; they were too easily manipulated by the priests who administered them, yet as sanctified ceremonials, proofs were not easily dispensable, and they were both quick and profitable to the crown. Ordeal by battle, however, was too dangerous, not only to life and limb but to the security of vested interests, to endure without providing an alternative form of proof for the settlement of disputes. Battle was also becoming too inequitable and farcical. In civil cases, such as disputes over property, the employment of champions, which was once exceptional, had become routine. Champions to do battle on behalf of a litigant arose when one of the parties was unable, for reasons of age, sex, or physical infirmity, to represent himself. The champion was at first a witness who could prove the case of the litigant, but in time champions became professional fighters available for hire in all civil cases, regardless of the physical capacity of the party. Sometimes champions were used as "approvers" to get rid of gangs of criminals.[9]

Henry II did not abolish older forms of proof; he sought, instead, to supersede them in as many instances as possible, by discrediting them and by making available to litigants an alternative and more equitable form of proceeding. Innovations began in 1164, when the Constitutions of Clarendon prescribed the use of a recognition by twelve sworn men to decide any dispute between laymen and clergy on the question whether land was subject to lay or clerical tenure. The Constitutions of Clarendon provided also that laymen should not be sued in ecclesiastical courts on untrustworthy or insufficient evidence, but that if the suspect were someone whom no one might dare to accuse, the sheriff on the request of the bishop must swear a jury of twelve to declare the truth by bringing the accusation. In the Constitutions of Clarendon, then, there is the glimmering of the civil jury in cases of land disputes and of the grand jury of criminal presentment or accusation.[10]

The Assize, or ordinance, of Clarendon, which Henry II promulgated two years later, on the centennial of the Conquest, provided for the firm foundation of the grand jury and instituted a variety of significant procedural reforms. The king instructed the royal judges on circuit or "eyre" to take jurisdiction over certain serious crimes or felonies presented to them by sworn inquests, the representative juries of the various localities. Twelve men from each hundred of the county and four from each township or vill of the hundred, were to be summoned by the sheriff to attend the public eyre. They were enjoined to inquire into all crimes committed since the beginning of Henry II's reign, and to report under oath all persons accused or suspected by the vicinage. The parties who were thus presented, if not already in custody, would be arrested and put to the ordeal of cold water. Even if absolved, those of very bad reputation were forced to abjure the realm. In certain cases, then, mere presentment was tantamount to a verdict of banishment, but generally was no more than an accusation which was tried by ordeal. The Assize of Northampton, which was issued in 1176, recodified the Assize of Clarendon, extended the list of felonies, and provided that the accused felon who was "undone" at the ordeal should lose a foot, his right hand, his chattels, and be banished. The Assize of 1176 made permanent, at least at the pleasure of the king, the revised procedure of accusation by twelve knights of the hundred or twelve freemen of the hundred and four of the vill.[11]

The Assizes of Clarendon and Northampton, by establishing what became the grand jury, offered a royally sanctioned option to the old system of private accusations by appeals of felony. Trial by battle, which was begun by an appeal of felony in criminal cases, continued; but it was undermined by the king's jury of criminal presentment as the model way of beginning a criminal trial. Henry II also made available an escape route from trial by battle in cases begun by an appeal of felony. On the theory that the security of the king's peace could not be safely left to accusations brought by private initiative, many of which were motived by malice, the writ de odio et atia, "of spite and hatred," was provided for appellees. For a price, the writ could be obtained from the king's court by one who claimed that his appellor proceeded from spite and hatred. A jury of recogniters would then be impaneled to render a verdict on this plea; if the jury sustained it, the appeal was quashed and battle avoided. What was practically a jury's verdict was therefore substituted in some instances for trial by battle. Nevertheless, the trial jury in criminal cases was unknown during the twelfth century. The trial jury in civil cases developed first, providing a model that could be copied later in matters of crime.[12]

Reformation of the machinery of civil justice at the expense of trial by battle was one of Henry II's foremost achievements. Once again his instrument was the sworn inquest or jury. Its use in cases of property disputes contributed to the stability of property rights, extended the jurisdiction of the royal courts at the expense of the feudal courts, aided the cause of justice at the same time that fees for the privilege of using the royal courts contributed to the exchequer, and sapped trial by battle in civil cases. The Constitutions of Clarendon in 1164 provided the precedent for turning to twelve men of the countryside for a verdict on a question concerning property rights. Such questions, especially in relation to the possession and title of land, were probably the most common and surely the most important on the civil side of the law. Henry II gradually introduced what became the trial jury for their solution. In 1166 the assize of *"novel disseisin,"* or recent dispossession, established the principle that no one might be evicted or dispossessed of his land without the approval of a jury verdict. This assize created a legal remedy for one who had been dispossessed. He could obtain a writ commanding the sheriff to summon twelve free men of the vicinity who presumably knew the facts of the case, put them under oath, and then in presence of the itinerant royal judges, require them to render a verdict on the question whether the tenant had been dispossessed. A verdict in the tenant's favor restored him to possession of his land. If, however, a lord seized the land of a tenant who died before the tenant's heirs might take possession of it, the assize of *novel disseisin* provided no remedy. The assize of *"mort d'ancestor,"* which was instituted in 1176, did the job. The heir might obtain a writ which put before a jury the question whether the decedent died in possession of the land and whether the claimant was his rightful heir. In the same reign, the assize of *"darrein presentment"* provided for a verdict by jury on questions involving rival claims to the possession of certain ecclesiastical benefices which were regarded as a form of real estate.[18]

Possession, though often indicative of right, was not synonymous with it. One might be "seissed" of land without having title to it. The dispossessor, not the dispossessed, might be the rightful owner; the heir might have a defective title. Thus, settlement of the question of possession was merely provisional, for it left the main question of ownership undecided, and that question was settled by battle. The claimant obtained a writ of right, the civil analogue to the appeal of felony in criminal cases, and challenged the possessor to a duel, with both parties represented by champions. But Henry II's Grand Assize, which was introduced in 1179, opened the way to peaceable settlement. The challenged party, in any case involving a question of proprietary right, might obtain a counterwrit transferring jurisdiction to the royal courts; he thereby consented to having the question settled by a jury which was chosen with great care to insure disinterestedness. The sheriff selected four knights who in turn chose twelve others of the same neighborhood, where the land was located, and the twelve, mainly from their own knowledge, declared which party had the better right to the land. Glanvill, chief justiciar to Henry II, described the procedure of the Grand Assize as a "royal benefit . . . whereby life and property are so wholesomely cared for that men can avoid the chance of the combat and yet keep whatever right they have in their freeholds."[14]

By the time of Magna Carta, the trial jury in civil cases was fairly well established, although in criminal cases was hardly known, if at all. The petty or possessory assizes of *novel disseisin*, *mort d'ancestor*, and *darrein presentment* had proved to be so popular that chapter eighteen of Magna Carta guaranteed that the circuit court would sit four times a year in each county for the purpose of getting verdicts on disputes which they settled. Civil disputes of virtually any description, not merely those named in the petty assizes, might be referred to the verdict of local recog-niters if both parties would consent to the procedure. On the criminal side of the law, Magna Carta in chapter thirty-six pro-vided that the writ *de odio et atia*, which by 1215 had become known as the writ of life and limb, should be granted without charge. It was by no means uncommon by then for one accused by private appeal to demand a jury verdict on any number of "ex-ceptions," such as the writ of life and limb, in the hope of getting the appeal quashed. In such cases, however, the jury decided only the question whether the "exception" was valid; the main question of guilt or innocence, which the appeal had raised, was still settled by battle if the exception was not sustained. Criminal accusations which were presented in accord with the grand inquest provided by the Assize of Clarendon were tried by ordeal. Magna Carta, in chapter thirty-eight, insured that no one could be put to the ordeal unless formally accused by the jury of presentment before the royal judges on circuit. This was the implication of the provision that "credible witnesses," members of the presenting jury, must corroborate the fact that there had been an indictment. The cele-brated chapter thirty-nine did not guarantee trial by jury for the simple reason that its use in criminal cases was still unknown in 1215. At best that chapter insured that indictment and trial by whatever was the appropriate test, whether battle or ordeal, must precede sentence.[15]

The course of history was affected at the same time by events in

Rome. The Fourth Lateran Council in 1215 forbade the participation of the clergy in the administration of ordeals, thereby divesting that proof of its rationale as a judgment of God. As a result, the ordeal died as a form of trial in western Europe and with its death arose the need for some procedure to take its place. While the continental nations and the Church turned to the inquisition, England found in its own form of the inquest a device at hand that would fill the gap. The absence of heresy and therefore of a papal inquisition allowed the alternative.[16]

With the ordeal abolished, battle remained the only means of trying a criminal case. But the movement of the law was away from battle. The same reasons of "equity" which led Glanvill in 1187 to say that the right to a freehold "can scarcely be proved by battle" spurred the search for an alternate means of proving an accusation of crime. Thus Magna Carta had made the writ of life and limb free, but still reflected traditional thinking in terms of ordeals and battle. Battle could never be had, however, in cases where one of the parties was aged, crippled, sick, or a woman. With the ordeal gone, English criminal procedure, in the words of Pollock and Maitland, "was deprived of its handiest weapon." Not only was there no way to try those who could not engage in battle; there was the greater quandary of what should be done with persons who had been accused by the sworn verdict of a grand inquest. Battle was possible only in the case of a private appeal of felony. As Stephen said, "When trial by ordeal was abolished and the system of accusation by grand juries was established, absolutely no mode of ascertaining the truth of an accusation made by a grand jury remained."[17]

The crown's bewilderment was revealed in a writ of 1219 giving instructions to the circuit judges: "Because it was in doubt and not definitely settled before the beginning of your eyre, with what trial those are to be judged who are accused of robbery, murder, arson, and similar crimes, since the trial by fire and water has been prohibited by the Roman Church," notorious criminals should be imprisoned, those accused of "medium" crimes but were not likely to offend again should be banished, and those accused of lesser crimes might be released on "pledges of fidelity and of keeping our peace." The writ concluded, "We have left to your discretion the observance of this aforesaid order . . . according to your own discretion and conscience," a formula that left the judges further perplexed but free to improvise.[18]

Treating an accusation as a conviction, when an accusation was little more than an expression of popular opinion, was a makeshift that fell so short of doing justice that it could not survive. In retrospect it seems natural that the judges on circuit should have turned to a sworn inquest for help. An eyre was a great event, virtually a county parliament. Present were the local nobles and bishops, the sheriffs and bailiffs, the knights and freeholders, and a very great many juries. From every hundred of the county there was a jury of twelve men, and from every township four representatives. Surrounded by various juries, the obvious course for the judges in any criminal case was to seek the sense of the community. The original jury of presentment was already sworn, presumably knew most about the facts, and was a representative group. Its indictment had not necessarily voiced its own belief in the prisoner's guilt; it rather affirmed the fact that he was commonly suspected. Although practice varied considerably at first, the judges began to ask the jury of presentment to render a verdict of guilty or not guilty on their indictment. Because the jury of presentment was more likely than not to sustain its indictment, even though it had sworn only that the accused was suspected and not that he was guilty, the judges usually swore in the representatives of the surrounding townships and asked whether they concurred; the jury of another hundred might also be conscripted to corroborate the verdict. In effect a body of the countryside gave the verdict. This practice of enlarging the original jury of presentment or seeking a series of verdicts from different juries was common during the thirteenth century. What became the petty jury was thus initially larger than the grand jury. The practice was too cumbersome, the body too unwieldy. Twelve was the number of the presenting jury and twelve the jury in many civil cases; gradually only twelve jurors were selected to try the indictment, but they always included among their number some of the original jury of presentment. The unfairness inherent in this practice and the theory that the accused must consent to his jury eventually led to a complete separation of the grand jury and the trial jury.[19]

Consent, even if induced by coercion, was an ancient feature of accusatory procedure. In Saxon times the accused party had to appear personally before his accuser and the assembled community, and agree to submit himself to whatever proof was assigned, or be outlawed. When Henry II introduced the sworn inquest in civil cases, it was available to those who secured a writ requesting it; so too, parties who sought to escape battle consented to abide by the verdict of a jury under the process of the Grand Assize or of the writ of life and limb. Indeed, in such cases where a trial jury was known, it was available only after consent. But no man would be likely to consent to the verdict of his accusers if he thought that they sought his conviction. And no man, it was thought, should be forced to accept the verdict of accusers except freely. Before ordeals died, if an accused refused to submit himself to the proof, he was considered to have repudiated the law and might, therefore, be punished as if he had outlawed himself. But the inquest acting as a trial jury was a novel and extraordinary device, making the reasoning that had led to outlawry for rejection of the ordeal seem repugnant if a man refused to put himself to the test of a jury. He might think the jury would not fairly decide, or that his chances of getting a verdict of not guilty, for whatever the reasons, were hopeless.[20]

To cope with such cases the law developed in two completely different ways, one barbaric, the other salutary. Before the judges turned to a second jury to decide the question of guilt or innocence, they would ask the accused whether he would submit to the final verdict of the "country," that is, of the inquest of the countryside or whole county. Most men consented, but some did not, quite likely because conviction meant the forfeiture of chattels and goods. Some judges proceeded with the trial anyway, in such cases; others treated the prisoner as if he were guilty; but most felt that it was unreasonable to compel a man to submit unless he consented. If he refused to consent, the law was nonplussed, the proceedings stymied. At length, in 1275 a statute supplied the answer: extort his consent. The statute read, "that notorious felons who are openly of evil fame and who refuse to put themselves upon inquests of felony at the suit of the King before his justices, shall be remanded to a hard and strong prison as befits those who refuse to abide by the common law of the land; but this is not to be understood of persons who are taken upon light suspicion." It is noteworthy that the trial jury, here called the inquest of felony, is described as the common law of the land by 1275. By the same date, incidentally, anyone appealed of felony might avoid battle if he put himself "upon his country," letting a jury decide the question of guilt or innocence.[21]

The notion of consent to trial by jury incredibly remained the law of the land until 1772. A prisoner who refused to plead to the indictment simply could not be tried, though he was subjected to a peculiar form of torture that was calculated to change his mind. Imprisonment strong and hard (*prison forte et dure*) within a quarter of a century of its introduction in 1275 degenerated into punishment strong and hard (*peine forte et dure*). At first the prisoner was stripped, put in irons on the bare ground in the worst part of the prison, and fed only coarse bread one day and water the next, which was surely cruel enough. Then the refinement of "punishment" was added; he was slowly pressed, spread-eagled on the ground, with as much iron placed upon his body as he could bear "and then more." The punishment by pressing, exposure, and slow starvation continued until the prisoner "put himself upon his country" or died. What made this barbarity so peculiar is that it derived from the admirable though rigid rule that the trial could not proceed without the prisoner's consent; moreover, that the worst felon should have an opportunity to prove his innocence. That is, the purpose of *peine forte et dure* was not to extort a confession, but simply to extort a plea; the law did not care whether he pleaded guilty or not guilty, only that he plead. In 1772 a new statute provided that a prisoner standing mute to the indictment of felony should be treated as if he had been convicted by verdict or confession, thus ending *peine forte et dure*. Not till 1827 was that rule altered to direct the court to enter a plea of not guilty for a prisoner who stood "mute of malice" and refused to plead.[22]

The other path taken by the notion of consent led to the emergence of the petty jury in criminal cases. This was the outcome of permitting the prisoner to challenge members of the presenting jury who were impaneled to serve on his trial jury. Bracton, writing about 1258, noted that the defendant might object against the inclusion of false and malicious accusers, and Britton, near the end of the thirteenth century, said that he might object if the jurors included enemies who sought his destruction or had been suborned

by the lord who sought his land "through greediness of the es-
cheat." In 1305 Prince Edward, later Edward II, acting on behalf
of a friend who had been indicted for murder, requested the judge
to provide a jury which excluded all members of the accusing jury.
With increasing frequency defendants challenged petty jurors who
had first served as their indicters, although the king's justices resisted the challenges because indicters were more likely to convict.
For that very reason Commons twice protested in the 1340's
against the inclusion of indicters, but it was not until 1352 that the
king agreed to a statute which gave the accused a right to challenge members of the petty jury who had participated in his indictment. As a result of this statute the two juries became differentiated in composition and function. From about 1376 the custom of requiring a unanimous verdict from twelve petty jurors
developed; by that time the size of the grand jury had been fixed
at twenty-three, a majority of whom decided whether accusations
should be proffered.[23]

By the middle of the fifteenth century criminal trials were being
conducted by rational principles that seem modern. Although the
law of evidence was still in its rudimentary stages, the trial jury
was losing its character as witnesses, men who of their own knowledge or from knowledge immediately available from the neighborhood, might swear to the guilt or innocence of the accused. The
jury was beginning to hear evidence that was produced in court,
although the jurors still continued to obtain facts by their own
inquiry. As late as the 1450's it was common for the jurors to visit
a witness at his home in the country to take his testimony, but
they were also beginning to pass judgment on evidence given in
their presence in court. More important, they were regarded as a
body of objective men, triers of fact, whose verdict was based on
the truth as best they could determine it. According to the ro-
manticized view of Chief Justice John Fortescue in the mid-fifteenth century, an innocent man need fear nothing because "none
but his neighbours, men of honest and good repute, against whom
he can have no probable cause of exception, can find the persons
accused guilty." He was no doubt additionally assured because he
might challenge without cause as many as thirty-five potential
jurors. Witnesses for the crown—the accused was allowed none—
gave evidence "in open Court," wrote Fortescue, "in the presence

and hearing of a jury, of twelve men, persons of good character, neighbours where the fact was committed, apprised of the circumstances in question, and well acquainted with the lives and conversations of the witnesses, *especially as they be near neighbours, and cannot but know whether they be worthy of credit, or not."* The prisoner knew the charges against him, confronted his accuser, and had freedom to give his own explanations as well as question and argue with the prosecution's witnesses. He suffered from many disadvantages—lack of counsel, lack of witnesses on his own behalf, lack of time to prepare his defense—yet the trial was supremely fair judged by any standard known in the western world of that day.[24]

The year 1215, which is celebrated in Anglo-American history because of Magna Carta, is notable too for an ecclesiastical event of sinister import, the regulations of the Fourth Lateran Council in Rome. The one ultimately symbolized the liberties of the subject; the other, ultimately, the rack and the auto-da-fé. The Council was dominated by that imperious autocrat, Pope Innocent III, who charted a new course for the criminal procedure of the canon law which would later be opposed by the English common law. The Church in the thirteenth century—and long after—was a world power, the only world power, and Innocent III (1198–1216) was more than its head; he was its master. One of the great legislators of the canon law, he was also the scourge of heretics, the man responsible for the Albigensian Crusade which slaughtered thousands, and for starting the Holy Inquisition on its bloody path. As John H. Wigmore said, Innocent III—a name scarcely apt—"established the inquisition of heresy, by warrants extending into every corner of Europe—a form of terrorism which served to extirpate those who dissented from the church's dogmas for the next four centuries." The same pope, a maker and breaker of kings, wielded a political authority over the whole of Christendom and sovereignty over its temporal monarchs. It was Innocent III who absolved King John for assenting to Magna Carta, which he thought shameful and detrimental, and for a time reduced England to the status of a vassal of the papacy. Under his leadership the Fourth Lateran Council defined the attitude of the Church toward heretics, the obligations of secular authorities to exterminate them, and a new code of criminal procedures which incorporated both the *"inquisitio,"* precursor of the Holy Inquisition, and a new oath that was self-incriminatory in nature.[25]

The *inquisitio* originated in the decrees of Innocent III at the close of the twelfth century and the beginning of the thirteenth, triggering a steady transition in the canon law from the old accusatorial procedure to the new inquisitional procedures. In English law the inquest had led to the double jury system; in canon law and in the civil law—the secular law of continental nations, which followed the suit of the Church—the inquest took a completely different form, one that left in its wake a trail of mangled bodies, shattered minds, and smoking flesh. The inquisitional procedure, which at first was aimed at discovering and punishing misconduct among the clergy, was speedily adapted to the overweening need of preserving the faith against heresy. As late as the twelfth century, however, the Church had an equivocal policy toward heretics, a substantially accusatorial system of criminal procedure, and an abhorrence of some of the very features that shortly proved most characteristic of the Inquisition. Heresy was not yet a crime of mental state or conscience; or, rather, only external acts of worship or doctrinal differences were punished as heresy, and the Church possessed no special machinery for detecting the guilty, let alone those with guilty thoughts or secret doubts. Back in the fifth century, Saints Chrysostom and Augustine, although urging the suppression of heresy, spoke against the death penalty, against torture, and against forcing men to accuse themselves. One should confess his sins to God, said Chrysostom: "I do not say to thee, make a parade of thyself, nor accuse thyself before others. . . ." These views were endorsed by Gratian's *Decretum* in the mid-twelfth century. Gratian espoused the penalties of exile and fine for heretics, repudiated torture, and declared, like Chrysostom, "I say not that thou shouldst incriminate thyself publicly nor accuse thyself before others." As late as 1184 Pope Lucius III merely excommunicated obstinate heretics and turned them over to the secular authority for severe penalties—exile, the confiscation of the properties, destruction of their houses, and loss of all rights—but the penalties did not touch the persons of the guilty; they were neither physically harmed nor imprisoned.[26]

By the mid-thirteenth century, however, all had changed. St. Thomas Aquinas required truthful answers to incriminating questions and advocated death for heretics in order to save the faith from their corruption; and Pope Innocent IV explicitly sanctioned the use of torture. In the period between Gratian and Aquinas, heresies had spread alarmingly, especially in the South of France among the Cathari, and the faith had found a champion, Pope Innocent III, who used his spiritual sword and administrative genius, however malevolent, to smite the enemies of Christ. Innocent III heralded a new attitude toward heretics. He considered their crime as the most execrable, the most damnable of all, *crimen laesae majestatis divinae* or high treason against God. By comparison it purified Sodom and Gomorrah, justified the infidelity of the Jews, and made the worst sins holy. The Christian's highest duty was to help exterminate heretics by denouncing them to the ecclesiastical authorities, regardless of any familial or human bonds. The son who did not deliver up his parents or the wife her husband shared the heretic's guilt. Faithfulness to a heretic, according to Innocent III, was faithlessness to God. The living must die; the guilty who were already dead, if buried in consecrated ground, must be dug up, cursed, and burned.[27]

The procedures available to the Church for the discovery and prosecution of heretics were archaic and ineffective before the reforms of Innocent III. In the main these procedures were of the same primitive accusatory character as those that were employed by the secular authorities in England and on the Continent during the early Middle Ages. Private accusation led to exculpation by the oath of the party, supported by compurgators (the "*purgatio canonica*"), or by ordeal (the "*purgatio vulgaris*"). In addition the Church very early resorted to an inquest by synodal witnesses which, as Adhémar Esmein observed, culminated in an inquisitional procedure which was "the anti-type of the 'inquisitio' from which sprang the English grand jury." In this ecclesiastical inquest, the bishop, who was the ecclesiastical judge, on visiting a parish within his jurisdiction, would convene a synod or gathering of the faithful. He selected some and swore them to denounce all persons guilty of offenses requiring investigation; then he closely interrogated the denouncers, or synodal witnesses, to uncover malefactors and, at the same time, to test the reliability of the testimony. It was but a short step for the ecclesiastical judge to conduct the prosecution against the accused and to decide on his guilt or innocence. Innocent III took that step, which the Fourth Lateran Council confirmed.[28]

The remodeled criminal procedures of the canon law, after 1215, described three modes of prosecution. The first, the *accusatio*, was the traditional form. A private person, on the basis of some information or evidence available to him, voluntarily accused another and thereby became a party to the prosecution, taking upon himself the task of proof. He also took upon himself the risk of being punished in the event that the prosecution failed. The second form of prosecution was the *denunciatio* which enabled the private accuser to avoid the danger and burden of the *accusatio*. Either an individual or the synodal witnesses played the role of informer, secretly indicting or denouncing someone before the court. The judge himself then became a party to the suit *ex officio*, by virtue of his office, and conducted the prosecution for the secret accuser. The third form was the *inquisitio*, by which the judge combined in his person all roles—that of accuser, prosecutor, judge, and jury. Technically the judge could not institute a suit unless an important preliminary condition had first been met; he must satisfy himself that there were probably grounds for the *inquisitio*. This was the canon law's equivalent of the grand jury of presentment of the English common law. The canon law required that an accusation must rest on *"infamia"*—infamy or bad reputation—which was established by the existence of either notorious suspicion (*"clamosa insinuatio"*) or common report (*"fama"*) which was some sort of public rumor. But the inquisitor himself was the sole judge of the existence of *infamia*, and his own suspicions, however based or baseless, were also adequate for the purpose of imprisoning the suspect and putting him to an inquisition. The Fourth Lateran Council prescribed no form for the establishment of *infamia* if the judge decided to proceed *"ex officio mero"*—of his own accord or at his discretion.[29]

One of the "most odious features," as Esmein said, of the whole inquisitional procedure which was introduced by the Fourth Lateran Council was the new oath which the suspect was required to swear. It was the oath *de veritate dicenda*, to tell the truth to all interrogatories that might be administered, a seemingly innocuous obligation which in reality was an inescapable trap, a form of spiritual torture, *"tortura spiritualis,"* calculated to induce self-incrimination. Confession of guilt was central to the whole inquisitional process, and the oath, which was administered at the very outset of the proceedings, was reckoned as indispensable to the confession. The accused, knowing neither the charges against him, nor his accusers, nor the evidence, was immediately placed between hammer and anvil: he must take the oath or be condemned as guilty, yet if he took the oath he exposed himself to the nearly certain risk of punishment for perjury—and his lies were evidence of his guilt—or condemning himself by admissions which his judge regarded as damaging, perhaps as a confession to the unnamed crime. The oath *de veritate dicenda* was thus virtually a self-incriminatory oath. Because it became associated with the Inquisition, it became known as the inquisitional oath; and because it originated in connection with a proceeding in which the judge served *ex officio* as indicter, assailant, and convicter, it was also called the oath *ex officio*.[30]

In the aftermath of the Inquisition, the Church which originated the oath turned against it. In 1698 the pope commissioned a study of the "expediency of abrogating the custom of requiring accused persons, prior to interrogation, to take an oath to tell the truth." Franciscus Memmius, the author of the study, concluded that the oath was both "violent and unjust" and should therefore be abolished. He emphasized the difference between the involuntary oath *de veritate dicenda* and either a voluntary oath or the old oaths of purgation in the medieval *purgatio canonica*. By the old procedure, the accused party swore an oath to his innocence, supported by his compurgators, and thereby ended the controversy. The significant character of the old oath, in other words, was its effect: it won a decision for the oath-taker, because it was thought to possess a sort of supernatural or divine character which proved innocence, like a successful ordeal. By contrast, as Memmius pointed out, the oath *de veritate dicenda* thrust the oath-taker in jeopardy and fear to which he ought not be exposed. It was, according to Memmius, a form of torture more cruel than physical torture because it tormented one's soul by tempting a man to save himself from punishment by perjuring himself at the expense of dishonoring God's name and risking eternal damnation. In 1725, as a result of such criticism, the Council of Rome abolished the oath of the criminally accused and declared null and void all confessions that might thereafter be extracted by its use, mainly because coerced confessions were unreliable.[31]

When the inquisitional oath was first introduced by the decretals of Innocent III and endorsed by the Fourth Lateran Council, it signalized, in the words of Wigmore, "an ephochal difference of method." Nevertheless, the accused retained some freedom of defense bcause the old accusatory procedures did not all die at once; some lingered for about a century, slowly withering. Originally the accused, when summoned, was acquainted with the testimony which established the *infamia* and was permitted to challenge it by witnesses proving his good repute. But as the Inquisition spread throughout Europe, terrorizing whole populations, this defense proved useless because no one would dare speak up for anyone unfortunate enough to fall into the inquisitor's hands; to support the victim inevitably came to mean that one shared his guilt and therefore became next in line to share his wretched fate. The defense of proving good repute simply died out. It never was available anyway when the judge proceeded *ex officio mero*, which was initially the exceptional procedure but quickly became the very ordinary, indeed almost the only, procedure, supplanting the *accusatio* and the *denunciatio*. The *accusatio* was systematically discouraged precisely because, being accusatory or litigious, it assured the defendant some means of defense. The *denunciatio* seems to have merged with the inquisitional procedure when a new ecclesiastical functionary, the "promotor," arose to assist the inquisitor in his tasks by denouncing individuals, thereby setting in motion the inquisitional process.[32]

The opportunities for self-defense which were originally available to the accused included a right to be informed of the charges against him, to know the names of the prosecution's witnesses, and to have copies of their depositions. He was then in a position to dispute the charges, to challenge the evidence and even the admissibility of testimony from witnesses who were his enemies. In the ordinary episcopal courts these defenses, as well as the right of counsel, remained unimpaired, but in cases of heresy, which were especially handled by the inquisitors in secret hearings and trials, the accused was denied all the usual rights one by one. The prosecution's witnesses were always examined secretly and out of the presence of the accused. As early as the mid-thirteenth century,

Pope Innocent IV empowered the judges to withhold the names of witnesses at discretion, and by the end of the century Pope Boniface VIII unreservedly ordered the suppression of their names. Their depositions were no longer produced for the accused's benefit except at the discretion of his judge, who became a law unto himself, operating in secrecy. Every defense was trammeled, every avenue of escape closed, leaving the accused at the complete mercy of his judge, the inquisitor.[33]

The role of the judicial inquisitor and the nature of the crime which he sought to establish and punish explain the severe procedures of the Inquisition as well as its gross atrocities. The judge was commissioned to perform a sacred mission, to avenge God and purify the faith by extirpating the ultimate sin, the heresy of disbelief or doubt. He was not merely a judge of overt acts of crime; he was also father-confessor to his victim, seeking to extract from him a confession of his guilt so that his soul might be saved despite wanton or ignorant errors of conscience which could lead only to eternal damnation. The inquisitor's task, therefore, in the words of Henry Charles Lea, was the nearly impossible one "of ascertaining the secret thoughts and opinions of the prisoner. . . . The believer must have fixed and unwavering faith, and it was the inquisitor's business to ascertain this condition of his mind." The defendant's behavior proved little except outward conformity, and that might be illusory, certainly inconclusive proof of the "most unbounded submission to the decisions of the Holy See, the strictest adherence to orthodox doctrine, the freest readiness to subscribe to whatever was demanded of him. . . ." Despite his verbal professions, his regularity at mass, his punctuality at confession, he might be a heretic at heart, fit only for the stake. His guilt was an unquestioned presumption which could lead only to a foregone conclusion, his condemnation. Legal niceties, procedural regularities, and forms of law counted for little when the objective was to obtain a conviction at any cost in order to fulfill a sacred mission.[34]

On the other hand the canon law, influenced by the Roman law of the later empire, developed a highly sophisticated system of evidence, later known as the theory of legal proofs, supposedly for the benefit of the accused by preventing the conviction of the innocent. The burden of proof, as in the accusatory system of old, was wholly upon the accuser or prosecutor, but the canon law required an unusual degree of proof in both kind and quantity. Innocent III, for example, cautioned inquisitors against convicting on merely "violent presumptions" in a matter as heinous as heresy. What the canon law required was perfect or complete proof which in a later day was specified with considerable complexity and quasi-scientific exactness. Complete proof was proof clearer than the sun at midday. It consisted, ideally, of the testimony of two eyewitnesses, neither impeached nor impeachable, to the same fact; they must have seen the prisoner commit the crime in order to complete the proof in a capital case. Proof so stringent and certain was nearly impossible to procure even when the crime was some overt act, certainly impossible in a heresy case when the crime was essentially one of thought. Documentary evidence such as heretical writings carried weight, but was rarely available. "Proximate indications" or "half proofs," such as many hearsay witnesses, and weighty presumptions or conjectural proofs were insufficient to support a conviction. The prisoner's confession was needed for corroboration.[35]

The tyranny of the system of legal proofs together with the inquisitor's zeal to snatch a soul from Satan led irresistibly to the tyranny of the Inquisition, making the confession the crux of the trial. The secret interrogation, the requirement of a self-incriminatory oath, and, finally, the employment of torture had as their single objective the confession of the prisoner. "The accused," reported Bernard Gui, one of the leading inquisitors of the early fourteenth century, "are not to be condemned unless they confess or are convicted by witnesses, though not according to the ordinary laws, as in other crimes, but according to the private laws or privileges conceded to the inquisitors by the Holy See, for there is much that is peculiar to the Inquisition." The judge who was convinced of his prisoner's guilt but lacked the necessary proof was driven to extort a confession by any means, however repulsive. In the interest of defending the faith the most unspeakable punishments were sanctioned. The Inquisition was the classic case of the ends justifying the means. In 1252 Innocent IV issued his bull, *Ad extirpanda*, directing the establishment of machinery for systematic persecution and authorizing the use of torture. The bull empowered the civil authorities to torture suspects in order to force them to name their accomplices as well as to confess their own guilt of heresy. Four years later, the pope authorized ecclesiastical judges to absolve each other and mutually grant dispensation for "irregularities," thereby enabling them to administer torture directly.[36]

The rules of the Inquisition prohibited the repetition of torture in any single case, but by casuistical interpretation a "continuance" rather than a repetition made possible repeated and prolonged applications of the rack, regardless of the intervals between separate torments. Confessions extorted by torture had to be "freely" repeated after torture, and in the event of a retraction by the prisoner, he was returned to the rack for a "continuance." Torture certainly was an efficacious system of interrogation, saving time and trouble for the inquisitors, but they had other means of persuading the prisoner to confess. He could be imprisoned indefinitely, often for years, in a dark dungeon, in solitary confinement, and be kept half starved, frozen, and sleepless, incapable of defending himself when brought before the inquisitor for a fresh interrogation.[37]

The usual course of a trial, which consisted of the secret examination of the accused under oath, was to confront him with the mass of surmises and rumors and hearsay against him and demand his confession. The indictment was built from the testimony of secret informers, malicious gossips, self-confessed victims, and frightened witnesses who, anxious to save themselves from being racked, revealed from their frantic imaginations whatever they thought the inquisitor might wish to hear. Convicted heretics, whose infamy disqualified them as witnesses in all other cases, gave the most prized testimony in heresy cases for the prosecution only. A prisoner who confessed, abjured heresy, and proclaimed his penitence could prove his sincerity—and escape the stake if not prison—by betraying friends, neighbors, and family. If he refused, the inquisitor considered him impenitent and put him to torture again to reveal their guilt—and then dispatched him for execution. By such methods *infamia* was established for an inquisition against fresh batches of victims. With his dossier of suspicions against the prisoner, the inquisitor cunningly examined him to obtain from his own lips the final proof of guilt. Guile, deceit, entrapment, promises, threats, and, if necessary, the rack managed inevitably to triumph. Lea reported that the entire history of the Inquisition reveals not a single instance of complete acquittal. In sum, "Abandon hope, all ye who enter here" best described the chances of an accused person under the inquisitorial system of criminal procedure which operated throughout the Continent. The Church had been the first authority to switch to the inquisitorial system from the accusatorial, and its supreme example speedily inspired European nations, excepting England, to reform the procedures of their secular criminal law in Rome's image. Everywhere the secret examination, the inquisitional oath, and torture became the standard, at first used only in "extraordinary" cases but quickly degenerating into a completely routine procedure for all cases but the most petty.[38]

The English system, which was based on the presentment by grand jury, the written indictment, and trial by jury, differed most markedly from the continental system in the role played by the judge. In the case of a felony, the officers of a French court, like the ecclesiastical judge in a case of heresy, completely dominated the proceedings at every stage from arrest to verdict. The English judge, by contrast, remained essentially a referee of a private fight, enforcing the observance of the rules by both parties. As an appointee of the crown, he was naturally partial to the prosecution and by his conduct often showed his favoritism, but he had neither a personal nor an official stake in the outcome of a criminal proceeding and little ability to command a verdict of guilty. He had no authority whatever to initiate or promote a prosecution, nor to make an accusation of crime against anyone.

In the inquisitorial system, the accusation and prosecution rested entirely with the court which was also the accuser, to the extent that any accuser was known. He was in a sense nameless and faceless, hidden beneath a hood that was called *"fama"* or *"clamosa insinuatio"*—common report or notorious suspicion. In England the name of the accuser had to be as definite as the accusation itself. The accuser was a witness who instigated the prosecution, and his direct and open participation in the case was indispensable. Unless an officer of the crown of his own knowledge suspected a man's guilt, he could not make an arrest without the sworn complaint or the physical presence of the witness who brought the accusation. The witness himself, as a matter of fact, had virtually the same powers of arrest as a crown officer. Without the accuser there could not even be a prosecution. A suspect might confess his guilt to a justice of the peace at a preliminary examination, be indicted by a grand jury, and yet plead not guilty at his arraignment perhaps because he planned to retract the confession at his trial. When the trial opened, if his accuser was not present to testify against him or if the justice of the peace, to whom he had confessed, did not testify either, "although the malefactor hath confessed the crime to the justice of the peace, and that it appear by his hand and confirmation," wrote Sir Thomas Smith about 1565, "the twelve men will acquit the prisoner. . . ." The accuser's role was so vital that he even had the same power of prosecution as a crown attorney. In England and in England alone the prosecution of crimes, in Stephen's words, was "left entirely to private persons, or to public officers who act in their capacity of private persons and who hardly have any legal powers beyond those which belong to private persons." By contrast, wherever the inquisitorial procedure prevailed, the court or its officers were alone empowered to institute accusations and prosecutions. Every criminal case was an official inquiry into the guilt or innocence of the accused.[39]

In England the grand jury made the formal presentment of crime against the accused on the basis of information known personally to its members, and the crown attorney framed an indictment accordingly; or the attorney, on the basis of an accusation brought to his attention, drew the bill of indictment for the grand jury's verdict, and if the evidence indicated the suspect's guilt, the grand jury approved of the indictment. Without its approval, however, there could be no prosecution for treason or felony. The judge had no part in the bringing of the presentment, the framing of the indictment, or the verdict of the grand jury. The grand jury not only stood between the suspect and the government which sought to prosecute him; the judge himself subjected the indictment to the most exacting scrutiny. It was the only written document in the entire proceedings which were in all other respects oral. The indictment inherited the characteristics of the old appeal of felony by private accusers seeking satisfaction by battle. It had to be a rigorously formal document that met every exacting technicality of the law, describing the accusation with the utmost particularity and accuracy. The specific crime charged against the accused and the time, place, and manner of its commission had to be precisely defined. Although the English common law recognized such vague crimes as seditious libel, conspiracy, and compassing the death of the king, it was generally inhospitable to dragnet definitions, which jeopardized personal security, and to crimes of mental state like heresy. The courts demanded strictness in indictments and treated the crown as if it were scarcely more than a private appellor bringing an appeal of felony, although every indictment was framed in the name of the king. Such strictness threw upon the crown the obligation of stating and proving its case in a manner unknown to a court of the inquisitorial system, which knew no such thing as the rule of law enforceable even against the sovereign. There was no security whatever against the arbitrary power of an inquisitor of the Church or a French magistrate. They were not even required to notify a prisoner of the crimes charged against him, let alone when, where, and how he was alleged to have committed them. The English judge had no discretion in such matters; his continental counterpart was governed by discretion alone. In England the entire indictment was read to the prisoner, who was free to make exceptions on grounds of law, though without the aid of counsel. The judge, at least in theory, served as his counsel, and on questions relating to the sufficiency of the indictment or informing him of the charges against him, the theory was realistic.[40]

The English judge presided over a criminal trial that was a symbolic reenactment of the old trial by battle. The proceeding was adversary in nature, and though the crown possessed several important advantages, its position was like that of the plaintiff in a civil case. Indeed, a criminal prosecution resembled in most respects the most ordinary litigation between private parties disputing the title to an estate. The trial was preeminently litigious, following substantially the same rules of procedure and pleadings as a civil trial. The defendant was completely free to make his defense as best he could, and he was tried publicly and before a jury, advantages of inestimable value compared to a secret inquisition. Again, the role of the English judge is most significant. He was in the main an impassive observer. It was not his duty to collect evidence against the prisoner, to evaluate it, to interrogate him—though he could do so, of course—or to judge him. The English judge was neither accuser nor prosecutor; he conducted no inquest against the defendant, was not a party adverse to him, and rendered no verdicts. Without reason to be powerfully biased against him, to strain for a conviction, or to presume guilt, the judge could afford to be neutral or, at least, relatively fair.

English judges of the Middle Ages tended to be harsh and sometimes abused the defendant by scornful remarks, but they were comparatively just. The crown's attorney had the task of conducting the prosecution and proving his case against the prisoner. The trial was a running argument between prosecution and defense, as if they were engaged in a combat before the jury. The examination of the defendant was the focus of the proceeding. If the defendant had the wit and the tongue he could give as well as he got from counsel against him, disputing and denying point for point, calling for production of the evidence, criticizing it, demanding to be confronted with the state's witnesses or to see their depositions. As Stephen says, "The trials were short and sharp; they were directed to the very point at issue, and, whatever disadvantages the prisoner lay under, he was allowed to say whatever he pleased; his attention was pointedly called to every part of the case against him, and if he had a real answer to make he had the opportunity to bring it out effectively and in detail. It was but seldom that he was abused or insulted." The judge simply presided, ruled on points of law, and, when the oral combat was over, summed up the evidence for the benefit of the jury and instructed them on the law that governed the case. The jury was then free to decide as it pleased on the question of guilt or innocence. The entire proceeding stood in merciful contrast to the inquisitorial procedure which cast the judge in every role and in every one an implacable enemy of his victim. Lea's remark about the spirit that infected an inquisitor of the canon law applies with equal force to an inquisitor of the French royal court: he conducted himself as if "the sacrifice of a hundred innocent men were better than the escape of one guilty." By contrast, the humanity of the English judge even in an age of cruelty persuaded him that the cause of justice was best served by bending over backwards to avoid convicting the innocent. As early as 1302 it was said that the best course was to relinquish the punishment of a wrongdoer rather than punish the innocent. Chief Justice Fortescue, in the mid-fifteenth century, expressed a standard that became a maxim of English law: "Indeed, one would much rather that twenty guilty persons should escape the punishment of death, than that one innocent person should be condemned, and suffer capitally." A century and a half later even the Star Chamber professed to believe in the maxim that "it were better to acquit twenty that are guyltie than condempne one Innocente."[41]

The humanity of the English judge was above all marked by his abhorrence of torture. The horrible punishment meted out to a prisoner who refused to plead either guilty or not guilty was undoubtedly a form of torture, yet *peine forte et dure* was never imposed except to force one to consent to being tried by a jury. It was never employed to extort a confession or to force the prisoner to incriminate himself in any manner. It was the proud boast of the English judge that torture was illegal in a common-law proceeding. Fortescue's panegyric of English law turned him to French law again and again for a chauvinistic comparison. The French, he said, do not think it enough to convict the accused by evidence, lest the innocent should thereby be condemned; they choose, rather, to put the accused to the rack "till they confess their guilt, rather than rely entirely on the depositions of witnesses, who, very often, from unreasonable prejudice and passion; sometimes, at the instigation of wicked men, are suborned, and so become guilty of perjury. By which over cautious, and inhuman stretch of policy, the suspected, as well as the *really* guilty, are in that kingdom, tortured in so many ways, as is too tedious and bad for description. Some are extended on *the rack,* till their very sinews crack, and the veins gush out in streams of blood: others have weights hung to their feet, till their limbs are almost torn asunder, and the whole body dislocated: some have their mouths gagged to such a wideness, for a long time, whereat such quantities of water are poured in, that their bellies swell to a prodigious degree, and then being pierced with a faucet, spigot, or other instrument for the purpose, the water spouts out in great abundance, like a whale. . . . To describe the inhumanity of such exquisite tortures affects me with too real a concern, and the varieties of them are not to be recounted in a large volume." Other kingdoms, added Fortescue, similarly engaged in torture: "Now, what man is there so stout or resolute, who has once gone through this horrid

trial by torture, be he never so innocent, who will not rather confess himself guilty of all kinds of wickedness, than undergo the like
tortures a second time? Who would not rather die once, since
death would put an end to all his fears, than to be killed so many
times, and suffer so many hellish tortures, more terrible than death
itself?"[42]

Torture thrived in dark and secret places, but could not survive a public trial before a jury. Secrecy, having infected the entire
inquisitorial process, brutalized its judges. They cited, arrested,
accused, imprisoned, collected evidence, examined, prosecuted, tortured, convicted, and punished in secrecy. Only the final sentence
was publicized. By contrast publicity bathed the English common-
law procedure, at least through the mid-sixteenth century. Criminal procedure under the Tudors took on a definite inquisitorial
cast, though it remained essentially accusatorial. The unsettling
effect of the Reformation in England, intensified by the conflicting religious policies of succeeding sovereigns, and frequent riots,
rebellious factions, and general disorders motivated the Tudors
to increase the surveillance of the central government over the
entire country by stricter police control. Both torture and an inquisitorial examination of suspects entered into English practice,
although torture was undoubtedly used on a sporadic basis as early
as the fifteenth century. When Sir Thomas Smith later wrote that
torture "to put a malefactor to excessive paine, to make him con-
fesse of himselfe, or of his felowes or complices, is not used in England," he meant that it was not used at common law. Indeed, the
opinion of the common-law judges was that torture was illegal.
But it could be employed, and was, by the special command or
authority of the king in his prerogative courts. It was an extraordinary power of the crown which might be inflicted in extraordinary cases, at first only those involving the safety of the state;
but its brutalizing effect on those who practiced it and its unquestionable efficiency led inevitably to its use in cases of serious
crime that were unrelated to state security. Yet the use of torture,
until its abolition by statute in 1640, was always restricted to the
Privy Council and its judicial arm, the Court of Star Chamber.[43]

The principal incursion made by the inquisitorial system on the
common law itself was the preliminary examination of accused

persons. In 1554 and 1555 Parliament enacted statutes that were intended to safeguard against collusion between justices of the peace and criminal suspects whom they too freely bailed. This legislation, as it turned out, had the effect of increasing the efficiency of criminal procedure by filling an important gap. Grand jurors had lost their character as presenters of the names of those who were simply reputed publicly to be criminals and were losing their character as witnesses who of their own knowledge suspected certain persons of crime. More and more, grand jurors were becoming dependent upon the production of evidence before them by crown officers. Justices of the peace, those county officials who have been called the government's "men-of-all-work" and whose duties included police and administrative functions as well as judicial functions, were authorized by the acts of 1554 and 1555 to take the examination of all persons suspected of crime and of their accusers.[44]

By the close of the sixteenth century these examinations were becoming quite inquisitorial. The suspect was closely and strictly interrogated in private; his accusers and witnesses against him were examined out of his presence and their evidence was withheld from him until the trial. The purpose of examining the suspect was to trap him into a confession. Torture, however, as has been indicated, was never used in any common-law proceeding. Nevertheless the preliminary examination by the justice of the peace was a common-law equivalent of the secret inquisition used on the Continent. Moreover, any damaging admissions made by the suspect were produced against him at his trial. The record of the examination was usually introduced in evidence at the beginning of the trial, placing the defendant in an unfavorable light, to say the least. Fortunately the trial itself, even before the Star Chamber, remained public, and the defendant could always retract or deny compromising statements made to the justice of the peace. Neither in the preliminary examination nor the trial was the defendant required or permitted to make statements under oath. The requirement of a public trial by a jury and the minimal role of the trial judge saved English procedure from degenerating into an inquisitorial system. That the court was open to all who cared to attend, the interested and the curious, made a difference; but it was the authority of the trial jury that finally counted, not merely in the disposition of any case but in the retention of the accusatory system.[45]

Despite the preliminary examination by the justice of the peace, the indictment by the grand jury, the evidence submitted by the crown, and the instructions of the judge, the trial jury when locked up to reach a verdict were responsible only to their own consciences. They were completely free to return a verdict of their pleasure in accordance with what they thought right. The evidence was not binding upon them; the judge's charge was not binding; nothing was. The law did not concern itself with the question how they reached their verdict. This curiously irrational element in the jury system proved, of course, to be a great protection to accused persons in many cases, whatever their actual guilt. If a jury moved by whim, mercy, sympathy, or pigheadedness refused to convict against all law and evidence, the prisoner was freed, and that was that. The doctrine, as Thayer said, was "ancient that one should not be twice put in jeopardy of life or limb for the same offence."[46] On the other hand, a jury prejudiced against a defendant might return a verdict of guilty, but the judge, if convinced of unfairness in such a case, could reprieve the prisoner and recommend that the king pardon him.

The finality of the jury's verdict of not guilty, in a criminal case, probably derived from the fact that the jury originated when the older forms of proof—compurgation, ordeal, and battle—had not yet died out. The verdict of the inquest took on the same conclusiveness as any judgment of God, especially because the jurors were originally witnesses whose oaths were decisive. By the late fourteenth century the requirement of a unanimous verdict became settled practice, adding to the authority of verdicts. The rule of unanimity may have originated, as Pollock and Maitland said, because the test was the voice of the country, and the country could have but one voice. The origin of the rule may also be found in the fact that in early trials by witnesses and compurgators, there was a requirement of unanimity. If one compurgator failed to make the oath by just the right formula or perjured himself, the oath "burst." By the same analogy the failure of a jury to agree "burst" the verdict. A unanimous verdict by the inquest, which was regarded as representative of the country, an expression of its sense, carried a supernatural weight. In any case the sworn inquest, having succeeded the older forms of proof, inherited many of their characteristics, including that of finality.[47]

In civil cases, but never in the instance of a criminal verdict, when jurors were still regarded as witnesses, the court regarded a false verdict as a form of perjury, punishable by a special process known as the attaint. A special jury of twenty-four tried the civil jury that gave the false verdict, and its members, if convicted, could be punished severely. As jurors lost their character as witnesses, the attaint fell into disuse; by the sixteenth century it was rarely employed and then only rarely successful. Juries in criminal cases, though never subject to the attaint, could be threatened with punishment by the Star Chamber for a false verdict, but the threat was more often than not an idle one calculated to intimidate rather than force a verdict of guilty. In the first half of the sixteenth century, almost every term of the Star Chamber saw some grand inquest or jury fined for acquitting felons or murderers, but that also became an anachronistic practice. One of the last examples of its use occurred after the trial of Sir Nicholas Throckmorton in 1554.[48]

Throckmorton was tried for high treason because of his complicity in Wyatt's Rebellion, which grew out of opposition to the marriage of Queen Mary to Philip of Spain. A treason trial, above all others, most directly involved the security of the state, and even a common-law court of that period would conduct the trial in the interests of the sovereign, determined on a conviction. Throckmorton had been imprisoned for fifty-eight days preceding the day of the trial; he had had no opportunity to prepare his case and had been kept in ignorance of the evidence against him. He had to defend himself, extemporaneously; counsel was not permitted in such cases till 1695. He heard the indictment read against him but had no copy of it—not till 1696 did defendants in treason cases have a right to a copy of the indictment. He had no right to call witnesses on his behalf either; when he saw in the courtroom a man whom he wanted to give testimony, the chief justice ordered the man out. With only the slimmest opportunity of making an effective defense, Throckmorton nevertheless had the very great advantage of being tried publicly before a jury and the freedom to say whatever he wished, and he made the most of it. Defending himself with astonishing vigor and agility, he engaged in a spirited altercation with the crown's counsel and even with the chief justice, on points of law as well as fact. He was allowed the liberty of correcting the court's summation to the jury and of making a speech to the jury following the summation. He won an acquittal. The jury's verdict certainly proved the comparative fairness of even an imperfect accusatorial procedure.[49]

The jurors, however, were punished for their audacity. The court, unable to touch Throckmorton, imprisoned all twelve jurors. Four who "made their submission, and owned their offence" were freed, but the remaining eight, after six months in jail, were heavily fined by the Star Chamber and then were discharged. Sir Thomas Smith, about a decade later, observed that if a jury "having pregnant evidence" acquitted a defendant, "which they will do sometime," he went free but the judge rebuked the jurors and threatened them with punishment. "But this threatening chanceth oftener than the execution thereof, and the twelve answer with most gentle words they did it according to their consciences and . . . as they thought right and . . . so it passeth away for the most part." Alluding to Throckmorton's case, he noted the punishment of the jury, yet added, "But these doings were even then by many accounted very violent, tyrannical, and contrary to the liberty and custom of the realm of England. Wherefore it cometh very seldom in use. . . ." Thus, although the rule was not finally established until Bushell's case in 1670 that a jury could not be punished for having acquitted a defendant against the evidence or the direction of the court, juries were free to render verdicts of their choice, with impunity, after Throckmorton's case. Notwithstanding their sometimes erratic and even inexplicable behavior, their tendency to reflect public prejudice, and their capability of being intimidated by the court, trial juries were England's major barrier against the growth of the inquisitional mode of procedure.[50]

In sum, then, criminal procedure on the Continent, in both ecclesiastical and secular courts, was thoroughly inquisitorial, while England's procedure remained essentially accusatorial. The two systems originated in the same source, the inquest, and developed at the same time but in divergent directions. In one there was no definite accuser lest it be the judge himself whose suspicions were aroused by common report or secret information; in the other, there was a definite accuser whose charges led to a preliminary examination of the suspect by a justice of the peace. The inquisitorial system did not provide for a specification and revelation of the charges; the accusatorial system, utilizing the grand jury to screen the charges, provided them in a detailed indictment. The inquisitorial system surrounded every step in the proceedings with secrecy, making unchecked tyranny inevitable; the accusatorial system was substantially public. The former was nonconfrontative, revealing not even the names of the witnesses against the accused; the latter was essentially confrontative, naming the witnesses, producing their depositions in court, and with some exceptions in treason trials allowing them to give sworn testimony before the accused and the jury. One system presumed the guilt of the accused; the other, requiring the prosecution to prove its case, did not. The one forced the accused to submit to a self-incriminatory oath; the other did not even permit the accused to give sworn testimony if he wanted to. One tried the accused by secret interrogatories, the other by public evidence. One was an official prosecution by the judge; the other made the trial an oral combat before a jury of the accused's peers, with the public watching, the crown's attorney prosecuting, and the judge basically passive. One empowered the judge to decide the question of guilt or innocence, while the other permitted a jury to control the verdict. One routinely used torture; the other regarded it as illegal. One utilized a stringent and sophisticated law of evidence, the theory of "legal proofs," while the other was almost casual about the nature of evidence. One made an absolute differentiation between civil and criminal procedure; the other employed essentially the same litigious procedure for both. One, not recognizing the concept of double jeopardy, retried a suspect indefinitely, while the other would not place anyone in jeopardy more than once for the same offense in a capital case. Finally, one was cruel and arbitrary; the other was relatively fair and just.

What accounts for England's singular escape from the fate of the continental nations of Europe? The most likely answer is that the accusatorial system of procedure, based on the inquest, effectively served the needs of the state, making unnecessary the employment of the inquisitorial system. Fortuitous timing seems to have made a great difference. Pollock and Maitland wrote that

England had a narrow escape. The old forms of proof were breaking down. "Happily, however, the reforms of Henry II were effected before the days of Innocent III." Just how narrow was the escape is shown by the fact that Henry II died in 1189, only nine years before Innocent III became pope. But the great Angevin's reforms were instituted in the 1160's and 1170's. In something of an overstatement, Pollock and Maitland remarked that "the whole of English law is centralized and unified" by the establishment of royal judges, their frequent eyres throughout the land, and "by the introduction of the 'inquest' or 'recognition' and the 'original writ' as normal parts of the machinery of justice." Not only was English law centralized early; the English state itself was centralized earlier than that of any other country, and one of the foremost means of achieving that centralization was the system of royal justice employing the inquest which became the grand and petty juries. Sir William Holdsworth best made the point: "Thus it happened that the delegates of royal power could make their influence felt all over the country, and royal justice everywhere superseded the justice administered by the local courts. One of the most important instruments of the royal power was the inquisition held under the supervision of a royal judge by means of a jury. And, wherever the royal justice was introduced, this method of determining facts accompanied it. Thus the jury system spread as rapidly and as widely as the justice of the royal courts, and as the rules of that common law which those courts were both making and administering. But the rapidity of the development of the common law caused it to develop a set of fixed principles before the ideas of the civil and canon lawyers had time to exercise an overwhelming influence upon the substance of its rules."[51]

Thus English rules of criminal law retained many archaic ideas, keeping the new jury procedure as accusatorial as the older modes of proof. The jury system was a new mode of proof, or at least was treated as if it were a mode of proof. It was therefore based on consent, and its results were taken as final. The judges took the path of least resistance by accepting verdicts rather than by making their own inquiries, a step that would have led to an inquisitorial system. The unsophisticated state of the law of evidence, which was indeed in its rudimentary stages, made it additionally easy for the judges to accept the findings of a band of witnesses

—the sworn inquest. Not the least result was that the English judge, relieved of the necessity of making his own determination of guilt or innocence, gained enhanced dignity and impartiality. These wholesome benefits would have been impossible had the crown not been able to adapt the accusatorial system of justice to the needs of the state. The sworn inquest, however, did serve to augment the exchequer, control local feudatories, and enforce the king's peace. By contrast, the French monarchy, a century after Henry II centralized England, had extended royal jurisdiction over the royal demesne only. The inquisitorial system became a powerful instrument for centralizing France as the accusatorial had in England. England was also less susceptible to the influences of the canon and civil lawyers of the Continent because of its isolation. For the same reason, perhaps, the contagion of heresy scarcely infected England; her orthodoxy in religion was also a settling force, a bulwark against the need for ecclesiastical inquisitions.

It would be misleading, however, to say that the inquisitional system became England's road not taken, for England did not escape. True enough, the only inquisitional process that entered the common-law system was the preliminary examination which to this day has never completely shaken its inquisitional cast. However, the common law was not the only law in England; in the later Middle Ages prerogative courts, such as the Star Chamber, were established which did not employ the ancient common-law writs, forms of action, or procedures. Some of these prerogative courts, which were erected by royal commission, exercised criminal jurisdiction. Their system of criminal procedure was decidedly inquisitorial, at least until 1640. By special warrant from the king or his Privy Council, they even used torture, as has already been noted. Their proceedings were by no means unconstitutional. England's judicial system, having become extremely complex by the sixteenth century, utilized more than one set of criminal procedures. To some degree the prerogative courts and the common-law courts were competing rivals. In any case, the employment by the prerogative courts of the oath *ex officio*, the inquisitional oath, provoked the struggle that eventually led to the creation of the right against self-incrimination.

Maitland's epigram that the "seamless web" of history is torn by telling a piece of it,[52] is borne out by any effort to explain the origins of the right against self-incrimination. The American origins derive from the inherited English common-law system of criminal justice. But the English origins, so much more complex, spilled over legal boundaries and reflected the many-sided religious, political, and constitutional issues which racked England during the sixteenth and seventeenth centuries: the struggles for supremacy between Catholicism and Protestantism, between Anglicanism and Puritanism, between King and Parliament, between arbitrary rule and limited or constitutional government, between the suppression of heresy and sedition and freedom of conscience and press. Even within the more immediate confines of law itself, the history of the right against self-incrimination is enmeshed in broad issues of great import: the contests for supremacy between the accusatory and the inquisitorial systems of criminal procedure, between the common law and the royal prerogative, and between the common law and its canon and civil law rivals. Against this huge canvas the origins of the concept that "no man is bound to accuse himself" (*nemo tenetur seipsum prodere*) must be understood. As noted earlier, when in 1532 John Lambert defied his inquisitors by refusing to swear an oath that would have forced him to accuse himself, he stood on several centuries of English experience with an accusatorial system of criminal procedure.

MILTON CANTOR

The Writ of Habeas Corpus: Early American Origins and Development

"A COUNTRY WHICH IGNORES ITS LEGAL HISTORY," wrote Dean Rippy of the New York University Law School, "is like a captain of a vessel at sea who neglects periodically to take his latitudinal and longitudinal position in order to be sure that he is on his true course."[1] Such admonitions notwithstanding, American historians have left their nation's early legal history largely unexplored. In part, this neglect is due to special difficulties embedded in the subject—the knowledge of legal technicalities and of the law itself; in part, it is due to the absence of court and statutory records; and, finally, the deterrent inheres in the colony-to-colony variation in legal practices and principles, which makes even regional generalizations less than compelling. This diversity in legal usages and institutions is an unyielding, almost insurmountable initial problem. Such diversity makes it essential to engage in a study of individual colonies. It leads to the disheartening conclusion that the colonies were by no means the neat, tidy places some historians imagine them to have been, and that the findings of a page-by-page and law-by-law examination are applicable only to the colony examined.[2]

This inability to generalize is, to be sure, as understandable as it is discouraging. The colonies, after all, were not only separated from the motherland, they were also physically distinct from one another. Consequently, localism was the dominant reality. Each

55

colony regarded itself as a disconnected and virtually autonomous unit for purposes of administration; each developed its own customs, traditions, usages; each regarded the laws of the others as "Foreign law."[3] Hence every student of colonial legal culture will recognize that his subject is one of paradoxes, inconsistencies, divergences.

The extent of the practice of English common law is possibly the most important controversy in colonial legal history, and the most difficult to resolve. Any student addressing himself to this inquiry must contend with the magisterial Roscoe Pound, who has affirmed that English common law, as known to the colonists, was "heavily burdened with the formalism of the strict law . . . [and, therefore] quite out of line with the needs and ideas of men who were opening up the wilderness." This claim, somewhat misleading because of its too sweeping tone, has also been the conclusion of Paul Reinsch, William Hamersley, and others.[4] Equally misleading for the same reason have been the conclusions of their scholarly adversaries, chief among them being Herbert Pope, Charles Hilkey, Francis Aumann, Julius Goebel, and John T. Farrell.[5] These authorities have challenged the "frontier theory," finding it "an artificial and labored explanation," and affirmed instead the transplantation of either English or Biblical law. Such a counterclaim has much to recommend it. Legal practices, such as habeas corpus, do not spring like Athena, fully armed from the head of Zeus. They are victims and possessors of the past. They are rooted centuries-deep in the soil of history, exfoliate slowly, and defy any all-inclusive generalization. To the contrary, all scholarly propositions about this haphazard accumulation of precedents and obscurities called the common law must be scrutinized in the light of actual conditions and practices in each colony. Then, it will be seen, these propositions will be qualified in one way for Massachusetts, in another for Virginia, in a third for Maryland, and so forth.

One qualification is that the transit of legal practices and institutions to many of the colonies was accomplished without the crudity that might have been expected and that votaries of the "frontier theory" have alleged. Further, insofar as certain guarantees of personal liberty were concerned, this transit did not discourage conformity to the spirit and substance of English common law. These guarantees, moreover, do not reflect the pluralistic character of the colonies' legal order nearly as much as most common-law practices. Certainly the writ of habeas corpus, a privilege at the vital center of Anglo-American liberties, is less vulnerable to colony-by-colony variation. Writing of the writ, W. F. Bailey has affirmed that the colonists brought it in their legal baggage, claiming it among the immemorial rights descended to them from their ancestors.[6] Bailey's work is superficial, simplistic, outdated; yet this categorical statement has retained its resilience and validity. To support Bailey's claim properly, it would seem necessary to explore English precedents—to determine whether this particular common-law practice remained a viable libertarian bulwark; or whether it suffered any changes in transit; or even whether, *mutatis mutandis*, it was anything like its great English counterpart.

Before doing so, however, something further wants saying of habeas corpus itself, of what Blackstone has called "the high prerogative" writ.[7] "The inviolability of the physical person," as Pound has observed, "is universally put first among the demands which the individual may make."[8] Such inviolability, that is security of person, has long been considered essential to the Anglo-American legal tradition. It has taken the form of protection against arbitrary seizure and detention, and against certain procedural violations. Like many rights and privileges, therefore, it was essentially a negative conception but, as two recent authorities have observed, "liberty must, indeed, mean absence of certain external restraints before it can mean anything better."[9]

Most notably, the right of personal liberty is inextricably enmeshed with the writ of *habeas corpus ad subjiciendum et recipiendum:* literally, that "you have the body for submitting to and receiving which," declared Blackstone, was "the great and efficacious writ in all manner of illegal confinement."[10] This writ was, in essence, little more than a judicial command to the respondent, usually penal authorities, to produce a named prisoner together with the cause of his detention—in order that the legal warrant detaining him may be judicially examined. Hence it was in the nature of a writ of error to examine the legality of a commitment. It was a writ of inquiry, and it did not automatically guarantee the petitioner's prayer. But it made mandatory that the parties should appear before the court for clarification of the facts of the case. If the examining magistrate found no justification in law, absolute discharge must result; and the writ, therefore, became the legal remedy for the enforcement of personal liberty, the means for speedy release from imprisonment without sufficient cause.[11] The judicial command for release, it should be understood, did not involve an inquiry into the alleged criminal act itself; nor was it followed by punishment for the wrongful act of restraining the petitioner.[12] On the same footing with other prerogative writs— *mandamus, quo warranto, certiorari,* etc.—habeas corpus has nonetheless been deemed the major guarantor of personal liberty since it supersedes all other writs and orders.[13]

The roots of the writ of habeas corpus lie in a very confusing period of English legal history. Sir William Holdsworth, in his luminous classic, quite properly affirmed that "the judges of the courts of common law . . . , in the twelfth and thirteenth centuries, laid the foundations of that common law. In fact, it is difficult to assign a limit to the antiquarian excursions it is necessary to make in order to find a starting point."[14] Sir William's assertion, so pertinent to the common law, appears particularly applicable to the great writ, which was first practiced in a dark and hazy past. Like all personal liberties assuming legal guise, it derived from tradition, trial-and-error usage, and compromise arrangements rather than statutory mandates.

Until legal scholars examined the conclusions of Edward Coke and William Blackstone, among others, it was generally understood that habeas corpus and Magna Carta were indissolubly linked.[15] When doubts were first raised, the modified claim became, "Magna Carta [was] the first royal recognition of this writ, but it came to us as a part of the common law."[16] More recently, however, historians have completely severed the writ from the barons' achievement at Runnymede.[17]

Perhaps the question—whether habeas corpus springs from Magna Carta—is irrelevant, since scholars have found that its usage predated 1215. Pollock and Maitland, in their monumental *History of England,* tell us that as early as 1187, "if a man was arrested he was usually replevied or mainprised; that is to say, he was set free as soon as sureties undertook or became bound for his appearance in court."[18] And they found "those famous words *habeas corpus* are making their way into divers writs." Two court orders of 1199, sixteen years before Magna Carta, commanded one party to have another named party appear before the court at Westminster.[19] The *Coram Rege Rolls* yield another definite instance, Tyrel's case of 1214 which, the record suggests, was neither unique nor unprecedented.[20] By the first quarter of the thirteenth century, there was a considerable body of evidence indicating that royal judges widely used the writ. Witness the *Curia Regis Rolls* for 1219–1220, which records specific orders directing a royal official (usually a sheriff) to produce a specified party so that litigation could be completed.[21]

Thus the writ functioned to expedite judicial processes and was issued at judicial command. It was at the outset merely an administrative order from superior judicial authority to subordinate courts or officials, directing them to give information or to do something.[22] But it was adapted to legal purposes and had libertarian overtones, even when issued without request by any petitioner. A man could hardly feel secure in his rights if legal processes might be carried on or concluded in his absence. The courts' hesitancy about proceeding without all parties to a cause, as Robert Walker has emphasized, served as indirect protection of the liberty of litigants.

The writ's practice altered, becoming broader in application, with the passage of time. Very gradually habeas corpus evolved to the point where it served a prisoner by directing his jailer to produce him before the court—to show the cause of detention and, inseparably joined to this procedure, to enable his judges to inquire into the lawfulness of the commitment. This practice developed over several centuries, and there was no one dramatic turn of events. By the 1350's, the concept of due process at common law was becoming familiar to Englishmen, particularly to lawyers and judges. Their awareness was partly inspired by the evolution of medieval towns into cities, which helped alter the old freedom from arrest and detention pending trial. Extended commitment, without due process administered by common-law courts, became a growing practice in the burgeoning and increasingly complex urban centers.

Changes in the court system paralleled unfolding urbanization. The royal courts assumed greater powers and jurisdictions for themselves. Habeas corpus adjusted to the developing legal and social order, being resifted and reshaped. Hence the Habeas Corpus Act, when Parliament finally passed it in 1679, merely bore testimony to a *fait accompli*. By this time, the functions and procedural intent of habeas corpus were widely known and widely accepted, another element in that body of practices known as the common law, which theoretically at least formed part of the heritage of British America.

Earlier commentary upon the sharply differing legal culture of most colonies deserves emphasis; likewise, the observation that law in these colonies was a combination of volatile and varying factors—overseas experiences, scriptural commands, local necessities. But caution is also warranted, since certain common-law practices—by reiteration, publication, and the fairly meticulous practice of some English administrators in America—assumed a colony-wide dimension, achieved stability and, in colonial eyes, became inherited and universal "rights." Listening to statements repeated since 1693, when King's Bench affirmed that Englishmen carried their law with them, eventually confirmed the fact to the settlers; so, too, did Blackstone, whose *Commentaries*, more than any other legal text, was read as a breviary, a repository of immutable truths, especially when personal liberty was threatened. At such times, the colonists exploited all the legal devices at their command; and possibly foremost among them was habeas corpus, "the most important human right," according to Zechariah Chafee.[23]

Given the great esteem with which the writ was held in England by the 1600's, we might expect some knowledge of habeas corpus to percolate early into the colonial consciousness. Its importance in seventeenth-century legal-political conflict in England, even more than the presence of settlers with legal experience, would seemingly guarantee awareness and practice of habeas corpus. But it is impossible to find any reference to the writ as a means of testing the validity of commitment prior to the 1680's.

The work of legal historians is of little help on the subject of the writ's reception. One scholar has contended that habeas corpus was not part of colonial practice prior to 1710, when Parliament formally applied the English act of 1679 to Virginia; another has found an effective common-law writ in existence by the

1670's; a third has placed its reception a decade later.[24] This last contention would seem the soundest, though habeas corpus probably was not fully operative until the 1690's. Such a delay is striking—until one begins to place the writ's usage within the context of the earlier and larger theme; namely, the common law and its reception in English America. The shaping factor of environment remained a constant, and it made the writ impracticable at an earlier date. The fact of a primitive society, rather than ignorance of habeas corpus or an insouciant disregard for the right of personal liberty, is mostly responsible for the belated appearance of this prerogative writ. Survival came first. Hence Dale's laws in Virginia, quasi-martial law in Connecticut, the built-in severities of Hebraic canons, the sense of emergency that governed many communities, dictated laws and regulations suitable for war or for settlement.[25]

In sum, early conditions inevitably retarded the use of habeas corpus. Its existence implied complex legal practices, and these would have been unrealistic in the 1600's. Habeas corpus, after all, presumed a reasonable separation of powers, an independent judiciary in particular. But a simple governmental system functioned in the first years of settlement. There was no distinct separation of powers anywhere. The Massachusetts General Court, for example, had judicial as well as legislative and quasi-executive functions. Maryland's governor and council were at "the apex of the [colony's] . . . judicial hierarchy."[26] Governors' councils, whatever their titles, generally combined administrative, adjudicative, and policy-making responsibilities.

Other relevant factors include the absence of professional legal groups and the paucity of legal knowledge. Further impeding the writ's reception, Massachusetts' Puritans distrusted lawyers as a class and viewed some aspects of the common law with hostility.[27] In Virginia, the landed gentry did most of its own law work, which discouraged the rise of an independent body of professionals. New York's merchants and large landowners were equally vigilant in guarding their powers. Quakers, seeking to avoid legal process entirely, used laymen as "common peacemakers." Judges of South Carolina were all laymen in the late seventeenth century, because no trained lawyers could be found there.[28] Then, too, the colonies lacked a single headquarters of appellate litigation and a center where ambitious apprentices in the law could learn. Rather, there were thirteen different centers, as Boorstin has asserted, and "no American London where lawyers could consolidate their monopoly." Nor should the absence of intricate commercial and mercantile operations be neglected, since these were the mainstays of a thriving legal business. Consequently, the colonies lacked a trained bar and had few law books. The principal texts in use at the outset which dealt with high prerogative writs were Coke's *Institutes*, Michael Dalton's *The Country Justice*, *Coke on Littleton*, *Coke on Magna Carta*, Fortescue's *On the Laws of England*.[29]

One final factor accounted for the writ's belated reception. Habeas corpus usage usually is crisis usage, and only in the late seventeenth century, when direct royal control was first asserted, did it become quantitatively important. Prior to this period the colonists, within their simple legal structure, had sufficient guarantees against arbitrary rule insofar as it meant illegal detention prior to formal adjudication. Pre-trial conditions were similar to England's at a comparable stage of development (in the twelfth and thirteenth centuries), when modest-sized agrarian communities prevailed, when polity was simple and unitary, when equity usually was sufficient, and when justice was easily expedited and highly decentralized. In such rural societies, imprisonment before or after trial was unusual. The colonists lived in isolated settlements, with little opportunity to escape constituted authority. Their possessions, both real and personal, could be readily attached if they failed to appear for hearing and for trial; they could be banished or otherwise punished for deliberate and continued flouting of authority.[30] Indeed, the courts seemed to find almost any form of punishment preferable to commitment. Alternatives included fines, whipping, branding, and the stocks. Imprisonment was infrequent by comparison, pre-trial commitments almost nonexistent, and few languished in jail without resort to expediting legal practices.[31] It followed, therefore, that the application of habeas corpus would be slowed down or deferred.

The colonists, however, were hardly unaware of their rights. Their concern for laws and legal practices in harmony with Magna Carta was evident as early as 1635 when, John Winthrop recorded, "the deputies have conceived great danger to our state in regard that our magistrates, for want of positive laws, in many cases might proceed according to their discretions, [and] it was agreed that some men should be appointed to frame a body of grounds of laws, *in resemblance to a Magna Charta*, which . . . should be received for fundamental laws."[32] Nathaniel Ward's Body of Liberties of 1641 was built on the common law and its guarantees, the first two sections deriving directly from Magna Carta, rather than from the Bible. And when the General Court sought to revise this legislation, it relied upon Coke's commentaries on the great charter. The second draft, consequently, gave a larger role to Magna Carta and a smaller one to scripture than the first. Massachusetts' example was soon followed in the New Haven Code of 1656, the Charter of Fundamental Law of West New Jersey of 1677, South Carolina's charter of 1712, and North Carolina's of 1715. The Rhode Island charter, with Roger Williams as its guiding spirit, eschewed all use of Holy Writ in favor of Chapter 39 of Magna Carta. This chapter was mentioned in New York's Charter of Liberties (1683), which was "very much an English document," particularly in its guarantees for liberty of person.[33] Colonists elsewhere were untiring in their assertion of rights coeval with those of all Englishmen, and frequently relied upon this provision.[34]

Such assertions were increasingly popular after the 1670's, when royal officials first began to consider restricting the autonomy of colonial legislatures. Until then, the profits of Yorkshire turnpikes, successive crises of empire, and recurrent troubles on the Continent took precedence at Westminster. Each colony, as a result, became accustomed to pursuing its own policies, though it derived legal existence from the crown. It was a simple dichotomy to enforce, since England had encouraged the principle that her overseas dominions should be self-governing, virtually disconnected from each other. It permitted these dominions a popular assembly, chosen by freemen or freeholders, to develop and sink roots deep into colonial soil. Distracted elsewhere, the motherland appeared indifferent when these legislative bodies increased the scope and number of their powers, and proclaimed the traditional privileges of their great prototype, the House of Commons.

By the time England turned her attention westward across the seas, a strong sense of legislative independence had developed. Believing themselves able to manage their own affairs, the colonists naturally turned to those legal instruments which they had found efficacious in contests with royal authority that antedated settlement. They looked to the union of Magna Carta and habeas corpus, that mismatch made inseparable by the demands of English constitutional debate. This interpretation, which had so plagued royal prerogative in the motherland, would continue to do so in her thirteen colonies.

The nascent conflict over the limits of Parliamentary authority took many forms: hostility to royal commissioners, antagonism toward royal governors, disallowance of colonial laws, struggle for control of the purse, usurpation of executive power by the colonial legislators, and passive resistance to externally imposed revisions on colonial statutes. The first crisis came in 1686 with the appointment of Edmund Andros as governor of the Dominion of New England. Ambitious and determined to impose direct royal authority, he was immediately resisted by the colonists. This opposition drove Andros to measures of unprecedented severity. His insistence that all land titles be reexamined and that the payment of a quitrent be a condition of regrants evoked intense opposition, which was exacerbated by his arbitrary imposition of what were considered unjust assessments. When an Ipswich town meeting resisted these impositions, Andros arrested and fined its leaders, issued an order limiting town meetings to one annually, and placed the militia under his direct control.

One result of this collision between Andros and the colonists was the Ipswich tax case (1687).[35] It arose out of the refusal of the Ipswich town meeting to pay a levy imposed by order of the governor's Council, on the grounds of illegality. Ipswich's minister, John Wise, and four prominent townsfolk, were thereupon arrested and imprisoned for "contempt and high misdemeanor." They applied for and were denied a writ of habeas corpus, trial judge informing them that they "must not think the Laws of England follow [petitioners] to the ends of the earth or whither [they] went." And when the defendants invoked Magna Carta, they were told that their only remaining privilege was "not to be sold as a slave."[36]

Major William Vaughn's conflict with the governor of New Hampshire in 1684 did not end with denial of the writ. But there is no firm evidence that habeas corpus was issued. What is significant about the New Hampshire proceedings and about the Ipswich case as well is that the writ had a role, and it suggests that habeas corpus may have been used on a common-law basis in the colonies. Certainly the settlers looked to it when confronted by the growing constitutional crisis. By the 1680's, therefore, it was a familiar legal device in all the colonies. Habeas corpus was prominent in the 1683 Beverley case in Virginia. Major Robert Beverley, clerk of the Burgesses, was arrested for refusing to produce the assembly's journals without its permission, and Governor Henry Chicheley committed Beverley to a frigate, "there to remain until further ordered." Challenging his detention, Beverley claimed that as "a free borne subject of England, I ought not to be committed prisoner without deserved crime." Shifted to an English prison, he was unable to secure a writ of habeas corpus. William Fitzhugh, a Virginia attorney who acted as Beverley's counsel, wrote a reassuring letter to his client before the trial. It affirmed that Beverley had a right to the privilege, being an Englishman, and he should be comforted by the knowledge that his detention was contrary to Magna Carta, the Resolution of the Judges, "the Petition of Right, and the diverse statutes made in confirmation of the first. . . ."[37]

Fitzhugh's arguments are illuminating. They indicate the growing awareness of English rights and, by their preciseness, tell us something of the sharpening character of constitutional discussion. Whitehall's decision to reshape and redirect colonial law and mores further intensified the debate. This new royal policy, when considered together with Andros' measures, clearly represented an effort to broaden royal prerogative at a time when it was being contained in England proper, and influenced the reception of habeas corpus.

After Massachusetts, which suffered under Andros' rule, New York was most severely affected by these unprecedented royal policies. Surprisingly, crown officials—rather than those alleging unjust detention—introduced the writ into the province. Theirs was a tactical move in the overall plan to guide New York law into the path of English jurisprudence, thereby entirely eliminating Dutch influence. Consonant with this objective, the colony's Charter of

Liberties of 1683 contained the provision that "the inhabitants of New York shall be governed by and according to the Laws of England." It seemed a likely assumption, and New Yorkers made it, that this clause embraced Magna Carta, the English Habeas Corpus Act, and other measures protecting individual liberty.

But this attempt to anglicize New York's legal system clashed with another design—that of allowing broad scope for royal prerogative. Consequently, in 1684, the Privy Council disallowed the charter with the terse observation: "this privilege [of habeas corpus] is not granted to any of his Majesties Plantations where the Act of Habeas Corpus and all other such Bills do not take place."[38] The same fate met attempts by Pennsylvania, Massachusetts, and South Carolina to make the writ formally operative.[39] Privy Council's reasoning was commonplace at the time: unless a Parliamentary measure contained specific reference to the colony or colonies, it was inapplicable to them.

In addition to the publicized reasons, however, there was another one that prompted the Council, and it was political rather than legal. The likelihood of maintaining the colonies subordinate to royal prerogative would be diminished if they were armed with due process, high prerogative writs, and other instruments of personal liberty. Such thoughts seem to have induced the following instruction of 1706 to the royal governors:

And whereas great mischiefs may arise by passing bills of an unusual and extraordinary nature and importance in the plantations, which bills remain in force there from the time of enacting until our pleasure be signified to the CONTRARY; we do hereby will and require you not to pass or give your consent hereafter to any bill or bills in the assembly of our said province of unusual and extraordinary nature and importance wherein our prerogative . . . may be prejudiced (until either (1) the royal pleasure has been signified, or (2) unless the bill contained a suspending clause delaying its effectuation until the royal will was known).[40]

The writ of liberty would clearly fall under the ban.

In this manner, habeas corpus became a debatable topic in the late seventeenth century, though its actual status is uncertain. Nor was Whitehall's policy clear-cut and consistent. Rejecting the Bay Colony's attempt to adopt the English Habeas Corpus Act of 1679, it permitted South Carolina to do so in 1692.[41]

Reiteration is in order, before turning to the eighteenth century: local court practices, while blurred and circumspect in the use of habeas corpus, did adopt the writ or one of its variations even in those colonies where legislative attempts to appropriate the English Habeas Corpus Act had been revoked. Common-law usage in such instances highlighted the fact that modern legal scholarship has disregarded the maxim: "the law under which the people of any particular time or place live must be sought for, in the last analysis, not in what the written laws, or even the courts say, but in what the courts *do.*"[42] Haskins, Reinsch, Hilkey, *et al.* have made the same error. They have restricted their studies to legislation alone, basing descriptions of the judicial system, the civil procedure, the legal *modus operandi* of a single colony or colonies almost entirely upon published codes and records. Taking statutory evidence at face value, they have neglected to check upon the actual implementation of the laws. Only the court records themselves can indicate the extent to which colonial law was English law. Thus Connecticut courts in the 1750's entertained actions for contracts and torts thoroughly familiar in English common law. The Beverley case of 1682, and one or two others of less importance, suggest that the writ was practiced in Virginia even before 1710, when Parliament officially extended the 1679 act to the province. Similarly, the writ was first used successfully in Massachusetts in 1686—in order to remove the defendant, in an action in trover, from one jurisdiction of the Court of Pleas for Suffolk to Superior Court; and in 1708, it was issued by Assize to remove a prisoner to a safer detention.[43] In another commitment case, noted above, the petitioners led by John Wise, in 1687, applied for (and were denied) habeas corpus, before the Massachusetts General Court conferred it by law five years later.[44]

Then there were instances when judges admitted *habeas corpus ad respondendum* or *ad prosequendum*, rather than *ad subjiciendum*. The Provincial Court of Maryland, for example, used *ad respondendum* as early as 1665, in order to secure the appearance of a prisoner already committed for debt, so that he might answer another action. Massachusetts' assembly, in 1686, instructed the Superior Court to issue a *habeas corpus ad prosequendum* in order to remove an action from the Suffolk Court of Pleas to its own jurisdiction. These writs of habeas corpus were not qualified by the respective legal bodies as *ad respondendum* or *ad prosequendum*, which has contributed to a misreading of the reception of *ad subjiciendum*. It also suggests that judicial reluctance to grant the writ was waning.

Nonetheless, such reluctance is characteristic of the late seventeenth century. Caution with respect to the open and avowed practice of habeas corpus was evident in New York; and it was understandable in view of the previous disallowance. That the writ was functional in the 1690's is apparent but, Goebel and Naughton have concluded, "the frequent incompleteness of the records in habeas corpus cases may be mere accident, but it conveys an impression of furtiveness which leads one to wonder whether or not an issue was deliberately avoided."[46] The same observation was applicable to Maryland, where one or two incomplete references to habeas corpus, such as *Short v. Gardiner* (1696), suggest judicial reticence and flaccid usage.[47]

A sprinkling of cases began in New York in 1691. The first one of importance, that of Hendrick Fransa, approximated a writ of error use of habeas corpus, and was an attack on the form of mittimus (by which Fransa was committed). Two years later, the writ was invoked to determine bailability, but the court's action was not indicated on the record. The only other report extant in this decade involved pre-trial transfer—in the Thomas Spurr case of 1691. This flurry of cases represented the first actual implementation of the writ on record in the province. Although the remedy may have been available, at least to secure a reasonable bail, in all common-law jurisdictions earlier than charters and statutes may have suggested, the South Carolina act of 1692 and this group of cases in the 1690's, mark the writ's actual reception in the colonies.

Edward Randolph, the Surveyor-General of South Carolina, recommended to the Board of Trade in 1700 " 'that, it being the practice for governors to imprison the subjects without bail, the habeas corpus act should be extended as fully to the colonies as it is in England.' "[48] His proposal received endorsement a decade later, when the privilege was formally extended to Virginia. Governor Spotswood, on instructions from Queen Anne in 1710, issued a proclamation which could legitimately be called America's first habeas corpus act:

. . . Whereas We are above all things desirous that all our Subjects enjoy their legal Rights, You are to take especial care that if any person be committed for any Criminal matters (unless for Treason or felony plainly and especially expressed in the Warrant of Commitment), he shall have free liberty to petition by himself or otherwise the chief Barron or any one of the Judges of the common pleas for a writt of Habeas Corpus.[49]

In other colonies, however, increasing though sporadic employment of the writ began without specific authorization; and recall its modest use in New York in the 1690's. After 1700, habits of circumspection began to disappear in a number of colonies. In Massachusetts, for instance, Chief Justice Sewall denied application for a writ in 1706, but on grounds that do not intimate petitioner's action was unusual.[50] Two years later, the Court of Assize granted the writ, to order a sheriff to transfer his prisoner to "better and more safe keeping." Habeas corpus, issued in New York in 1701, compelled "the Sheriff to bring ye defendant immediate" before the court.[51] Three years later, a special court of Oyer and Terminer and General Gaol Delivery "ordered that the Sheriff bring John Johnson, the prisoner in his custody immediately to the Barr."[52] In 1707, Lord Cornbury, the governor, directed that two ministers—Francis Makemie and John Hampton—be arrested for preaching without licenses and committed them under a warrant to the sheriff instructing them to be "safely" kept "till further orders."[53] The Chief Justice issued the writ on application of the defendants; and the sheriff was furnished with another warrant specifying the offense. Presumably he might have made a return stating that this executive warrant was his sole authority for commitment, the sort of return presented in Darnel's case—namely, per speciale mandatum Domini Regis. But the issue of detention on an executive order was not raised.[54]

If the writ began to be used with growing frequency without official sanction early in the eighteenth century, the sanctions themselves were soon forthcoming from Westminster and from colonial assemblies. In 1712, for example, instructions similar to those given Spotswood resulted in a firm statutory foundation in North and South Carolina.[55] Obviously royal policy had changed. As a result, habeas corpus began its rapid assimilation into colonial jurisprudence. It did so, moreover, in recognizably English fashion.

Witness, for example, the manner in which South Carolina's lower house shaped its mandate to use the writ—by a measure of 1733 suspending habeas corpus in cases of parliamentary privilege.[56]

The issue at stake was a facsimile of the century-old conflict between Parliament and the common-law courts. It was, once again, *lex parliamente* v. *lex terrae*—though the protagonists in South Carolina were the chief justice and the lower house.[57] The colony, even before 1733, had been the scene of tumultuous developments. In 1726, Chief Justice Thomas Hepworth had denied the petitioner, the venerable landgrave, Thomas Smith, a writ of habeas corpus. Smith, a council member, petitioned to the lower house for relief, criticizing the chief justice for refusing to issue the writ. The assembly, acting in Smith's behalf, examined his petition. Angry words passed between House and Council, the latter finally standing on royal prerogative.[58]

New York court cases further illustrate the rising applicability of habeas corpus. Counsel for the defense in *McCullogh* v. *Walker*, in the New York Mayor's Court (1729), claimed that the English Habeas Corpus Act was legally relevant to the province. After a five-year period when the writ does not appear to have been used in any cases adjudicated in New York, it was invoked in the historic case of *King* v. *Zenger*. Arrested and imprisoned under a warrant issued by the Governor and Council "for printing and publishing several Seditious Libels," Zenger was held incommunicado for three days before his friends secured a writ of habeas corpus. His counsel, William Smith and James Alexander, insisted, in the return, on the right to bail on the grounds of Magna Carta, the Petition of Right, and the Habeas Corpus Act of 1679.[59]

After the dramatic circumstances of this case, the writ was not employed again until 1750, when the records indicate that habeas corpus functioned once more to shift a case—*King* v. *Sackett*—from a JP to the Supreme Court of Judicature; and that it was used in 1754 to determine bailability and to remove a prisoner from commitment pending his appearance at the Court of Oyer and Terminer and General Gaol Delivery for Orange County.

The leading authorities on New York adjudicature can cite only one or two other post-1750 instances of the use of the privilege, which prompted them reluctantly to "conclude that habeas corpus was not often resorted to."[60] In the Bay Colony, too, there are only a few cases mentioning habeas corpus after mid-century, and an act of 1757 even watered down the writ's effectiveness by returning to the outmoded English practice of recommitments.[61] Certainly habeas corpus usage for bailment would be infrequent since, with the exception of treason, murder, and grand larceny, the principal courts were willing to bail. Nor was bail normally excessive, barring cases with political implications. Zenger, for instance, quite properly complained that bail was fixed too high.

Another New York case, that of Alexander McDougall, did as much as Zenger's to publicize the cause of freedom of the press. Also a seditious libel case, McDougall's had a greater dimension, duplicating as it did the Smith trial in South Carolina, and the conflict between Parliament and common-law courts that had been going on in England. It highlighted the question of whether someone committed by legislative order could be released by judicially-granted relief in the form of habeas corpus.[62] After the common-law prosecution against McDougall collapsed, he was arrested on a warrant issued by Assembly Speaker John Cruger, by order of the house, and the legislators voted him in contempt of their parliamentary privilege. Sentenced to an indeterminate term, McDougall obtained a writ of habeas corpus, but to no avail, since the sheriff—who was ordered not to obey its mandate—notified the court that the matter was outside his jurisdiction.[63]

Seditious libel became the occasion for the use of habeas corpus in Pennsylvania as well as in New York. Each provincial assembly entertained the same low opinion of freedom of speech and press, and willingly used its punitive powers in an attempt to curb what the lawmakers considered seditious expression. One such instance occurred in 1758 and, like the South Carolina events of 1726, dramatized a schism between judiciary and assembly, and then between governor and assembly, with the legislative branch asserting, in contempt cases, its primacy over the executive. The case developed out of the hostility toward Quaker principles of warfare on the part of the Anglican chief judge of Court of Common Pleas for Chester County, William Moore, which earned him the antagonism of the Quaker-dominated assembly.[64] William Smith, a prominent Anglican and also a member of the "war party," became involved when Moore, his relative, enlisted his support. The founder of a German-language paper, Smith complied with

Moore's request for publication of his reply to the assembly in his newspaper. Both Anglicans were then arrested, in 1758, on order of the lawmakers, for crimes against the previous assembly. Convicted before the bar of the House, Moore was turned over to the sheriff for an indeterminate time, with the latter directed not to honor any writ of habeas corpus that might be issued for him.[65] The legislative ukase was as unnecessary in this case as it had been in McDougall's, since the court ruled that the petitioner had been committed for a breach of privilege and that the writ could not be granted or plaintiff bailed while the House was in session.[66] The rift that widened between governor and councillors on one hand and assembly on the other, as the Smith-Moore drama played itself out, involved habeas corpus, the powers and privileges of the legislature, and limitations on the right of the chief justice and governor to use the writ.

Hence habeas corpus takes on the same axial role in the New World as it did in the Old. It was used by petitioners, perhaps less successfully than in England, to block those arbitrarily claiming prerogative rights at the expense of personal liberty. Although its users were often frustrated, the writ was becoming an inherent property of American legal thought, much in the same way that constitutional conflict made it a reality in English law. Any attempt to curtail its applicability evoked a hostile response. The Quebec Act of 1774, by which Westminster denied habeas corpus to Quebec, is illustrative. Cited as a grievous imposition on man's unalienable rights in the Declaration of Independence, the act was attributed to George III. Jefferson condemned him "for abolishing the free system of English Laws in a neighboring Province, establishing therein an Arbitrary government, and enlarging its Boundaries so as to render it at once an example and fit instrument for introducing the same absolute rule to these colonies." Hence the colonists were in effect affirming the opinion of Sir Mathew Hale that habeas corpus ought to extend to all the King's domains.[67]

The writ's importance in colonial legal thought is attested to by the fact that four of the original eleven states framing constitutions took cognizance of it and that, by 1800, seven of the original thirteen gave it statutory foundation. Such action preceded the Revolution in four of the colonies, and the others followed rapidly after 1776.[68] The Massachusetts Constitution of 1780, memorable because of the meticulous democratic procedures utilized in its ratification, perhaps most completely epitomized the American attitude when it declared that the writ ought to be provided ". . . in the most free, easy, cheap, expeditious, and ample manner."[69]

In summary, habeas corpus was deeply embedded in the interstices of colonial thought, much like the common law itself. It was, to be sure, mentioned in less than half of the state constitutions by 1787; but possibly this is simply because, as Chafee has surmised, the writ "had been so long and solidly established" that state constitutional provisions were "probably considered unnecessary."[70] Americans, after all, had become thoroughly acquainted with its functions and benefits. If not always aware of intermittent provincial court practices in relatively minor civil and criminal causes, they were familiar with the widely publicized Zenger, McDougall, and Smith-Moore cases. On the eve of the Revolution, colonists understood how the writ contributed to Lord Mansfield's decision in Somersett's case, which delivered a Negro from slavery in England. They had committed themselves to John Wilkes's cause, identifying it with their own; and they had rejoiced when he was released from the Tower on the writ issued by Mansfield's adversary in Common Pleas, Charles Pratt, on the ground of privilege. (Wilkes had been in Parliament while writing the abrasive *North Briton No. 45*, and his arrest, therefore, had been a violation of privilege.) Pennsylvania's Quakers were not the only avid readers of *People's Ancient and Just Liberties*, which contained a record of the trial of William Penn and William Mead (1670). John Hawles's account was in Madison's hands, and those unacquainted with the case might have learned about it from Andrew Hamilton, since he had exploited its implications during Zenger's trial. One way or another, the colonists learned about Penn and Mead's Old Bailey ordeal, their jury's imprisonment because it voted for acquittal, and its release on habeas corpus proceedings.

Mention of Madison's name carries us to the Constitutional Convention. Doubtless the delegates were aware of the role of habeas corpus in the seditious libel cases. They were well read in history and in the law, and they were conscious of being part of a great stream of historical change. They knew about such legendary events as Titus Oates's continued recourse to habeas corpus; the controversy surrounding John Wilkes's struggle with Crown and Commonwealth, which taught a clear lesson about the writ's usefulness; the Francis Jenckes case that led directly to England's Habeas Corpus Act of 1679. They had wrestled with the *Second Institute* and had no reason to doubt Coke when he legitimized popular rights, identified "due process" with "*legem terrae*"; and confounded habeas corpus with the older writ *de odio et atia*, which, after all, had been used at the time of Magna Carta to release persons wrongfully committed.

Habeas corpus was the only common-law process explicitly written into the Constitution, which is the most complete measure of its reception by the colonists and the high regard in which it was held. Indeed, the delegates' vote on Article 1, Section 9, Clause 2 had been unanimous that "the privilege of the writ of Habeas Corpus shall not be suspended." And then they added, by a vote of seven states to three, the qualifying proviso, "unless in cases of rebellion or invasion the public safety may require it." Gouverneur Morris had introduced this version, which was a refinement of Charles Pinckney's original proposal to the Committee on Detail.[71] This proposal, substantially the same wording as that of the Massachusetts Constitution, provoked the only debate on the writ; i.e., whether a suspension clause was necessary; and, such being the decision, how it might be phrased so as to grant maximum protection to the individual without adversely affecting the nation in event of emergency.[72]

Habeas corpus never made the charmed circle of "natural rights," but it stood on the threshold in being an "immemorial right." The writ resembled the great natural rights in the sense that it was also taken for granted by the delegates. Natural rights required specification in the form of a Bill of Rights because the framers, taking these rights for granted, had neglected to incorporate them into the Constitution. Habeas corpus was missing from the first-draft version of the Constitution; and convention records do not suggest that the delegates were unduly concerned or even had reservations about a clause which prohibited the writ's suspension but failed expressly to grant the privilege.[73] Such apparent neglect is understandable when one learns that the writ was not constitutionally granted in positive terms in many state constitutions, and that it was only recognized indirectly by a limitation placed upon the authority to suspend its operation.[74] The delegates, reasoning by analogy, may have assumed that the non-suspension clause in the federal document also functioned in oblique fashion, implicitly conferring the right of the privilege. Or else, as in the spirited debate over ratification, when discussion turned on the absence of the great substantive and procedural rights, the framers may have believed that habeas corpus, existing in the several states under common or statutory law, provided adequate protection for the individual.

And, after all, each state was regarded as a sovereign entity, each could provide for the writ itself, and apparently each did, in fact, have the writ available as a result of custom or mandate. Hence any person under commitment anywhere in the Union was afforded the protection of habeas corpus—even if the petitioner had been imprisoned by federal authorities.[75] Understandably, therefore, the delegates exhibited little desire to place a positive and elaborate statement about habeas corpus in the federal document.

Whatever the hypothesis, the provision, when finally adopted, left the writ as a federally recognized privilege in an equivocal position. From what has already been observed about the writ's widespread usage, there is something to be said for the argument that the framers did not intend a federal habeas corpus. The states apparently thought this way, for they accepted the role carved out for them, and the habeas corpus provision in the federal constitution had been anticipated by or would be copied by the constitution-makers in the thirteen original states.[76]

The question in a real sense is academic, whatever the framers' intent. For habeas corpus remained to all practical purposes a concern of state adjudication, at least until the national 1789 Judiciary Act. By this measure, the first Congress established a system of federal courts. These courts were authorized, in section fourteen, to issue "writs of scire facias, habeas corpus. . . . And that either the justices of the Supreme Court as well as the judges of the District Courts, shall have power to grant writs of habeas corpus for the purpose of an inquiry into the cause of commitment."[77] According to the record, there was no congressional debate as to the desirability of authorizing the federal judiciary to issue habeas corpus. The writ was mentioned only in connection with the broader argument denying the necessity of a separate federal court system.[78] The one specific restraint provided that this federal writ be available only to persons committed by federal authority; it would not "extend to prisoners in gaol, unless where they are in custody, under or by colour of the authority of the United States, or are committed for trial before some court of the same, or are necessary to be brought into court to testify."[79] But responsibility for interpretation of this restricting clause, as well as of other procedural and jurisdictional questions, went to the federal judiciary.

One major question remained before it could be affirmed that the writ was a thoroughly established and effective instrument of federal law; namely, whether, given Marshall's ruling on original jurisdiction in *Marbury v. Madison* (1803), when mandamus was at stake, the habeas corpus clause of the 1789 Judiciary Act was constitutional. The Chief Justice disposed of the issue when the first opportunity presented itself. Responding affirmatively in *Ex parte Bollman* (1807), he found that the authority to issue habeas corpus was a necessary adjunct to supreme judicial power, that it had been properly granted by statute and recognized by precedent. He affirmed:

Acting under the immediate influence of this injunction [*habeas corpus* provision in the Constitution], they [legislators in the first session of Congress] must have felt, with peculiar force, the obligation of providing efficient means by which this great constitutional privilege should receive life and activity; for if the means be not in existence, the privilege itself would be lost, although no law for its suspension should be enacted. Under the impression of this obligation, they give to all the courts the power of awarding writs of *habeas corpus*.[80]

Distinguishing between Marbury's and Bollman's plea to the Court for original jurisdiction, Marshall found the latter's was a request for appellate action which Congress had properly authorized.

Marshall's reasoning in *Ex parte Bollman* was strained and evasive. He avoided such vexatious questions as the Court's jurisdiction in treason cases. Nor were the opinions of his colleagues reassuring or the precedents cited—though Marshall was always weak in this area. Nevertheless, the case was of historic significance, for it rounded out an evolutionary process that, in America alone, was over a century in the making. The reception of habeas corpus into the mainstream of American law was complete.

WILSON SMITH

John Locke in the Great Unitarian Controversy

THERE IS STILL MUCH for historians to do with the theme of John Locke in nineteenth-century American thought. Merle Curti's now classic essay on "The Great Mr. Locke: America's Philosopher" is a model for those who prefer to continue charting specific appeals to Locke by prominent writers and public men.[1] Louis Hartz's brilliant survey, *The Liberal Tradition in America*, perceives Lockian ideology throughout the American "ethos" in ways that suggest further speculation and a lot more hunting for evidence.[2] Those interested in the history of American or Anglo-American philosophy have yet to explore some parts of the problem of Lockian empiricism as it underwent modification, change, and erosion beneath the impact of Scottish common-sense realism, transcendentalism, and later Kantian idealism.[3] We have no clear picture of the place of Locke's essays in nineteenth-century college curricula.[4] The relationship between Locke's educational thought and the development of teaching practices in American schools needs examining.[5] The argument for the Lockian "natural right" to property needs to be traced, particularly where it is found in our constitutional history.[6] And Locke's influence upon the growth of experimental psychology in the United States has yet to be fully described by historians of science or of the higher learning in America.[7]

To list these topics so neatly in our present intellectual climate that has somehow become impatient with even the more recent

78

and presumably more sophisticated intellectual leadership of Darwin, Freud, Mannheim, or Niebuhr is perhaps disadvantageous to new and exciting scholarly inquiry. It is like invoking the name of Locke himself in modern "rational" discourse: these topics seem narrowly conceived just as Lockian psychology alone seems to give a one-dimensional picture of the human mind. But these topics surely can still be handled with subtlety and finesse, although I doubt that they can be approached effectively in the old monographic way of the standard American doctoral dissertation. For this reason my reconsideration here of John Locke's name in the Great Unitarian Controversy from 1805 until about 1840, though restricted to one theme by space limitations, touches upon or cuts across some of these unexplored areas.

I choose this subject, however, mainly for two reasons that have much to do with the ambiguous relationship between intellectual and social history. For one, we have come to the time when social historians can profitably disinter old theological debates. Controversy between partisan denominationalists over the name of Locke can disclose, at least from one perspective, the connection between theology and social thought. Secondly, the Great Unitarian Controversy puts Locke in an institutional context. There is an advantage here for the social historian who, without surrendering his belief that men transmit ideas, wants to assess the role of institutions as effective transmitters or custodians of a culture. We need fresh points of view upon a rapidly changing nineteenth-century American society wherein certain crude ideas may have been taken up more readily and protected by institutions—in this case by denominations—than by individuals. Moreover, since twentieth-century historical writing in the liberal Parringtonian tradition, including Professor Commager's memorable biography of Theodore Parker, has already described how Lockian ideas were grasped and manipulated or rejected by men of thought,[8] it remains to be asked how liberal and, on occasion, even orthodox institutions captured and retained Lockian principles as mottoes or symbols for mass appeal. Effective ideas that are commandeered by impersonal institutions are as inviting for the social historian to trace to their outcome as they are attractive to the intellectual historian in their structure and relationships. It is indeed with a mutual concern for social ideas that intellectual and social historians sometimes come to their work in parallel if not altogether similar ways.

The major episode of the Great Unitarian Controversy occurs during the 1820's. Although it is located within the national arena of early denominational rivalries, one must turn first to New England where Unitarians were beginning to promulgate Lockian ideas as "denominational" doctrine around 1800. Without repeating an old story to the disadvantage of this untold one, we should briefly recall that Unitarians at first preferred only to call themselves liberal Christians; they did not organize a formal denominational body until 1825; the Lockian precepts they upheld as a faction within the New England-way Congregational churches had been common intellectual coin in New England since the 1720's; but when they set these principles firmly at the center of institutional discourse, the Great Controversy began.[9] The orthodox regarded the liberals as Lockian conspirators bent on subverting the faith.

Clearly associating liberal Congregationalism with Lockian psychology in a way that would put an institutional trademark upon Unitarianism was a sermon preached by Samuel Spring of Newburyport in March, 1805. Spring spoke for orthodoxy only a month after Henry Ware, Sr., had been elected to the Hollis Chair of Divinity at Harvard College, a victory for the liberals that customarily dates the beginning of the Great Controversy. After Ware's election, polemical sermons and parish political maneuvers increased while pamphlet warfare broke out between liberal and orthodox Congregationalist factions. Since orthodox opposition to a Lockian reappraisal of Calvinism would later find its great strength in Presbyterianism, it was indicative of things to come that Spring was a graduate of the Presbyterian College of New Jersey at Princeton. In his New England career Spring was one of the founders of Andover Theological Seminary and beside Jedidiah Morse one of the most powerful spokesmen for orthodoxy. Even so, there is irony in Spring's modified Calvinism. As a Hopkinsian in theology, Spring was partly concerned with human happiness under the principle of "disinterested benevolence."[10] Although this was really more a matter of ethics than of theology, it suggests how much Calvinism had been softened by the American Enlightenment and how ironic for changing Calvinism was the Great Controversy with Unitarianism in the nineteenth century. Men like Spring were nevertheless embittered by the Lockian liberals in their midst. Unitarians, he claimed,

compare man as he comes into the world, with a blank sheet of paper, destitute of any impression good or bad; and upon this blank they teach us that every person, by his "self-determining power," independently of help, impresses and displays his real character. For these theorists deny the necessity of special influences to prepare sinners to embrace Christ. No wonder then, that they explode the necessity of an infinite atonement, and the consequent necessity of an infinite personage to make it. For pride loves specious consistency, because self-interest is nearly concerned. I do not assert that no Unitarians are good men. But I am compelled to believe that they are destitute of religion, if their hearts correspond with their peculiar theory. If Unitarians are good men, it must at times be deeply mortifying that free thinkers, latitudinarians, universalists and not a few infidels, love to move in their parochial circles, and to refresh and to regale themselves under their arbor. Is it not a fact, that men will not long support social, intimate intercourse, unless their views and enjoyments are coincident and congenial?

. . . Let us also review the primitive College of Cambridge. How dignified her ancient Electors and Overseers, who spared no pains to establish evangelical officers at the University, and to fence it against the most distant approach of every species of Heresy. Were they afraid of the leading doctrines of Calvinism? . . . We ask the present Electors and Curators whether their distant predecessors were in the habit of preferring a Theological Instructor, whose sentiments were either too orthodox or too heterodox to be publicly mentioned? Did they ever fall below the dignity and high responsibility of their office in this manner? Oh Harvard, thou seminary of science, thou seat of gospel instruction, how didst thou shine like the rising day, when it was thy care to teach our sons to embrace the doctrines of God's incarnation![11]

Three of these charges were to be repeatedly used by Calvinists in the Controversy that would swell until the 1820's. One was that self-styled "liberal Christians" are indeed Unitarians; another was that a Lockian psychology is insufficient for revealed religion; the third was that Unitarianism results in moral laxity.

It would have strengthened the liberal position if in first answering these charges Henry Ware had been more outspoken. But he was not. He was a mild-mannered man given to the Arminian point of view that man can win salvation through moral effort and, more importantly in these circumstances, to the Socinian point of view that the Scriptures are the revelation of God's word and rationally defensible. Ware was always willing to converse in a scholarly fashion with the Trinitarians, as was his son who came to the Harvard Divinity School faculty by 1830, but only willing to converse by analyzing different passages of scriptural text. This was early American "higher criticism" of the Bible. It followed English latitudinarian methods of inquiry as much as it did eighteenth-century German Biblical criticism. Yet Henry Ware, Sr., and most Unitarians of his generation never brought their opponents to the central issue of Lockian argument in religion. Ware did not reply to Spring on the question of the *tabula rasa*. Even fifteen years after his appointment, when he was engaged in his renowned pamphlet debate with Leonard Woods of Andover Seminary and when liberals held the majority of the pulpits in Boston, Ware's arguments, like those of Woods, were strictly exegetical. In this debate, known then as the Wood'n Ware Controversy, the relevance of Locke to a "reasonable" faith for Unitarians was scarcely mentioned.[12] Ware's failure to go beyond exegesis or scriptural interpretation into the meaning of Lockian free inquiry and empirical rationalism for the historical development of liberal Protestantism typified Unitarians in the first encounter of the Great Controversy. Unwilling to press home Lockian arguments, they kept American Unitarianism in its youth from acquiring strong intellectual foundations. They did have an institutional frame of mind, but it was more Congregational than Unitarian. In finding the substance of the Great Controversy, it is then more helpful to ask why rather than how the name of Locke was virtually ignored in theological discourse.

In its formative years American Unitarianism espoused a negative theology. It was *anti*-Trinitarian and it was *anti*-predestinarian. These negative convictions toward the Calvinism of their fathers and their own younger days were compelling and immediate for the older liberals who carried the fight against orthodoxy into their own churches and who finally rejoiced in Ware's appointment in 1805. The slowness of Henry Ware's founding generation of Unitarians to advance Lockian arguments characterizes the handicap under which they labored in their disputes with the Calvinists. To be read out of their mother church for irreligion did not come easily to them. The name of heretic was particularly unsettling in a region where filiopietism and past-mindedness were customary. Whatever sense of guilt they felt in having renounced the family faith was a burden that put them theologically on the defensive. Their only positive conviction was the ideal of free inquiry or, as they called it, "the private judgment of reason." But as Vernon Parrington wrote, this was more a state of mind than it was a systematic doctrine carefully worked out upon a base of Arminianism and Lockian or eighteenth-century liberal theology. For us to emphasize an aggressively liberal theology in the first generation of American Unitarians without accounting for their greater psychological and social defensiveness is in my judgment to misread their history. They were really apostates who were trying somehow to reform their church from within. Locked in a struggle with Calvinism on its own ground, only a few scholars of this first generation could successfully advocate free scriptural inquiry. Theological reform was improbable without a clean break from orthodoxy. Moreover, their sympathy for a moral philosophy sanctioned by the laws of nature rather than by scriptural law opened them to the taunts of the orthodox in rural New England where devotion to creed had long been the ultimate test of morality.

The second generation of Unitarians, however, obtained an independence and institutional integrity that the pioneers never achieved. It is in this group of generally younger men that we must test the institutional effectiveness of Unitarian claims upon the Lockian tradition of religious toleration (within a Protestant context) and free inquiry (within the limits of scriptural faith). None of the leading founders of the American Unitarian Association in 1825 was over forty years of age.[13] James Walker and Henry Ware, Jr., were then thirty-one years old; Ezra Stiles Gannett was only twenty-four; John Gorham Palfrey was twenty-nine; John Pierpont was forty; Andrews Norton was thirty-nine; and Jared Sparks was thirty-six. All of them, except Andrews Norton (Harvard Class of 1804) and John Pierpont (Yale Class of 1804), graduated from Harvard College during Ware Senior's professorship and during the illustrious presidency of John Thornton Kirkland. Locke's *Essay Concerning Human Understanding* was a part of their studies. One of their generation of alumni, Edward Everett, recalled from his sophomore year in 1808: "We recited from Locke's *Essay* three times a day, the first four days of the week, the recitation of Thursday afternoon being a review of the rest. We were expected to give the substance of the author's remarks: but were at liberty to condense them and to use our own words. . . ."[14]

Harvard students had been exposed to Locke's *Essay* in this way since at least 1743.[15] Retention of the *Essay* under increasingly milder climates of Calvinist opinion on the eighteenth-century Harvard boards of control perhaps only underscores its use in support of moral philosophy and mental discipline and the degree to which the liberal arts and sciences there, as Samuel Eliot Morison has always maintained, were unfettered by Calvinist orthodoxy. Knowing this, the second generation of Unitarians in the 1820's may sometimes have wondered why all the fuss over Ware's election occurred in 1805. Most of them were too young, however, in 1805 to realize how crucial to the institutional prestige of orthodoxy was the Hollis appointment. The professorship of divinity in the ancient home of orthodoxy was as sacred to Calvinists as a battle flag. Orthodox clergymen fought Ware's appointment because they sensed that his theology was based partly upon a rational inquiry into the scriptures and upon the kind of sentiments found in Locke's *Letter on Toleration*. The image of the *tabula rasa*, learned even by the orthodox ministers in their own Harvard days, was transformed into a vision of heresy, a clear and present danger to the faith.

The battle for the Hollis chair, the first in the Great Controversy, was neither a personal experience nor an institutional memory for most of the founders of the American Unitarian Association. By 1825, Ware's beliefs were orthodox liberalism. All of the younger founders of the Association except Palfrey had at least one year of divinity studies under Ware. Free scriptural inquiry and confidence in man's moral freedom and goodness became a normal part of the theology they took into the institutional life of the Unitarian Church. From their important Boston pulpits in the 1820's they saw that the fears and animosities of orthodox Congregationalists, especially in the New England hinterland, were far from quieted; but they no longer tried to cope with orthodoxy from a defensive position. A Lockian assent to faith was their institutional weapon. How well they employed it was to determine their fortune in the significant battles of the Great Controversy.

One person who tried early to prepare firm ground for Unitarians was Andrews Norton. Older than most of the Unitarian second generation, Norton nevertheless belonged to it even though he chose to remain aloof from the Association after initially supporting its founding. His eminence as a Biblical scholar and his defense of the Unitarian establishment in the late 1830's during the transcendentalist revolt are well known. But the Norton who concerns us here is the younger man of twenty-six who, while tutor and lecturer on the Bible at Harvard, sought almost singlehandedly in 1812 to institutionalize the name of John Locke for Unitarianism. By establishing and editing the first distinctly Unitarian journal in this country, Norton fought the second major engagement of the Great Controversy.

Named the *General Repository and Review*, Norton's journal ran for only four volumes, but in it the views of "liberal Christians" were promulgated. Norton began his attack on Calvinist orthodoxy in his first volume by pleading the "Defense of Liberal Christianity." He admired "Locke's metaphysics" and Bishop Joseph Butler's "reasonings" while he described Locke as the champion of "free inquiry."[16] By free inquiry he meant the liberty to find religious truth in a rational or deductive way from the first principles of Biblical authority. Little wonder that the first Boston edition of Locke's *Reasonableness of Christianity* was also published in 1812. Norton was insisting then as he always would that only "enlightened reason" can interpret Biblical revelation. "Reason," he wrote, "must not humble itself before our faith."[17] He wanted to awaken his fellow liberals to the tradition of Locke, and of Grotius, Butler, Lardner, Paley, and Priestley—all of whom he saw as "liberal Christians."[18]

Norton was optimistic about the growth of Unitarianism in America. His confidence in the manifest destiny of liberal religion was not unlike the commitment of some American statesmen to continental expansion on the eve of the War of 1812. Moreover, he tied the institutional expansion of his faith to the unilinear concept of progress then becoming popular. Liberal Christianity, he asserted, would produce throughout the whole character "a gradual but constant progression in excellence."[19] It would one day take its place at the peak of the gradual upward ascent of knowledge and freedom of inquiry that has been the story of Christendom since the Reformation.[20] Rejecting the psychology of the evangelical sects and denominations, which produce "an unnatural excitement of feelings," Norton espoused a rational and reserved religious attitude. In his opposition to enthusiasm even his orthodox opponents agreed with him. But before long many of them would be won over to evangelicalism, which in the coming decades would set the tone of American Protestantism. In 1812, however, his major incentive was to convince not only the orthodox Congregationalists but also his fellow liberals that liberalism was not infidelity. Each time that Norton denied the charge of infidelity, the orthodox raised it anew. Particularly bitter on this issue was his dispute in the *Review* with Abiel Holmes, who had included a reference to young Norton's "Defense" in a sermon on infidelity.[21]

Notwithstanding Norton's occasional rancor in the columns of the *Review*, his arguments were generally incisive and constructive for a Unitarian platform of belief. He rejected any authority in religion other than the Bible. He spurned proselytism on every ground except that of rational persuasion. He claimed that orthodoxy "is intolerant ignorance that pretends to dogmatize," and that Liberal Christianity "has no sectarian air, no habitual look of gloom and repulsion, no assuming of censorship and superiority." He dismissed "the barbarous jargon" in the "technical theology" of Calvinism. He was optimistic that candid religious inquiry (within the limits of eighteenth-century liberal Protestantism) in the name of Milton and Locke would free theology from error. He acknowledged the importance of "the checks and balances of [competing] religious parties" in the young nation, but he insisted that "a liberal and catholic spirit" was on the rise.[22]

These assertions were clearly an attempt to give "liberal Christians" an institutional identity. They fairly entitle Norton's *Review* to be called the institutional foundation of American Unitarianism even though it expired for lack of funds within two years. To be sure, Unitarianism would not emerge as a denomination for another thirteen years, and William Ellery Channing would not deliver his famous sermon at Baltimore, which was based more upon Platonic than upon Lockian philosophy, for another seven years. But in the four volumes of his *Review* Norton put himself and Unitarians squarely in the Lockian religious and moral tradition. This tradition had already been alive for half a century in New England Arminianism, or in what Conrad Wright terms "supernatural rationalism."[23] What Norton did, however, was to show his fellow liberals that they could assert this tradition with precisely the vigor and conviction that could overcome their negative psychology of anti-Calvinism. From this time until his death in 1853 Andrews Norton became known among New England men of intellect as the leading disciple of John Locke in America.

If Norton's *Review* was the first institutional journal of Lockian Unitarianism in this country, the dispute between Jared Sparks and Samuel Miller from 1820 to 1823 became the institutional testing time of Unitarian commitment to Lockian preconceptions. The Sparks-Miller debate is in my view the third major milestone in the Great Controversy and its most significant event because it took the Lockian theme into the area of national denominational rivalries. Moreover, it replaced the first two institutional problems of Unitarianism, free scriptural inquiry and the question of the divinity of Jesus, with the problem of finding a liberal religious basis for ethics in Jacksonian America. In facing the first two problems Unitarians generally followed Lockian and Arminian guidelines, but until the time of Norton's *Review* they rarely gave as good an account of their understanding of Locke as their opponents like Samuel Spring gave. During the early 1820's Unitarians made frequent appeals to the name of Locke. But his ideas were virtually ignored. This was the Unitarian failure of nerve in the Great Controversy.

The dispute between Jared Sparks and Samuel Miller was in one limited sense a Harvard-Princeton debate. After his graduation in 1819 from the Divinity School at Harvard where he was the student of the elder Ware and of Norton and one of the bright young group of second generation Unitarians of whom great things were expected, Jared Sparks was called to the new Unitarian church in Baltimore. Channing's memorable sermon at Sparks's ordination is of course an important event in the established history of American Protestantism. But its aftermath in Baltimore and Princeton has gone unrecorded. When in 1820 William Nevins came to the pulpit of the First Presbyterian Church in Baltimore, Samuel Miller of the Princeton Theological Seminary was called to deliver the ordination sermon. Miller, since 1812 one of two professors at the new seminary, had been increasingly recognized as a leading spokesman for Old Light Calvinist orthodoxy. By summoning this Presbyterian divine from Princeton to quell the Unitarian blaze in Baltimore, Presbyterians and their orthodox Congregationalist allies anticipated a strong response to Channing's sermon. They were not to be disappointed. What may have astonished the orthodox, however, was the line of Miller's argument. In attacking Unitarianism, Miller broke free from the theological bounds in which both liberal and orthodox Protestants long had disputed each other. He turned instead to the issue of maintaining orthodoxy in an urban environment or, in his title words, to "The Difficulties and Temptations Which Attend the Preaching of the Gospel in Great Cities."[24] This was an increasingly important problem for all churchmen as they began to witness the rapid growth of city life following the War of 1812. But Miller, more than most churchmen early in the twenties, sensed that denominational rivalries would be sharpened in the eastern cities, even though he was a professor at the leading seminary that was preparing young men for ministries in the South and West. With a foresight that was as accurate as his arguments were aggressively pointed toward Unitarians, Miller turned from the eighteenth-century dispute over Arminianism and away from the Harvard-Princeton divinity school axis of debate toward the range of ethical problems facing denominational clergymen in a new secular age. It was a shrewd gambit.

Miller's central theme was that the morally weak doctrines of Unitarianism are the result of urban surroundings. His preliminary statements were that the wealth, luxury, and dissipation of a great city "form a serious obstacle to the plain and faithful preaching of the gospel."[25] He claimed further that the "refinements of philosophy . . . are unfriendly to the preaching and success of the gospel"; that the alliance of a city pastor with "polished and fashionable society" makes for "smooth and superficial preaching"; and that the circumstances of populous cities tend to "harden the heart."[26] Miller was leading to the assertion that city life had resulted in a "fatal decline" from orthodoxy and an alliance with the "soul-destroying errors of Arius or Socinus."[27] He flatly stated that "great cities have commonly been, in all ages, the hotbeds of error."[28] He had opened the way for his attack on Unitarians. It began:

We might easily illustrate and confirm this position, by examples drawn from our own country, had we time to trace the history of several sects among us, and especially of American Unitarianism. But I forbear to pursue the illustration farther: and shall only take the liberty to ask, as I pass along—How it is to be accounted for, that the preaching of those who deny the Divinity and Atonement of the Saviour, and who reject the doctrines of Human Depravity, of Regeneration, and of Justification by the righteousness of Christ—How, I ask, is it to be accounted for, that such preachers, all over the world, are most acceptable to the gay, the fashionable, the worldly minded, and even the licentious?[29]

In order to answer these accusations, Jared Sparks began what was a common practice for intelligent clergymen who wanted to engage in debate. He followed Andrews Norton's precedent and started a magazine, this one a monthly called *The Unitarian Miscellany and Christian Monitor*. In his first reply to Miller's ordination sermon, Sparks accused Miller of having said in effect that Newton, Locke, and Chillingworth were "no Christians in any correct sense of the word."[30] What Miller actually had said was that "the real and profound science of such men as Bacon, and Boyle, and Newton, and Locke, and many others" demonstrated that knowledge in itself is "a handmaid to religion, a friend to faith." Yet he hedged in adding that "the pride of knowledge, and the speculations of false science, are diametrically opposed to the humility and simplicity of the gospel."[31]

Despite Miller's unwillingness to brand Newton and Locke and most eighteenth-century Anglican churchmen as infidels, he was evidently nettled by Sparks's belligerency (though it is hard to see what else he could have expected) and by Sparks's insistence that the liberal piety of these famous English minds was really a crucial question at all. So he chose to continue the debate. In the next round Miller readily agreed that he would not call Unitarians Christians. To justify his stand he took up the old argument that whoever rejects the Calvinist doctrines of man's guilt and depravity by nature really rejects Christianity—as really, he said, as any Deist ever did. Such a person, he charged, is on just as dangerous ground as was Lord Herbert or David Hume. He granted that Unitarians are not all licentious or immoral, but he did hold that "the Unitarian mode of preaching is more acceptable to the taste of carnal, worldly men, than any other kind of preaching."[32]

As the debate grew warmer it appeared that both men wanted to argue chiefly about Unitarian morality. But to gauge its level they were only willing to question the reputedly unitarian persuasions of Newton, Locke, and the hymn-writer Isaac Watts. Miller maintained that the frequent inclusion of their names in Unitarian catalogues did them a great injustice.[33] He was probably right about Watts, whose theology, despite its anti-Trinitarian leanings, was as much a religion of the heart as of the intellect.[34] When one of his clerical colleagues, James Renwick Willson from Newburgh, New York, pointed out to him that their cause rested upon the "infallible word" of Holy Writ and not upon Watts any more than upon Priestley, Belsham, or Lindsey, Miller may have welcomed the reminder.[35] For by this time Miller saw that he was on the weaker side in the great names game. Even if to him Newton and Locke were not unitarians, he had to accuse them of "gross idolatry" as members of the Church of England and as subscribers to its Articles. And he admitted that Mr. Locke was indeed no Socinian for he solemnly denied it while he lived. Trying to extricate himself from this corner of the dispute, Miller claimed inconsistently that prejudice founded on the authority of great names is fruitless and makes a plea of no force at all because investigations of this kind will always turn out with a proportion of "five-hundred to one in favor of orthodoxy and against Unitarianism."[36] His final word of capitulation was that if Newton and Locke were unitarians, they acted an "unworthy part."[37]

In the short view, Sparks came off better than Miller in this dispute. He had avoided the main argument of Miller's Baltimore sermon and instead had brought Miller into the great names game. Here he successfully put the burden of proof upon Miller, admonishing him:

In your sermon you speak of Locke as a Christian; but you certainly cannot suppose the definition of this term, which is contained in your Reply, will apply to the sentiments of Locke. . . . Locke must still be considered a Unitarian, till he can be proved a Trinitarian; a task which it is not likely you will soon undertake. At all events, he had no faith in the assemblage of articles, which you denominate the essence of Christianity, and without believing which, you say, no one can be called a Christian. His whole treatise on the Reasonableness of Christianity bears witness to this truth. . . . He says nothing about total depravity, the atonement . . . nor any of your peculiar doctrines. Yet who has done more to elucidate the Sacred Scriptures, or to prove the consistency and reasonableness of the religion of Jesus? Your rule, however, will take from him the Christian name.[38]

Through his final letters to Miller, Sparks kept insisting that it was up to the Trinitarians to prove that Newton and Locke were not unitarians. His references to Locke's *Reasonableness of Christianity* emphasized that its primary object was "to ascertain the kind of faith necessary to make a man a Christian."[39] There was nothing in this or in any other of Locke's writings to show that he leaned to the doctrine of the Trinity. For Sparks, this was simple proof enough that Locke believed in none of the doctrines of high orthodoxy. "The principles," he wrote, "by which Locke was guided in explaining the religion of the Saviour, and interpreting the word of God, are in all respects the same as those of Unitarians." "It is enough," he concluded, "that Locke has been accounted a Unitarian, that his writings confirm this sentiment, and that no adequate evidence has been offered to the contrary."[40]

Were these assertions really enough to strengthen American Unitarianism as a Lockian institution? I think not. They led only into the old channel of argument over the Trinity; they judged the character, if not the ethics, of great men to be synonymous with their views on the Trinity; they forestalled discussing the consequences of the right of private judgment in the present generation. Nor can we believe that Sparks was satisfied with this line of debate, even though he had invited it. Of course, he claimed freedom of Biblical interpretation through the use of reason; and of course Miller insisted that Unitarians studied the Scriptures chiefly as "a cold intellectual exercise."[41] But Sparks would go no further into the implications of this problem for liberty of thought and speech or for social ethics. And surely Miller would not: he was dedicated to the Calvinist view of freedom as commitment to one's creed.[42] Their exchange over the religious affiliations of great Englishmen long dead amounted to no more than sectarian bickering.[43] The dispute was particularly unfortunate, moreover, when we recall that both men were historians. Samuel Miller's *Brief Retrospect of the Eighteenth Century*, in which he had mentioned admiringly the importance of Locke's *Essay*, had been published back in 1803. It was the first significant work in intellectual history of our national period. Sparks, too, was to mark out a milestone in American historical scholarship with the first competent edition of George Washington's papers. Despite their mutual interest in the past, however, they used history poorly. They wanted to possess figures of the past as factional ornaments on their own shelf of history. They made Locke, Milton, and Newton, and the whole array of eighteenth-century English churchmen into figurines to be taken down only for display. No matter how either man regarded Locke's religious views, he was not using Lockian ideas effectively; he was embalming them. Despite his youth and his newness to clerical debate, Sparks was at fault here simply because he had the education in liberal theology to enable him to break out of the old deadlock with Calvinism. That he did not entirely do this was, in the long view, damaging to the institutional foundations of Unitarianism outside New England. To be sure, strong Unitarian churches were established in other southern and western cities. For a while they prospered. But no Unitarian minister beyond New England again had Jared Sparks's opportunity to engage one of the professors from the very center of Presbyterian power in open theological combat.

After the Sparks-Miller debate, Lockian ideas in the Great Controversy generally follow two different courses. Each course can be traced back to the crucial years, 1820–1823, and to the Lockian issues raised or implied but left unprobed by Sparks and Miller. One channel runs through Unitarian theology in the 1830's and ends in the debate between members of the Unitarian establishment and the young rebels who left it for transcendentalism. This final conflict of the Great Unitarian Controversy was basically a rebellion against Lockian sensational psychology as the basis for Unitarian belief. The transcendentalist revolt has been well described by historians and students of American literature.[44] It need only be emphasized here that Unitarians were ill prepared for it within the broadest Lockian terms. They never really had thought through the empirical side of Locke's writings to their own institutional advantage. Since the time of Henry Ware's election and Andrews Norton's *Review* their appeals had been first to the Lockian "reasonableness" of scriptural belief and next to the Lockian argument for toleration among Protestant denominations. Indeed, the Andrews Norton who in 1838 called transcendentalism "the latest form of infidelity" was not the latest form of Andrews Norton. He was theologically the same Norton who had been using Locke's writings to bolster his own rationalism in Biblical studies for the preceding twenty-five years.

In judging the degree to which Unitarians institutionalized Lockian themes in the 1830's, we must nevertheless credit them with fortitude and with partial success. When evangelicalism was dominating American church life, they clearly assessed and announced their own position on reason and toleration in religion. Alexander Hill Everett in the *North American Review;* James Walker, W. B. O. Peabody, Francis Parkman, and Francis Bowen in the *Christian Examiner* (the Unitarian house organ); all published articles that plainly identified Unitarian belief with Lockian precepts of rational inquiry and religious freedom.[45] Unlike Sparks, their first purpose was not to claim that Locke was a unitarian in his personal religious views, although they usually assumed that he was. Rather their pleas were for freedom of religious thought, for regarding Unitarianism as free of skeptical tendencies, and for "rational conviction" instead of "trust" as the basis for faith.[46] One of them stated their case in 1831:

The distinction between the Unitarian and the Trinitarian is not, that the former thinks himself supported by reason, and the latter by Scripture. Each thinks himself supported by Scripture, and the only difference . . . is, that the Unitarian thinks himself supported by reason too. . . . [Unitarians] make a distinction . . . between being inspired and being omniscient.[47]

This writer made it clear, however, that in the matter of Christian revelation, Unitarians substantially followed Paley, the liberal divines of the Church of England, and "almost the entire body of German theologians at the present day, the professed Rationalists excepted."[48] "Reason" then for Unitarians was neither entirely intuited in the Kantian way that transcendentalists soon would follow nor was it entirely empirical or experiential in the Baconian tradition. This was indeed the Lockian position; but here lay both their advantage and their difficulty in the use of Locke. His theological rationalism meant to them "the free right of the individual reason to interpret the Bible."⁴⁹ Beyond this they did not try to balance Locke's theology with the psychology of his *Essay*.

If modern criticism has held that even Locke himself could not bring all his writings into logical harmony, is it fair then to ask this of the American Unitarians? Perhaps not, but this is not quite the point. What is relevant here is to ask why Locke's two essays most used by Unitarian pamphlet writers, *The Reasonableness of Christianity, as delivered in the Scriptures* (1695 and later editions) and *A Letter Concerning Toleration* (1689 and later editions), were not considered in conjunction with the empiricism of *An Essay Concerning Humane Understanding* (1690 and later editions) or in the light of all that was going on in American sacred and secular affairs. The question, I think, points up again the strategic place of Jared Sparks's letters to Samuel Miller. In their importance for the potential development of Unitarianism as a Lockian institution in this country, they far outweigh the debates almost two decades later between angry, tired, or complacent Unitarians and lively transcendentalists.

Jared Sparks was clever, if not exceptionally courageous, in carrying the religious opinions of Newton and Locke to a Unitarian frontier beyond New England and into a public dispute with a more experienced clergyman who represented Presbyterian orthodoxy. He knew that in the study of man and matter the names of Locke and Newton for a century had been virtually above reproach in the English-speaking world. Borrowing upon their prestige to blunt and to divert the arguments of Miller's Baltimore sermon was well worth the debater's risk he took when he surely knew that Locke's and Newton's religious sentiments would be suspect to Miller. What better move than to force Miller to attack the religion of two Englishmen revered by most educated Americans? Sparks did not have a weak case, but he presented it weakly. He championed Locke only as an anti-Trinitarian and as one who believed that "the truths revealed by Jesus [are] adapted to the understanding."⁵⁰

Why then in his fifteen letters to Miller did Jared Sparks exemplify the Unitarian failure of nerve that runs into the 1830's? One plausible reason for his limited use of Lockian themes may be that the young man, fresh from the security of divinity school, was closer to the apologetic Arminianism of eighteenth-century

New England than to the "free" or liberal religions of the later nineteenth century. To be sure, he was being attacked by a latter-day Calvinist; so he could not extricate himself entirely from the old deadlock of Arminianism with Calvinism. He himself had been reared a Calvinist, but he had left this far behind him. Another plausible reason is that Sparks did not want openly to repudiate or to embarrass the great Channing, who had come to ordain him and whose premises were more Platonic than Lockian.[51] But Channing could defend himself if need be; Sparks was on his own. These reasons for Sparks's limited Lockian argument misread, I think, his intelligence, his social awareness, and the importance of the 1820's for American Protestantism. In this decade he was equally distant from the earlier and the later periods of liberal Protestantism. He was not caught between two centuries—a cherished apology for second-rate men. He knew that he was beginning his career in a unique period of institutional development. Moreover, he was asserting Lockian religious ideas at a time when Locke's views were being tested and reinspected in other fields— in state constitutional assemblies, in political argument over the natural rights of man, in college curricula, and in general philosophical speculation. Sparks well knew that his pulpit and his location made his presentation of the Lockian religious point of view crucial to the national development of Unitarianism. He had an important post in the middle states, in that area where varieties of denominational and institutional growth and competitions among cultural and economic groups were to decide much of the future of nineteenth-century America.

The reason for Sparks's failure to use broader Lockian arguments goes, I believe, straight to the heart of the problem of incorporating ideas into new social institutions in a competitive society. He was an ambitious young man trying to institutionalize Lockian arguments for Unitarianism in the South and West.[52] To do so he had to be cautious. Around him in an era of sectarian evangelicalism and denominational beginnings were all kinds of traps for men of "reasonable" theology, set by both Old Light and New Light preachers. To evade them he had to voice the Lockian theme with moderation, not to avoid shocking Unitarians but to enable emerging Unitarianism to gather institutional strength before it was smothered by adverse public opinion. Even Boston

Unitarians, who we too easily assume were secure against orthodox attacks, for the next two decades did not venture much
farther into Lockian speculation. The irony of their predicament,
first illustrated by Sparks in Baltimore, was that they needed support from the broader Lockian ideology they thought they had
to avoid. Simple appeals to the rational authority of Locke's name
alone, though unified and well composed in the early 1830's as
we have noted, were not enough for their institutional cause.

The point here is not, I trust, present-minded or unhistorical.
No one then expected Unitarians to surrender their belief in New
Testament miracles, in which Locke too had believed, for Deism
or for an empirical humanism. The point is that Sparks could
well have used his knowledge of Locke's Essay to support his pleas
for Lockian toleration among denominations. Not only the tabula
rasa of infant understanding but also the record of collective human experience in seeking religious truths was at issue. Locke's
plea for religious toleration, like Milton's great Areopagitica, was
that religious error could be avoided by freedom of Christian inquiry. Sparks could well have gone to this theme, especially since
he was pitted against a dogmatic man.[53] On the way he could
have shown himself to be a far better historian than Miller by
reviewing the historical experience of Protestant dissent. His careful tracing of Locke's unitarian tendencies showed that he already
was a competent student of English religious history.[54] Sparks indeed spoke for toleration, but he chose not to appeal for it in terms
of the entire Protestant historical experience. There were two institutional reasons for this. For one, Unitarians, like all church
people, wanted articles of belief, not only an ideal of toleration.
For another, appeals to religious history in Lockian terms would
inevitably invite the old conflict between historical evidence and
scriptural authority. Although Unitarians in New England, after
the manner of Locke, had settled this conflict to their own satisfaction by simple belief where reason stopped, Sparks could
scarcely hope to advance his institutional cause by raising this
problem in new and alien territory. He surely did not want Miller
to charge that Unitarians professed Deism or Hume's skepticism.
Yet the major intellectual and institutional issue that Sparks
evaded was Lockian empiricism. He and Unitarians for two decades failed to exploit the implications of Lockian epistemology

for religious toleration in the Jacksonian period.[55] Sparks may have won the third battle of the Great Unitarian Controversy despite this failure, but in the long run his argument arrested the growth of Unitarianism as a national institution.

The second course of Lockian ideas after the Sparks-Miller exchange of letters was initiated by Samuel Miller's Baltimore sermon and furthered by opponents of the New England Unitarians. Even though Miller earlier had admired Locke, his sermon prepared the way for the later charge that Lockian psychology is undemocratic. If he could clinch the point that Unitarian clergymen, who were disciples of Locke, preached to "the gay, the fashionable, the worldly minded, and even the licentious" in cities that were "hotbeds of error," then Locke too would be associated with urban evil. Miller, in effect, was tying the name of Locke to the whole crowd of sophisticated and morally lax Unitarians, as he saw them, in Baltimore, Philadelphia, and of course in Boston. He knew that rural and small-town Calvinists suspected urban Unitarians of being snobbish, exclusive, and affected. But we know too that before his removal to the bucolic surroundings of the Princeton Seminary in 1812, Miller in his New York City pastorate had been admired for his sophistication and urbanity.[56]

By not disputing the title thesis of Miller's sermon, Sparks made another debater's decision that would penalize Unitarianism. For one aspect of the transcendentalist revolt against Unitarianism— one that has not usually been emphasized by scholars of the subject—is the extension to 1838 of the charge that Miller first made in 1820. Through his *Boston Quarterly Review* Orestes Brownson best expressed the argument. His major contention, like that of all the transcendentalists, was that with Locke there is an absence of "spiritual experience." Building his case against Lockian sensationalism, Brownson charged also that Locke and his followers think that knowledge only comes from human teachers, that the masses have no ideas because of the Lockian individual *tabula rasa.*[57] The Lockian philosophy is not democratic, he contended; it "disinherits the mass" because it refers us only to recognized historical authority, not to the "light of reason universal in all men." The disciple of Locke, Brownson asserted, cannot trust the people. He must "scout universal suffrage, and labor to concentrate all power in the hands of those he looks upon as the enlightened and respectable few." The history of Harvard, he wrote, "may tend to confirm this conclusion. . . . As long as Locke is her textbook, she will have no faith in democratic institutions."[58] Six months later Brownson, whose fame rests partly upon his several changes of religious opinion, confessed in July of 1839 that to him Unitarianism was "the progressive party." He exclaimed: "We love this party, not because it is said to be Unitarian, not for any of its actual dogmas, but for its liberality, because it is the *Liberal Party*."[59] He was satisfied by then that the appointment of James Walker to the Alford Chair at Harvard and the adoption there of Cousin's eclectic *Psychology* as a textbook to accompany Locke would contribute to the spread of "a more worthy philosophy of the human mind."[60]

By 1839 Locke had not been as completely dismissed from the American academic scene as transcendentalists wished. Although the *Essay* lingered as prescribed reading at Harvard, its sensational psychology was explained there and in most American colleges mainly through the textbooks of Scottish common-sense realism, which had been replacing William Paley's moral philosophy, a popularization of Lockian theological utilitarianism.[61] Acceptance of the Scottish philosophy at Harvard may be called the fourth stage in the Great Unitarian Controversy. The Scottish philosophy had been constructed in the eighteenth century in large part upon Locke's *Essay*. But in ethics it had added an innate moral faculty to man. This characteristic well fitted the romantic, intuitive, and evangelical public temper of Jacksonian America. In such a climate of opinion Brownson's charge that Lockian psychology was undemocratic doubtless had its supporters, though no one replied to him that this was a curious way to view a founding father of American political theory. Doubtless too, most New England urban Unitarians who appealed to the name of Locke stood in the Federalist-Whig political tradition; some of the older ones retained their earlier distrust of democracy. So when the transcendentalists charged that Unitarians were complacent, exclusive, and unconcerned for humanity, they were partly right—though the force of their indictment is founded more upon their style and the intellectual excitement they aroused than upon a valid social generalization. There were always the Charles Follens, the Samuel Mays, the Horace Manns, or the Peabody sisters to show that transcendentalists were also partly wrong about Unitarian social attitudes. But by this time the argument, as far as Lockian thought goes, had passed the point of relevance for Unitarianism. The surrender of a well-entrenched Lockian position had been made a lot earlier. Unitarians were indeed complacent to the point of intellectual flabbiness in their Lockian premises.

The problem of the Protestant ministry and urban social attitudes did not begin with Jared Sparks in Baltimore. But it was there first clearly put before Unitarians and connected with Lockian ideas by Samuel Miller. Failing to take up Miller's theme, Sparks missed his opportunity to state that Lockian Unitarianism did indeed have a thoroughly American social ethics to offer city people. Democracy in the early 1820's was beginning to mean that more people were participating in the experience of the republic; democratic republicanism was being built upon recognition of the diverse experiences of many people in urban and rural situations. If it was anything, experience was a Lockian word. By answering Miller in this way, Sparks could have demonstrated that the great Mr. Locke's understanding of human behavior, like Newton's understanding of natural science, was readily accessible to public use.

This criticism of Sparks is not directed primarily at his debating tactics. Though limited, they perhaps were excusable. After all, he did well for a young man championing the name of Locke when denominational partiality was dearer to most church people than the ideal of religious toleration. Nor do I think that his lack of institutional strategy can be attributed to some traditional and easy, perhaps for him too easy, explanations. He may have been intellectually closer to Calvin than to Thomas Huxley; he may have been closer to Federalist elitism than to the Jacksonian temper; he may have been uncertain, as we may still be today, of the difference between Lockian psychology and Lockian philosophy. These explanations, however, simply do not nullify criticism of young Sparks's ambitious but incomplete strategy for his liberal church, particularly in the South. He was a sociable young man; he was well liked; he was intellectually alert; he was precisely what Unitarianism needed as a church leader outside New England, perhaps in some ways even more than it needed the scholarship of Andrews Norton at home.[62] Seeking the name of Locke as his institutional standard, Sparks knew that, for Locke, freedom meant not just liberty of choice; it meant liberty of action based upon choice. The institutional challenge to Unitarianism was for it to act by carrying into the vortex of American denominationalism the message of reason and toleration based upon knowledge of the common historical experiences of competing faiths.

The short view of Lockian ideas displayed by Sparks in this episode was not nearly as significant for his career as it was for the institutional future of Unitarianism. Sparks left the ministry in 1823 for the editorship of the *North American Review*. Yet Unitarianism went on its indecisive way with Locke. The Sparks-Miller debate, as I see it, was the crucial point for the potential institutional growth of Unitarianism in the young nation. It was far more important in this respect than the final dispute Unitarianism as a declining regional institution had with the transcendentalists. The course of Lockian ideas in American theology and academic philosophy was determined not in the next few decades, as we sometimes assume, but in the 1820's when the power of evangelical denominationalism North and South turned Locke aside. And in secular political affairs, by 1832, Lockian and Jeffersonian ideas also were defeated in the debate over freedom of thought in the Old South. In that region perhaps there would have been little that Sparks or a dozen like him could do to keep alive the ideas of liberal religion into the antebellum period. The mood of public discourse by then was to be so changed that it would only re-emphasize the peculiarly American way in which the name of Locke could be used opportunely and superficially.

Fortunately, Lockian thought was not permanently dismissed from American life. It was reinvigorated in the abolitionist movements of the 1830's and the 1960's. It reappeared in its empirical form within American philosophy, psychology, and theology during the late nineteenth century. And its spirit of freedom for truth-seeking in the middle of our century has marked the work of the historian to whom the essays in this volume have been dedicated.

JOHN D. WRIGHT, JR.

Libertarianism's Loss: The Case of Horace Holley and Transylvania University

BETWEEN THE YEARS 1818 AND 1827 there occurred at Transylvania University in Lexington, Kentucky, what has been called the classic case of the continuing struggle in the early nineteenth century between liberal higher education and the forces of intellectual and class leveling and denominational control.[1] The value of this particular example of a not unfamiliar pattern in the educational history of that period in the South and West is the dramatic character of the struggle and the inclusion within this one situation of most of the controversial issues that beset other college campuses only in part.

While this struggle at Transylvania may appear, in retrospect, to be one over academic freedom in its largest sense—the right of free inquiry unhampered by sectarian dogma or political or class interests—it cannot be so viewed in its historical context for the reason that such a concept of academic freedom was but barely emerging in the academic mind at the time. The issues of free speech, right of assembly, and religious toleration involved in the debate over the Bill of Rights appended to the new Constitution were only vaguely associated with the educational institutions and learning process in the land, and the transfer of civil liberties to the academic scene was an imperfect and controversial process. The alliance of religious institutions with higher education was especially strong in the English tradition, and there was no attempt to divorce these elements in the beginnings of American

101

higher education. There had not yet developed a tradition of independent and protected faculty freedom in the classroom and on the campus. Indeed, the very status of the college professor was improving only at a snail's pace, as forward-looking college presidents began to recommend that the tutorial-recitation method be replaced by more learned lectures, if not research. There were no significant faculty organizations, neither within the colleges nor between colleges, established to define and defend academic freedom and the individual faculty members.[2]

Nor were the college presidents in a much stronger position. Despite the fact that the status of the college president in the colonial and antebellum periods was considerably higher than that of the teacher, he likewise suffered from the lack of a tradition to protect his independence of thought and action, one which might have supported him in his defense of intellectual freedom on his campus. Thus, in 1654, when President Henry Dunster of Harvard found himself at doctrinal odds with the college overseers "he never argued that a college is a place in which the search for truth is to be carried on through free inquiry and the exchange of views. . . . It is a place in which received truth is to be passed on."[3] There was no higher law to which he might have appealed, and he resigned quietly. Only gradually did the concept of intellectual freedom develop in the intellectual milieu of the eighteenth century, and there was no attempt at that time to attach such freedom to the teaching function. The American college, as Richard Hofstadter points out, differed from the European college and university in being, firstly, a mixture of private denominational sponsorship with some state supervision; secondly, in lacking professional faculties such as the European universities had; and, thirdly, in the creation of lay, non-resident governing boards. None of these elements were conducive to the development of academic freedom, not because they embodied anti-intellectual forces necessarily, but because, as in the case of the governing boards, they were outside of the academic community as such. These factors, therefore, should be kept in mind when we consider the reasons for Holley's failure at Transylvania University to preserve the independence of the school, academic freedom, and his own position as president against outside forces.

At the time that Transylvania was originally chartered by the

Virginia legislature in 1780, there was no reason to anticipate that it would be substantially different from a number of other academies and seminaries of learning that were being chartered so frequently at the time. Though the Presbyterians were responsible for persuading the legislature to charter this school for Virginia's western county of Kentucky, the charter, interestingly enough, contained no reference to the denomination nor did it attempt to make any provision for denominational representation on the Board of Trustees. The charter was amended in 1783 appending the name Transylvania to the institution and adding additional acres of confiscated loyalist real estate to the original grant.[4]

Widespread pioneer settlements and continual Indian attacks were not the most favorable conditions for supporting schools, and Transylvania endured through a haphazard career as a grammar school under Presbyterian auspices into the 1790's, moving then from its original location near Danville to Lexington. A temporary loss of control of the school motivated the Presbyterians to erect a rival institution not far distant, but the disaster confronting both schools as a result of this action persuaded cooler heads to unite their efforts, once again under Presbyterian control. The Kentucky legislature amended the original charter once again to combine these two schools into Transylvania University in 1799, attaching to the infant academic department law and medical departments. Lack of inspired leadership as well as inadequate support from the intellectual and financial community resulted in slow progress. In 1815 the liberal trustees mounted an attack against the domination of the Presbyterian influence in the school's affairs, with the aim of ousting the Rev. James Blythe, long-time acting-president. This action may have been provoked by Blythe's vehement denunciation of the War of 1812, a minority position extremely unpopular in Kentucky. In any case, the liberal trustees so effectively persuaded the Kentucky legislature of the need for a change that a bill was passed discharging the existing Board of Trustees and replacing them with a new board, among whom was Henry Clay. The liberals were now in full control. As they had done before, the defeated Presbyterians countered their loss with the establishment of a rival institution a few years later. This institution was Centre College, and the Presbyterians firmly committed themselves to it, turning their backs once and for all on Transylvania. Unfortunately for the latter institution, certain Presbyterian leaders would not remain content until they had destroyed what they could not control. In this instance, as in many others like it across the country, the struggle centered on a controversial individual. Ignoring ominous threats, the new Transylvania trustees embarked upon a vigorous program to improve the university. They gave top priority to securing an outstanding president. Their choice was the Rev. Horace Holley of Boston.[5]

How did the Board of Trustees of a distant western college decide to appoint a Boston Unitarian minister to the presidency? The records do not provide us with a clear answer except to show that there was wide correspondence to individuals across the country asking for suggestions for individuals who might qualify for the post. Boston and Cambridge, traditional centers of learning and educational leadership, were natural sources to turn to for capable men in this field. It was known that Holley was active in educational affairs in Boston. Holley had another major qualification for being a college president. He was a Yale graduate and a minister. Yale and Princeton graduates, particularly clergymen, supplied the bulk of the college presidents for the West and South during this period.[6] As early as 1815, the old Board, under the misconception that Holley was an orthodox theologian in the Timothy Dwight tradition, had appointed him president, but then changed their minds. Holley apparently gave the overture no serious consideration at that time. However, on November 15, 1817, the new Board again elected Horace Holley to the presidency. They sent a letter to him informing him of their action. This technique of appointing a man to a position as college president and then surprising him with the news seemed to be typical of the time. It was a time-consuming procedure since many such impromptu appointments were refused by the recipients.

In their letter to Holley the trustees described the current status of the institution, financial and otherwise, with particular emphasis on the possibility of growth under dynamic leadership. They offered a salary of $2250, which they pointed out was $250 higher than any civil officer received in Kentucky. They urged Holley to visit Lexington in the spring of 1818.[7]

Horace Holley was a native of Connecticut, born in 1781 in

the quiet farming community of Salisbury.[8] His father and mother were both native New Englanders, the former rising successfully from poor beginnings as a farmer and schoolmaster to being a reasonably well-to-do business man, the latter the daughter of a Baptist minister. The Holley homelife provided intellectual interests, sound morals, and unusually mild and liberal religious background. Horace's intellectual bent became increasingly evident as he grew older, and his father provided him with an education at an academy at Williamstown and then at Yale. Timothy Dwight praised the academic achievements of this promising student who, after a brief tour to New York to investigate the possibility of law as a career, returned to Yale to study divinity under Dwight. For a period of time, Holley moved into the most conservative position of Calvinist theology, and began his ministry in Dwight's old pastorate in Fairfield County as quite an orthodox pastor. However, his theological views began to undergo a substantial change from his Yale days, a change which Mrs. Holley described later as a slow process beginning while still in his first pastorate in Connecticut and accelerated later by contact with lively minds in Boston.[9] How far his religious views had changed is evidenced by the fact that his next pastorate was at the Unitarian South End Church on Hollis Street in Boston. There he began to develop his oratorical talents which won him considerable fame in his church (the size of the congregation doubled and they had to build a new church) and in the surrounding area. He held strong Federalist sympathies at this time, 1809–1818, and was on good terms with the aging presidential patriarch of Quincy. Later, John Adams was to write a letter to Jefferson introducing and commending Holley to him. Holley's interest in community affairs resulted in his becoming a member of the Boston School Committee, a member of the Board of Overseers of Harvard, and a member of various literary, scientific, and benevolent organizations and institutions. To these causes he gave liberally of his money, time, and talents.[10]

Why, then, did Holley give serious consideration to the offer from Kentucky to become president of Transylvania University? His position in Boston was an enviable and secure one. His wife Mary, now entering her second pregnancy, was perfectly content with her situation and most disturbed at the prospect of changing it. The answer to the question is neither surprising nor original.

Holley was attracted to the offer by the challenge it presented, by the sacrifices it demanded, and by the possible rewards that it might offer. For Holley was not only a talented man, he was also an ambitious man. He was nearing the completion of a decade of service at the Hollis Street Church. He may have felt the urge to move out and conquer new worlds. "I did not expect to increase my happiness by taking a more important station, but anticipated some privations and difficulties," he recalled later.[11] After he had surveyed the scene in Lexington and decided to accept the position, he wrote his wife that

there can be no doubt that it is my duty as a philanthropist to accept of the station which is offered to me here. I believe it is in my power to do more good in this region than in any other at this moment. My life has not been half so useful in Boston, though it has been of some value there, as I am persuaded it will be in Lexington. . . . For the sole purpose of doing good, I had rather be at the head of this institution than at the head of an Eastern college. The field is wider, the harvest more abundant, and the grain of a most excellent quality. I may become what you call a martyr, but it is not my intention to be one. I shall make a sacrifice in many things, but I shall do my duty, and if I meet with success it will be glorious. I am not about to bury myself, nor take my talents, humble as they are, from an active and conspicuous sphere. This whole Western country is to feed my seminary, which will send out lawyers, physicians, clergymen, statesmen, poets, orators, and savans, who will make the nation feel them.[12]

On his first trip to Lexington in the spring of 1818, Holley was impressed by the town and its hospitality. "The town is handsomer than I expected," he said, "and has a more comfortable and genteel aspect. It has not the pretension without the reality, that so many small towns have through which I have passed."[13] Henry Clay acted as the official host, showing Holley the attractive countryside and introducing him to the influential members of the community, including a visit to Frankfort and Governor Slaughter. He made a short address to the students, professors, and trustees of the college, and then toured the small campus and buildings. The limited resources did not discourage him. "Everything is to be done, and so much the better, as nothing is to be reformed," he wrote. "Almost the whole is proposed to be left me to arrange."[14]

Holley realized that all segments of the community were not equally happy at the prospect of his becoming president. Most suspicious and hostile were the Presbyterian leaders in the area, already distressed at losing control of the Board of Trustees. Holley's Unitarian connections only intensified their suspicion and hostility. While the churches of other denominations in the area invited Holley to speak from their pulpits, the Presbyterians appeared adamant in refusing him theirs until the elders of one of the most important Presbyterian churches in Lexington voted unanimously to invite him to preach. Large crowds from Lexington and surrounding areas flocked to hear him as he had become the center of considerable controversy. "Persons came from neighboring towns," reported Holley, "eager to learn whether I am a heretic or not. As I am no heretic, they went away satisfied, I hope, of the truth."[15] In the exhilarating fervor of the moment Holley convinced himself that not only might he prove himself as an educational leader but also as a uniting force among sectarian differences. Henry Clay wisely warned him against becoming involved in any such activity, however, and, for the most part, Holley took his advice.[16] Yet, undoubtedly, Holley underestimated the devastating effect of a united and dedicated sectarian hostility. In April, 1818, Holley formally accepted the position as president of Transylvania University. The trustees, more impressed by Holley than ever, guaranteed him a salary of $3000, which was $750 more than they had originally offered him, and which made him one of the highest paid academic officials in the country.[17]

Three major obstacles were to confront Holley in his attempt to develop Transylvania into a successful state university: 1) denominational hostility, primarily Presbyterian, 2) political attacks, primarily from Governor Joseph Desha and his exploitation of the common man vs. aristocrats issue, and 3) economics, primarily Kentucky's acute depression and the Relief controversy. Niels Sonne, in his excellent study on *Liberal Kentucky, 1780–1828*, describes clearly the changing character of the Kentucky intellectual atmosphere from its early days through the Holley controversy. The Virginia men, states Sonne, who provided the leadership in the development of Kentucky as it moved through the early tribulations toward statehood in 1792 carried with them into the western country a political philosophy that emphasized individual liberty and states' rights, a religious philosophy that advocated toleration and separation of church and state, and a liberal intellectualism which shared in the diversity of enlightened European thought. It is Sonne's contention that a period of relative religious liberalism prevailed between 1780–1820, but that this liberalism was seriously, indeed successfully, challenged in the latter part of that period, and a time of Protestant orthodoxy replaced it; that this orthodoxy placed on the defensive not only religious liberalism but intellectual liberalism as well, thus affecting the political and educational issues of the day.[18] The ultimate defeat of liberalism was due as much to the fact that its strength lay mainly among the upper classes and their inability to win support among other classes, as it was due to the conquest of liberal thought by orthodox thought in even debate. Indeed, the religious hold of the churches on the early settlers of Kentucky was so weak that the orthodox church leaders in their conflict with the liberal leaders had to incorporate into their attack economic, class, and political issues, irrelevant to religious dogma, in order to muster sufficient strength to win the battle.

In the contest between liberal and orthodox groups in Kentucky, and in other states as well, the Presbyterian leaders led the forces of orthodoxy. Despite a perpetual numerical inferiority, the Presbyterians wielded an influence acknowledged by friend and foe alike, and evidenced time and again by their successes. Sonne attributes this influence to the fact that the Presbyterians were largely of the upper classes, or on their way up, that they adhered to a strictly defined Calvinism, and that they concentrated a good deal of their efforts on education and the establishment of educational institutions, not only as a means to provide them with an essential educated ministry but also to provide them with leaders in other fields as well.[19] Why their attacks should have intensified in the early part of the nineteenth century is debatable. Their minority position, the challenge of eighteenth-century European thought and the rise of Unitarianism, and the threat of the new, unlettered, and powerful revivalism are factors that are relevant to the answer.[20] The growing freedom from the Indian threat provided them with a more secure atmosphere in which to engage in religious controversy.

The Baptists, and to a large extent the Methodists as well,

concentrated more on the lower classes who tended to remain unchurched and who would have found little appeal in the intellectualized theological approach of a learned clergy. The battle lines, therefore, tended to be drawn between the educated and articulate Presbyterians on the one hand and the educated and articulate non-Presbyterian "infidels" on the other. Unfortunately for the progress of higher education in this country, the schools were frequently the arena for this contest. Ironically, many of the new schools had to turn to Presbyterians for their faculty and presidents, not out of preference so much as because of the short supply of educated men. Hofstadter points out that "of all the churches, the Presbyterians were by far the most vigilant and censorious as men like Jefferson, Thomas Cooper, Horace Holley, and Frances Lieber painfully learned. The history of collegiate education in the South and West is in large measure the history of the struggles in which that church played a central part."[21]

So we find the Presbyterians in the curious position of being leaders in the establishment of schools while acting frequently as deterrents to educational progress by their sectarian obstruction. Jefferson made no secret of his attitude toward that denomination. In 1820, at the very time the Presbyterians in Kentucky were heating up their attacks on Holley, he wrote: "The Presbyterian clergy are the loudest, the most intolerant of all sects, the most tyrannical and ambitious. . . . They pant to re-establish by law the holy inquisition which they can now only infuse into public opinion."[22] To denounce categorically the Presbyterian Church at this time as being wholly innocent of any liberal members would be not only unjust but inaccurate. Yet it seems indisputable that too frequently their organized hostility proved far more successful against liberal opposition than any liberal stirrings in their own camp could ever hope to balance.

The second major obstacle to Holley's success was political. Because Transylvania had been chartered without any reference to religion or denominational affiliation, it was assumed that the Virginia legislature intended it to be a non-denominational state institution. The Kentucky legislature certainly acted as if the school were a child of theirs, at least for the first few decades of the nineteenth century. This connection with the state legislature brought to focus upon Transylvania the lively forces of political controversy. The Presbyterians quite clearly understood the necessity of mustering political support for their attack on Holley and Transylvania. Thus, though many claimed to be Republican in their political sympathies, they found it difficult to avoid being classified as Federalists, particularly during the War of 1812 when many leading Presbyterians, especially in the ministry, supported and advocated the New England position of dissent.[23] The denunciation of the war by the Rev. James Blythe, president of Transylvania and a devout Presbyterian, has already been alluded to. It became necessary for the Presbyterians to mask their former Federalist identification by accusing Transylvania of catering to the rich and aristocratic, and, by implication, of being immoral and atheistic. Such strategy, however, would never have been successful if the material for its exploitation had not been available. There had not yet developed in the southern states a tradition of state support of public education. The state legislatures were willing enough to charter private church-supported academies of all types, but this proved nothing and was little more than a manifestation of their opinion that education was probably beneficial and that it was a private matter. They showed little willingness to support financially educational institutions except by land grants which, though appearing generous in retrospect, were at the time cumbersome and unproductive sources of income. The grants for the most part were inaccessible, unsurveyed, unwanted by affluent purchasers, and plagued by legal entanglements, especially in the case of the escheated lands acquired during the Revolution.

Kentucky showed a natural tendency to subordinate educational concerns to the priorities of survival in the early years of her settlement. Defense against the Indians and the speculation in, and settlement of, the new lands commanded most of the inhabitants' interests. Kentucky's early governors were soldiers and planters. The first three governors were members of the Board of Trustees of Transylvania, but Governor Shelby (1792–1796, 1812–1816) was dropped because he failed to attend the Board meetings, nor did he in any of his official messages to the legislature so much as mention education or the need for schools.[24] Governor Garrard (1796–1804) followed this unfortunate precedent, but Governor Greenup (1804–1808) broke this silence by urging the Kentucky legislature to fulfill its responsibilities to educate the state's youth.

He was an active member of Transylvania's Board, acting as its legal adviser, frequently serving as its treasurer, and he headed some of the more difficult committee assignments. Governor Slaughter (1816–1820), who as lieutenant governor came to office following Governor Madison's death after one month in office, made a notable one-man campaign for legislative support for education in Kentucky. His efforts were largely vitiated by legislative opposition, created in large part by his mistake in appointing a most unpopular individual to an important state post. His recommendation that the populous parts of the state be divided into school districts of four or five miles square was the most progressive suggestion so far, but it died at its presentation. Another suggestion of his adopted by a later legislature was to put the proceeds from the sale of public lands into a literary fund to be dispensed as the legislature saw fit to support public schools and a state university. Though over $140,000 was accumulated in this fund, it is significant that not one major appropriation was made out of it for the support of the schools.[25]

Finally, as far as this relates to the Holley period, there was the split which occurred during the administration of Governor Adair (1820–1824) between those of his administration who supported his position on the importance of providing state support for Transylvania and those who favored some state support for education but favored the public schools, or common schools, over the college. The legislature made no move to establish a common school system and its haphazard support of Transylvania shortly came to an end. One cannot but conclude that there was no firm conviction on the part of the legislature that the state could or should support a system of public schools, or that it should even place itself firmly behind its most promising established university. Such an attitude was easily exploited by Governor Joseph Desha in his desire to injure, if not actually destroy, Transylvania and Holley, and along with them the "aristocratic" privilege of higher education.

The third obstacle confronting Holley, in addition to the Presbyterian and political hurdles, was the economic crisis in Kentucky. The period of 1816–1836 was one in which controversies over banks, the debt relief laws, the court decisions on replevin laws and the struggles over the courts resulting therefrom, played a central role. Following a period of unparalleled prosperity sparked by the trade restrictions prior to the War of 1812 and then the war itself, the Kentucky economy was severely depressed by the return to peacetime conditions. To relieve a money shortage, the Kentucky legislature chartered forty-six banks in 1818 authorized to issue $26,000,000. Within a year, the drop in the value of such bank notes was disastrous.[26] Only the two branches of the Second Bank of the United States located in Louisville and Lexington provided any financial stability and a dependable currency. The Kentucky legislature granted brief stays of judgment executions, closed most of the unsound banks, and passed a replevin law which gave the creditor the distasteful choice of either accepting notes of the Bank of Kentucky in payment of a debt or granting the debtor a two-year stay. In Governor Adair's administration, 1820–1824, growing political polarization around these controversial economic issues reached its peak as a new Bank of the Commonwealth was chartered, and, even more significant, as the replevin laws were declared unconstitutional by a number of the state courts, a position upheld by the state's highest court, the Court of Appeals. With the election of Desha in 1824 as head of the so-called Relief forces in the state, backed by a Relief majority in the state legislature, attacks on the Court of Appeals and its decision on the replevin laws began. Failing to impeach the judges, the legislature repealed the laws establishing the court, a dubious constitutional measure at best, and established a New Court manned by supporters of the Relief position. The Old Court would not relinquish its position, the New Court proved to be ineffective and controversial, and within little more than a year a new election brought the Old Court forces into power and the legislation establishing the New Court was repealed. The state was thus split between the Relief-New Court forces and the Antirelief Old Court forces. Though Henry Clay attempted to avoid embroilment in these state issues in order to obtain bipartisan support for his presidential hopes in 1824, he was soon identified with the Antirelief forces. The situation became embarrassing when Desha and the Relief majority in the legislature, 1824–1825, directed the Kentucky delegation in Congress to cast their votes for Jackson. When Clay and the Kentucky delegation "defected" and cast their support to Adams, Desha and his Relief followers denounced this betrayal and became vehement opponents of Clay.[27] Clay's friendship with Holley, and his influential role as a trustee of Transylvania, made the New England Unitarian president and his university tempting targets for Desha.

In the fall of 1818, Horace Holley and his family, accompanied by young John Everett, brother of Edward Everett and a recent graduate of Harvard whom Holley had engaged as a tutor in the classics, arrived in Lexington with considerable fanfare. The main college building was illuminated, committees of welcome had been assembled, and the usual formalities were extended the new president. The Holleys stayed at the home of Henry Clay until their own residence was ready. On December 19, 1818, Holley was formally inaugurated into office at the Episcopal Church, the college chapel being too small to hold the large crowd.[28]

On assuming office, Holley threw himself energetically into the task of solving the host of large and small problems that inevitably crowd the desk of the college administrator. He proved to be an able administrator as well as a talented teacher in Transylvania's classrooms, conducting classes on mental and moral philosophy, and even giving a course of lectures in the Law Department. After creating some order in the college calendar and structure by insisting on the adoption of a two-semester plan and the organization of the student body into the traditional four classes, improving the physical facilities and their upkeep, and establishing effective rapport with the community, he concentrated upon recruiting as able a faculty as his personal influence could persuade to come to such an educational outpost. His letters to men like John Warren, Boston's outstanding surgeon, Benjamin Silliman, the cornerstone of Yale's science department, and Edward Livingston, public servant and able New York lawyer, all give evidence of his determination to start with top men.[29] That he had to settle for something less than the most famous scholars in America is understandable, but in his faculty for the Medical Department he achieved a success acknowledged by medical authorities throughout the nation and attested to by the remarkable influx of medical students who provided the larger part of Transylvania's enrollment during his administration. The names of Daniel Drake, Benjamin Dudley, Samuel Brown, Charles Caldwell, W. H. Richardson, and Charles Short will be familiar to

anyone acquainted with the medical history of this country.[30] To
the Law Department he attracted such men as Jesse Bledsoe and
William T. Barry, the latter becoming lieutenant governor of
Kentucky shortly after his career as a law lecturer had begun. Holley had asked Judge John Rowan and Edward Livingston of New
York to lecture in the Law Department, but they declined the
offer.[31]

One of the most bizarre members of the faculty was Constan-
tine Rafinesque, the unpredictable and controversial naturalist.
Born in Constantinople of a French father and German mother,
Rafinesque lived in France for a few years, visited Philadelphia,
returned to Sicily for a decade, and then returned to the United
States permanently in 1815. His energies were limitless, his hunger
for all aspects of natural history insatiable, and his penchant for
discovering, poorly preserving, and freely classifying all forms of
flora and fauna was the despair of his fellow naturalists. Add to
this a rather exotic personal appearance and eccentric manners
and you had a faculty member eminently qualified to annoy his
colleagues, irritate the administration, provoke the community,
and inspire and amuse the students. Yet Harvard's Louis Agassiz
wrote of Rafinesque that he

collected a vast amount of information from all parts of the States,
upon a variety of objects then entirely new to science. From what I
can learn of Rafinesque, I am satisfied that he was a better man than
he appeared. His misfortune was his prurient desire for novelties and
his rashness in publishing them, and yet both in Europe and America
he has anticipated most of his contemporaries in the discovery of new
genera and species in those departments of science which he has cultivated most perseveringly. . . .[32]

It was this man that Holley risked putting on the faculty, and
for a number of years the Holley home was a pleasant refuge for
Rafinesque, due especially to Mrs. Holley's sympathy for and
kindness to him.[33] Yet even Holley's forbearance had its limits,
and in 1825 the two men came to a parting of the ways.

Meanwhile, Holley maintained correspondence with friends in
the East as he sought for distinguished men to man his staff, and
spreading the word among his influential friends of the progress
and character of his university. He sent Jefferson a copy of a re-

port on common schools and professed his admiration for the Virginian's devotion to the new university in Charlottesville. Jared Sparks requested that Holley write a review of Marshall's *History of Kentucky* for an issue of the *North American Review*. Benjamin Silliman sent him reports on promising young scientists at Harvard and Yale that Holley might contact. John Adams thanked Holley for his note of condolence on the recent death of Mrs. Adams, saying that of all the notes he had received, none had been "so congenial to my own Sentiments and so consoling to my feelings, as yours. . . ." Dr. John Warren said that members of the Friday Night Club in Boston sorely missed Holley's presence, but that if he had to leave, then he deserved as distinguished a post as he had accepted. George Ticknor inquired about Transylvania's experiment with enrolling students who were not intending to go on for a degree, and thought Harvard should adopt a similar system. And Justice Joseph Story waxed poetic as he expressed his opinion to Holley that he looked "upon Transylvania as an institution which must have a very important influence upon the morals & the literature & the taste & the religion & the public feeling of that interesting portion of our country." Here lay the "destinies of an empire," he said, and it was important that the people there acquire intellectual discipline, eloquence, classical literature, and "that rational Christianity, which enobles & exalts. . . ." It is to be expected, he consoled Holley, that opposition would develop "from prejudice & from misrepresentation, & from innocent delusion," but he was confident that in five years Holley's "perseverance will completely triumph; . . . [and his] fame be as highly estimated as it deserves."[34] Encouragement from such a source must have been welcomed by Holley. It was unfortunate that Story's predictions proved to be so wrong.

While there does not appear to have been much argument between Holley and his opponents over his educational philosophy, certain of his ideas smacked of educational novelty and may have disturbed those groups which composed his dedicated opposition. First and foremost was his ambition to make Transylvania a leading state university in the West. This was in accord with his view of higher education nationally. Holley believed that there should be a federal system of higher education reflecting our federal form of government. With James Madison and John Quincy Adams, he believed that heading the system should be a national university, reflecting not only the national and international character of learning but acting as a unifying agent among the diverse regions of the nation and developing great leaders for the country.[35] Supplementing the national university should be one major university in each state and only one, for the limited resources of most states did not permit them to be dissipated among many institutions. By concentrating upon one university, a state might erect a strong institution and, in addition, counteract the forces of sectional prejudices and conflicting parties which would undermine the strength of an institution. Holley was convinced that Kentucky was in a remarkably good strategic position to create a strong state university which could influence the entire Mississippi Valley. "It is intellectual capital alone," he said, "that can confer on her genuine and enduring greatness and power."[36] And falling into the cliché of the time and place, Holley suggested that Kentucky was the Attica, Lexington the Athens, of the West. Nor was he worried about the decline of business and population in Lexington, which was suffering economically from the rapid growth of the river towns of Cincinnati and Louisville. A people less involved with business might be more open to the development of the intellect and the spirit, he believed. Indeed, the whole economic and cultural interrelationship between Transylvania and the Lexington community was an interesting and significant one.[37]

Holley expounded his educational views at some length in an article he wrote for the *Western Review* entitled "Education in the Western States."[38] His views were marked by flexibility and practicality. He emphasized the need for adjusting education to the needs and character of different sections of the country. He condemned the tendency of many parents to hurry their sons through their education, to send them to college at too early an age. He also advocated that young students should concentrate on memory disciplines such as languages, and postpone the development of their scientific, speculative, and analytical capacities until college. Again, he emphasized the danger of multiplying academies and colleges in the western states, a trend that accelerated beyond all reason in these decades. He urged the development of adequate libraries, pointing out, as George Ticknor was doing at the same time in Boston, the vast difference between the holdings of American and European university libraries.[39]

Given a student enrollment which had increased under Holley from 60 students to 418 in 1826, matching, if not surpassing, that of Harvard, Yale, or Princeton; given a Medical Department as distinguished as any in the country; given a president whose stature and influence were indisputable; given its strategic location and its success in drawing students from all over the South, although as many as twenty-one states and two foreign countries were represented at one time or another; it is fair to assume that as a state institution Transylvania needed only the continued moral and financial support of the Kentucky legislature to make it the leading university in the West. Such was not to be.[40]

The first and most persistent attacks on Holley came from the Presbyterians. This is understandable. For the second time the Presbyterians had lost control of the school they had been instrumental in establishing, a mistake for which the Rev. Robert Davidson, the Presbyterian apologist and historian of that period, blamed his fellow Presbyterians as much as anyone.[41] The basis of the struggle was not whether there should be any college chapel or religious instruction at Transylvania, or at any state university, but whether the chapel services and religious instruction would be dominated by a single sect and permeated by its creedal peculiarities. Some years earlier the famed Philadelphia physician, Benjamin Rush, had written his belief "that the only foundation for a useful education in a republic is to be laid in Religion. Without this there can be no virtue, and without virtue there can be no liberty, and liberty is the object and life of all republican governments. . . . A Christian cannot fail of being a republican."[42] It can be assumed that such a viewpoint was widely held by many educators and legislators of Holley's period. The prevalence of Bible classes, daily prayers, compulsory chapel, and revivalism at most of the state universities was hardly evidence of religious indifference.[43] Yet, the more militant sects were not content with this situation, and either attacked the state universities as dens of iniquity or fought vigorously to bring them under sectarian control. Thus, Holley's situation was not unique, but he was more successful than other college presidents in attracting a greater combination of adversaries.

The usual media used by the churches in launching their attacks were letters to the editors of the local newspapers, sectarian journals, and special pamphlets which could be cheaply printed and widely distributed. Thus, within two weeks after Holley's inauguration as president of Transylvania University, there appeared in the Chillicothe, Ohio, *Weekly Recorder* (a rather distant gun, it would seem, but perhaps the only one available at the time and one close enough to fire on the outposts) a series of articles by anonymous authors that leveled at Holley and Transylvania what were to become the all too familiar charges in the years ahead. These centered on Holley's supposed infidelity, a term used by the Presbyterians to define a non-Presbyterian and did not imply sexual impropriety, his attempts to disseminate his heretical religious views in the classroom and the college chapel both by affirmation and by sarcastic ridicule of the students' orthodox beliefs, his private "high life" which included worldly social gatherings at his home where improper conversation was heard, undraped female statuary displayed and carefree songs sung, and his attendance at the races and plays.[44] Holley was a man who enjoyed balancing his periods of serious intellectual work with a lively social schedule. He entertained as much as his limited financial resources allowed, and the fact that he had to move to considerably more modest quarters after his first year in Lexington indicates that he was not exceptionally affluent. During his term as president he played host to President Monroe, Jackson, and Lafayette, to mention only the most familiar names. He took special delight in entertaining visiting scholars whom he liked to engage in intellectual dialogue that gave him great satisfaction. All evidence points to his success in these matters, and Mrs. Holley believed that her husband's superiority in these talents merely infuriated his opponents.[45] It was indicative of the desperation of his critics in their no-quarter attack on Holley that these aspects of his private life were exposed in this fashion.

As has been mentioned earlier, Henry Clay had advised Holley to avoid becoming embroiled in sectarian controversies and concentrate upon educational matters, and for the most part, Holley restrained himself. His alert critics did not miss a trick, however. Thus, in May, 1823, when Holley delivered a memorial funeral oration for Col. James Morrison, a wealthy and distinguished Kentuckian and a great benefactor to Transylvania, his words were carefully scanned by hostile readers. There appeared paragraphs describing Morrison's liberal beliefs which sounded a good deal like a defense of Holley's own views on freedom of thought, and in commenting on Morrison's religious views Holley said:

Col. Morrison was a Christian in his sentiments and practice, but did not consider the peculiarities of any of the sectarian creeds in religion, whether papal or Protestant, ancient or modern, as necessary, or as useful, or as ornamental to his character. He had large views and philanthropic feelings, and recognized the wisdom, authority, goodness, and impartiality of the Deity in all relations of life. . . . With him a life of virtue was the most suitable homage to the Deity. He knew and felt that the end of all genuine religion is to make men good, useful and happy.[46]

The above quotation is cited for two reasons. Firstly, it reflects quite accurately the basic religious outlook and profession of Holley himself.[47] Secondly, it gives us some idea of why such a religious outlook irritated the Presbyterians. To the Calvinist, such expression of goodwill as a basis for religious belief was nothing but benevolent banality. They identified it with the whole unhappy, French, enlightened, deistic intellectual influence on American thinking. A few months later, a number of Presbyterian ministers banded together to issue a special pamphlet known as *The Literary Pamphleteer* to carry the barrage of anti-Holley material that a number of the local newspapers would not print. Thus, in the fall of 1823, a new Presbyterian offensive was launched, using Holley's funeral oration as a starting point. One writer managed to read into the oration that Holley intended that

such as enjoy the education of a University, and improve it, though there be no knowledge given of Jesus Christ, will not only be saved, but shall be perfectly happy, and most highly exalted in heaven, whilst such men as Col. J. Morrison, whose education is principally by observation and experience, shall be saved, but shall occupy a lower place.[48]

The same writer accused Holley of removing the cross from Christianity, placing Jesus on the same level with other religious leaders, and joining together Jew, Greek, Mohammedan, and Christian. Interestingly enough, not only did Holley's religious position come under attack but his alleged aristocratic leanings as well. Transylvania was indicted as being not only a quagmire of infidelity, but of being the special educational preserve of the rich as well. The introduction of such a tactic at this stage was extremely well timed for this was on the eve of the 1824 national election. The age of the Jacksonian common man was emerging in Kentucky politics with the Relief controversy and the demagoguery of Joseph Desha.

Although parochial prejudice is always difficult to determine statistically, it cannot be excluded entirely from the Holley controversy. One concerned Presbyterian not only identified Holley with infidelity but Boston as well: "Boston, that seat of infidelity, the fountain of that poisonous stream of western Socinianism spreading its baleful influence thro' our State beginning at Lexington."[49] Even Holley noticed that during the tension aroused by the controversy over Missouri in 1819–1820 "the word Yankee has been used here of late, with a tone of uncommon severity. But it is going down since the compromise, and promises not to do permanent harm."[50] One thing Holley did not import to Kentucky from New England was abolition. In an article he wrote for the American Colonization Society he expressed views on slavery surprisingly similar to those of his friend Henry Clay. He condemned the slave trade but condoned humane ownership of Negroes for service in the fields and homes until gradual colonization should again restore them to their original condition. He purchased a few servants for his own household after coming to Kentucky.[51] Despite the admirable record of the Presbyterians in the matter of antislavery, beginning with the courageous leadership of the Rev. David Rice who led a vigorous battle in the early Kentucky constitutional conventions to abolish slavery in the new state, the issue never came up in the long controversy with Holley. This was probably due to the fact that by 1820 the issue had become too sensitive and involved. Indeed, all three of the denominations—Baptists, Methodists, and Presbyterians—which had taken strong stands against slavery in the late eighteenth and early nineteenth centuries, backed away from the antislavery position, at least as far as enforcing such a policy on their members was concerned.[52]

That Holley may have erred in underestimating the danger of the Presbyterian attack was generally acknowledged by his wife and friends later. But in 1820, Holley was all optimism:

Our University is prosperous. We have many students, and gain upon the public mind. We are without rival in the West, and probably shall be for some years. We are hated by a sect, but are out of its power. Presbyterianism is bitter as gall, but dares not bite, although it growls in its den, and waits for a favorable moment to leap out upon its prey. This remark, of course, refers to the leaders, priests, and bigots, and not to all people. The people of all sects are about the same.[53]

The most concrete threat that the Presbyterians leveled at Transylvania was the establishment of a competing college not fifty miles away at Danville. Centre College was chartered in 1819, but only after successive tries did the Presbyterians bring the new school under its complete denominational control. The Methodists, meanwhile, had established a school in eastern Kentucky at Augusta in 1822, and the Catholics two schools. The familiar pattern of institutional multiplication was already taking form. Yet Transylvania had a good lead, if it could keep it.

The economic problems which plagued Kentuckians during this period and which led to the Relief-New Court Party versus the Antirelief-Old Court Party struggle, have already been briefly described. To Transylvania these economic difficulties presented concrete problems as the income of the school was substantially affected. The bonus from the Farmers and Mechanics Bank which had been assigned by the legislature to Transylvania disappeared with the repeal of the charter of independent banks in February, 1820. The income from 134 shares of stock of the Bank of Kentucky amounting originally to some $2,200 disappeared for the same reason. A substantial appropriation to the school from the legislature of $20,000 in 1821 was accompanied by a warning that Transylvania would have to go it alone in the future, thus confirming the suspicion that the legislature did not recognize it as its state university, deserving of continued and increasing support. Meanwhile, as tuition was raised to compensate for these losses of income, the accusation that only rich students could afford to go to Transylvania was heard more frequently. Holley was identified with the Antirelief-Old Court Party, as was Henry Clay. The political denouement was imminent.[54]

While the sniping at Holley from the Presbyterians continued rather steadily, no real damage was evident until the incessant attacks forced the issue upon the attention of the state legislature, particularly as wild charges of mismanagement and improper use of funds were made. The legislature established a special committee to investigate Transylvania in January, 1824, but outside of a critical comment that the accounts had not been kept with sufficient care, no major discovery of bad administration or misappropriation of funds was made then or later.[55] However, repeated legislative investigation certainly did not improve the public image of the school, and it opened the door for more oblique and damaging attacks.

After a bitter election campaign in the summer of 1824 which included a riot in Lexington, Joseph Desha was elected governor of Kentucky. This prosperous farmer had already served six terms as U.S. Representative, being one of the Kentucky War Hawks during the War of 1812, and his political ambitions appeared limitless. His campaign techniques revealed a ruthless, wily, and effective demagogue. How far he might have gone as a political figure we will never know, for within two months after his inauguration in the fall of 1824, his son committed a brutal murder and was tried, found guilty, and sentenced to hang. Two additional trials only confirmed the first verdict, and Governor Desha resolved this intolerable personal and political dilemma by commuting his son's death sentence to life imprisonment.[56] The pressure this event placed on Desha, and the handicap it placed on his political future (he went into political retirement after his one term as governor), only intensified his hostility toward persons, institutions, and causes that he had never favored in the first place. Into this category fell Henry Clay, Holley, and Transylvania University. While Desha's opposition to Clay was primarily political, Clay's important role as a trustee in recruiting Holley for the college presidency and his encouragement of the institution's progress, made the school and Holley convenient targets. And as if this were not enough, Desha was informed that a student at Transylvania had delivered a vehement denunciation of the Governor and his political principles in the college chapel in the presence of Holley.[57]

As a matter of fact, Holley had been surprised by the speech and had in no way condoned it, but he had not interrupted the student because it had been his policy to grant the students the freedom to deliver extemporary speeches on current issues in the chapel, and all shades of political opinion were expressed by the students. The timing of this particular speech was unfortunate, however, and all the arguments mustered in favor of free speech and intellectual debate would not have mollified Desha. Heading the Relief forces which identified the debtor classes with the "common man," Desha had little difficulty in designing charges against Transylvania. In his November, 1825, message to the legislature, Desha accused the college of serving only the rich and excluding the poor, of overpaying its president, of parasitically absorbing funds from the state that should go to support a common school system.[58] The official attacks were supported by heated denunciations of Transylvania in the administration's mouthpiece, Amos Kendall's *Argus of Western America.*

Did no one come to Holley's defense? In retrospect, the defending forces appear quite formidable. The Board of Trustees ably defended Holley and the operation of Transylvania. They submitted to repeated legislative investigation, if not harassment, and attempted openly and honestly to answer all inquiries and charges. Paradoxically, the fact that Henry Clay was a member of the Board may have reduced its effectiveness as a shield for Holley. It is doubtful that Clay ever intended to use his position as a trustee for his political advantage, but any hopes he might have had of keeping his political role separated from his service as a trustee dimmed with every partisan attack that saw Clay's support of Holley a move to gain New England's support for his presidential ambitions.[59] Whatever political embarrassment it may have caused Clay to be associated with Holley, he sided with the New Englander throughout the controversy and opposed his resignation, holding out the hope to Holley that future state administrations might be more favorably disposed toward Transylvania.[60]

With the exception of the resignation of the unhappy Robert Bishop, and the unfortunate and dramatic break with Rafinesque, the faculty supported Holley, and a number of them signed various depositions to Holley's ability and the competence and honesty of his administration. The Rev. Robert Bishop, a Presbyterian faculty member who had stayed on even after Holley came, although he had to relinquish some of his classes to Holley, ultimately became too involved with the president's opponents, and finally resigned in 1824 to assume the presidency of Miami College in Ohio. It is difficult to measure the effectiveness of faculty support for Holley as far as influencing public or legislative opinion is concerned, particularly so as professorial status in Kentucky may have been at a lower premium than in New England. Holley's critics counterbalanced faculty influence by stating that while the faculty might be intellectually competent, they could never be accused of being religious.[61]

The students represent a more mixed picture. Some of the more religiously orthodox had unquestionably been offended on occasion by Holley's sophisticated approach to religious inquiry and lighthearted sarcasm toward the fanatical. They signed affidavits supporting the anti-Holley group. The majority of the students, it would appear, found Holley tolerant, well-balanced, sympathetic with various views, non-dogmatic, and a challenging and able teacher. They signed statements to this effect.[62]

The Lexington elite favored Holley, and the local press proved to be fair during the controversy, even going to the extent of excluding for months articles and letters relating to either side. But the newspapers could not maintain a policy of exclusion forever, and the vituperative attacks and warm rejoinders boiled up in their columns. Editorial opinion generally favored Holley and Transylvania. The business community saw in an expanding and prosperous college a substantial economic benefit to the town, especially at a time when Lexington was suffering from a loss of population and income. Generous financial support came occasionally from these sources, but it was limited and could never hope to be a substitute for state support.

Holley's personal response to attack was usually a dignified silence. Such a stance was doubtless urged upon him by men like Clay. Mrs. Holley, in retrospect at least, thought a more vigorous response on the part of Holley would have been more effective.[63] Dr. Caldwell, though himself a most ardent polemicist, believed, however, that "had President Holley been less independent in spirit, less firm and resolute in purpose, and less frank and intrepid in disclosing his sentiments, he would have been more fortunate, and Transylvania more prosperous."[64] A greater accommodation to public opinion might have been more judicious, he believed. It is difficult to see at this distance what tactic would have guaranteed Holley's safety except wholesale surrender. It was only rarely that Holley in public addresses defended his position and the course of Transylvania. Such an occasion as Col. Morrison's funeral address is an example. During the Desha attack, however, he told the Kentucky Institute that "while my tongue can move, or my pen form its ink in intelligible characters, I will assert and pursue the liberty of philosophical, political, and religious investigation, unawed by civil or ecclesiastical power."[65] Yet, on December 23, 1825, Holley wrote out his resignation and sent it to the Board. Why?

The final straw was Desha's attack on Holley and Transylvania in the fall of 1825, and the apparent willingness of a loyal legislature to accept Desha's viewpoint. Holley had gone to Frankfort to see Desha and talk with members of the legislature, but the unveiled hostility he met there made such overtures fruitless. This defeat, placed on top of the constant harassment from other sources over the years, was too much to endure. In his final report he said:

Our personal and local jealousies, our political contentions, and our sectarian divisions, have thus far prevented a result which all enlightened men must acknowledge to be eminently desirable. This is a State institution, declared so repeatedly and solemnly by the State itself, assembled in its representatives; and they will doubtless refuse to let it pass out of their hands. What then is the result? Plainly this: the State must endow it amply, and endow it speedily or bear the disgrace of its decline, and perhaps of its fall. Individual efforts have heretofore chiefly maintained it, and large subscriptions have been collected from among yourselves and your neighbor. This resource is exhausted, or nearly so; and especially the motives are wanting, which are to rekindle private exertions.[66]

He agreed, reluctantly, to stay for another year, but the news of his imminent departure resulted in a sharp drop in enrollment for the following term. In the spring of 1827, Holley left Lexington for New Orleans, his mind filled with plans for a trip to Europe and perhaps a new school to establish in Louisiana. Finding the heat of the New Orleans' summer unbearable, he set sail for New York, died of yellow fever aboard ship on July 31, 1827, and was buried at sea off the Dry Tortugas.

The failure of Holley to establish at Transylvania a liberal state university was really the failure of the Kentuckians and their state legislature to overcome the divisive forces of sectarianism, class jealousies, and political rivalries. It showed the lack of a fundamental commitment to higher education in the form of a single state university, and the multiplication of small denominational colleges was the result. What had also gone down to defeat with Holley was liberal thought and the atmosphere of academic freedom essential for its existence. Holley's valiant proclamation to "pursue the liberty of philosophical, political, and religious investigation, unawed by civil or ecclesiastical power" appeared quixotic in an atmosphere growing increasingly hostile to its fulfillment. To have preserved such liberty at Transylvania, free of denominational control, would have required a handsome financial endowment, which it did not have, or generous and consistent state support, which it never received. In the light of the subsequent retreat from its previous liberal position of the same Board which had secured Holley in 1818, it is difficult to see how Holley's continuance as president of Transylvania would have been anything but a futile rearguard action. We can only conclude that Holley saw the signs of the times realistically. The atmosphere of academic freedom, the progress of liberal thought, and the development in Kentucky of a great state university were thus postponed for decades to come.

AUGUST MEIER

卐

Frederick Douglass' Vision for America:
A Case Study in Nineteenth-Century
Negro Protest

THE MOST DISTINGUISHED NEGRO in nineteenth-century America was Frederick Douglass. His fame rests chiefly upon his work as a brilliant antislavery orator and newspaper editor. Yet Douglass was also deeply concerned with developing a program to secure full citizenship rights and acceptance in American society for the free Negroes—both for the minority who were free before the Civil War and for the great masses after emancipation. With his thinking rooted in the principles of American democracy and Christianity—in the Declaration of Independence and the Sermon on the Mount—Douglass' life was a moral crusade for the abolition of slavery and racial distinction, the attainment of civil and political rights and equality before the law, and the assimilation of Negroes into American society. However his specific tactics and programs for racial elevation might vary—and they did undergo significant changes over the years—Douglass was ever the militant agitator, ever the forthright editor and orator, who consistently worked toward these goals through his half-century (1841–1895) of leadership.

Douglass' antislavery career has received detailed treatment at the hands of other scholars,[1] but his ideologies concerning the advancement of free Negroes have not yet been the subject of systematic analysis. This paper, therefore, is limited to a discus-

127

sion of the programs he advocated for the achievement of full racial equality, and the relationship of these programs to the dominant patterns in nineteenth-century Negro thought.

Today Negro protest is expressed in the form of demands rather than appeals, in terms of power as well as justice, and is identified with a strategy of direct action rather than one of oratory and propaganda. The character of modern Negro protest is founded on the international pressures raised in behalf of American Negroes, the growing support for civil rights in the white population, and the increasing power of the Negro vote, which now acts as a balance of power in national elections. Throughout the nineteenth century, however, Negroes lacked leverage of this sort. They utilized the written and spoken word as their major vehicle of protest, combining denunciation of the undemocratic and unchristian oppression under which they lived, with pleas directed at awakening the conscience of white Americans in order to secure redress of these grievances and recognition of their constitutional rights. Instances of what we would today call direct action did occur, but they were rare. Where conditions warranted it—as in those states where the antebellum Negroes could vote, and especially during Reconstruction—advocacy of political activity, in itself the central constitutional right which Negroes asked, was a leading theme, supplementing and lending weight to written and oral agitation, to conventions and meetings, to petitions and resolutions.

On the other hand articulate Negroes in that era ordinarily gave nearly equal emphasis to urging Negroes to cultivate good character, to be thrifty and industrious, and to acquire as much property as possible. It was believed that by thus achieving middle-class moral and economic respectability, Negroes would earn the respect of the whites, counteract prejudice, and ease the way toward recognition of their manhood and their citizenship.

Many nineteenth-century advocates of thrift, industry, and economic accumulation placed special emphasis on the value of industrial education or training in mechanical trades. Most prominently associated with the accommodating ideology of Booker T. Washington at the end of the century, industrial education had been seriously advocated by prominent Negroes as early as the 1830's. Many Negro and white abolitionists viewed manual-labor schools, where the students earned their way through the productive work they performed while learning a useful trade, as an instrument for uplifting the lowly of both races and assimilating them into the mainstream of American middle-class society. Such schools, it was believed, would inculcate the values of thrift and industry at the same time that they provided the students with the means of making a living. At mid-century, the economic crisis facing unskilled Negro workers fostered a resurgence of interest in industrial training.

Underlying the moral and economic program was a theme of individual and racial self-help that in turn overlapped with an ideology of racial solidarity—of racial cooperation and racial unity. This ideology of racial solidarity was one that caused considerable division and argument among articulate nineteenth-century Negroes. While a few went so far as to question the advisability of Negro churches and social organizations, the debate raged chiefly over whether or not Negroes should form their own protest organizations, and establish and support their own protest publications, rather than rely solely upon cooperation with sympathetic whites. This division of opinion was due to more than the attitudes and policies of the many white abolitionists who failed to concern themselves with the Negroes' citizenship rights, who objected to employing Negroes in other than menial positions, and who even refused to allow Negroes to participate fully in the decision-making process of the antislavery societies. It was more than an argument over the question of whether or not it was consistent for Negroes to ask for integration and for acceptance into the mainstream of white society, and at the same time segregate themselves into separate organizations. Beyond these matters the debate was rooted in a fundamental ethnic dualism—an identification with both American society on the one hand, and the persecuted Negro group on the other. This dualism arose out of the contradiction in American culture as Negroes experienced it: the contradiction between the American dream of equality for all and the reality of American race prejudice and discrimination.

Racial solidarity and self-help were always most characteristically associated with the advocacy of morality and economic accumulation, and like these doctrines tended to be especially popular in periods of greatest discouragement, particularly during the 1850's and again at the end of the century. During the decade before the Civil War, the passage of the Fugitive Slave Law of 1850, the decline of the antislavery societies, the increasing competition for menial and laboring jobs offered by Irish immigrants, the southern ascendancy in the national government which culminated in the Dred Scott decision, all made the outlook appear increasingly hopeless. Later, after the overthrow of Reconstruction, the increasing disfranchisement, segregation, and mob violence in the South and, by the 1890's, the growing evidence of prejudice and discrimination in the North, again "forced the Negro back upon himself," as contemporaries expressed it. In the latter period, protest efforts declined sharply, and the advocacy of racial solidarity, self-help, and economic and moral uplift tended to be most often coupled with an ideology of accommodation, especially in the South. This combination of ideas received its most notable expression in the philosophy of Booker T. Washington.

Proposals for racial union, self-help, and solidarity are generally recognized as a variety of Negro "nationalism." It was a form of nationalism which insisted upon the Negro's American citizenship, and viewed the cultivation of race pride and unity as a prerequisite for Negroes organizing themselves for the struggle to obtain equality and integration in American society. Related to this kind of ideology, though eschewing ethnic dualism and the notion that Negroes could ever hope to achieve freedom and equal rights in the United States, was the philosophy of emigration or colonization. Its advocates held that the only solution to the problems facing American Negroes was to emigrate and create a national state of their own, either in the Caribbean area or in Africa. Such proposals, especially popular during the 1850's, cropped up with varying intensity throughout the century. Actually the function of colonization as an ideology is ambiguous. While its advocates protested vigorously against race discrimination in America, they nevertheless favored a form of withdrawal that was in effect an escapist accommodation to the American race system, rather than an assault upon it.

Except for colonization, Douglass enunciated all of these ideologies—agitation, political action, the practice of morality and economy, the acquisition of property, self-help, and racial cooperation. Like other Negroes he shifted his emphasis as the changing situation seemed to warrant. Yet Douglass' views are not simply a reflection of what Negroes generally were saying. Ever the independent thinker, he was willing at times to diverge widely from the patterns of thought ascendant among his friends and contemporaries.[2]

The Antebellum Era

While in the latter part of the century Douglass was a symbol rather than a man of broad influence, during the years prior to the Civil War he was undoubtedly the most powerful leader in the northern Negro community, and his views roughly paralleled the ascendant ideologies among the antebellum free people of color.

Because there was an interrelationship between his program for securing the emancipation of the slaves and his proposals for advancing the status of free Negroes, a brief recapitulation of his antislavery career is in order. Born a slave on the Eastern Shore of Maryland, Douglass succeeded in escaping from his Baltimore master in 1838. By 1841 he had entered the ranks of Massachusetts abolitionist orators. His public career during the abolitionist period may be fairly neatly divided into two parts: the 1840's when he followed the moral suasion tactics of the Garrisonians, and the 1850's when he espoused the cause of political abolition. The four years following the establishment of his weekly newspaper, *North Star*, in Rochester, were a period of transition during which, influenced by western abolitionists like Gerrit Smith, he reexamined his views and finally came to support political abolition, openly breaking with Garrison in 1851.[3] From then on, agitation for political rights and stress upon the value of political activity became one of the most important themes in his thinking, and one which he articulated consistently for the rest of his life. Moreover, it was probably from his abolitionist role that Douglass derived a belief in the value of verbal agitation, and a social philosophy which saw the world in essential moral terms, explaining social institutions and social change as based on the good and evil propensities in human nature. To Douglass the solution of America's race problem lay not in any fundamental institutional changes, beyond the destruction of slavery. Rather, the solution lay in a sincere effort to apply the moral principles upon which the Republic was founded. How to activate these moral principles was his major lifelong concern.

In the years from the founding of *North Star* to the election of Lincoln, Douglass' program for the advancement of free Negroes consisted of three principal elements: a major emphasis on protest and citizenship rights, and secondary emphases on self-help, race pride, and racial solidarity on the one hand, and economic development on the other. First and foremost, he regarded Negroes as Americans: "By birth, we are American citizens; by the principles of the Declaration of Independence, we are American citizens; within the meaning of the United States Constitution, we are American citizens; by the facts of history . . . by the hardships and trials endured, by the courage and fidelity displayed by our ancestors in defending the liberties and in achieving the independence of our land, we are American citizens."[4] Only on the rarest of occasions did his alienation and anger lead him to declare that "I have no love for America," that he could feel no patriotism for a country like the United States,[5] or to warn that the oppressed black men might some day rise up and "become the instruments of spreading desolation, devastation, and death throughout our borders."[6]

Douglass constantly condemned the prejudice and discrimination which Negroes met daily: the segregation, the lack of economic opportunity, the exclusion from churches and schools, from juries and armed forces, and above all the disfranchisement. He denounced the "shameful" and "diabolical" Black Laws of Ohio as "the servile work of pandering politicians." He called upon the white people of Ohio to repeal the Black Laws and enfranchise the Negro, thus wiping out "a most foul imputation" upon their character and making Ohio "the paragon of all the free States."[7] In 1860, in the midst of a campaign to abolish the discriminatory franchise qualifications of the New York State Constitution, he declared:

It is a mockery to talk about protection in a government like ours to a class in it denied the elective franchise. The very denial of that right strips them of "protection," and leaves them at the mercy of all that is low, vulgar, cruel, and base in the community. The ballot box and the jury box both stand closed against the man of color. . . . The white people of this country would wade knee-deep in blood before they would be deprived of either of these means of protection against power and oppression.[8]

Not satisfied with mere resolves and declarations, Douglass was constantly in active rebellion against segregation and discrimination in all its forms, and was one of the few men of his time who engaged in what today would be regarded as nonviolent direct action. While residing in Massachusetts in the early 1840's he refused to ride on the Jim Crow railroad car, and was forcibly removed from the white coach.[9] He withdrew his daughter from school rather than permit her to attend segregated schools in Rochester, and agitated for their elimination until he was successful.[10] As his biographer says, "He made it a point to go into hotels, sit down at tables in restaurants, and enter public carriers."[11] A well-known incident was his insistence upon being admitted to the reception President Lincoln held on the eve of his second inauguration, even though the guards tried to keep him out.[12]

Douglass was interested in more than protesting against discrimination and agitating for citizenship rights. Firmly in the American middle-class tradition he also campaigned for "education, that grand lever of improvement," and for moral elevation and economic independence.[13] While "not insensible" to the "withering prejudice" and "malignant and active hate" that placed obstacles in the Negro's pathway to respectability "even in the best parts of the country," he nevertheless believed: "The fact that we are limited and circumscribed ought rather to incite us to a more vigorous and persevering use of the elevating means within our reach, than to dishearten us." What Negroes needed, he went on, was character, and this they could only obtain for themselves through hard toil. "A change in our political condition would do very little for us without this. . . . Industry, sobriety, honesty, combined with intelligence and a due self-respect, find them where you will, among black or white, *must be looked up to.*" With character would come power, in the sense that with it "we may appeal to the sense of justice alive in the public mind, and by an honest, upright life, we may at least wring from a reluctant public the all-important confession that we are men, worthy men, good citizens, good Christians, and ought to be treated as such."[14] True, hostility was directed not at the lower-class Negroes whom whites found acceptable in their subordinate status, but against respectable Negroes; but this, he asserted, was only because color had for so long been associated in the public mind with the degradation of slavery. If Negroes generally acquired middle-class ways, whites would cease to couple undesirable qualities with a black skin.[15]

Along with this emphasis on Negroes helping themselves through moral elevation and the cultivation of good character went a decided interest in economic matters—an interest greatly intensified by the growing competition from immigrants who threatened the Negroes' hold upon even the unskilled and service occupations. Accordingly, Douglass emphatically urged the acquisition of skilled trades to stave off impending disaster. Dramatically he called upon Negroes to "Learn Trades or Starve." In phraseology that was remarkably similar to that which Washington employed a half-century later, Douglass insisted:

We must become valuable to society in other departments of industry than those service ones from which we are rapidly being excluded. We must show that we can *do* as well as *be*; and to this end we must learn trades. When we can build as well as live in houses; when we can *make* as well as *wear* shoes; when we can produce as well as consume *wheat*, corn and rye—then we shall become valuable to society. Society is a hard-hearted affair. With it the helpless may expect no higher dignity than that of paupers. The individual must lay society under obligation to him, or society will harbor him only as a stranger. . . . *How* shall this be done? In this manner: Use every means, strain every nerve to master some important mechanic art.[16]

Neither classical education, nor "holding conventions and passing strong resolutions" could prevent the "degradation of Negroes. . . . The fact is . . . the education of the hand must precede that of the head. We can never have an educated class until we have more men of means amongst us."[17] Negroes could not become merchants or professional men "in a single leap," but only "when we have patiently and laboriously . . . passed through the intermediate gradations of agriculture and mechanic arts."[18] Backed by an offer of financial assistance (later withdrawn) from Harriet Beecher Stowe, Douglass presented a proposal for a manual-labor school to the National Convention of Negro leaders which met at Rochester in 1853. The conferees, convinced that a strong emphasis on racial solidarity and economic accumulation was essential to the securing of citizenship rights, enthusiastically endorsed Douglass' plan.[19]

The hopes of the Rochester Convention proved illusory. Nevertheless, it is significant that over a generation before industrial education became a major plank in Booker T. Washington's platform of accommodation, arguments almost identical to those later employed by the Tuskegeean had been utilized by the noted protest leader, Frederick Douglass, to justify emphasis on training for the trades over education for the learned professions.

For Douglass, of course, the advocacy of character development and economic accumulation was no substitute for agitation for citizenship rights. When Horace Greeley in 1855 urged Negroes to stop agitating for the vote and instead direct their energies toward achieving the economic standing necessary for them to meet the discriminatory franchise qualifications of New York State, Douglass replied:

Why should we be told to break up our Conventions, cease "jawing" and "clamoring," when others equally "*indolent, improvident, servile and licentious*" (all of which adjectives we reject as untruthful . . .) are suffered to indulge . . . in similar demonstrations? In a word, why should we be sent to hoeing, and planting corn, to digging potatoes, and raising cabbages, as the "*preferable and more effective*" method of abrogating the unjust, anti-Republican and disgraceful race restrictions imposed upon us, in the property qualification?[20]

Thus, for Douglass the acquisition of morality and property was a supplemental instrument in the struggle for equal rights. Character and wealth certainly did not take precedence over protest and agitation, or an appeal to the conscience of white America, based upon its democratic and egalitarian values.

Deteriorating conditions also led Douglass to place considerable emphasis on self-help and racial solidarity. *North Star* in fact was founded in a period when the advocacy both of these ideas and of colonization was on the rise. In fact, in the very first issue Douglass urged his "oppressed countrymen" to "remember that we are one, that our cause is one, and that we must help each other, if we would succeed. . . . We are indissolubly united, and must fall or flourish together."[21] He criticized Negroes for depending too much on whites to better their condition. True, he counselled Negroes to "Never refuse to act with a white society or institution because it is white, or a black one, because it is black. But act with all men without distinction of color. . . . We say avail yourselves of *white* institutions, not because they are white, but because they afford a more convenient means of improvement."[22] Nevertheless, he maintained that "the main work must be commenced, carried on, and concluded by ourselves. . . . Our destiny, for good or evil . . . is, by an all-wise God, committed to us. . . . It is evident that we can be improved and elevated only just so fast and far as we shall improve and elevate ourselves."[23]

Douglass perceived that race prejudice produced among Negroes what in today's terms would be called an awareness of a separate identity. He held that while all men were brothers, and were "naturally and self-evidently entitled to all the rights, privileges and immunities common to every member of that family," nevertheless "the force of potent circumstance" made it proper for him to address Negroes as "our own people."[24] Indeed, he referred to Negroes as an oppressed "nation within a nation," slave and free alike united in a "destiny [that] seems one and the same."[25] He proposed a "Union of the Oppressed for the Sake of Freedom," to organize Negroes in order to obtain their rights and elevate themselves through collective effort.[26] His propaganda bore fruit when the Rochester Convention of 1853, which marked the high tide of enthusiasm for racial solidarity among the antebellum Negro conventions, organized an abortive Protective Union to coordinate race interests and efforts.

Douglass defended his plans for racial union against charges that such a segregated organization would create a "complexional issue." It was not the colored men but whites who, by their policy of discrimination, had created a "complexional issue." As he put it in 1855, in roundly criticizing that class of abolitionists who kept Negroes subservient to whites in the movement: "Every day brings with it renewed evidence of the truthfulness of the sentiment, now . . . gaining the confidence and sympathy of our oppressed People, THAT OUR ELEVATION AS A RACE, IS ALMOST WHOLLY DEPENDENT UPON OUR OWN EXERTIONS. . . . The history of other oppressed nations will confirm us in this assertion . . . the oppressed nation itself, has always taken a prominent part in the conflict."[27]

Douglass, with his feeling that prejudice and discrimination made Negroes a "nation within a nation," resembled many other articulate Negroes of this period in exhibiting strong ethnocentric tendencies. Yet he never went as far as did a number of others who completely rejected American society and advocated colonization. It is not unlikely that a majority of Negro leaders at one time or another in the 1850's espoused emigration,[28] but Douglass consistently affirmed that

Nothing seems more evident to us, than that our destiny is sealed up with that of the white people of this country, and we believe that we must fall or flourish with them. We must banish all thought of emigration from our minds, and resolve to stay just where we are . . . among white people, and avail ourselves of the civilization of America.[29]

Born in America, Negroes had fought and bled for the country: "We are here; . . . this is our country; . . . The white man's happiness cannot be purchased by the black man's misery. . . ."[30] Even during the fifties, when colonization sentiments were making strong inroads into the thinking of articulate Negroes, he opposed them. Writing to Henry Highland Garnet, the eminent Presbyterian minister and abolitionist who had become an emigrationist, Douglass maintained that the emigrationists actually weakened the efforts to elevate Negroes in this country, since they channeled their energies, which might have helped Negroes in the United States, into visionary colonization schemes.[31]

Yet the pressure for expatriation was exceedingly strong. As the fifties drew to a close, conditions seemed to grow worse. Lincoln's policy after his inauguration appeared to Douglass to be one of appeasing the slaveholders, and he was bitterly disappointed.[32] Discouraged, he finally lent an open ear and eye toward emigration, and agreed to undertake a trip to Haiti; not with the intention of settling there himself, but to obtain information that might be useful to those who, alarmed at the persecution and hardships that were becoming "more and more rigorous and grievous with every year," were "looking out into the world for a place of retreat," and were "already resolved to look for homes beyond the boundaries of the United States."[33]

Even before this editorial appeared in print the attack on Fort Sumter occurred. To Douglass this was a welcome event and one which completely changed his plans. To him the war presaged both the emancipation of the slaves and the attainment of racial equality. As he said in a speech in Philadelphia in 1863, "The Mission of the War" was twofold: "the utter extirpation of slavery from every facet of American soil, and the complete enfranchisement of the entire colored people of this country."[34]

Reconstruction and After

Douglass' wartime efforts to secure the emancipation of the slaves, and the admission of Negro soldiers to the Union armies, have been amply described by other scholars.[35] Both of these activities were, in his view, but a prelude to the larger task of securing full citizenship rights and ending all forms of race discrimination. Speaking at the thirtieth anniversary meeting of the American Anti-Slavery Society in December, 1863, Douglass warned that the struggle was not over; "that our work will not be done until the colored man is admitted a full member in good and regular standing in the American body politic."[36] Merely to abolish slavery was no solution to the race problem. Rather, "the question is: Can the white and colored peoples of this country be blended into a common nationality . . . and enjoy together in the same country, under the same flag, the inestimable blessings of life, liberty, and the pursuit of happiness, as neighborly citizens of a common country."[37]

Over the course of the next two decades, during Reconstruction and the years immediately following, Douglass' philosophy retained the broad scope of the pre-Civil War decade, but with some differences in emphasis. Basically, Douglass demanded the immediate and complete integration of Negroes into American society. He held to a vision of the United States as a "composite nation," in which all races of men participated without discrimination. "In whatever else other nations may have been great and grand," Douglass explained, "our greatness and grandeur will be found in the faithful application of the principle of perfect civil

equality to the people of all races and creeds."[38] Addressing the
Massachusetts Anti-Slavery Society in the spring of 1865, he called
for the " 'immediate, unconditional and universal' enfranchisement of the black man." He pointed out that Negroes wanted
the suffrage

because it is our right, first of all. No class of men can, without in-
sulting their own nature, be content with any deprivation of their
rights. . . . Again, I want the elective franchise . . . because ours is
a peculiar government, based upon a peculiar idea, and that idea is
universal suffrage. If I were in a monarchical government, or an aristocratic government, where the few ruled and the many were subject,
there would be no special stigma resting upon me because I did not
exercise the elective franchise. . . . But here, where universal suffrage
. . . is the fundamental idea of the Government, to rule us out is to
make us an exception, to brand us with the stigma of inferiority, and
to invite to our heads the missiles of those about us.

Later, when men hitherto friendly toward the Negroes became
critical of their stress on political rights, alleging that their interest in politics was "far more lively than is consistent" with their
welfare, he conceded that no intelligent person could want to see
the Negroes "look to politics" as their proper vocation, or to government as their only means of advancement." But he also insisted that "scarcely less deplorable would be the condition of this
people, if among them there should be found no disposition . . .
for political activity. That man who would advise the black man
to make no effort to distinguish himself in politics will advise
him to omit one of the most important levers that can be employed to elevate his race."[39]

Meanwhile, Douglass placed greater emphasis on the gospel of
wealth and racial cooperation than did most of his articulate contemporaries, though these ideas were less prominent in his ideology than formerly. As president of the national conventions
held by Negro leaders at Syracuse in 1864 and at Louisville in
1883 (Douglass presiding over both of them), he replied to critics
of the idea of holding a race convention by calling attention to
the prejudice and discrimination which Negroes still encountered,
in spite of the Emancipation Proclamation and in spite of the legislation and constitutional amendments enacted during Reconstruction.[40] When he and others established a newspaper known

as *The New Era* in 1870, he appealed for Negro support for a
race journal on the basis of self-help and racial solidarity: "Our
friends," he declared, "can do much for us, but there are some
things which colored men can and must do for themselves." Later
he grew irate when Negroes failed to support the publication, and
he criticized them because they were "not conscious of any associated existence or a common cause."[41]

On economic matters his thought remained unchanged. In
1864 he advised the freedmen "to shape their course toward fru-
gality, the accumulation of property, and above all, to leave un-
tried no amount of effort and self-denial to acquire knowledge,
and to secure a vigorous moral and religious growth." Sixteen
years later, in a rhetoric typical of the age, and in words that
Booker T. Washington would have fully approved, he was still
uttering the standard pieties of middle-class Americans:

Neither we, nor any other people, will ever be respected till we respect
ourselves, and we will never respect ourselves till we have the means
to live respectably. . . . A race which cannot save its earnings, which
spends all it makes . . . can never rise in the scale of civilization. . . .

. . . This part of our destiny is in our own hands. . . . If the
time shall ever come when we shall possess in the colored people of
the United States, a class of men noted for enterprise, industry, economy and success, we shall no longer have any trouble in the matter of
civil and political rights. The battle against popular prejudice will have
been fought and won. . . . The laws which determine the destinies
of individuals and nations are impartial and eternal. We shall reap as
we shall sow. There is no escape. The conditions of success are universal and unchangeable. The nation or people which shall comply
with them will rise, and those which violate them will fall.[42]

Douglass' basically middle-class orientation toward the solution
of the problems facing American Negroes is revealed in the way
in which he expressed his very genuine concern with the problems of the Negro working classes. Basically he believed that the
ordinary person, of whatever race, should strive to become an
entrepreneur. He admitted that "the disproportionate distribution
of wealth certainly is one of the evils which puzzle the greatest
national economists," but thought that attacking capital was to
attack a "symptom" rather than a cause. "Real pauperism," he

continued, existed only in those states "where liberty and equality
have been mere mockeries until lately." Workers had the right
to strike, but Douglass thought it "tyranny" when they tried to
prevent others from working in their places.[43] Douglass' attitudes
were perceptibly reinforced by a personal experience—the exclusion of his son from the typographical society of Washington.[44]
Yet on occasion he could express a vague consciousness of the
identity of interest between white and black workers, as when he
argued in 1883 that the white labor unions should not isolate
themselves and "throw away this colored element of strength."
Labor everywhere, regardless of race, wanted the same thing: "an
honest day's pay for an honest day's work." Unity among black
and white workers was desirable, he concluded, because "Experience demonstrates that there may be a slavery of wages only a
little less galling and crushing in its effects than chattel slavery,
and this slavery of wages must go down with the other."[45]

After the failure of Radical Reconstruction and the restoration
of white supremacy in the South, Douglass' philosophy did not
change; if anything, he became more vigorous in his denunciations
of caste and oppression and proscription. Writing in the *North
American Review* in 1881, he denounced the growing repression
in the South in scathing terms:

Of all the varieties of men who have suffered from this feeling [of
race prejudice] the colored people of this country have endured most.
. . . The workshop denies him work, and the inn denies him shelter;
the ballot-box a fair vote, and the jury-box a fair trial. He has ceased
to be the slave of an individual, but has in some sense become the
slave of society. . . .

Ridiculing the inconsistencies of the color line, he pointed out
that the Chinese were hated because they were industrious, the
Negroes because they were thought to be lazy. Southerners
thought the Negro so deficient in "intellect and . . . manhood,
that he is but the echo of the designing white man," and yet so
strong and clearheaded "that he cannot be persuaded by arguments or intimidated by threats, and that nothing but the shot-
gun can restrain him from voting. . . . They shrink back in hor-
ror from contact with the Negro as a man and a gentleman, but
like him very well as a barber, waiter, coachman or cook." Two

years later, when the Supreme Court declared the Civil Rights Act of 1875 unconstitutional, Douglass, speaking at an indignation meeting in Washington, called the decision a "shocking" sign of "moral weakness in high places," a "calamity" resulting from the "autocratic" powers of the court that embarrassed the country before the world. If the Civil Rights Act was "a bill for social equality, so is the Declaration of Independence, which declares that all men have equal rights; so is the Sermon on the Mount, so is the Golden Rule . . . ; so is the Apostolic teaching that of one blood, God has made all nations . . . ; so is the Constitution. . . ." Douglass became so bitter that in 1884 he suggested that Negroes might resort to retaliatory violence. Unfortunately the "safety valves" provided by American institutions for the peaceful expression and redress of grievances—free speech, a free press, the right of assembly, and the ballot box—did not exist in the South. Only such institutions made violence and insurrection, daggers and dynamite, unnecessary for an oppressed people; and he warned the South that ideas were contagious, and that the black man was aware of the example set by revolutionists in European countries. Such statements were extremely rare in Douglass' speeches; that he made them at this juncture reveals the depth of his disillusionment and anger as he observed the worsening situation of southern Negroes.[46]

Meanwhile, Douglass had developed misgivings about the compromising course of the Republican party in regard to protecting the rights of southern Negroes, even though Presidents Hayes, Garfield, Arthur, and Harrison appointed him to political office.[47] Sharply criticized for his supposed support of the Compromise of 1877, Douglass, at the Louisville Convention in 1883, felt it necessary to defend himself from charges of indifference to the Compromise. He described himself as "an uneasy Republican," who had opposed Hayes's policy. He was quoted as saying that "Parties are made for men and not men for parties. . . . Follow no party blindly. If the Republican Party cannot stand a demand for justice and fair play it ought to go down. . . ." Six years later, in a widely circulated address delivered before the Bethel Literary and Historical Society of Washington, the most celebrated forum in the American Negro community, Douglass defended the favorable comments he had made about Cleveland in 1885, and argued that even though the Republican party had recently returned to power in Washington, "past experience makes us doubtful" that anything would be done for Negro rights. To Douglass the question was purely a moral one: the Republican defeat in the Congressional elections of 1890, like Blaine's defeat in 1884, was due to the fact that the party had deserted the Negro's cause. "The success of the Republican Party," he averred, "does not depend mainly upon its economic theories. . . . Its appeal is to the conscience of the Nation, and its success is to be sought and found in firm adhesion to the humane and progressive ideas of liberty and humanity which called it into being."[48]

Douglass had traveled a long road indeed from 1872 when he had uttered his famous phrase, "The Republican Party is the deck, all else is the sea."[49] Yet he never deserted the party, and during the eighties campaigned vigorously on its behalf. "I am sometimes reproached," he once wrote, "[for] being too much addicted to the Republican Party. I am not ashamed of that reproach." Negroes, he continued, owed a great deal to the party, and to desert it would be to ignore both this debt and the atrocities suffered at the hands of southern Democrats.[50] Indeed, in the final analysis the situation in the South, where the Democrats dominated, demanded loyalty to the Republicans,[51] and at election time he expressed nothing but contempt for those Negroes who were Democrats—men whose talks were "rank with treason to the highest and best interest of the Negro race."[52] Yet continued loyalty was not rewarded, and by 1892 Douglass confessed that he was only lukewarm in his support of the party.[53]

The Final Decade

It is a noteworthy fact that during the 1880's and 1890's, as conditions grew worse, as Negro thought veered from emphasis on political activity and immediate attainment of equal rights to doctrines of self-help, racial solidarity, and economic advancement, Douglass' thought moved in an opposite direction to a position more consistently assimilationist than at any time since the founding of North Star in 1847. More than ever he stressed assimilation and amalgamation as the solution to the race problem, and he constantly asserted that it was not a Negro problem, to be solved largely by the Negro's efforts to acquire morality and wealth, but the problem of the nation and the whites who had created the situation. It should be stressed that these ideas were not new in Douglass' philosophy; what is notable is the shift in emphasis, for in the last years of his life he discarded almost completely the idea of self-help, ignored the theme of race solidarity, declaimed against race pride, and said little of the gospel of wealth.

One may surmise that this shift came about as a result of one or both of two factors. Undoubtedly he was deeply concerned about the rising ascendancy of an accommodating ideology which accepted white stereotypes of Negroes as ignorant, immoral, lazy, and thriftless; blamed Negroes themselves for this state of affairs and for the white prejudice they suffered; placed the principal burden of Negro advancement upon Negroes themselves; accepted segregation; depreciated agitation and politics; and stressed self-help, character-building, the frugal virtues, and the acquisition of wealth as a program for achieving the respect of the white man and thus ultimately, it was implied, "earning" the "privilege" of enjoying citizenship rights. Accordingly Douglass may well have decided to cease stressing those aspects of his philosophy which had been appropriated by the accommodators.

More likely his ideological change was due largely to the influence of his second wife, a white woman, Helen Pitts, whom he married in January 1884. Douglass had earlier expressed the view that race intermixture would increase,[54] and the year preceding his second marriage he had declared: "There is but one destiny, it seems to me, left for us, and that is to make ourselves and be made by others a part of the American people in every sense of the word. Assimilation and not isolation is our true policy and our national destiny."[55] The marriage caused quite an uproar among many Negroes, who accused Douglass of lacking race pride. As he wrote to his friend and supporter, George L. Ruffin: "What business has any man to trouble himself about the color of another man's wife? Does it not appear violently impertinent—this intermeddling? Every man ought to try to be content with the form and color of his own wife and stop at that."[56] Two years later he explicitly predicted that amalgamation of the races would be the "inevitable" solution of the race problem.[37]

In a widely reprinted address, originally delivered before the Bethel Literary Association in 1889, Douglass summarized the views he held during the last decade of his life. In the first place, he said, the problem was not one for Negroes to solve themselves: "It is not what we shall do but what the nation shall do and be, that is to settle this great national problem." Admittedly Negroes could in part combat discrimination "by lives and acquirements which counteract and put to shame this narrow and malignant" prejudice. Indeed, "we have errors of our own to abandon, habits to reform, manners to improve, ignorance to dispel, and character to build up."

Douglass then went on to specify, even though he ran "the risk of incurring displeasure," other errors committed by Negroes which contemporaries usually listed as virtues—race pride, race solidarity, and economic nationalism (or the advocacy of Negro support of Negro business). First among them was the "greater prominence of late" being given to the "stimulation of a sentiment we are pleased to call race pride," to which Negroes were "inclining most persistently and mischievously. . . . I find it in all our books, papers and speeches." Douglass could see nothing to be either proud or ashamed of in a "gift from the Almighty," and perceived "no benefit to be derived from this everlasting exhortation to the cultivation of race pride. On the contrary, I see in it a positive evil. It is building on a false foundation. Besides, what is the thing we are fighting against . . . but race pride . . . ? Let us away with this supercilious nonsense."

A second error was the doctrine "that union among ourselves is an essential element of success in our relations with the white race." Douglass held that "our union is our weakness," that the trouble was that when assembled together "in numerous numbers" rather than scattered among whites, "we are apt to form communities by ourselves." This, in turn, "brings us into separate schools, separate churches, separate benevolent and literary societies, and the result is the adoption of a scale of manners, morals and customs peculiar to our condition . . . as an oppressed people." Moreover, "a nation within a nation is an anomaly. There can be but one American nation . . . and we are Americans."

Negroes should yield as little as humanly possible to the circumstances that compelled them to maintain separate neighborhoods
and institutions. "We cannot afford to draw the line in politics,
trade, education, manner, religion, or civilization." Douglass then
went on to ridicule as "another popular error flaunted in our faces
at every turn, and for the most part by very weak and impossible
editors, the alleged duty of the colored man to patronize colored
newspapers . . . because they happen to be edited and published
by colored men." Though he continued to believe that an "able"
Negro paper was "a powerful lever for the elevation and advancement of the race," colored journals like colored artisans should be
supported only on the basis of the "character of the man and the
quality of his work."[58]

In short, during his last years, Douglass was the protest and
assimilationist leader epitomized.

Yet interestingly enough he was on friendly terms with Booker
T. Washington. In 1892 he gave the Commencement Address at
Tuskegee Institute, and two years later obtained a substantial gift
for the school from an English friend.[59] At the same time he
proudly recalled his earlier advocacy of industrial education.[60]

There is no reason to believe that Douglass would have favored
Washington's ascendancy as a race leader, which began a few
months after Douglass' death with Washington's famous address
at the Atlanta Exposition in September 1895. It is true that during the 1850's, and even for some years after the Civil War,
Douglass had frequently expressed himself in terms that were remarkably similar to those that Washington enunciated at the
end of the century. Like Washington, and using the same arguments and clichés, Douglass had stressed the middle-class virtues
and middle-class respectability; the importance of trades and industrial education; the necessity for self-help and racial solidarity.
But unlike Washington, Douglass was always clear and explicit
about his desire for full equality. In fact he always subordinated
these aspects of his philosophy to his advocacy of agitation and
political activity. He never employed the flattering and conciliatory phraseology of the Tuskegeean; he never put the principal
blame on Negro shoulders, nor did he make Negro self-improve-
ment a panacea for the solution of the race problem. Finally, un-

like Washington, he never permitted his ends to be obscured by his emphasis on the means.

We have pointed out that as the constellation of ideas which Washington epitomized was achieving ascendancy in Negro thought during the years after Reconstruction, Douglass' writings and speeches moved in an opposite direction. Integration, assimilation, protest against segregation and all other forms of oppression, and spirited advocacy of political rights and political activity were the hallmarks of his creed. Washington's ascendancy symbolized Negro acquiescence in segregation and disfranchisement and a soft-pedaling of political activity. And if there was one thing which Douglass had emphasized consistently, from mid-century on, it was the importance of political rights and political activity as essential for protecting Negroes and advancing their status in American society.

To raise Negroes to the highest status in American society, to secure their inclusion in the "body politic," to make them integrally a part of the American community, had been Douglass' aim, his vision, his dream. In constructing his program he naturally stressed and utilized the basic values and ideologies of American culture. If whites treasured political and civil rights, Negroes as a minority group treasured them even more. If white Americans valued self-help, independence, virtuous character, and the accumulation of property, these things would also be of inestimable aid to Negroes in their struggle for advancement. If white Americans were proud of their nationality and what they had achieved by the collective effort of the nation, Negroes also needed to be proud of themselves and cooperate with each other in order to advance and progress. Douglass, like his friends and associates, thus fashioned the basic ideologies of American civilization into a program for the elevation of a minority group that would secure its acceptance into the larger society. Beyond all else Douglass was the moralist, constantly appealing to the democratic and Christian values of brotherhood, equality and justice—values which Americans cherished but which, for Negroes, remained unfulfilled. As Douglass put it in 1889: "The real question is whether American justice, American liberty, American civilization, American law and American Christianity can be made to include and protect alike and forever all American citizens. . . . It is whether this great nation shall conquer its prejudices, rise to the dignity of its professions and proceed in the sublime course of truth and liberty [which Providence] has marked out for it."[61]

HAROLD M. HYMAN

The Narrow Escape from a "Compromise of 1860": Secession and the Constitution

SOON AFTER LINCOLN'S ELECTION, lame-duck President James Buchanan complained to a visitor at the White House: "I think it is very hard [that] they can not let me finish my term of office in peace, at my time of life."[1] There was to be no peace in the sense of stability for which Buchanan yearned, and at the end of 1860 the close of his tenure in office stretched distantly ahead. The curious rhythm that the Constitution imposed upon the electoral process required that he hold his office a third of a year after the election had chosen a successor whose policies differed markedly from his own. During this interregnum Buchanan had little power. But he might have influenced events in constructive manner.

Tragically, the limitations of Buchanan's vision denied the nation the only possible effective national leadership. On Capitol Hill the hangover Congress was caught up in rancorous contention and repetitive debate. The Supreme Court was discredited in the North because of the Dred Scott decision, and had nothing more to say to the South and so was disregarded there. If sectional reconciliation was to come forth its source had to be the White House. Leadership failing to come from there meant failure, on the part of every ordinary institutional resource that the national government possessed, to cope with the worst crisis the nation had ever faced. Resort to some extraordinary expedient—

149

peace congress or constitutional convention—was an implicit acceptance of incapacity on the part of President, Congress, and parties.

Attention focused on the White House because then as now America was a President-centered political society. All other elected officials, including United States senators and representatives, were essentially states' men. The public was not deceived by the existence of the anachronistic Electoral College into misreading the character of the presidential office. It had come to be the only wholly national possession. Despite weak Democratic Presidents and the Whigs' theory of the need for a weak executive, the heritage of Washington, Jefferson, and Jackson provided Buchanan with a tremendous reservoir of potential effectiveness in defining desirable public policy, even, men hoped, to the point of dealing constructively with the determined southern spokesmen.

It was also apparent that enormous obstacles stood in the way of such accomplishment. Buchanan had proved unable to hold together his own party. Unless he swiftly altered his constitutional views he could not hope to win Republican support. Alteration was unlikely in a man who during the election just past had supported the dissident Breckinridge Democrats. After the balloting the southern Democratic party apparatuses with which Buchanan had identified himself were energizing the secession process in half-a-dozen states. In the North the public had sustained the Douglas Democrats and the upstart Republicans, implicitly repudiating the President. Fretful at such treatment from the North, Buchanan felt betrayed by his erstwhile friends in and from the South, and with much cause. Aging, querulous, belatedly suspicious of men of good will when earlier he had been too uncritical of other men's purposes, the President found it difficult to alter his course.

Buchanan's ignorance of American history, especially of the nationalist line of constitutional development, added heavily to the odds against his taking effective action. He confessed to a confidant who advised him ". . . to show the Country a grand example of the teachings of the Jackson school in which we were educated," that he did not know his predecessor's position during the 1832 nullification crisis. "I was out of the country as Minister

to Russia during the Nullification times and I really don't know
the arguments on the question," Buchanan admitted.[2]

To his credit, the President sought instruction although he did
not follow through on his new mentors' precepts. He had brought
into his cabinet men of anti-secession attitude to replace defectors
of southern persuasion. In stormy cabinet sessions and in more
intimate private meetings at the White House, the new cabinet
officers tried to bring the old man to a more respectable Unionist
posture.[3]

These counselors were partially successful. They lessened the
flaccidity that had characterized Buchanan's manner and public
utterances under earlier pro-southern tutors. But the degree of
tautness that the new advisors possessed and thereby could im-
part to Buchanan, or the novelty of what they communicated to
him, is easily overestimated. As example of the limits that men
close to the heart of affairs believed existed on the permissible
arena of national action to oppose states' secessions, consider the
following testament by Joseph Holt, the new Secretary of War.
In mid-January, 1861, Holt wrote to a Louisiana friend:

The thought of employing force to oblige a state to remain in the
Union has never been entertained by the President or any member of
his cabinet—he has held, as I do, that it is his duty to protect the public property in his charge as well as he can—but this principle is virtually an abstraction since with two or three exceptions the arm[ories]
and forts of the Un[ited] States have been seized throughout the
South. . . . No effort to regain them will be made. . . . The Union is
passing away like a band of fog before the wind. But the fate of the
South will be that of Sampson. She will pull down the temple, but she
will perish amid the ruins."[4]

In its most extended posture during the secession winter, the
Buchanan administration held to limits similar to Holt's, on what
the national government might do to combat secession of states.
Early in December, 1860, Buchanan addressed the lame-duck session of the Thirty-sixth Congress on the sorry state of the Union.
In his presentation Buchanan revealed that his basic constitutional position was unchanged from what it had been before the
elections. His view was classic dual federalism. The federal system
contained functional orbits for the national government to travel
that, because of the Tenth Amendment, never interacted with

those of the states. Existence of these discrete pathways allowed no means to the central government to halt secession. The unhappy legislators heard the President's dismal conclusion that secession was unconstitutional but that no branch of the national government could do anything to impede the process. Coercion was out of reason. The ". . . power to make war against a state is at variance with the whole spirit and intent of the Constitution," the President insisted in what the scholar John W. Burgess later described as ". . . one of the most unfortunate state papers of our history."[5]

Buchanan's speech deserved Burgess' description because it left no alternative but to accede to pre-election southern demands as the price of evading dismemberment. To Buchanan the possible destruction of the Union from efforts by the national government to stem secession by force was worse than the certain destruction of the Union by acquiescence in illegal secession. Therefore, even if the Constitution allowed the central government to wage war upon a state or states in order to thwart secession, Buchanan opposed recourse to this desperate expedient. "War would not only present the most effectual means of destroying it [the Union] but would banish all hope of its peaceable reconstruction," he stated. Only mutual good will between the sections would serve.

But this happy improvement could occur only when the South's terms were met. If the Dred Scott decision had been accepted as a finality in constitutional law, as Buchanan believed it should have been, then southern views on the issues "settled" by that case might have rested where they were in 1857. Unfortunately ". . . a very large proportion of the people of the United States still contest the correctness of that decision, and never will cease from agitation and admit its binding force until [the Court's restrictive interpretation of Congress's power over slavery in the federal territories was] established by the people of the several states in their sovereign character," the President said crossly, careless of his own earlier concern over the need for a consensus. Northern recusancy made understandable the South's raised sights beyond the 1857 level to the Breckinridge Democratic heights in the campaign just past. Now the rest of the nation must give evidence that secession was unnecessary as well as unlawful.

In the face of the ballots, so recently counted, which meant a northern mandate to Congress to halt the westward march of slavery, the President brought forth a proposal to reverse the basic verdict of that election and to nullify the Republican and Douglas Democratic positions. He wanted Congress and the states to add an "explanatory" amendment to the Constitution. Among the omnibus provisions he wished to include, the President specified a confirmation of the legitimacy of slave property in slave-owning states (in 1860 it was under attack in none); congressional protection for slave property in all national territories until state constitutions with or without slavery replaced the territorial condition (the Kansas troubles had occurred because men were convinced that a slaveowning territory must become a slaveowning state); and a reaffirmation of the 1850 fugitive slave law coupled with a clause voiding obstructive personal liberty laws of northern states.[6]

In the North the President's message unleashed what was to be a new wave of criticism of the Constitution. The critics were front runners among the literati of the nation, who, sickened by what they considered to be the craven course of action—or inaction—in Washington, began to wonder what was wrong with American institutions.

Until this time, despite implicit agreement that slavery had extended far enough, little effective cooperation had existed between Republican "professionals" and the congeries of patrician intellectuals, humanitarian reformers, and literary pace-setters, who thenceforth plunged into politics. By today's inapplicable standards, many of these men and women exhibited curious mixtures of antislavery and Negrophobe attitudes. They opposed secession yet revealed patrician antipathies to democracy's excesses. Some penmen blended incongruously pacifism and militant patriotism.

The fact remains that in mid-nineteenth century terms these people were the consciences of American society, in the same sense that the Republican party was the only on-hand vehicle with which to oppose in politics the western advance of slavery.[7] The President's dualistic view of the federal system and his overblowing of the Tenth Amendment in manner likely to have pleased Calhoun, pushed many men of letters into more effective political action than had been thought to be possible. Of course, affiliation was possible only with Republicans because the common fear was that the South's blackmail would win. If the Republican party backtracked from its central principle and accepted a "compromise" of the character of those agreed to in 1820 and 1850, free society was impossible.[8] To be sure, definitions varied widely of the nature of free government. Orestes Brownson, Charles Eliot Norton, Francis Lieber, and James Russell Lowell were far apart in social purposes from John Brown, William Lloyd Garrison, Wendell Phillips, or Charles Sumner. But aristocrats and egalitarians shared a growing conviction that the Constitution was at crossroads. A wrong turn in direction of acquiescence to Buchanan's constitutional invocations, on the part of the Republican party, would mean disaster for all purposes.

Now was the time for men to stand up to the South; perhaps the last time when a stiff spine might save American society if it was worth saving. To paraphrase the title of a sermon by Rev. Henry W. Bellows, a prominent Unitarian minister, there was advantage to be gained by testing without further delay American principles. Possibility existed to overcome the South's long-time customary lead and to purify a society grown flabby from preoccupation with things.[9]

Concern that the doughsoul's servile nature had taken over not only in the White House and the Supreme Court but also in Congress, with consequent total corruption in store for the Constitution, led intellectuals to conclude that confrontation was a morally superior alternative to continued cowardice. As example, Lowell expressed this reaction to the President's constitutional appeal of December, 1860:

Is it the effect of democracy to make all men cowards? An ounce of pluck just now were worth a king's ransom. There is one comfort, though a shabby one, in the feeling that matters will come to such a pass that courage will be forced upon us, and that when there is no hope left we shall learn a little self-confidence from despair. That in such a crisis the fate of the country should be in the hands of a sneak [Buchanan]! If the Republicans stand firm we shall be saved, even at the cost of disunion. If they yield, it is all up with us and with the experiment of democracy.[10]

The diffusion among men who like Lowell were normally cautious and conservative, of such belligerent sentiments, has impressed twentieth-century commentators. One historian concluded recently that "It was obvious by 1860 that . . . intellectuals were ready to welcome a great national catastrophe . . . [or] a 'chastising calamity,' [and] . . . hurried the country along toward civil war."[11]

Certainly it is true that by 1860 many "intellectuals"—though by no means all—welcomed a confrontation at last that might bring forth a decent resolution of the country's difficulties. Decency required that secession stop and that the Juggernautish western advance of slavery grind to a halt. If force was necessary to realize these ends then these men were at the point of welcoming the abstract notion of war in the belief that if possessed of superior virtue the North's cause must win.

But they did not advocate that Americans plunge into a civil war—certainly not into *the* Civil War—as a solution to problems for which in their view the Constitution already offered remedy, or in order to burn evils out of the American system. Superficial similarities in language notwithstanding, the nineteenth-century reformers were not predecessors of repellent *sturm und drang* notions that twentieth-century militarists espoused. In 1860 Americans lived in an age of innocence with respect to the nature of mass war, and in the least military society the world then knew. Certainly intellectuals of reformist bent did not look forward to a war as a desirable step in social change or in preventing further change.

When war did come the intellectuals' concern remained what it had grown to be by the time of the secession winter. They wanted to employ the power of the Constitution and the facilities of the national government on behalf of the old Federalist idea of stability, or in search of whatever improvements in American society they advocated, especially to keep the territories free from slavery. Obviously the Democracy had no appeal for this new breed of liberal. Once convinced that politics was the only practical way to win goals, even abolitionist reformers, who had in some instances been fiercely anti-political and in other instances anti-democratic and anti-Union, moved into Republican ranks. At least they shared with Republican "pros" the assumption that the Constitution was a source of power, not limitations. The reformers' problem was to bend the Republican party to their purposes. Meanwhile they kept close attention on Congress and the White House.[12]

In December, 1860, holdover Republicans in Washington had the heavy burden of conducting a rearguard operation so that the Lincoln administration might have a capital to come to.[13] Rising to the challenge, party front runners revealed how unpalatable they found Buchanan's suggestion for constitutional amendment. Speaking on December 17th, Wade spotlighted the jerry-built nature of the President's proposal. The Ohioan stressed the inability of political democracy to survive if losers of elections employed subsequent constitutional amendments to reverse popular verdicts. Republicans would not compromise away the responsibilities that the recent balloting had imposed on them. But Wade insisted that southerners had no justification to take their states out of the Union merely because Republicans intended once in office to obey the popular voice.[14]

Wade was a member of the special Senate committee of thirteen that was seeking a viable formula for sectional conciliation. Prospects were dismal for the success of the committee's efforts when the distance is realized not only between Wade's constitutional views and Buchanan's, but between the Ohioan's position and that of some of his colleagues on the special committee. One of Wade's committee-mates was Toombs of Georgia. Toombs proposed to the group that it report out for the Senate's approval a draft of an irrepealable, unamendable amendment to the Constitution. It would embrace perpetually the essentials of what the southern Democrats had demanded as the price of party unity in the elections just past, as well as what President Buchanan had outlined in his speech to Congress.

The concept of an unamendable amendment—a fatally constrictive "Chinese shoe" Von Holst later called it—was and is novel in America. That it should have received serious consideration during the weeks following Lincoln's election is the measure of how low secession had depressed the constitutional ethics of many Americans, and of how frightened the country was.[15]

Toombs insisted that the Constitution receive unalterable amendment to read that slave property was to enjoy the same status within national jurisdictions as any other legitimate chattels. Citizens were to have the right to move into all present and future national territories "with whatever property they may possess, including slaves," and receive protection for their goods, human and otherwise. Then, coming to the heart of burning public issues, Toombs proposed a perpetual, irrevocable alteration in the nature of the federal system. He wished permanently to change interstate relationships especially with respect to the current practices of comity, so that the slave and criminal codes of southern states would apply in free-soil states. In Toombs's words:

Persons committing crimes against slave property in one State, and fleeing to another, shall be delivered up in the same manner as persons committing crimes against other property, and that the laws of the States from which such persons flee shall be the test of criminality; that fugitive slaves shall be surrendered under the provisions of the Fugitive Slave Act of 1850, without being entitled either to a writ of Habeas Corpus, or trial by jury, or other similar obstructions of legislation in the state to which they may flee; and that Congress shall pass efficient laws for the punishment of all persons in any of the States who shall in any manner aid and abet invasion or insurrection in any other State, or commit any other act against the law of Nations, tending to disturb the tranquility of the people of government of any other State.[16]

Thereupon, Kentucky's Senator John J. Crittenden essayed Henry Clay's former role of sectional pacificator, with intention primarily to placate the South. Resorting again to the traditional border-state practice of balancing interests, Crittenden proposed to escalate the pattern of crisis legislation made familiar in 1820 and 1850 into an irreversible constitutional principle. He brought forth a proposal for a "compromise of 1860" that in essential matters followed the Buchanan-Toombs lead.

As was true of them, Crittenden's notion of acceptable compromise was to attach to the Constitution an unamendable amendment. He revived the old 36'30" line as a viable partition of the national territories that were then in hand or that the nation might acquire in the future. North of that line no slavery could ever exist. But south of it an enormous expanse was always to be open to slavery. There, Congress must protect slave property so long as the territorial status continued. To be sure, Crittenden prescribed that future states carved from territories south of 36'30" might come into the Union with or without slavery as residents chose. However, it was sure that enfranchised inhabitants of a slaveholding territory would choose to enter as a slave state.

Going further, and despite the fact that no one in 1860 who rated a hearing in terms of political realities suggested that Congress could reach into states to end slavery, Crittenden specified that it could never do so. Similarly, he would perpetually disarm Congress of a power it did possess, to abolish slavery within the District of Columbia or in other national enclaves that were located inside slaveholding states. Slaveowners who were unable to recover runaways because of popular antipathy in northern states to enforcement of the fugitive slave law, would receive compensation from the national government. It would then extract a like amount from the county in which the fugitive had found succor because of local interference with the federal statute. In all events and for all time, Congress must rigorously enforce the fugitive slave ordinance, which in a sense thereby also became unrepealable. Last, Crittenden wanted his amendment to declare null and void the personal liberty laws of northern states.[17]

A tenacious tradition has come into existence that the Crittenden proposals were decent, honorable, and reasonable ways to peace and stability between the sections. But this judgment reflects certain dubious assumptions. It suggests that in 1860 most white Americans felt able to live harmoniously in a situation in which slavery's western enlargement was not merely permitted but guaranteed, and placed forever beyond limitation by future political action. Second, a favorable view of Crittenden's propositions requires faith that political institutions and processes would have been done with the slavery-extension question even if a compromise drawn to the Kentuckian's specifications went on the books. Next, kudos for Crittenden's formula calls for conviction that any peace is better than any war. Last, a favorable estimate of his proposals rises easiest from retrospective knowledge that war was in the wings—indeed, that the Civil War was waiting—and must come onstage in absence of a settlement agreeable to the South.

Consider first the last point. Admitting all imperfections in public opinion sampling in the past, it appears that in December, 1860, and January, 1861, when Crittenden made his bid, few Americans anywhere seriously anticipated war despite bellicose rhetoric. Men on the inside of the best information then available, who received warnings of the possibility of armed strife, found incredible the notion of large-scale, formal trial at arms between the sections.[18]

But even in light of the war that was to come, the Crittenden proposals were unrealistic and wretched levels on which to fix, as permanently as men knew how to do, the constitutional law of the United States. Clearly, Crittenden and those who supported him meant exactly what they said. They were establishing perpetuity for slave property in the regions with which he dealt. It is difficult to understand how a revision in 1860–61 of the Constitution in Crittenden's terms could have opened in the foreseeable future opportunities to deal peaceably through politics with subjects that he excluded from future political consideration. It also strains credulity to rank as a constitutionally or morally superior alternative to the Republican position of holding the line, Crittenden's proposal to enlarge areas open to slavery, unless prejudgment exists that anything is preferable to confrontation.

In the last days of 1860 confrontation was not the necessary consequence of rejection for the Crittenden package. He and his coadjutors, as well as those who backed other proposals of similar nature, were not desperately trying to fend off a war the onset of which they did not seriously anticipate. It appears more reasonable to say that the would-be compromisers were structuring as permanent a peace as they felt able to do. They were peacemakers in the exact meaning of the word, not war-avoiders.

What confuses is that Crittenden employed a constitutional idiom for a political purpose. Because in the South's opinion slavery was too delicate an institution to allow its involvement in the processes of political democracy, Crittenden wished to provide it a permanent sanctuary in the Constitution. Without awareness of the inconsistencies involved in his desire to sever the Constitution from politics, to cut from the former the capacity to receive from the latter continuing relevancy to popular needs, Crittenden pressed for a way to remove the major causes of the South's unease.

His way was to freeze the Constitution into a catatonic condition. With respect to certain tender functional arenas of the national government and vital federal-state relationships, Crittenden wished to rewrite the 1787 Constitution into terms agreeable to the South. No fool, he knew the extent of northern distaste for what he proposed. Crittenden knew also how fearful and shaken northerners were by the ongoing process of secession in the South. Perhaps actual secession would lever out of the North what threats of seceding had failed to force.

Secession's incredible reality in darkest winter days shook men so deeply that many northerners were willing a few weeks after the election to abandon their positions of November and to support Crittenden's way. Recent Constitutional Unionists swung away from their campaign slogan of "The Constitution and the Union" to approve a Constitution and Union reshaped to the South's demands. Douglas Democrats generally followed their leader's post-election shift in favor of perpetually exempting from the principle of popular sovereignty the vast lands south of the 36'30" partition line, agreeably to the Crittenden proposals and apparently without worrying overmuch about the incongruities involved.[19]

In sharp contrast, Republicans held fast to their election position and to the constitutional position that underlay it. Indeed, in early 1861 the Republicans—and most northerners—were exactly where a dozen years earlier the Wilmot Proviso had pointed for a tiny minority of northerners; at a conviction that slavery's expansion had gone on long enough and that Congress could and must call it to a halt. The Republican imperative derived partially from party professionals' understanding that the precarious coalition achieved in 1860 would shatter into futile fragments if members did not hold fast on the root issue of slavery containment. In this instance, party welfare and the nation's welfare were synonymous; political self-interest served the best interests of most Americans. Admittedly, the concern of Republicans was to maintain for white men the most open possible society. The result of racial selfishness was opposition to freezing that society perpetually to benefit a minority among whites. Black men were the pawns in all these matters. Southern whites wanted their pawns in the West; most northern whites wanted the West for whites only.

But by the standards of 1860–61 the Republican position contained elements of idealism adequate to fire the imaginations of hard-bitten political "pros" as well as of Negrophobes and reformer-intellectuals. Unlike Buchanan, Crittenden, Douglas, or Toombs, the Republicans assumed that practical alternatives existed to ignominious capitulation. These alternatives could be reached through the continuing operation of the ordinary processes of political democracy, not by closing them off or resorting to extraordinary expedients. The Republican belief was that the Constitution deserved a better fate than to be welded forever to slavery; the Republican position was simply better than the on-hand alternatives. Reflecting on this matter of the Republicans' tenacious concern with alternatives, Joshua Giddings recalled how "Mr. Crittenden appeared to think that the Union could only be preserved by so amending the Constitution as to change the essential character of the Government, making it a slave-sustaining federation, instead of adapting its energies to securing liberty."[20]

A sense of injured nationalism and a conviction about the Constitution's adaptability were the essence of the new political liberalism and of the old constitutional attitude that by 1860 had attracted into the Republican party all sorts and conditions of northerners. During the early weeks of 1860 the question rose whether the leaders of the party, especially the President-elect, would withstand the lure of the Crittenden sort of proposal, leading to immobility in the Constitution.

Pressures grew on Lincoln to accept such a course. Influential elements within his party were coming to favor acquiescence in Crittenden-like formulations. Similar solutions for the nation's woes came forth from a variety of *ad hoc* groups that had come into existence since the new year, and that were groping for ways to ward off secession. Special committees of the House and Senate, a governors' conference, and a prestigious though fumbling peace congress at Washington, added to the confusion and increased the verbiage. All these efforts lifted hopes, only to dash them down to more intense disappointment as failures became evident.

As much as possible during the interregnum Lincoln avoided the limelight. He refused to commit himself or his future administration to anything less or more than his party's platform and his previous statements specified. A caller at Willard's Hotel late in February, 1861, after seeing the President-elect, described how "Everybody here seems to look to Lincoln and Lincoln says 'delighted to see you &c &c.,' but no one gets his tongue and every-one has his ear. . . . The peace Congress is a humbug."[21]

Agreeing implicitly with the last judgment, Lincoln saw to it that his position was known on the basic issues that the election results should have settled, but that the Crittenden proposals had again brought into the public dialogue. In knowledge that the information would be broadcast, Lincoln wrote to a member of the special House committee of thirty-three members that was searching for a path to sectional reconciliation:

Entertain no proposition for a compromise in regard to the *extension* of slavery. The instant you do, they have us under again; all our labor is lost, and sooner or later must be done over. . . . Have none of it. The tug has to come, and better now than later.

For dissemination among states' governors then convened, Lincoln let it be known that as President:

I will be inflexible on the territorial question; . . . I think either the Missouri line extended, or Douglas' . . . Pop[ular] Sov[ereignty] would lose us everything we gained by the election; that filibustering [by southern whites in Latin America] for all South of us, and making slave states of it, would follow.

To be sure, Lincoln was not immune to the need to placate southern opinion with respect to his alleged bellicosity and to prove to many northerners that he and Republicans generally were not radical about duties that the Constitution imposed. Writing on February 1st to his Secretary of State-designate, the prominent New Yorker William H. Seward, again with intention that the information leak to the public, Lincoln adverted to his imminent responsibility as President to enforce the fugitive slave law. Of this tender matter, of the interstate slave trade generally, ". . . and whatever springs of necessity from the fact that the institution [of slavery] is among us, I care but little, so what is done be comely, and not altogether outrageous," he stated. But always he returned to what was basic that year; "I am for no compromise which assists or permits the extension of the [slave] institution on soil owned by the nation."[22]

Lincoln's consistency on this critical position and its appropriateness for 1860 made him acceptable among almost all the numerous shades of Republicans.[23] Evoked by the spectre of expanding thralldom and made urgent by the shock of secession, this position had at its center the assumption that the national government under the Constitution possessed power to hold the line between free and slave regions, and a duty to do so arising out of the election results. The year 1860 was one of those points in the history of this nation when a party's constitutional position was so much in harmony with the nation's needs as to render irrelevant efforts to separate them.[24]

Yet, so powerful was secession as sectional blackmail that it squeezed even Republican stalwarts. A proposal to amend the Constitution in direction of a perpetual commitment to the sanctity of slave property in states where it then existed, under Seward's sponsorship came from the special House committee on sectional conciliation. By terms of the proposed addition, "no amendment shall be made to the Constitution which will authorize or give to Congress the power to abolish or interfere, within any state, with the domestic institutions thereof, including that of persons held to labor or service by the laws of said state."[25]

In the House and then in the Senate an impressive number of Republicans supported this suggestion. It appeared to be in harmony with the plank of the Republicans' 1860 platform that pledged against interference by the national government with the internal concerns of states, although during the past November the party had not offered this pledge in form of a proposition for an ordinary amendment to the Constitution, much less a perpetual one. Nevertheless, the 1861 Seward amendment offered hope of stabilizing one uneasy element in federal-state relationships. Perhaps approval for it would halt secession without requiring abandonment of the primary Republican concern with keeping the territories free from slavery.

By March, 1861, the proposed amendment had passed through both houses of Congress. It reached the White House before going out to the states for ratification in time for Lincoln to refer to it in his inaugural address. Such a restriction on Congress' power was already "implied constitutional law," Lincoln said. Therefore he could not object "to its being made express, and irrevocable."[26]

Failing to receive approval by the requisite number of states in time irrevocably to alter the Constitution in manner to protect slavery in the states, the proposed amendment became a casualty of the war it was designed to avert. Less than two years after the amendment's proposal the idea had become anachronistic of any national protections for slave property in the southern states, with such exceptions as Lincoln noted in his Emancipation Proclamation. Further, abolition pressure was increasing even in the loyal border states where slaveholding existed. By the close of 1865 a Thirteenth Amendment to the Constitution, embracing all the states as well as territories, contradicted directly the terms of the 1861 proposal that would have become the thirteenth article of amendment, if events had gone other ways.[27]

The Civil War crushed not only the specific subject matter of the 1861 amendment proposal but also its novel and unsuitable method. After 1861 Americans never again attempted seriously to add unamendable amendments to the Constitution. Posterity remained free from this unsuitable device. And white Americans were saved from the ignominy in history of having bought peace for themselves at the price of cementing forever into the Constitution slavery for black men.

It had been a narrow escape. Perhaps this sense of the tight squeeze underlay Burgess' criticism of Lincoln and of his party for having gone too far in search of peace. Accepted into the Constitution, the irrepealable amendments would have formed "a rotten spot" to taint the whole, Burgess believed.[28]

During the secession crisis, in addition to proposing unamendable amendments to the Constitution, conservatives suggested employment of plebiscites—national referenda and/or constitutional conventions—to reverse verdicts by ballots. Edward Pollard, the effective chronicler of the Lost Cause, in 1867 recalled how during pre-secession arguments in Congress, then-Mississippi Senator Jefferson Davis revived one of Calhoun's "most beautiful and ingenious theories." Calhoun had ". . . proposed that in cases of serious dispute between any State and the General Government, the matter should be referred to a convention of all the States for its final and conclusive determination." Such a convention would rein in democracy's excesses through exercise of "august guardianship" by the states. And Calhoun, Davis, and Pollard professed to believe that a convention of states super-added to the federal system, would provide ". . . that principle of adaptability to circumstances which is the first virtue of wise government."[29]

Responding to a similar conviction, on January 3, 1861, Crittenden had suggested in the Senate that it initiate a nationwide referendum to register, as advisory only, popular opinion on his earlier propositions irrevocably to amend the Constitution. Douglas added his still heavy weight on the side of the Kentuckian's plebiscite innovation, insisting that arguments from Republicans were unconvincing that the preceding November's balloting had already registered public opinion.

For Republicans, Seward retorted that it was frank blackmail for Democrats to exploit post-election secession as a partisan opportunity to reverse the election's verdict. He condemned as unconstitutional any delegation of Congress' inescapable responsibilities to govern, by a ruse such as the one Crittenden wished the Senate to approve.[30] Perhaps as a diversionary tactic designed to lift from Republicans any onus of insensitivity to avenues of conciliation, Seward himself had put forward a notion of an appeal to the public with a view to overall reconsideration of the Constitution. Back in December 1860, with the election results just in, in a public speech Seward had evaluated the causes and cures of America's mounting difficulties. The elections had decided the single immediate constitutional issue involved in slavery extension, he stated. Sober study was in order of why this issue had achieved such magnitude and what steps were needed to hold to manageable political limits other unsettled questions.

Therefore, Seward had advocated initiation of a national constitutional convention that would take on the task of modernizing the 1787 document that secession had proved was obviously deficient. A reporter paraphrased his appeal:

He [Seward] referred to the fact that every municipality and state in the nation had been compelled to alter its organic law repeatedly in order to meet the changes wrought by advancing time, and deduced the very obvious conclusion that alterations in the organic law of the nation itself might be necessary; and added that, however perfect the national Constitution might have been at the time of its adoption, it would be a marvel if what was perfectly adapted to the country when its population was three million should be equally suitable when its population was ten times that number.[31]

In the Senate on January 12, 1861, Seward reaffirmed his conviction that a national constitutional convention was in order. He held to his December position that the convention should not be a substitute for present politics. Instead, it must be an opportunity to repair what was defective in the Constitution, to excise what was obsolete, and to add what experience had shown was needed to permit politics to function better.[32]

Like Lincoln, Seward was holding Republican constitutional doctrine pretty much where it had been since the party assumed national prominence four years earlier. This position acknowledged that the Constitution required study and repair. It denied the southern rejection of the Constitution and of politics, as well as the border-state tinkering that would have amputated functional arenas.

All proposals failed for national constitutional conventions or plebiscites, and for unamendable amendments to the Constitution. However, almost no one accounted as much of a triumph the Constitution's passage, unaltered, through the trials of the secession winter. Instead, the unopposed progress of secession and unimpeded creation of the Confederacy appeared to be irrefutable proofs that the 1787 Constitution was hopelessly defective as a frame for government. At best, it was a weak reed, not a staff from which patriots could derive firm support. With a great civil war in the wings it is difficult to imagine a longer road for the Constitution to travel than the one stretching from Sumter to Appomattox. And it is more difficult to explain the successful transit without appreciation of the narrow escape from capitulation during the secession winter, which the Republicans' constitutional position made possible.

MARIAN McKENNA

Some Catholic Churchmen as Americanizers

WRITING OF THE 1890's, which he names "a watershed between two eras of American thought," Professor Henry S. Commager, in his *The American Mind,* concludes that: ". . . the Catholic church was, during this period, one of the most effective of all agencies for democracy and Americanization."[1] In his brief but characteristically provocative assertion, historians, social scientists, and the increasing number of scholars using an interdisciplinary approach will find enough subject matter for a whole shelf of monographs and essays.

The Commager thesis is arresting because it casts the Catholic Church in the role of an Americanizing institution, a role with which very few writers have associated it. On the contrary, nineteenth-century immigration and social history is replete with references to the "Romish" church as a foreign institution, wholly authoritarian in structure and demanding the allegiance of all its members to a foreign ruler, a loyalty incompatible with national patriotism. Moreover, the Church, because of its authoritarian organization and its close connection with the despotic monarchies of Europe, was regarded as the inveterate enemy of political liberty and democracy. Even into the twentieth century some Americans continued to believe in a far-ranging papal plot to subvert the government in the United States.

Works of major or minor importance in immigration, church history, and American social history yield no more than an occasional reference to the Catholic influence on Americanization.

167

In his study of assimilation in American life, Milton Gordon refers to the general neglect in the investigation of the nature of
ethnic communal life in the United States. More particularly he
finds that Catholic communal life has been little researched; indeed, until Will Herberg's perceptive study, *Protestant-Catholic-
Jew*, appeared, that subject had been little articulated in the public
consciousness. The question whether Catholics, Jews, Negroes, or
Mexican-Americans should maintain or lose their group identity
in the America of the future is one which, for the most part, has
received no thoughtful attention or has been dealt with largely in
clichés. John Higham's entire chapter on "The Crusade for Americanization" in *Strangers in the Land* mentions neither the Catholic nor any other church. In his analysis, the institution above
all others on which nineteenth-century Americans relied to further
such ethnic unity as they required was the common school. Education, it was confidently believed, would solve every problem of
national life, even that of assimilating our foreign elements. But,
as it turned out, the schools made almost no effort to single out
immigrant children for special attention. The focus in Higham's
study, therefore, falls on the social settlement houses. They faced
the problem from a human perspective. Further, the growth of
organized patriotic hereditary societies, such as the Sons and
Daughters of the American Revolution, whose movement for
Americanization reached its height around the time of World
War I, was one more indication of a growing urgency of the nationalist impulse.[2]

The subject of the Catholic Church as an Americanizing agency
has been treated, at least tangentially, by a few writers but a comprehensive study of the problem is needed. The method followed
here will be to survey the late nineteenth-century manifestations
of Americanizing in the Catholic community, and to suggest the
various approaches which could be profitably pursued. A fuller investigation might also treat such related aspects as the Irish influence in the Catholic community, including the impact of clashing
nationalities within the Church, the Americanizing of the Catholic
Church itself, and the Church's response to the separation of
church and state in the United States.

One of the many useful aspects of Gordon's study is its survey
of a wide sample of accumulated usages and meanings of the terms

assimilation, acculturation, and amalgamation, which are often and loosely used to describe the processes and results of the meetings of people. If nothing else, his exposition provides a greater appreciation of the true complexity of the assimilation process.[3] For the sake of simplicity, the term Americanization will be equated with assimilation and the definition of assimilation formulated by the American sociologist, Robert E. Park, will serve as base. Assimilation, Park wrote, is

> the name given to the process or processes by which peoples of diverse racial origins and different cultural heritages, occupying a common territory, achieve a cultural solidarity sufficient at least to sustain a national existence.[4]

In a further effort at a definition of terms, consider Gordon's assessment of the primary goal of assimilation, e.g., adaptation to the core society and culture. In this connection it is profitable to turn for a moment to the question, to what preferred goals of adjustment could the influx of 41 million diverse peoples into the United States be expected to look for guidance? This is a question requiring answers before understanding is possible of what Catholic Americanizers hoped to accomplish. And here again a barrier exists to convincing replies, to whose formulation little explicit attention has been given. As Gordon points out, the problem is confounded by the paucity of material, the ambiguities of meaning, and the incompleteness of analysis which the record reveals. Happily, Gordon has gone a long way toward eliminating ambiguities in terminology. In clear form he presents the goal systems of assimilation as grouping themselves around three main axes, or three ideological tendencies: (1) Anglo-conformity, (2) the melting pot, and (3) cultural pluralism.[5]

The first of these, Anglo-conformity, has for its leading tendency the pressure to mold a differentiated whole into one people, whose leading characteristics are English as altered on American soil. It demanded complete renunciation of the immigrant's ancestral culture in favor of the behavior and values of the Anglo-Saxon core group. In varying guises, it has been the most prevalent ideology of assimilation in the American historical experience, and it will therefore not be surprising to find it the primary goal, however ambiguously enunciated, of the Catholic Americanizers.

The second, or the melting pot metaphor, anticipated the biological merger of Anglo-Saxons with the other immigrant groups and a consequent blending of their respective cultures into a new, indigenous American type. In the general optimism and progressive spirit of the nineteenth century, it was believed that the newcomer underwent a complete transformation upon his arrival. The notion was best expressed by Crèvecoeur, in answer to his own question, who is an American?

He is an American, who leaving behind him all his ancient prejudices and manners, receives new ones from the new mode of life he has embraced, the new government he obeys, and the new rank he holds. . . . Here individuals of all nations are melted into a new race of men, whose labors and posterity will one day cause great changes in the world.[6]

The third, cultural pluralism, postulated the preservation of the communal life and significant portions of the culture of later immigrant groups within the context of American citizenship and political and economic integration into American society. As an articulated goal system of assimilation, this idea was a relative latecomer on the American scene, predominantly a development of the experience and reflection of the twentieth century. However, there were at least a few leading churchmen in the Catholic community, as we will see, who anticipated, if they did not articulate, notions of cultural pluralism in the nineteenth century, showing that the fact existed in American society before its formulation as a theory. The cultural pluralist justifies the anticipated result as providing a more democratic, a more interesting, and a more dynamically fruitful culture for all Americans than the one in which conformity is the norm.[7]

While attention remains focused on efforts to assimilate the newcomers into the core culture, sight should not be lost of the fact that the core culture itself was irrevocably affected by the presence of the immigrants and minority groups. The distinction has been made between the impact of members of minority groups as individuals, and the specific impact on the American culture of minority cultures themselves. In the first instance, the impact of individuals has been so considerable that it is no longer possible to conceive of what American society or American life would have been without it. In the second instance, the impact of minority group culture has been of modest dimensions, but significantly extensive in one area, that of institutional religion. From a distinct minority, Catholicism has now emerged as one of the three great faiths. Allegiance to one of the three has become the norm in American life. In the course of taking root in American soil, Catholicism and Judaism have themselves undergone changes in form and expression in response to the forces and changes of American experience.[8]

John Tracy Ellis, in his brief study, *American Catholicism*, asserts that the primary problem and most pressing preoccupation of that church before the century's turn was how best to mold the nationalities that composed the faithful of the nineteenth century into a stable element of the Catholic population. Studies have convincingly shown that specifically national aspects of most ethnic groups, except where color is involved, in significant terms rarely survive the third generation. Mixed neighborhoods and intermarriage, both common in the United States, even among Catholics, have worked steadily to dilute the strongest national traditions. But ordinarily, with first and second generations of immigrants, with which this essay deals, thought processes and culture patterns were not radically altered by transplantation and adaptation in the new locale. The overwhelming number of immigrants clung to their customs, simultaneously becoming citizens and contributing their labor and ideas to the new country.[9] Some, of course, and especially the "new immigrants" after 1885, came here with no intention of staying, of becoming citizens, or of making America their home.

If no complete transformation took place or was possible, then what did the leading Americanizers, particularly the Catholic Americanizers, hope to accomplish? While Americanization, in its various stages, had more than one emphasis, essentially it was a consciously articulated movement to strip the immigrant of his native culture and attachments and make him over into an American along Anglo-Saxon lines—all this to be accomplished with great rapidity. In the phrase of a later day, it was an attempt at "pressure-recooked assimilation."[10]

To the Cleveland Americanization Committee, Americanization meant

. . . assimilating into the American life of the community. . . . The keystone to Americanization is learning the language of our country. . . . Americanization is the cooperative process by means of which "many peoples" become "one nation," united in language, work, home ties and citizenship, with one flag above all flags, and only one allegiance to that flag. . . .[11]

To Samuel Rea, the president of the Pennsylvania railroad system, the task of producing good U.S. citizens from the millions of aliens reaching these shores resolved itself into two problems. America must be made to seem to these people "a good place, not merely to make money in, but to live in." Second, they must be induced to give up the language, customs, and method of life which they had brought with them across the ocean, and adopt instead the language, habits, and customs of this country, and the general standards and ways of American living.[12]

On this question, we can also with profit listen to the native-born convert to Catholicism, Isaac Thomas Hecker, founder of the Missionary Society of St. Paul the Apostle (the Paulist Fathers). In his view, Americanism stood for nothing more than the loyal devotion of American Catholics to the principles on which their government was founded, and their deep conviction that these principles offer the Catholic valuable advantages for the promotion of the glory of God, the development and expansion of the Church, and the salvation of souls.[13]

How then did the Church go about converting its huge immigrant flock to American ways? In the course of doing so did it attempt to deprive them of cherished Old World customs? As preliminary to an effort toward replies, attention is in order to the several interwoven strands which made up the cloth of the Americanization program. For the Church, the principal means employed were parochial schools, Catholic institutions of charity (orphanages, hospitals, parish poor societies, homes for the aged, etc.), the Catholic press, and the personal counsel of bishops, priests, and nuns.[14] Add to these the numerous fraternal, benevolent, and social organizations which multiplied in Catholic communities over the land, such as the Knights of Columbus and the German Central Verein (which still conducts evening classes in the English language in St. Louis), and a visualization emerges of the program in its true dimensions.

The concern for political loyalty and external manifestations of patriotism dominated the emotional tone of the later stages of the Americanization program. But running through the whole, even before the turn of the century, were more prosaic instrumental programs of instruction. These included tutelage in the use of the English language, elementary American history, the nature of American government, etc. According to Gordon, however, "Both the patriotic appeals and the instrumental materials . . . were embedded in a framework of either explicit denigration or implicit disregard of the immigrant's own native culture and the groups and institutions which, with his fellows, he had created on American soil."[15]

No program of this nature could, of course, be scientific. The Catholic program was perhaps least scientific of all, owing to the large number of recent immigrants in its clergy or teaching in its schools. The pastoral letters issued periodically by the American bishops, instruction in English, civics, and moral conduct in Catholic schools, and the information circulated through the Catholic press, had an inevitable effect on the cultural or behavioral assimilation of immigrants into the American way of life. Reception of the sacrament of penance (oral confession), in particular, afforded a natural channel for priestly guidance and direction in the countless difficulties encountered by Catholic newcomers. Of secondary importance were the sermons preached at Sunday Mass and the occasional parish missions conducted by visiting clergymen who usually scheduled week-long instructions.[16]

For example, in May, 1852, the pastoral letter of the bishops assembled at the First Plenary Council of Baltimore, addressed to the clergy and people, exhorted the faithful to continue service as good Americans, "not that there is reason to fear that your feelings could change from what they have always been but, rather that you may find in your religion more profound reasons to fulfill your civic duties."[17]

Bishop John England of Charleston first realized the possibilities in a vigorous Catholic press. Armed with the journalistic experience acquired in his native Cork, he launched the *U.S. Catholic Miscellany* in June, 1822—the first American Catholic weekly. Its columns served as a medium for answering nativist attacks and misrepresentations of Catholicism as well as to enlighten Catholics on their duties as citizens. The recurring theme in England's editorials was that no Catholic doctrine conflicted with republicanism. Newspapers as popular as the Catholic Miscellany exerted a powerful influence on American Catholic opinion and the effectiveness of the Charleston bishop's courageous stand in the face of nativist opposition emboldened Catholics elsewhere to avail themselves of opportunities afforded by the press.[18]

Although all four aspects of the Church's Americanization program are important, this essay will emphasize the influence and personal counsel of American bishops. This aspect of the program could be effectively examined through the life and work of the native-born John Carroll, first Bishop (and later Archbishop) of Baltimore, or Bishop John England of Charleston, or Bishop Martin J. Spalding of Louisville, or James Cardinal Gibbons of Baltimore. Indeed, lay Catholic leaders, Orestes Brownson, founder and editor of the American Catholic Quarterly Review, and the previously mentioned Father Isaac Hecker, would supply the focus for fruitful studies of the Americanization program in both its formal and informal features. I have chosen to concentrate on the prelate John Ireland (1838–1918), the Irish-born Archbishop of St. Paul, as the central figure, because he had a remarkable ability to enter into the mainstream of American life, and though not a university graduate, he was esteemed by scholarly men within and outside the Catholic community. The Chicago Post (February 22, 1895) referred to him as "the one Metropolitan of all whose intense devotion to American institutions has been constantly conspicuous."

The three great struggles of Ireland's battle-scarred career as a churchman were for temperance, reconciliation of the common school system with the parochial schools, which by his time educated almost half the Catholic children in the Midwest and were demanded as an essential feature of Catholic life in America, and the colonization movement. Colonization societies organized for the Catholic emigrant were generally more successful among the Germans than the Irish. These societies urged westward migration to relieve congestion and misery in the overcrowded cities of the East. Between 1876 and 1881 Ireland was their most conspicuously successful organizer and colonizer. He negotiated with the railroad companies the purchase of huge tracts of Minnesota lands, parceled them out to colonizers on easy payment plans, for which he made himself responsible, served as land agent, provided religious succor to rootless immigrants, and in general made Minnesota "the center of Catholic culture for the entire northwest."[19]

John Ireland's patriotism first manifested itself when during the Civil War he enlisted as chaplain of the fifth Minnesota Volunteers. At the battle of Corinth, when the cry went up that the supply of ammunition was failing, he was seen hurrying down the lines, heedless of the bullets flying around him, carrying a box and shouting: "Here are your cartridges, boys, don't spare them."[20]

At a time when the Grand Army of the Republic was regarded with suspicion by some members of his Church, Ireland accepted membership in it, frequently attended its meetings and encampments and was elected Chaplain-in-Chief in 1906. One Protestant minister who served with him during the War always referred to him after it as "My Archbishop." At ease with mixed groups of Protestants and Catholics, Ireland at these meetings did not wish to be called by his former companions in arms "Your Grace," preferring the title "Archbishop." He would not even permit the members of his old regiment to kiss his ring—"It is not American," he said.[21]

Of all the speeches delivered throughout a long, active career in which he championed, if he did not instigate, at least a hundred different civic and religious projects, none were more stirring than those extolling the glory of patriotism. He was passionately devoted to the land of his adoption and fiercely proud of his American citizenship. Ireland's impact, as a Catholic prelate and as an American, on the Americanization of immigrants, was chiefly generated through his speeches.

At a meeting of German Societies at Chaska, Minnesota, Archbishop Ireland directed his remarks not only to the Germans in his audience but to all ethnic groups in America. He paid tribute to the cultural value of the German language, but he reminded them that English is the language of this country, and that the political unity of the United States, the economic future of their children and their religious interests, demanded its employment.

Americanization, he believed, did not mean the sudden extirpation of foreign languages and cultures, or the forgetting of the old land. Setting aside of previous traditions and inspirations was unnecessary. Instead, the filling of the heart with love for America and her institutions, so that immigrants would not be as "strangers in a strange land," was in order. "It is," he said, "the knowing of the language of the land, and failing in nothing to prove our attachment to its laws, and our willingness to adopt as dutiful citizens all that is good and laudable in its social life and civilization."[22]

Archbishop Ireland expressed regret that in certain German-American newspapers the word "Americanization" was held up as an opprobrious term, synonymous with dangerous tendencies, to be deplored and avoided. There were in America certain self-constituted leaders of foreign-born citizens who used Americanization as a term of reproach. With these men, public opinion should deal severely. To Ireland, the United States was a providential nation whose mission was to prepare the world by example and moral influence for the reign of liberty and human rights.[23]

From his cathedral pulpit he gave his congregation sound advice. Catholics should be models of Americanism and personal righteousness. Like de Tocqueville, whom Ireland greatly admired, he believed that the power of religion in America and the surest guarantee of its permanent hold upon the people depended on its absolute divorce from political parties. But Catholics should be, in the best sense of the word, American—loving America, loving its institutions, devoted to her interests, chary in blaming but ardent in her defense.[24] In another message, he went beyond this to say:

America demands that all who live on her soil and are protected by her flag be Americans, and she cannot do less than to demand this; beyond this, she proclaims the sacred right of liberty. The individual who does not . . . proclaim this right of liberty for his fellow citizens is no true son of America. American loyalty and fitness for office— these must ever be, and these alone, the conditions which determine an American's vote.[25]

Not all the immigrants who came to America were prepared to participate in political life. And yet, liberal Catholics, like Ireland, were quick to recognize that more was expected of residents in America than passive obedience to the laws. Nativists and partisans of democracy were demanding of all newcomers professions of patriotism unqualified by devotion to fatherlands, and they expected each citizen to share in the responsibility of governing. The reluctance of many Catholics to meet these demands, liberals insisted, was seriously jeopardizing the Church's apologetic mission to American culture.[26] In a country where the Catholic Church was still regarded in some quarters as a foreign menace, whose members spoke diverse languages, clung to their alien traditions, and owed allegiance to a foreign authority whose laws overrode those of American lawgivers, it was all the more novel to hear a Catholic bishop proclaiming:

Next to God is country, and next to religion is patriotism. Patriotism is a Catholic virtue. I would have Catholics be the first patriots of the land.[27]

Lofty patriotic considerations did not constitute the only reason why the persistence of immigrant loyalties to other lands disturbed liberal Catholics or troubled the Americanizers. They were moved as much, perhaps more, by their hopes and fears for the future unity of the Church in America. Some suspected that French and German parishes were trying to maintain their old national attachments for no better reason than to assert their independence of the liberal leaders who were more fully Americanized. John Ireland and John Keane presented a countermemorial to the memorial of 1886 in which Father Abbelen of Milwaukee and fourscore German priests from St. Louis asked the Pope to make German parishes altogether independent, so the rectors of "Irish" parishes could exercise no rights over the Germans. John Ireland protested against the insinuation that there was a conflict in America between the Irish and Germans. The countermemorial stated:

The Church will never be strong in America; she will never be sure of keeping within her fold the descendents of immigrants until she has gained a decided ascendancy among the Americans themselves. She must be presented in a form attractive to Americans. The great objection which they have until now urged against her—an objection which at certain periods of her history they entertained so strongly as even to raise persecutions—is, that the Catholic Church is composed of foreigners, that it exists in America as an alien institution, and that it is consequently, a menace to the existence of the Republic.[28]

Orestes Brownson feared that the Church would be less able to attract converts if, like some of the Presbyterian and Reformed churches in America, it was, in effect, divided along national lines. The Paulist father, Isaac Hecker, devoted himself and his order to winning for the Church the confidence of the American people, some of whom continued to look with suspicion upon it as a foreign institution. In short, Hecker attempted in the United States what Cardinal Newman tried to do for the Church in England.[29]

The prime objection liberal Catholics had to the persistence of immigrant loyalties to other lands was that so long as there was any reason to doubt the loyalty of a single Catholic immigrant, many patriots would challenge the right of the Church to bid for American acceptance.

Archbishop Ireland devoted his life to prevent such a dismal future. His address on "American Citizenship," delivered to the Chicago Union League Club (February 22, 1895), established his reputation as "the biggest Republican" in America. In it, Ireland urged the need for fully assimilating all who come here seeking asylum. Cardinal Gibbons believed this speech deserved to rank as one of the most significant achievements of Ireland's fruitful career. In it, Ireland had rung the changes on the theme of pure patriotism. "Never was there another title equaling it in sublimity of meaning and in copious wealth of rights and privileges . . . American citizenship in American manhood," he declaimed.[30]

Attending next to the moral and religious aspects of patriotism, he told his audience that morality is the very soul of good citizenship. Religion gives life and power to morality. Ireland distinguished between two kinds of patriotism. The first he described as an attachment arising principally from instinctive, disinterested, and indefinable feelings that bind the heart of man to his home and traditions. The second is a more rational attachment, less ardent perhaps, and less generous, but more fruitful and more lasting. Born with the spread of knowledge, nurtured by laws, matured by the exercise of civil rights, it is, in the end, identified with the personal interest of the citizen. It arises as men comprehend the influence which the prosperity of their country has upon their welfare and whatever they hold most dear.[31]

Intelligence, which is essential to democracy, implies manhood suffrage, instructed Ireland. He issued a warning to Americans lest the education so profoundly dispensed to their children be only of the mind, and not also the discipline of a moral soul. Insufficient attention was given in American schools and colleges to instruction in the nature and functions of representative government, in the duties of citizenship, and in the elements of political economy, Ireland asserted.

All this was preliminary to the central idea in his address; that the casting of the ballot is the supreme act of citizenship. There are other attributes but the ballot is the pride of the true American, and its proper use is a sacred duty. The man who refuses to vote, said the Archbishop, deserves disfranchisement or exile. Any American boasting of his political indifference proclaims his own shame.[32]

Answering those who were pressing for immigration restriction, he asserted that the difficulties arising from immigration were sufficient to awaken vigilance but not to cause alarm. He did not believe a well-directed immigration would be detrimental to the American spirit or loyalty. "The spirit of our institutions should, of course, be made to pervade our foreign-born populations." But, he maintained, in no state of the Union should immigrants be prematurely authorized to vote (an obvious swipe at his neighboring state of Wisconsin).[33] No one should be invested with the franchise until a sufficient residence in the country had given him full opportunity to understand its institutions and laws. These views were in decided contrast to the activities of eastern ward and block leaders accustomed to whisking immigrants from New York's wharves to vote in city elections before they even had a chance to unpack.

Ireland frowned on all efforts to concentrate immigrants in social groups that were retarding their Americanization. No encouragement was to be given to social and political organizations which perpetuated in America foreign ideas or customs. He declared: "An Irish-American, a German-American, or a French-American vote is an intolerable anomaly." In many European countries the formation of Catholic parties had proved very effective in bringing to the attention of statesmen and voters the relevance of Christianity to current social problems. With the important exception of German-American Catholics, some of the conservatives in the

United States gave many signs of favoring such an activist policy, though some were distrustful of the existing parties. Liberals, on their part, left no doubt among Catholics that such a move was neither desirable nor necessary in America. As it was, Catholics were already commonly charged with bloc voting. William Onahan, who enjoyed a successful career in Chicago politics, declared that the fewer religious or national groups that existed in American politics, the better.[34]

If the measures Ireland outlined were taken, he assured them, no harm would come from immigration. The material resources of the continent seemed limitless. American institutions easily won the esteem and love of those who chose to link their destiny with hers, and there is, he said, in the plastic nature of all men, under proper influence, a wondrous susceptibility to civil and political liberty.

And if no encouragement was to be given to political organizations which perpetuated in this country foreign ideas and customs, neither should Americans be permitted, in Ireland's phrase, "to become foreignized" by importing foreign fashions:

American citizenship implies a sincere love for America, a strong devotion to political democracy, an earnestness in advancing the interests of the country. These vital features of American citizenship we do not discern in the thousands of Americans who, professing that in their country there is no salubrity of air, no sublimity of mountain scenery, no beauty of landscape, roam annually from one end of Europe to the other, scattering broadcast on that continent a hundred millions or more of American dollars. They are not Americans, except inasmuch as they draw their gold from America, who colonize the so-called American quarters in the capitals of Europe. Nor are they Americans who glory in importing foreign fashions of language and dress, and who are willing to pay treble prices for ornaments of home or person, merely because these ornaments are of foreign fabrication. And they surely are not Americans who covet, above all that is American, foreign titles for their fortunes or their daughters? There is room among Americans for the work of Americanization.[35]

At this same banquet, the main speaker was asked to make a reply to the toast: "The churchman as a citizen." The Archbishop said he was not at all sure that churchmen did not stand in need of the lessons on their civic duties he had just finished reading to other citizens. Of the churchmen, he stated the opinion:

. . . they belong, I fear, to the class I made mention of . . . the educated and the refined, who, perusing leisurely at home their morning or evening paper, lament the corruption of politics, but are never found striving by word or act to mend politics.

Ireland was convinced that there were ways in which churchmen could exercise civic responsibility without the smallest infringement upon clerical propriety. Let churchmen, in teaching their fellow men religious and moral duty, preach good citizenship, which is certainly a great religious and moral duty. Let clerics not only preach good citizenship, let them practice it. Let them be glad to cast ballots on election day, and prove by their presence at the polls that they are proud of their American citizenship:

And when he does vote, let it be known far and wide that he votes for good men, pure-minded men, honest and capable men. To be patriotic in words is of small avail; to be patriotic in deeds, whether on the battlefield in time of war, or at the polls in time of peace, is what saves the country.[36]

Perhaps some churchmen deserved Ireland's harsh inferences, but the Catholic clergy in the United States had generally escaped this kind of criticism. De Tocqueville, who spent two years in America from 1831–33, wrote of the Catholics: "They constitute the most Republican and democratic class in America. . . . They, especially the clergy, are a living sample of the adage, 'Render unto Caesar that which is Caesar's and unto God that which is God's.' " Beginning with John Carroll and going forward to the present, it is difficult to find a single bishop who did not extol patriotism. One might even say that the American hierarchy is distinctive for its particular American national character. A century ago Henry Adams pondered over the nature of national character, concluding that, of all historical problems, it is the most difficult and yet the most important.

Ireland was not altogether realistic when he protested that there was no conflict of nationalities (he used the term races) between the Germans and the Irish. Much the same kind of conflict as existed in the 1890's had threatened the unity of the Church earlier in the century when the Irish first began to challenge the French-dominated clergy and hierarchy. In this connection, the instance is noteworthy of the learned Sulpician, Monsignor Dubois, founder of Mount St. Mary's Seminary in Emmitsburg, Maryland. The Irish-born priest, John Power, may have been slightly exaggerating when in 1829 he complained that Dubois had lived ". . . thirty-six years in America, and when he attempts to give common instructions, thirty-six of three thousand [parishioners] cannot understand a word of what he says. Hundreds leave the Church and go into the Rum Shops while he is speaking. . . ."[37] In contrast, we have Dubois' heartbroken declaration when, elected Bishop, he was charged with being "French":

If I had not been an American for such a long time through sworn loyalty, custom, gratitude and affection which bind me to this land, then the 35 years I have spent in America as a missionary and teacher ought certainly to give me the right to exclaim: "I, too, am an American." But all of us are Catholics. In this common profession, are not all differences of birth and homeland pardoned us?[38]

Clearly, the Irish were becoming the dominant and pervasive element in the gradual emergence of a pan-Catholic sub-society in America. But both Ireland and Gibbons were as much opposed to Irish agitations as they were to the German, or almost as much. On several occasions Archbishop Ireland warned the Irish that they must not set themselves up as a class superior or apart, for it was their duty to become completely identified with the American spirit and institutions. Cardinal Gibbons hoped, as did Ireland, that the Irish Benevolent Society would drop the word "Irish" from its title, in the expectation that the action would set an example for the Germans. How different the attitude of Archbishop Michael Heiss of Milwaukee, who, in August, 1887, spoke of the need for more German bishops!

Undoubtedly these antagonisms represented a natural phase of adjustment in a country that was growing to maturity, and moving toward a more pluralistic society. But the Irish, noticeably, displayed no patience with immigrant groups lacking their facility in the English language. And the English Catholics were never numerous or prominent enough, after John Carroll's pioneering episcopacy, to exert a mediating influence. The Church's response to the problem of clashing nationalities was to set up the so-called "national parish," or ethnic parishes whose congregations consisted of all persons within an area who possessed a particular nationality background and whose priest sprang from the same tradition and language.[39]

James Moynihan's life of John Ireland is uncritically hostile to the Germans (who could claim at that time only one Archbishop, Heiss of Milwaukee, and eleven bishops in the American hierarchy), while Colman Barry's treatment of German Catholics is, conversely, sympathetic to the Germans. But both writers agree that an increasing number of Americans in the late nineteenth century believed the recognizably foreign to be unfit for citizenship.[40]

A. Lawrence Lowell, in criticizing Irish nationalist activity, argued that the crucial step in the Americanization process was the liberation of the individual from the past. "The country is not safe," he asserted, "until all groups of foreigners have become so merged in the American people that they cannot be distinguished as a class, by opinion or sentiment on any subject, from the mass of the population."[41]

This called for a very large order but in sentiment it echoed Baltimore-born Archbishop Gross of Oregon. He became incensed over an interview given by Archbishop Heiss in which he stated that ". . . the church desires to keep up the German language or any other language for the spiritual welfare of its children, and for no other purpose. It will do this so long as it is found to be necessary." Complained Gross: ". . . Archbishop Heiss makes every Bishop and Archbishop in the United States to be an Englishman, Frenchman, Irishman, German, or Belgian—there is not an American among us."[42]

The first stage in this discussion of Americanization has been concerned with what certain liberal Catholics hoped to accomplish in their task of creating simultaneously religious and national unity among the immigrants of Catholic Europe. The next stage concerns the more refined considerations of time. How long should it take for an emigrant to become assimilated into the American way of life? The merging of which Lowell spoke was not to be long drawn out. In Professor Cross's apt phrases, "an era that found the melting pot a suitable metaphor of the process of acculturation did not think it should take several generations to produce an acceptably American individual."[43]

Most liberal Catholics shared these convictions. One exception was John Lancaster Spalding, Bishop of Peoria. He expressed his cultural pluralist position in his introduction to Peter Abbelen's life of Mother M. Caroline Friess, published in St. Louis, in 1893. In an era when the American Catholic hierarchy was torn by ethnic hostilities, Spalding publicly espoused both the right of the "Germans" to retain their own culture and the zeal of the "Irish" to embrace American culture, without winning the affection or support of either party. But the overwhelming sentiment opposed his stand. The strongest words of all, perhaps, were used by the *Catholic World*, which believed that the unassimilated populations were "like undigested food in the human stomach, painful and weakening to the body politic," and argued that the Church's duty was to "smooth and hasten the process of Americanizing."[44]

Archbishop Ireland thought that no nationality unwilling to be *immediately* assimilated deserved admission into the country. At the Chaska *Katholikentage*, he said that any immigrant who does not thank God that he is an American and who cannot rejoice in the American way of life "should in simple consistency betake his foreign soul to foreign shores, and crouch in misery and abjection beneath tyranny's sceptre."[45] At Dubuque on another occasion, Ireland acknowledged that the work of transition for Catholic immigrants must necessarily take time and he said he was certainly willing to allow the time, but he demanded, in the name of religion, that it be not retarded.[46]

The Americanizers and their spokesmen in leading Catholic journals assumed that, while each immigrant contributed unique cultural elements to the American type, the final amalgam would be a virtual continuation of the dominantly English culture. They thus met the argument frequently advanced by Archbishop Heiss and other German Catholics, to wit, that immigrants need not hurry to conform to the merely transitional present type. This argument also helped remove any doubts that the liberals themselves were fully Americanized.[47]

In the 1890's the German-speaking group caused by far the greatest tumult. "To a great extent," writes one student of ethnic movements in America, "the Germans used their language to ward off Americanization and assimilation, and used every social milieu, the home, the church, the school, the press, in the fight to preserve the German language, even among their children and grandchildren." Since the Germans presented the only significant challenge to Irish-American domination of the hierarchy, the liberals' offensive against them may have stemmed in part from nothing more exalted than the desire to eliminate their resistance. But this was an era when Pan-Germanism was becoming an alarming European phenomenon. The persistence here of a group fiercely proclaiming its consciousness of nationality and of the fatherland, and linking it closely with their Catholicism, gave the liberals a more exalted justification for their "crusade to Americanize." Bishop McQuaid of Rochester, however, thought liberal leaders secretly favored everything Irish. Most other conservative Catholic leaders flatly disagreed with the premises of "Americanization." Archbishop Michael A. Corrigan of New York once told a German convention: ". . . we do not feel called upon to trumpet our patriotism . . . many things may well be taken for granted. An honest man does not . . . feel bound to prove the legitimate marriage of his parents" at every turn. "Enough for us that we have been born here, or that we have voluntarily made it our home, that our patriotism should not be challenged without good reason."[48]

Other spokesmen, particularly among the German-Americans, were even less conciliatory to American expectations of loyalty and devotion to democracy, not merely as a political system but as a way of life. One of them was the Rev. Anton H. Walburg, pastor of St. Augustine's Church in Cincinnati, and author of the influential pamphlet, *The Question of Nationality and Its Relation to the Catholic Church in the U.S.* (St. Louis, 1889). In it, he attacked Anglo-conformity and made the distinction between what he called true and false Americanism. "True Americanism," he writes, "consists in the promotion of the peace, the happiness, and the prosperity of the people, and in the advancement of the public good and the general welfare of the country." As virtue is the principal support of a Republic, he reasoned, true Americanism aids and encourages whatever promotes the growth of virtue and morality. It makes no distinction between natives and foreigners, considering all born free and equal. And since the Catholic religion promotes virtue, piety, and morality, true Americanism should desire the growth of the Catholic Church.

False Americanism, he maintains, "is a spirit of pride and self-conceit, and looks with contempt upon other nationalities. It is . . . boasting, arrogant. . . . It glories in the biggest rivers, the tallest trees, the grandest scenery, and considers this country superior to every other country on the face of the globe. . . . It is a spirit of infidelity and materialism. False Americanism is mammon worship. . . ." Walburg was only one of scores who observed that the ideal set before every American youth is money.

And with its vaunted independence, this spurious Americanism, in its ostentatious display of wealth, stoops to Foreignism, copies European fashions, imports a Parisian cook, and considers itself fortunate to exchange its wealth for the musty title of some needy descendant of the nobility.

Though they were far apart in their notions of Americanism, Walburg's passage bears a strong resemblance to the remarks noted earlier, which John Ireland offered to the Chicago Union League club (see above, p. 180). After a scathing indictment of the Anglo-Saxon strain in the American nationality, which he considered the source of all vice, corruption, and criminality, to say nothing of fanaticism and intolerance, Walburg warned that assimilation with this element would prove totally detrimental to Catholics and the Church:

Denationalization is demoralization. It degrades and debases human nature. A foreigner who loses his nationality is in danger of losing his faith and character. When the German immigrant, on arriving in this country, seeks to throw aside his nationality and to become "quite English you know," the first word he learns is generally a curse, and the rowdy element is his preference to the sterling qualities of the Puritans.

Walburg blandly asserted that ". . . Germany stands foremost in the ranks of civilized nations," and he assured Americans that it was absurd to talk of waging war with Germany, since the American navy was patently too weak to defeat even a small Latin-American state, let alone a major European power. A midwestern editor, at the same time, noted with satisfaction that America had always belonged to Germany anyway, according to the papal grant of Charles V.[49]

Religion and nationality go hand in hand, asserted Walburg, and proof could be found in the fact that wherever the Irish, Germans, and French (here he was referring to French Canadians in New England) were isolated, and where their language and nationality were encouraged and fostered, they remained true to the faith. Conversely, they generally lost their faith as they Americanized. Five years earlier Walter Elliott, a lawyer converted to the clergy by a Hecker lecture, had gone to some lengths to denounce as malicious libel an English Jesuit's allegation that political freedom unsuited men for proper deference to ecclesiastical authority. On the contrary, Elliott contended, experience in freedom had promoted highly responsible participation in both political and religious life. The Church had known less difficulty with fractious democrats than with those immigrants "whose Catholicity had been maintained by a paternal civil government." Fortunately, thought Elliott, as immigrants become more Americanized, they become better Catholics.[50] Such a view, expressed by a native of Anglo-Saxon origin converted to Catholicism by a Hecker lecture, was, of course, irreconcilable with the arguments put forth by Walburg.

Even Walburg acknowledged, however, that no foreign nationality could permanently maintain itself in America, no matter how ardently immigrants may have wished to re-create their Old World villages and towns in the new land of their adoption. American nationality would eventually prevail as foreign nationalities were absorbed in it. Assimilation was inevitable. Nevertheless, he warned, the transition from one nationality to another is always a dangerous process, and it would not do to hasten it and force foreigners to Americanize.[51]

Basic to these rather overdrawn forecasts by Walburg and other German nationalists was a genuine fear that the certain consequences of a forced-draft Americanization, in which language and customs were sacrificed, would be extensive losses to Catholicism. Unhindered by reliable statistics, Walburg claimed that between 1870 and 1889 as much as two-thirds of the Catholic population of America had been lost to the faith. In striking contrast to his conclusions about transplantation to an American environment producing a loss of faith, are the clearly contradictory findings of a later study made by Bishop Michael O'Shaughnessy. He showed that the Church in the United States held the loyalty of the vast majority of immigrants, otherwise the growth his figures and statistics record would have been impossible.[52]

Many Germans firmly believed that only a clergy proud of its German origins would be able to hold adult German Catholics in the faith, and that only in German language parochial schools could immigrant children be rescued from demoralization and de-Catholicization. "Make these schools more intensely, thoroughly German," pleaded Walburg, who claimed distinction as the first native of German descent in Cincinnati to be called to the priesthood. Some of the best blood in the midwestern clergy was being drawn from these parochial schools, Walburg stated. Cultivate this soil, he urged, if you wish to build up the Church in America. To Walburg, the proper course for the Church to follow was to concentrate on "fanning the embers of faith" still smoldering in the hearts of recent immigrants instead of encouraging their denationalization, and thus jeopardizing their religious loyalty. Until the immigrant's faith had been safeguarded, churchmen should not look around for other responsibilities.[53]

The liberals refused to take this matter seriously. To suppose that souls could be saved to the Church in America by retarding Americanization was, to their way of thinking, "a suitable theme for comic opera." Their opposition only served to convince the Germans more completely that they alone were anxious to preserve the faith of their countrymen. According to the *Herald des Glaubens*, there were American priests in this country who would rather see several million Germans go to hell than forego the opportunity to convert a few hundred Yankees.[54]

In 1887, a group of about fifty German priests and leaders of the Central Verein met in Chicago. They organized the American German-Catholic General Assembly, which arranged annual mass meetings of the German Catholics of the United States. All this was in frank imitation of the conventions held annually in Germany, which had so effectively secured the triumph of the Center Party. The American society's avowed purpose was "to attain the same ends by the same means in this country as the *Katholikentage* organization in Germany." It sent representatives to the assemblies in Germany and leaders of Germany's Center Party (which was offering stout resistance to Bismarck's attacks on the Catholic Church) frequently visited and spoke in America.

In 1890, Ernst Lieber, a leader of the Center Party in the German parliament, spoke in Pittsburgh and warned against too rapid Americanization. "The world knows," he said, "that you attack no one when you assert your right to remain American citizens and Germans. . . . Suffer no injustice in the consciousness of your rights." According to Robert Cross, who has made a brilliant analysis of the bifurcation between liberal "Americanizers" and conservatives within the American Catholic body, in the period from 1890 to 1920, remarks so inconsiderate of American patriotic zeal would have provoked antagonism even had the speaker not been a leading political figure of a foreign country. Nor did Archbishop Ireland fail to alert the Associated Press to its responsibility for covering all the meetings of this German Assembly in order to keep watch on its "general un-American character."[55]

Ireland's impatience with the Germans could only with great difficulty be concealed. The efforts of more than three decades were being thrown to the wind! Walter Elliott, speaking on citizenship to Middle Western Protestant audiences, John Keane and Ireland himself pleading with Leo XIII not to encourage clashing nationalisms in the American Church, Father Hecker's untiring efforts to make Catholicism acceptable in a democracy—all were striving to show that, regardless of their immigrant origins, American Catholics were wholly patriotic.[56]

Ireland thought he had good reason to fear for the reputation of the American Church. The *New York Times*, already alarmed by the intransigence displayed by the Germans toward the public schools (even toward English-speaking parochial schools), and toward the Pope's loss of temporal power, found itself unable to recall any other body of American residents which had shown itself "so completely out of touch with American institutions. . . . They [the *Katholikentage* group] have kept themselves as clear of any taint of Americanism during their sojourn in this country as if they were so many Chinese laundrymen." The *Times* editorial concluded on this ominous note: ". . . it is not too much to say that, if the spirit of the Roman Catholic Church were that expressed in the proceedings of the Newark conference [of the German Catholic General Assembly], that Church would be a public enemy." The same editorial acknowledged that it would be most unfair to judge Catholicism in America by "the ridiculous persons . . . assembled at Newark, . . . who represent comparatively few Catholics except themselves."

It is no news to anybody that there are Catholics in this country, and men high in the councils of the Church, whose aim is to reconcile their obligations as Catholics with their obligations as Americans, and to persuade their countrymen of other Beliefs that a devout Catholic may be as good a citizen as if he were not a Catholic. These men are striving to win converts and friends to their Church by Americanizing it, and they are going about their work in a very enlightened and a very effective way. Among these men are Cardinal Gibbons and Archbishop Ireland. It is a very good augury for the Church in this country that they should have persuaded the authorities at the Vatican to favor, or to acquiesce in, the methods they have devised to reconcile the obligations of Roman Catholics and American citizens. Yet these patriotic and devoted Churchmen are the objects of a peculiar animosity on the part of the men represented at Newark. . . .[57]

The *cause célèbre* of the controversy was, of course, the storm which went under the title "Cahenslyism." During the 1880's and 1890's German Catholics, including Father Peter M. Abbelen, Vicar General of the Diocese of Milwaukee, had made strenuous efforts to persuade Rome to choose more German bishops for the American Church. His first memorial, which he carried to Rome in 1886, in the name of priests from the Milwaukee, St. Louis, and Cincinnati areas, and which had the approval of Archbishop Heiss, indicated strong German resentment over alleged inadequacies or discrimination in their treatment by the American hierarchy. It asked for equality for German parishes and their entire independence of Irish parishes or Irish pastors. The Abbelen Memorial immediately became a storm center of misunderstanding.

The earliest German Catholics had established themselves in the United States with relative ease. Arriving here at the same time as the Irish, they had settled on farms, mainly in Pennsylvania, or in sections of the cities where they could create German parishes. There were, in fact, a few German bishops. But the Germans who came later in the century found a more complicated situation. In cities where the Irish were already dominant they had trouble setting up churches of their own, and often found the bishops unsympathetic or hostile. This was the burden of a complaint thirty-two German priests had addressed to the Pope in 1884; and this was also the tenor of the argument set forth in the tearful pamphlet two years later by Father Abbelen.[58]

In addition to reflecting on the devotion of the "Americanizing" bishops, these attempts to make ethnic origin a primary criterion for American hierarchical appointments threatened to give the lie to liberal boasts about the Church's patriotism. Even the conservative Archbishop Corrigan was outraged. He had one of his doughtily conservative priests write a blistering attack, which the *Catholic World* was undoubtedly eager to publish. The Congregation of Propaganda, which took such matters under advisement, in April, 1888, gave its answer to the Abbelen Memorial. While granting the unimportant petitions—rights which the Germans already enjoyed—Rome rejected the main clauses which dealt with transfers from parishes and preaching in both languages.[59]

The liberals were especially critical when similar proposals came not from midwestern German-American priests, but from a group of European laymen led by Peter Paul Cahensly, the man from whom the next manifestation of the German movement took its name. He was a successful German merchant, and Secretary of the St. Raphael's Society, an organization formed by Germans to aid German emigrants in the United States. In fact, Cahensly had dedicated most of his life to the protection of the religious and social interests of German immigrants to America. Alarmed by what he regarded as the rapid alienation from the faith and fatherland of many Germans who settled in America—losses sometimes referred to in the literature of the time as "leakage"—he was one of the prominent laymen brought together from several European countries at the First International Conference of the St. Raphael's Societies in Lucerne, Switzerland, December 9–10, 1890. The outgrowth of the Lucerne Conference was a memorial addressed to Pope Leo XIII and forwarded to Rome in February, 1891. Among other things, it asked that immigrant groups of each nationality in the United States be united in separate parishes wherever numbers made this possible; that the administration of these parishes be entrusted to priests of the same nationality; that separate parochial schools for each nationality be set up wherever possible and include instruction in the mother tongue as well as English;

and that, whenever feasible, Catholics of each nationality have several bishops of the same origin so that every immigrant group would be represented in the assemblies of the bishops. This meant that more foreign language prelates should be installed in America.[60]

Ireland learned of the Lucerne Memorial through a series of press reports and Associated Press cablegrams. These communications purported to come from Rome, Brussels, and Berlin, but actually originated with Ireland's close friend, Monsignor Denis O'Connell, rector of the North American College in Rome, and Monsignor Boeglin, a correspondent for the Vatican news. The reports insinuated that "Cahenslyism" was a plot hatched by the Prussian government! After studying these reports, Archbishop Ireland immediately called in newspaper reporters, accused Cahensly of working to harness the Church in America into the service of German immigrants, and predicted to them that neither the Holy Father nor the American hierarchy would ever sanction the memorial's suggestions. He expressed his amazement at "the impudence" of Cahensly and other foreigners in meddling in American Catholic affairs. While indicting a German clique in the United States for its intrigue, he absolved the mass of German-speaking Catholics from any complicity. It was his feeling that the American bishops were quite capable of taking care of the matter themselves. This "unpardonable" attempt would be resented by all the faithful who, he carefully pointed out to the public, acknowledged no foreign loyalties. American Catholics, he explained, accepted the Pope of Rome as their chieftain in spiritual matters and were glad to receive directions from him, "but men in Germany, or Switzerland, or Ireland must mind their own business and be still as to ours."[61]

Ireland expected Rome to turn a deaf ear to Cahensly, because it was Rome's policy, he assured the press, to trust the hierarchy of each country. In proof of this, he quoted the words of Leo XIII: "The bishops should see that all men practice their religion in the language they understand, but, when this much is done, let the work be toward amalgamation and union." He charged that the promoters of German foreignism in America were certain journalists whose trade was gone if the German language ever lost its hold, and certain priests, who, upon coming to America in advanced years, never learned English and scarcely knew there was a country outside the German village surrounding their parsonage. In a second interview, he enlarged on this theme, but at the same time he admitted that some of Cahensly's demands, such as German parishes and German schools, were quite admissible.[62] Nevertheless, Ireland regarded as singular malice Cahensly's attempt to represent the Catholic Church in America as Irish, and to make such a fantastic charge, as stated in the memorial, that "the losses which the Church has suffered in the United States . . . number more than ten million souls."

Ireland believed that if Cahensly succeeded in his scheme of having "national" bishops appointed from Rome, the manifold elements composing the Church in America would become so many foreign colonies, living in weakness and isolation, shut off from one another by the barrier of diverse languages. In another interview Ireland said:

It is strange news for American ears that the Austrian and Prussian ambassadors in Rome had been instructed by their government to bring on the Vatican their influence in favor of Cahensly's plan. The Prussian ambassador, von Schloezer, declared that he viewed the appointment of Bishop Katzer of Milwaukee as favorable to German interests. M. Mercier, the Minister of the Province of Quebec, who met Cahensly in Rome, rushed to the Vatican to urge the appointment of Canadian bishops in the United States.[63]

Undoubtedly, the liberals deliberately exaggerated the threat of foreign political intervention in order to get non-Catholic support for their ecclesiastical battle with Rome to secure rejection of the Lucerne Memorial. The alternative, confided Ireland to O'Connell, was the "absolute subjugation of the American Church" by the German Catholics in Europe and America. Ireland was largely responsible for much of the bombast and exaggerations. He certainly knew that Denis O'Connell was serving up these juicy cablegrams coming across the Atlantic via the Associated Press. Moynihan points out that O'Connell, who had a decided flair for the sensational, was not always a safe guide for Ireland. Perhaps the Archbishop was not fully apprised of the extent of the intrigue; but he must have known that von Schloezer belonged to Bismarck's party, while Cahensly belonged to the Center party. Under these circumstances it is very unlikely the two were working together.

Tireless in his campaign, John Ireland at once set out to enlist the aid of Cardinal Gibbons. In a long, outspoken letter, he asked the Cardinal:

Is there no protest to be made by us as regards what has been so aptly called the "Lucerne conspiracy"? Is Mr. Cahensly, Herr Schlosser [sic], Premier Mercier, etc., to go on telling Rome how the Church in America is to be ruled, with our silence and apparent approval? Are we, by saying nothing, showing ourselves worthy of the trust which our people put in us? Will not Rome herself deem us worthless men, whom she need not consult on this or any other matter, in which we are concerned? . . . The American Church has been deeply insulted.

After inviting the Baltimore Cardinal to summon the Archbishops to meet and advise him, and then take proper action, Ireland went on:

You will say that I am hasty, and need to be repressed. Not so, this time I think. We are American bishops; an effort is made to dethrone us and to foreignize our country in the name of religion. The question will not be as to quarrels between us and Germans—or Canadians in America. . . . But it will be as to men daring to rule us from Germany or Canada. Our non-Catholic fellow citizens can well call us traitors if we are silent.[64]

Ireland made one other important move. He persuaded Senator Cushman Davis of Minnesota to attack Cahensly's "political aggression" on the floor of the United States Senate. Representing the more extreme liberal opinion, Ireland was sure that such strong measures were necessary in resistance to Cahensly. Vigorous liberal activism was needed to ensure that the Germans would not rule the American Church, and, what was obviously far more important, to make it possible that a Catholic Church could exist in America at all.[65]

Only a few weeks after Cardinal Gibbons had belabored "self-constituted critics" in Europe who undertook to prescribe the proper treatment of Germans in America, he had a chance meeting with Benjamin Harrison, who was vacationing at Cape May, New Jersey. As he was returning along the boardwalk to his cottage, the

President invited the Cardinal into his summer house. There Harrison introduced the subject of the Cahensly memorials and the agitation they were causing. According to Gibbons' own account, the President remarked:

I have followed the question with profound interest, and I regard it as a subject of deep importance to our country. . . . Foreign and unauthorized interference with American affairs cannot be viewed with indifference. I was very much pleased with the opinion that you expressed publicly in the matter. I had thought several times of writing to you, and offering you my congratulations on the remarks you had made, but I refrained from doing so lest I should be interfering with church matters. . . . This is no longer a missionary country like others which need missionaries from abroad. It has an authorized Hierarchy and well-established congregations. Of all men, the Bishop of the Church should be in full harmony with the political institutions and sentiments of the country.

The President told the Cardinal that he had his authority to make any use he thought proper of these remarks. For his part, Gibbons fully realized the implications of this chance meeting and the advantages to which it could be turned. He not only released the contents of the interview to the newspapers, but he promptly detailed the events of that July 11 meeting at Cape May to the Cardinal Secretary of State, Rampolla in Rome. When these views of the American National government were made known, the *coup de grâce* was given to the "national" movement in the American Church.[66]

But this did not come about until more fuel had been added to the fire. A second memorial appeared, drawn up by Cahensly and the Marchese Volpe-Landi, charging that sixteen million immigrants had lost their faith owing to the lack of priests and bishops of their own nationalities, want of societies to protect them, and the influence of the public schools. It went on to say that the whole question affected the interests of the countries from which immigration came and through these immigrants those nations were acquiring an influence in the United States. Such remarks convinced Ireland that forces in Germany were attempting to influence the Vatican. He gave his copy of the memorial to the Associated Press with an introduction of his own. Meanwhile, he continued urging Cardinal Gibbons to speak out on the matter.

For a while, Rome maintained a noncommittal attitude toward the controversy. In the end, however, the counsel of Ireland and his friends prevailed. In July, 1891, the Cardinal Secretary of State indicated to Cardinal Gibbons that the Holy See approved neither of Cahensly's propositions nor the rumor that the American hierarchy planned to consider the matter in a series of special meetings. Together with his fellow bishops, Gibbons was urged to work for harmony in the Church and the restoration of peace.[67]

Cardinal Gibbons realized that President Harrison and many other Americans needed repeated assurances of Catholic patriotism. Responding to this awareness, and heeding the advice given him by Rome, Gibbons took advantage of every opportunity to plead for greater unity and harmony. The first chance occurred when he was invited to Milwaukee to bestow the pallium[68] on Archbishop Katzer. While simultaneously preaching harmony, Gibbons delivered a stern warning to the German nationalists in their midwestern stronghold:

Woe to him . . . who would destroy or impair this blessed harmony that reigns among us! Woe to him who would sow tares of discord in the fair fields of the Church of America! Woe to him who would breed dissension among the leaders of Israel by introducing a spirit of nationalism into the camps of the Lord! Brothers we are, whatever may be our nationality, and brothers we shall remain. . . . God and our country!—this our watchword.

Although the Cardinal's brave plea may have fallen on some deaf ears, he enjoined them to avoid dissensions with either Church or state. He spoke to them as well of the luminous example set by the Old Testament figure, Ruth:

Let us glory in the title of American citizen. We owe our allegiance to one country, and that country is America. We must be in harmony with our political institutions. It matters not whether this is the land of our birth or the land of our adoption. It is the land of our destiny. . . .

When our brethren across the Atlantic resolve to come to our shores, may they be animated by the sentiments of Ruth, when she determined to join her husband's kindred in the land of Israel, and may they say to you as she said to their relations: "Whither thou hast gone, I also shall go . . . thy people shall be my people, and thy God my God. The land that shall receive thee dying, in the same will I die, and there will I be buried."[69]

Gibbons, the unofficial primate of the American Church, from the pulpit of St. John's cathedral, on this occasion spoke to seven hundred prelates and priests, representing every nationality in the Church. When he was finished speaking, they were aghast. Years later he looked back on the occasion as one of the most audacious things he had ever attempted, but it had to be done; there could be no compromise or hesitation.

Whatever effect his remarks may have had on the Germans, the response of the secular press was all that the liberals could desire. To most newspapers, Gibbons' sermon proved beyond any reasonable doubt that the leadership of the Church accepted wholeheartedly the first responsibility of American citizenship: unqualified and undivided loyalty to the United States.[70]

But Bishop John Lancaster Spalding, who was of an unquestionable American background and sympathy, had this significant comment to make:

It is simply laughable to see a kind of treason in this memorial against American liberty, and to accuse them [the Germans] of the intention of introducing foreign practices into the country. Actually Cahensly's plan does not entail any principal changes in America. It is certainly a prudent proposal to place the care of souls in the hands of priests of their own nationality, acquainted as they are with the language and national peculiarities. This does not by any means bring the Church into opposition with American institutions. Catholics emigrate to improve their living conditions, and this improvement makes them appreciate the value of American citizenship. Anything which makes immigrants more satisfied also makes them better citizens.[71]

Cahenslyism, so-called ever since for the German promoter of the scheme, was synonymous with efforts to fragment the Church in America along diocesan lines on a national origins basis. Such efforts, which would have effectively retarded the development of an English language pan-Catholicism, were decisively defeated in the closing decades of the nineteenth century by firm ecclesiastical action. From this point of view, Gordon has noted, ecclesiastical sanction of the "national parish," i.e., drawing parish lines to include only one predominantly ethnic group or requiring ethnic homogeneity for parish membership, was a more modest step than Cahensly proposed, and turns out in retrospect to have been an inspired "middle ground" position which met the needs of the immigrants themselves without compromising the future needs of their descendants.[72]

Of course, Cahensly's efforts were well meaning. He later maintained that he had no intention of interfering with American affairs or giving offense to American bishops. His only desire had been to protect European immigrants and keep them faithful to the Church. But even his friends questioned why the St. Raphael's Society had not addressed its complaints in the proper manner to the American bishops. Fortunately, the majority of Americans knew that Cardinal Gibbons was the representative of American Catholicism, and accepted his views as decisive in the controversy.

From the above we see how the Catholic attitude, like the American attitude, toward the assimilation process of the immigrant has passed through several stages. Throughout the early nineteenth century, in the absence of much theorizing about the problem, it was confidently assumed that assimilation would take place automatically. But this assumption, and the later brand of speeded-up or "pressure cooked" assimilation, showed no understanding or concern for the ethnic sensitivities of the minorities which composed as culturally pluralistic a Catholic community as American society itself. The assumption of a relatively facile Americanization indicated limited knowledge of the nature, origin, development, and survival potential of established cultural patterns.[73] Many ingredients in the American "melting pot" appeared to be highly resistant to the "purging flame." Groups made up of first generation immigrants did not "melt"—but maintained their respective communal subsystems and held out for priests of their own nationality and language. Geographic separation in "national" parishes helped to minimize the conflict among church members at the parish level, but it was not eliminated in the struggle for power or representation at the level of the hierarchy.[74]

When clashes of cultures did occur, as between the Germans and Irish, Archbishop Ireland blindly insisted that there was no conflict of nationalities or, as he put it, "races." Since the Irish and Germans arrived early in the century and were well established before the "new" immigrants arrived, they tended to think of themselves as natives, and Ireland's utterances bear some of the marks of prejudice acquired by a dominant, English-speaking group against later arrivals, mainly from southern Europe, whom they regarded as "foreigners." These attitudes, however, led to exacerbated animosities among national groups within the Church. There are to this day hundreds of active national parishes existing alongside of and even competing with the traditional territorial parishes. Second and third generation ethnics are more rapidly assimilated into a highly urbanized and mobile contemporary American society, and thus the separate ethnic communal subsystems, which heretofore existed as separate units in the social structure of American Catholicism, are breaking up and dissolving into the larger system of American pan-Catholicism, but the problem of minorities is now more acute than ever. Toward such relatively large subcultural groups as Negroes, Mexicans, Puerto Ricans, and Indians, racial prejudices are still so strong that they openly hinder the work of the Church. With regard to the inclusion of these racial and quasi-racial groups, pan-Catholicism as a sociological goal has been largely unrealized.[75]

In the absence of any demographic trend studies, it is not even known to what extent second and third generation Poles, Italians, or Slovaks, in the more socially mobile middle class, are moving away from the juridical national parishes, although the decline and disappearance of the national parish is projected as the result of current immigration policies of the United States.[76]

The Americanization of Catholic immigrants under Irish influence meant a substantial reshaping of the American Church's outlook in a way that reflected the influence of the American environment. The development of the Church along activist lines corresponding to the American ethos, its fusion with nationalism in the minds of its adherents, the modification of its traditional position on the desirability of state "establishment" of Catholicism, the de facto acceptance of, and empirical comfortableness with, the pluralism of American religious life with its "three great religions of Democracy"—all of these developments represent modifications in traditional Catholic orientations. They reflect the nature of the pervasive social forces emanating from American life and conditions, and constitute a measure of the substantial degree of acculturation which the institutionalized Catholic Church has undergone in America.[77]

With the emergence of a dominant middle class, which included the advancement of large segments of the Catholic community, the Church too advanced, becoming on its part more middle-class and more American—without losing its contact with the lower classes or ethnically unassimilated. As Herberg has noted: "It thus became possible to be an American not only without falling away from the church but (if one may so put it) precisely through and by way of being a Catholic."[78]

Reflecting the more perceptive American attitudes of the post-war era and recognizing the manifold diversity and complexity in the process of "becoming an American," the policy of the Church today is not to foster nationality communalism any longer than is necessary. To quote the words of Father Harte:

In general, the official position of the Church on this question of membership in juridical national parishes is clearly to encourage assimilation into a larger community by lifting all barriers to affiliation with the territorial parish for those who speak English.

At the same time [he goes on to add] however, the individual's right to make his choice freely is fully guaranteed, and the right of the national or ethnic group to perpetuate its culture is likewise protected.[79]

This moderate tone is in the greatest contrast to the nineteenth-century crusaders of Ireland's stamp who tried to force the immigrants to divest themselves of their heritages immediately and to take upon themselves a highly standardized American pattern in their lives. However well intentioned these Americanizers may have been, they were working toward denationalization and standardization (some, like Walburg, thought even demoralization), and not assimilation. This desire to enforce conformity, which has plagued generations of Americans, has been regarded by some historians as "a carry-over from Puritanism." In the words of Marcus Lee Hansen: "That was the essence of practical Puritanism—the restriction of others."[80] It is not surprising to find John Ireland transmitting the puritanical strain so often associated with Irish Catholicism in America.

The draconic Americanizing crusade characterizing the years

1914 to 1920 ran its course (although as we have seen, the inevitable Americanization process had set in among the German immigrants well before that time), and fortunately the crusade was eventually recognized as fostering a spurious Americanization. After 1920, social thought embraced notions of long-range cultural fusion, and more important still, cultural pluralism.[81] When the counterattack came, it came, not from the newcomers who were still far more concerned with their own survival than with sophisticated theories of adjustment, but from social workers in the settlement houses like Jane Addams, who saw the unfortunate effects demands for rapid Americanization had on the immigrants' children, who were frequently alienated from their parents.

An appreciative view of the immigrants' cultural heritage and of its distinct usefulness to himself and his adopted country received additional sustenance from yet another source: those intellectual currents of the time which, however overborne by their more powerful contemporary opposites, emphasized liberalism, tolerance, and internationalism.[82]

It may be, as Father Ong has speculated, that the American has only left Europe vicariously, perhaps ten or twelve generations ago. But Europe is still present in the American psyche. Every summer this presence draws thousands of Americans across the Atlantic, in spite of John Ireland's stinging reproach, to refresh their corporate memories, or to prove in some vague sort of way that they are not irresponsible, or that their ancestors were right in leaving Europe after all.

There can be little doubt that some kind of interior dialogue with Europe formed, matured, and finally opened for all the world to see the characteristic American attitudes of Father Hecker. Reared in America, converted from Protestantism in America, he felt intensely from the beginning the need for the Church to be at home in his native land. And yet he went to Belgium for his novitiate, and his Paulist community was actually first conceived in Rome. John Ireland attributed to the Paulists the primary responsibility for the "American" spirit which he thought was becoming more influential in the Church.

The striking thing about Hecker's dialogue with Europe was its open, developing character. He never worked back and forth to make Europeans Americans or Americans Europeans. Constant involvement in European-American problems only enlarged his field of vision more and more to horizons beyond both Europe and America. As St. Paul became the apostle not merely of the Graeco-Roman but of the entire Gentile as well as Jewish world, so, too, a widening international vision grew in Hecker's mind. It is revealed in the following passage from his private memoranda written in Europe during his illness in 1874–5:

What else has been my exile from home for unless to prepare my soul to make my life-experience applicable to the general condition of the Church and the world in its present crisis? The past was for the United States, the future, for the world. To this end all particular attachments to persons, places, labors, had to be cut off, not to give a bias to the judgment, and not to interfere with my action. It was with a deeper meaning than at first sight appeared to me that I now see why I called myself "An international Catholic."[83]

ARTHUR W. THOMPSON

American Socialists and the Russian Revolution of 1905–1906[1]

THE OUTBREAK of the much anticipated Russian revolt and the rise to national prominence of American socialism, both occurring in the first decade of this century, interacted in numerous and complex ways. Although American influence on the course of events in Russia was minimal and derived largely from non-socialist quarters, it should not be ignored. The response of American socialists to Russian developments during 1905 and 1906 shaped their own direction considerably more than it did that of Russia. To grasp these relationships and reactions, it is necessary to understand the general framework within which American socialism operated fifty years ago.

By the turn of this century, the movement toward political consolidation had gained considerable headway among socialists. Fragmentary groups remained, chief among them being Daniel De-Leon's Socialist Labor Party. Still, in 1900 the Social Democrats, largest of the socialist organizations, had gathered 98,000 votes toward putting Eugene V. Debs into the White House. Two years later, under the further integrated banner of the Socialist Party, their total national vote doubled. In 1904 Debs received over 400,-000 votes on the Presidential ticket, again doubling the Socialist national vote. Here was clear evidence that socialism in America

203

had arrived; it was no longer an impotent force to be ignored. Socialists were convinced that their political appeal was growing.
Their speakers had more drawing power and the circulation of
their magazines was on the rise.

The national organization of the Socialist Party was directed by
a National Executive Committee and quadrennial convention. By
1905, the national party was trying to coordinate the activities of
about thirty-five state and territorial organizations. These, in turn,
were subdivided into locals, run by a General Committee. In large
urban areas such as New York and Chicago, the General Committee had an Executive Committee that was in continuous contact with the Assembly or Congressional districts. The lower eche-
lons of this structure selected candidates for local elections, organized demonstrations and parades, ran lecture series, distributed
pamphlets—in English, Finnish, German, Italian, Yiddish, or whatever the occasion called for—visited trade union groups, sold tickets
for a variety of benefits, peddled party papers, and discussed the
most pressing topics of the day. There were also a number of
ethnic groups whose organizations or membership had varying
ties with the socialist movement.[2]

The Socialist Party drew its support from a variety of quarters.
From Oklahoma, Texas, California, Oregon, Washington, and Nebraska came the ex-Bryanites, and from a multitude of urban areas
came the "petty bourgeoisie." No easy generalization is really possible, for as David Shannon has rightly concluded, it "was composed of a little of everything—of recent immigrants and descendants of the *Mayflower's* passengers, of tenement dwellers and
prairie farmers, of intellectuals and unlettered sharecroppers, of devout ministers and belligerent agnostics, of syndicalists and craft
unionists, of revolutionists and gradualist reformers." Nevertheless,
party leadership consisted of lawyers, journalists, and teachers, or,
as a later Communist Party official bemoaned, the "non-proletarian
intellectuals."

Undoubtedly, the effectiveness of the socialist movement was
curtailed by the frequent, often bitter, political, ideological, organizational, and tactical differences among its leaders. Cleavages
within the Party were often as great as those between the various
socialist organizations. Midwestern factionalism was evident when
the more radical Charles H. Kerr, who issued the *International So-*

cialist Review, fired Algie M. Simons in 1906. At the same time, Simons was at loggerheads with the more moderate elements represented by Milwaukee's Victor Berger. Toledo's William Mailly, former national secretary of the Socialist Party (1903–1904), condemned Berger as a bully, a coward, and an unwelcome member in their midst. John C. Chase, of the Party's New York State Executive Committee, joined in the opposition to Berger.[3]

For all their differences, Socialist Party leaders managed to unite in venting their violent objections against Daniel DeLeon of the rival Socialist Labor Party. DeLeon's policies were often accused of being in perfect harmony with those of the Czar of Russia and the employers' associations of America. Frequently, DeLeon's rejoinders were even more colorful.

Newspapers and magazines published by each of the factions aggravated and perpetuated these intra-socialist conflicts. Among the magazines, the scholarly *International Socialist Review*, *Wilshire's Magazine* (whose efforts to secure a million subscribers finally brought the price down to twenty-five cents for three years by June of 1905), and Wayland's *Appeal to Reason*, reputedly the most influential of the periodicals, led the lists. There were the socialist, class-conscious labor journals: *The Industrial Worker* (IWW), *Miners Magazine* (Western Federation of Miners), and the *Voice of Labor*. Other Socialist Party organs ranged from Berger's moderate *Social Democratic Herald* to the aggressive New York *Worker* and *Chicago Socialist* to the more vociferous left-wing *Toledo Socialist*, and to Socialist Labor Party's *The Weekly People*.

Despite bickering between and within organizations, American socialists were encouraged by the growth of their party and electoral strength during the first years of the new century. Then, rumbling during the latter half of 1904 and exploding through 1905, came news of revolution in Russia.

The assassination of Viacheslav Plehve, the bitterly hated Russian Minister of the Interior, on July 28, 1904, was one in a series of murders of Russian leaders that began in the late nineteenth century. Plehve's death provoked widespread reaction in the United States. Among American socialists, not a single leader criticized the act. On the contrary, a certain delight swept through socialist ranks now that the "despot," the "bloodhound," had been disposed of. Only *Wilshire's Magazine* asked whether it was worth it, whether it might not entrench the autocracy further. During the rest of 1904, occasional and casual references to the developing Russian situation punctuated the press.[4]

News of "Bloody Sunday" brought American socialists to full attention. On January 22, 1905, several thousand unarmed Russian workers, accompanied by women and children, marched on the Winter Palace to petition the Czar for a redress of certain political and economic grievances. The response was a massacre. Hundreds of people were killed and wounded by the Imperial Guard. News of these and of continued Cossack attacks on the general populace during the next few days shocked many Americans. For socialists, however, shock and indignation were accompanied by a sense of exhilaration. It seemed obvious that the hectic days of late January marked the beginning of the long-awaited Russian revolution. For the moment, factionalism gave way to a common response. Headlines in the socialist press viewed Bloody Sunday as "The Morning Glow of Liberty." The storm had finally burst; czarism in Russia was doomed. A new day was ahead. The czar's divinity had at last been stripped away; now there was hope and enthusiasm, as well as consistent and anxious attention to news coming from Russia.

By February, Debs saw the revolution as having special significance for organized labor. It would, he felt sure, promote labor solidarity everywhere. The Debsian view, however, was too optimistic for many American socialists who believed that the job of spreading the principles of trade unionism and social democracy still had to be done. DeLeon was even less optimistic. He suggested rather contemptuously that the revolution was blocked, if only temporarily, by the "dumbness" and inability of the revolutionary class to see what was needed.

American socialists greeted with cheers news of the February 17 assassination of the Grand Duke Sergius. His death appeared to be a logical consequence of the Russian government's policy of repression after Bloody Sunday. Among American socialists it was generally agreed that Sergius was the worst of the "ducal cabal."[5]

Another encouraging sign was the *Potemkin* mutiny beginning in late June. Seizure of the Black Sea battleship by its crew on the twenty-seventh, followed by the bombardment of the port of Odessa, the execution of naval officers, and nearly two weeks of seemingly aimless cruising until the mutineers surrendered the warship to Rumanian authorities on July 9, provoked hurrahs for "the Navy of the Revolution." Algernon Lee condemned the "capitalist press" for calling these heroic sailors pirates. But in Chicago, Murray E. King bemoaned the ignorance and lack of class consciousness of the crewmen who threw away a precious opportunity. And Gaylord Wilshire believed the affair was "somewhat more dramatic than significant," arguing a little disgustedly that the sailors had rebelled because they were fed up with rotten food and not from any love of liberty or humanity.

In the meantime, the Russo-Japanese War, which was still raging in East Asia, brought forth condemnation from Americans. They adopted John Spargo's resolution branding the war "a crime against progress and civilization." By and large, however, the Socialists were interested in the conflict only insofar as it would have a bearing on the class struggle throughout the world. On this issue, American, Japanese, and Russian socialists joined hands in opposing the war. All three organizations also favored a Russian defeat. Most socialists, regardless of national origin, simply believed that a Japanese victory would help to undo the czarist autocracy.[6]

The successive waves of revolutionary violence that swept through large areas of Russia between Bloody Sunday and September, 1905 were welcomed in all American socialist circles. Their spokesmen either ignored or condemned ameliorative efforts by the beleaguered Czarist government. The March 3 ukase, for example, in which the Czar announced his intention to create a consultative assembly, or the Easter ukase, granting limited freedom of religion, were apparently not worthy of any comment by American socialists. A manifesto issued August 19, proposing another assembly—this one with deliberative powers—aroused much scorn and little enthusiasm. Virtually all socialists agreed it would be little more than "a coalition of all the feudalistic and capitalistic forces against the revolutionary working class of Russia. . . ."

The events of October, 1905 would gain unwavering attention in the United States. The increasing role of Russian proletarians in the politically motivated general strike that started in mid-October struck a responsive chord in America. Events were now going more as it was assumed they should. Workingmen had become more class conscious and were, therefore, in the vanguard of the revolution. Then came the thirtieth and the October Manifesto: newspapers across the United States blared in bold headlines that Russia was to have a constitution, a duma with legislative power, and civil liberties. Indeed, revolution had come to Russia! Even so, socialist responses in America varied from unrestrained joy to cynicism.

Perhaps Emma Goldman reflected the joyous views of a majority of the rank and file socialists when she wrote that the news was "electrifying and carried us to ecstatic heights." As for the Russian contingent in New York, she added:

The radical East Side lived in a delirium, spending almost all of its time at monster meetings and discussing these matters in cafes, forgetting political differences and brought into close comradeship by the glorious events happening in the fatherland.

Immigrant Russian Jews, whether socialists or not, were convinced that the Manifesto was one of those historic documents in the march of mankind. Wealthy settlement house socialists, including William E. Walling and James G. Phelps Stokes, more concerned with humanitarian than ideological considerations, were excited and deeply moved. Here was a major step in their dream "for the freedom of the whole human race from tyranny of every kind. . . ."

More moderate socialist leaders were almost equally delighted by the October Manifesto. For Victor Berger it was "wonderful news," tempered only by a few reservations. Obviously all socialist goals had not been won in Russia, but the beginning of a constitutional era there certainly indicated "a successful revolution." Berger believed that the manifesto was all part of an evolutionary process and that a nation could no more escape natural development than a human being. Therefore, he argued, "if I were in Russia . . . I would advise our comrades to accept the situation."[7] More doctrinaire socialist groups represented by Algernon Lee tended to minimize the revolutionary character of events.

According to Gaylord Wilshire, the wheels of history turned even more slowly. Czars and Count Witte would come and go, the peasants might even receive some land, but the socialist commonwealth was not yet discernible. "Socialism," Wilshire editorialized, "comes as the result of social evolution, and Russia has not yet taken the necessary steps." American industrial unionists were even less moved by the Russian events of late October. Not until "industrial liberty" had been achieved and the people were the supreme authority would there be any need to cheer. The most negative reaction came from the Socialist Labor Party. DeLeon forces first condemned the Russian general strike as inadequate for a real revolution and then proceeded to ignore the Manifesto entirely.

News of the bloody and brutal November and December days in Russia convinced more radical American groups that their pessimistic evaluation of the Manifesto had been correct. They cheered the Social Democrats' refusal to cooperate with Witte and followed the Moscow insurrection during the last ten days of December with pure joy. American socialists depicted the Moscow affair as a desperate and brave fight, as a glorious and heroic struggle against great odds; they viewed its failure as the real tragedy of 1905.[8]

The early months of 1906 were frustrating for American socialists. Most American citizens who managed a glance at Russian affairs were optimistic about the forthcoming Duma, but their socialist brethren followed the lead of the Russian Social Democrats by taking a dim view of the proposed legislative body. Then, having approved the boycott of the elections which resulted in a minimul radical representation, the American socialists condemned as a farce the first Duma, which convened on May 10. Still, the Duma was a reality. By June, American socialists finally embraced it as a "revolutionary Duma," in time to represent its dissolution on July 21 as another bitter blow.[9] The Czar's treachery was denounced; he was playing a dangerous game that now clearly sealed his doom. Once the hand-wringing stage passed, most American socialists returned to their earlier critique of the Duma. They assumed an "I-told-you-so" view. Many American socialists recognized, however, that they could not expect too much too quickly.

There was general concurrence with Victor Berger's views on the progress of the Russian revolution: at least the stage had been set and the second act could begin at any time.

Thus socialists here followed developments in Russia with considerable interest, week by week—sometimes even day by day—from Bloody Sunday of January 22, 1905, through the dissolution of the first Duma a year and a half later. Despite differences among themselves, response among American socialists to particular phases of the revolution did not fluctuate nearly as much as did those of most other American groups. Indeed, socialists were relatively consistent in their views of the major Russian personalities who tended to dominate the American news scene.

For example, American socialists were unanimous in their view of the Czar as a brutal and destructive immoral force and as a financial drain on the Russian public. He was devoid of any wisdom and was utterly hopeless. Unlike a large number of Americans, socialists were quite unwilling to distinguish between the Czar and the ducal bureaucracy at any time during the revolution. Contrary to the thinking of other Americans, socialists were clear in their demands for an end to the monarchy itself.[10]

Though considerably less violent, many socialists were adamant also in their opposition to Tolstoy. The Count's widespread popularity in the United States failed to engage them. They viewed his philosophical anarchism with suspicion, arguing that it tended to be too submissive to the autocracy. His economic views, like those of Henry George (whom he admired), were not to be taken seriously. Socialists were even more at variance with general American opinion on the matter of Count Witte. Generally speaking, he was virtually ignored in the socialist press, as compared to the broad coverage accorded him in the regular media.[11] Socialists believed Witte was a capitalist trimmer who did not deserve trust.

Consensus about personalities gave way to further discord about pogroms in Russia. Pogroms had become almost endemic in Russia during the late nineteenth century. The brutal massacre of Jews at Kishineff in 1903 climaxed their dreadful progression. In America, awareness grew that the 1905–1906 upheaval did nothing to reduce the terror. On the contrary, the revolution provided the

Russian government with an excuse to extend and intensify the slaughter of Jews.

The response of American socialists to these events and to Jews in general was infinitely more complicated than their reaction to Russian personalities and, in many respects, more closely paralleled the general, non-socialist reaction in America. To begin with, when the socialists took any stand at all, there was universal condemnation of the pogroms themselves. The socialist local in New York was joined by a few other branches, including, for example, the Sioux City local, in strong statements of disapproval. Yet the bloody episodes rarely consumed much space in the socialist press and even less in the records of their state and national organizations. At no time during 1905 and 1906 did the Socialist Party of America take any official stand or issue any statement on the pogroms. On a number of occasions, however, socialists criticized condemnations by others as hypocrisy. William Randolph Hearst and Theodore Roosevelt were among those whose sincerity socialists questioned. Generally, socialists ascribed "Jew baiting" in Russia and everywhere to the malevolence of the ruling class, which showed itself not only in economic exploitation, but also in its use of racial and religious prejudice. In America, socialists argued, the Negro and the immigrant were "used" as bulwarks of capitalism.[12]

The attitude of the organizational socialist toward the Jew per se was another matter, and not a simple one at that. There were occasional evidences of respect, even suggestions that the Russian Jew was worth a dozen of their "vodka-loving Slavonic oppressors." But implied anti-Semitism was a consistent socialist element. Socialists asserted that Jews were not popular because they were too smart; they were "born to be American lawyers." Jews were sharp, shrewd, and grasping, as was evidenced by their business tactics. Socialists were merely following the contemporary American pattern. But since socialists generally agreed that "racial" prejudice was a manifestation of capitalist exploitation and condemned capitalists at every turn, it was possible for them to condemn some Jews (those businessmen who paid "starvation wages") and to praise others (the young and enlightened ones who joined the socialist cause).

In the last analysis, American socialists who were not Jews opposed pogroms because they were opposing everything the Russian government did. Their views on the Jew in America often represented a form of covert anti-Semitism, modified on occasion to suit doctrinal needs and out of deference to a segment of their membership. Jewish socialists, on the other hand, were far more exercised than their non-Jewish colleagues about the pogroms, but for them religious indifference substituted for anti-Semitism.[13]

Socialists were not only in accord in their condemnation of the Czar, Tolstoy, Witte, the Bureaucracy, and the pogroms, but they also agreed that "the workers" constituted the key to a successful Russian revolution. The *Chicago Socialist* reflected the thinking of the Socialist Party when it argued that for forty years the Russian business and professional classes had been unsuccessful in their efforts to effect a revolution; that success waited until the workingmen joined the fray. Conviction was widespread that the mass strike did more to bring on the 1905 Russian revolution than the guns of Admiral Togo in the Sea of Japan. *The Miners Magazine*, the *International Socialist Review*, the New York *Worker*, and other socialist organs concurred in a judgment that the "factory proletariat" had succeeded where the bourgeoisie had failed.

Ideological predilections of American socialists convinced them of the crucial role that the Russian proletariat would play in any successful upheaval. These attitudes also produced an interpretation of the Russian revolution which differed significantly from that held by most Americans. To begin with, comparisons of one kind or another with the French Revolution of 1789, so much in evidence in the non-socialist newspapers and magazines, were not acceptable in American socialist quarters.[14] Instead, socialists viewed the late eighteenth-century upheaval as one stage in a vast, evolutionary scheme rather than as a valid point of comparison with twentieth-century events. Most agreed that Russia was an unfortunate "instance of arrested development on a national scale," but that her time in the scheme of things had arrived.

Again, unlike nonsocialist America (which could not make up its mind whether or not the Russian affair was a revolution), socialists here were convinced that it was the real thing. To them, progress and civilization in Russia were in mortal combat with despotic government and capitalistic exploitation.

But if socialists were sure they were witnessing a revolution, they were hopelessly divided—at least prior to the October Manifesto—as to the particular revolutionary stage they were observing. For approximately half of the socialist press, led vociferously by the *Chicago Socialist*, January 22, 1905 ushered in the era of twentieth-century proletarian revolutions. Skepticism characterized *Wilshire's Magazine*. Its writers were quite convinced that this was merely Russia's bourgeois stage. By contrast, Algernon Lee's New York *Worker* was sure that the revolution did not really start until October.

Victor Berger and the *Social Democratic Herald* were almost alone in a more moderate and consistent evaluation of Russian events. Even prior to Bloody Sunday, the Milwaukee paper argued: "Although the Czar's reforms will be calculated to temper the winds of despotism to the middle class, still there is an ultimate gain to the working class also."[15] This kind of logic was totally unacceptable to the bulk of the socialist spokesmen. Bloody Sunday did not change Berger's views. He insisted that the Russian cry had been for bread, not revolution, that that dreadful day had not been a revolt, but a massacre. Besides, the people were not prepared for a revolution on the scale of the French model. And then, to bolster his position, Berger invoked the Marxian dialectic, insisting that "the bourgeois state is a necessary phase of economic evolution," and Russia was not ready for the main event. Even after the general strike and Manifesto of October and the rioting of November, when socialist opinion began to solidify on the timetable of revolution, Berger refused to alter his position. Socialists, he agreed, should certainly help the cause, but up to a point.

The Russian revolution without any doubt is *not* a Socialist revolution. Russia at the present day is no more ripe for Socialism than is China. The Socialists do not form one-tenth of one percent of the population. At the most, the revolution will be simply a bourgeois revolution, and we cannot see why we American Socialists should strain our funds for a revolution which will mainly benefit the intelligent middle class and the peasantry of Russia.

Throughout 1905 and 1906 Wilshire agreed with Berger's analysis that the socialist dawn was not imminent. Russia's convulsions were merely part of the movement from feudalism to capitalism. Given the limited degree of industrialization and the mass of uneducated peasants, Russia's social revolution was at least twenty years off. In any event, there was little hope for socialism in Russia in advance of a Western European upheaval. For the present, the best that could be hoped for would be a little housecleaning, Wilshire insisted.[16]

The October Manifesto, with its promise of an effective Duma, and the appointment of Count Witte to the post of Premier, helped to bring the historical process into better focus for the American socialists. Most socialist organs, including the *International Socialist Review*, now perceived with greater clarity that the next stage would be a "capitalist 'liberal' government." The *Chicago Socialist* reluctantly concluded that its analysis during the earlier months of 1905 had been overly optimistic. But by December, as the nonsocialist American press increasingly decried the accelerated violence in Russia, the *Chicago Socialist* countered that Russia had always known violence. Now, however, it served a good cause.

Socialist penmen were specially angered by the willingness of the bourgeois press to settle for mere reforms. They reasoned that nonsocialist newspapers, especially the *Chicago Tribune*, wanted reform only because it would create a good field for investment. As if to heighten the contrast in outlooks, Algie M. Simons and the *Chicago Socialist* directed attention less to the present capitalist stage in Russia than to the forthcoming proletarian phase of basic revolution. Simons attacked Witte and stated categorically that the proletarian revolution was following hard on the heels of the capitalist. Indeed, the beginning of the world proletarian revolution was in process. By the end of January, 1906, even after the unsuccessful Moscow insurrection of late December, the *Chicago Socialist* continued to insist, "They have started the greatest of all revolutions, the revolution of the proletariat."[17]

One perceptible consequence of this view of an imminent proletarian victory was that it stimulated American socialists' faith in industrial unionism. Simons, Lucy E. Parsons, W. E. Trautmann, and other delegates at the organizational meeting of the IWW during June and July of 1905 adopted resolutions of support and endorsed industrial unionism for both countries. *The Miners Magazine* of Denver would settle for nothing less in Russia than "a republic, where labor shall be Czar." Chicago's *Voice of Labor* agreed. The IWW's *Industrial Worker* repudiated parliamentarianism as a waste of time and as a bourgeois device whereby the workers are "stripped of their social patrimony and the results of their toil." All avowed that the era of proletarian revolutions had started.

Despite varying degrees of optimism about the relative imminence of socialism, by early 1906 American socialists from Debs to DeLeon were reasonably certain of two things. First, they were convinced of the ultimate success of the Russian revolution, and second, that the Social Democrats were the vehicle through which that success would be attained.[18]

Responses of American socialists to the Russian revolution also shaped their views of contemporary America. To begin with, the firm conviction of inevitability on the part of the leaders and press of the American Socialist Party that history was on their side, contributed to their failure to perceive significant differences between conditions here and those in Russia. Equal or greater distortions affected the manner in which nonsocialist Americans estimated the aims and deeds of their socialist countrymen. To a large number of nonsocialist Americans, socialism was indistinguishable from anarchism and violence. The relative growth of the socialist vote during the first years of the new century augmented their fears about revolution here.

Faced with an American public that was not only hostile, but which also opposed its view of the revolution in Russia, American socialists indiscriminately consigned the political and economic systems of the two nations to the same pit of damnation. More radical socialists were quickest to make this association. Immediately after Bloody Sunday, the Socialist Labor Party cried, "Pobedonostseffism is international, like Capitalism." DeLeon drew what appeared to him to be certain obvious similarities: the "language" of the capitalists matched that of the Russian bureaucrats; the "brutality" of Colorado's Adjutant General Bell paralleled that of Grand Duke Vladimir; the condemnation of the socialists for talking "like wild men" came from the *New York Times* and General Dimitri Trepoff alike; and the American trade unions, like the zemstvos, were ineffectual in their efforts to achieve real changes. The argument that strikes and violence have no justification in countries where people participate in government, as in the United States, was repeatedly attacked.[19]

Then, as months followed the issuance of the October Manifesto, and as frustration and violence mounted in Russia and American aversion grew to the revolution, more moderate American socialists also came to see fewer differences between the two nations.

As result of these reciprocal blanket condemnations, the hostility of American socialists toward Russian capitalists became involved in their mounting attack on American capitalists. A number of analogies appeared in the socialist press again and again during 1905 and 1906. Plundering corporations here were organizing the middle class against labor in ways infinitely worse than anything ever attempted in Russia. Indeed, the Czar could learn a great deal about running a country from the Rockefellers, Belmonts, and Armours. American business leaders were no less brutal or averse to the use of violence than their counterparts in the Russian regime. Occurrences such as the rail strike of '94 and other unpleasant episodes proved that Chicago was not so different from St. Petersburg after all. Beatings administered to Russian workers by "an arrogant knout-wielding Czar" were horrible, but in America the knout of hunger stung no less. Certainly working-class Americans should be aware of the outrageous exploitations to which they were subjected. Even Andrew Carnegie's philanthropy aroused considerable misgivings among socialist scribes. The *Chicago Socialist* suggested that the $10-million Carnegie grant for the relief and maintenance of superannuated college professors might more appropriately have gone to old and worn out steelworkers whose labor produced the money in the first place.[20]

More inflammatory among socialists than any other issue were the arrests and trials of Charles H. Moyer, William D. Haywood, and George A. Pettibone of the Eastern Federation of Miners for the murder of Idaho's former governor, Frank Steunenberg. Socialist press accounts had earlier condemned Russian-style despotism in the Illinois coal mines and militarism in Colorado. Now American socialists saw Russian tactics surpassed in the Rocky Mountain region. When newspapers and magazines bemoaned labor's use of Russian terroristic methods, the socialist press insisted that Russian methods had been adopted first by capitalists in the western mining states. Local police and units of the United States Army were merely "American Cossacks," and the Mine Owners' Association was worse than the Grand Dukes. Even in eastern areas, such as the Pennsylvania coalmines, state police were "being used as private watchmen as well as Cossack patrols."

The operations of American politics as well as American economics left socialists cynical. According to Wilshire, "We Americans, in a way, are under a worse autocracy under our Constitution than the Russians are under their Tzar. The Tzar can be made to change his mind, but the Constitution must remain immutable no matter how great the necessity of change."[21] If socialists likened American magnates to the ducal bureaucracy, President Theodore Roosevelt was the counterpart of the Czar. He, too, posed as a liberator. Socialists damned the President for urging the reestablishment of the whipping post in the Army. They berated him for his failure to recognize the Republic of Lithuania, especially after the rapidity with which he had accepted the Republic of Panama. Wasn't the Baltic state the "real thing," something not made in Wall Street? Still, socialists felt some hope in Roosevelt. Progressive Democrats William Jennings Bryan and William Randolph Hearst talked a great deal, but a conservative like Roosevelt could well become a revolutionist if he succeeded in efforts to extend government regulation of corporate practices.

At times, the socialist attack on Samuel Gompers and the trade union movement was almost as strong as that directed against businessmen and politicians. More radical socialists, especially those committed to industrial unionism, were vitriolic in their barrages. Trautmann, General Secretary-Treasurer of the IWW, repeatedly denounced the American Federation of Labor. In a speech at Union Temple in Minneapolis, DeLeon condemned "The tyranny of the grand dukes of the AFofL." In such diatribes, socialists consigned "labor czars" to speedy and "well-deserved oblivion." John Mitchell's command of the United Mine Workers was little more than a lieutenancy of the capitalist class. Daniel J. Tobin's leadership of the Teamsters, and the work of the Machinists' James O'Connell, involved "reactionary imbecility." The major and most contemptible czar of them all was "Trade Union Pure and Simple, no Socialism Gompers." He had sold out to the capitalists, to August Belmont and the National Civic Federation, as well as to any other group that happened to be the subject of socialist wrath at the moment. Any Gompers pronouncement was an "imperial ukase." And when Gompers cabled Count Witte in mid-December, 1905, the period of virtual civil war in Russia, Simons looked upon the move "as the most damnable act of treason ever perpetrated upon the working-class of the world."[22]

Regardless of where they placed their primary tactical emphasis, American socialists were thoroughly sympathetic toward the 1905 Russian Revolution and the success of the workers. Socialist sympathy manifested itself in a number of ways during the year and a half following January 22. Meetings and demonstrations, resolutions, collections, and fund campaigns, and a seemingly endless flow of Russian revolutionary speakers to the United States were overt proofs of American socialist awareness concerning events in Russia.

A flood of meetings, especially in New York City, formed the initial domestic response to the news of January 22. Individual sessions varied, but the pattern was generally the same. Men and women gathered—a few dozen, a few hundred, a few thousand— to express their protest against the Czar and his government, their sympathy for the Russian people and their joy with the long-awaited turn of events, to draft resolutions of condemnation or of greetings, and to gather needed funds. The greatest excitement and enthusiasm was clearly present among the Russians and Russian Jews of the city's lower East side. For at least two weeks there was an orgy of sustained neighborhood activity.[23]

The first major gathering took place on Monday, January 23. More than four thousand angered, yet excited and expectant people paid a five-cent admission to join in proceedings at Clinton Hall. On Thursday, January 26, the Russian Social Democratic Society sponsored a rally at the Grand American Hall on Houston Street. On January 27, the Social Democratic Literary Club convened in Brooklyn's American Star Hall. On January 29, the American Friends of the Russian Revolution met at the Academy of Music. On the same day, the New York Central Federated Union adopted a resolution typical of many approved during that first week after the initial explosion in St. Petersburg.

Resolved, That we hereby denounce most vehemently the bureaucratic system of government prevailing in Russia as inconsistent with reason and incompatible with progress, and we call upon all broadminded and liberty-loving Americans to do their utmost on behalf of the men and women in Russia who are animated by the same spirit that led our forefathers in 1776 to undertake the great struggle for independence which laid the foundations for this great Republic.

At almost all of these meetings, speeches and printed sentiments were offered in three or four languages, and sometimes more. The January 26 meeting, for example, involved Morris Hillquit speaking in English, Alexander Jonas in German, G. Urieff in Russian, and the editor of the *Jewish Daily Forward*, Abraham Cahan, in Yiddish, while Italian-language throwaways littered the aisles.

The socialist response to news from Russia gained momentum more slowly in other areas of the United States. West and south of New York and other Atlantic urban-immigrant centers, the strong emotional content and sense of urgency was less. In Chicago and Boston, supporters of the Russian Social Democrats had rallied their sympathizers on January 26. By the twenty-ninth, the socialists of Portland, Maine, were denouncing the Russian Czar and the pogroms as phenomena comparable to Colorado's James H. Peabody and South Carolina's "terrible child slaughter in the mills." The Socialist Party of Worcester, Massachusetts, attracted four hundred persons to a protest rally. Discussions of "The Russian Situation" were held during February in many of Chicago's wards. William D. Haywood, Luella Twining, and J. Edward Morgan addressed a February 13 mass meeting in West Denver's Turner Hall. Benjamin Hanford, the Socialist Party candidate for Vice-President of the United States in 1904, and Abraham Cahan were the leading speakers at a Philadelphia mass meeting on February 19. Cahan confined himself to a condemnation of the entire Russian system, but Hanford drew a "deadly parallel" with the "tyranny" and "shooting of unarmed workers" in the United States.[24]

By the summer of 1905, the number of meetings had sharply declined, and intervals between them were farther apart. In March, the Brooklyn Labor Lyceum held a benefit ball; in May, Meyer London addressed a meeting of the American Bund in Cooper Union. Significantly, these sessions reflected the tenacious concerns to interested minorities rather than the Socialist organization as a whole.

Then, in the fall of 1905, the picture changed. The General Strike and October Manifesto, the riots and pogroms of November, and the Moscow insurrection of late December brought American socialists and their allied groups back to life. Russia's revolution had gained new impetus and, what was more important to the socialists, Russian Social Democrats had become more aggressive. The workers' star seemed to be in the ascendancy. Once again a flurry of meetings marked the American socialist scene. More protests, more resolutions, and more words of encouragement issued from American radical sources. Now the demonstrations were larger than ever. On October 7, thirty thousand supporters of the Russian Revolution converged on New York's Union Square. Other large gatherings followed during November and December in New York, Philadelphia, Chicago, Sioux City, and elsewhere.[25] By far the largest and the best organized of the socialist efforts took place on January 22, 1906, memorializing the first anniversary of Bloody Sunday.

American socialists' conciousness of Bloody Sunday played a more significant role than mere memorials to its victims. In America, one anniversary observation became a spark which provided socialists here with a temporary measure of superficial unity, lessening briefly the endemic animosities and factionalisms that separated socialists from one another.

The spark came out of San Francisco. On November 11, 1905, California socialists led by Anna Strunsky and Jack London addressed a public letter to the International Socialist Bureau in Brussels, calling for a worldwide commemoration of Bloody Sunday. The Bureau responded favorably on December 21, proclaiming January 22, 1906 as a day for demonstrations and the collection of funds to support the revolution. It eulogized the Russian worker and insisted that "moral and material support" was "the imperative duty of all Socialists regardless of race or nationality." In the United States, J. Mahlon Barnes, National Secretary, reacted to the call by issuing a proclamation for the National Executive Committee. Local committees were to make all necessary arrangements, and contributions would be filtered back to the national organization. The Socialist Labor Party also quickly approved the Brussels resolution.

Feverish activity in socialist circles marked the first three weeks of 1906; the entire socialist organization seemed to come alive. Socialist locals selected arrangement committees and voted necessary sums of money to help cover expenses of parades in which they would be participating. Municipal locals, as in the case of Schenectady, called on their state organizations to supply speakers. In New York City, preparations brought more and more participants into the projected demonstration until about one hundred groups of all kinds were involved—Socialist, Socialist Labor, and IWW; federations and societies; ethnic, religious, and benevolent associations of Lithuanians, Finns, Poles, Germans, Italians, Russians; trade-union locals of cigar makers, hat makers, vest makers, bricklayers, carpenters, and joiners.[26]

The parade held in New York on January 22 was a tremendous success. Partisan estimates suggested that thirty-five thousand participated under the auspices of the Party's local. In Chicago, the weather seemed to be in league with the Russian oppressors. A "procession of local Socialists and radical foreign groups marched five miles in slush and snow through the city's grey streets." Marchers sang the "Internationale" and other revolutionary hymns, carried banners, and waved red flags. Later, the Socialist Party of Cook County met at the North Side Turner Hall where Algie M. Simons, Seymour Stedman, and J. Mahlon Barnes addressed a large crowd. Brief talks in Russian and Yiddish were followed by a new declaration of independence against American and Russian capitalism. On the previous day, a Sunday, dozens of smaller rallies were held in and around Chicago. Six hundred German Socialists met at Uhlich's Hall, Trautmann and Simons talked to an IWW gathering at Aurora Hall, and the Bohemian Central Committee held forth at Thalia Hall. Similar sessions took place in Elgin, Waukegan, and Joliet. And the Chicago Socialist leadership looked forward to Jack London's lecture on "Social Revolution" on the following Sunday, January 28, to sustain enthusiasm and to encourage money contributions.

Milwaukee's Scandia Hall hosted the Scandinavian Central Committee on the twenty-second, and a large crowd heard speakers in English and Scandinavian. Cincinnati's IWW, Socialist, and Socialist Labor Parties joined hands long enough for a joint meeting. Other sessions took place in Boston, Bridgeport, Buffalo, Detroit, New Haven, Newark, Philadelphia, Pittsburgh, St. Louis, and San Francisco. Socialists asserted that every American industrial center had participated. They were sure that there had been no more extensive celebration in history so soon after an event than the Bloody Sunday demonstrations of January 22, 1906.[27]

Throughout the year which followed the tragic events of January, 1905, a succession of large and small meetings raised funds in support of the Russian revolution. The national effort was coordinated by a committee composed of Victor Berger, John C. Chase, Eugene V. Debs, Benjamin Hanford, Max Hayes, Morris Hillquit, Alexander Jonas, Algernon Lee, Jack London, Algie Simons, and J. A. Wayland. It was not easy to form the committee. As an example of the difficulties, William Mailly was willing to make a contribution, but refused the use of his name. In Mailly's case, he objected strongly to Wayland's method. Several socialist frontrunners agreed with Mailly. Other leaders, including Max S. Hayes, president of Cleveland's typographical union, were glad to have their names on Hillquit's circular letter, but monetary contributions were another matter. "Here, in Cleveland," Hayes wrote, "we are doing a bit of work through the unions to raise funds for the Russian revolutionists."

Money slowly filtered into different socialist headquarters. Locals and ward groups would donate $25, $100, or whatever the local treasury could sustain. Demonstrations, meetings, lectures, outings, and balls produced varying amounts, from small deficits to several hundred dollars. The money came from numerous and diverse sources—from New York's Executive Committee, from Colorado's Socialist Party, from the Brewers' Union, from German and Austro-Hungarian groups, from the Globe, Arizona local of the Western Federation of Miners, from the Alameda County Socialist Party of California. Contributions continued to flow in all year, from individuals, groups, and socialist locals from California to Connecticut, from Missouri to Montana, from Nebraska to New Jersey.[28] By March, 1905, the Socialist Party's fund for the Russian Social Democratic Society had reached $1,000; by summer it was over $3,000; and by the end of the year it had passed the

$5,000 mark. The January 22, 1906 memorial pushed it over $7,000 and the excitement of the Duma added another $2,000. By the end of 1906, the fund finally reached $12,000, with small sums trickling in during early 1907.

The Socialist Labor Party had its fund, too, with Henry Kuhn serving as national secretary. At one point, Wilshire had his own collection in progress. In larger cities, house-to-house canvasses were common.[29] The real problem was the distribution of the various collections. Different segments of the Russian Social Democratic Party undoubtedly received the bulk of the money raised. But there were many other recipients, perhaps because there were numerous channels of distribution.

New York socialists sent money through the Berlin *Vorwaerts*. Denver's Progressive Circle employed Cahan's New York *Jewish Daily Forward*. Some money went to "Comrade Axelrod" in Switzerland. Separate collections aided the Russian Social Democrats, the Jewish Bund, and the "Finnish Revolutionists." On occasion, instead of money, guns and ammunition reportedly went from America to where they would do the "most good."[30]

Visiting Russian revolutionary leaders provided a vigorous spur in mobilizing opinion and contributions. For example, Max Hayes complained at one point that the collection of funds was "slow work on account of the decreasing excitement." But, he added, "We expect to have Madame Breshkovsky here in about two weeks," and flagging spirits would soon revive. The flow of revolutionary leaders to the United States was not a new phenomenon, but the large number who came beginning in late 1904 was unusual. Generally, there were three kinds of political visitors: representatives of the Bund (the revolutionary organization of Jewish workers in Russia), the Social Revolutionaries, and the Social Democrats.[31] During the early years of the new century, a bond of sympathy had developed between the Bund in Russia and many immigrant Jewish workers in the United States. In 1906, Meyer London quickly "made the work of the Bund his chief interest," and shepherded a number of visiting Bundists from city after city, from one lecture and meeting to another. The most prominent of this group was Gregory Maxim, president of the short-lived Baltic Republic, who came to the United States in the spring of 1906.

More popular and more numerous were the Social Revolutionary visitors. Of this group Catherine Breshkovsky evoked the greatest public response. She enjoyed the advantage of helpful letters of introduction to and from prominent settlement-house workers, including Jane Addams, Helena S. Dudley, and Lillian D. Wald. Ernest Poole wrote a moving and poignant account of her suffering in Russian prisons for *Outlook*. The eruption of Bloody Sunday seemed to validate her accusations against the old regime. As a result, Catherine Breshkovsky spoke to packed houses in Boston, Chicago, New York, and Philadelphia. When she left in April, 1905, she had with her about $10,000 for the Social Revolutionaries. A year later, Nicholas Tschaikowsky made an impressive series of appearances, but his influence was largely confined to regular socialist groups.[32]

Among the third group of visitors, the Social Democrats, the best-known and most controversial was Maxim Gorky. The Gorky vogue in the United States had contributed to the initial American hostility to the old regime, as well as to the many protests against the writer's imprisonment after Bloody Sunday. Announcement a year later of a Gorky tour of the United States was greeted with tremendous enthusiasm. Numerous committees were formed, dinners planned, and lecture tours arranged. His arrival, on April 10, 1906, produced excitement and publicity which rivaled earlier welcomes accorded Kossuth and Garibaldi.

This auspicious effort to win sympathy and financial support was smashed to bits four days after Gorky landed. The *New York World* revealed in a page-one exposé that Gorky's legal wife and child were in Russia and that his traveling companion was the famous actress Maria Andreyeva. Efforts were futile to explain that Gorky had long been separated from his wife, that the Russian Church would not grant a divorce to one beyond the political pale, and that Madame Andreyeva was really his common-law wife.

All nonsocialist activities in honor of Gorky stalled to a halt. Most newspapers and magazines quickly turned against him. But the socialist press unanimously denounced American bourgeois morality. Socialist writers insisted that the *World's* revelations were the result of sinister intercessions by the Russian Embassy combined with the anger on Wall Street deriving from Gorky's telegram of support to the imprisoned Wobblies, Haywood and

Moyer. Probably the *World's* anger with Gorky was capitalist-inspired, for he had contracted with Hearst to write exclusively for the rival New York *Journal.*

The upshot was a reaffirmation of the conclusion that only Revolutionary America would aid Revolutionary Russia.[33] For the ensuing several months, as Gorky spoke at a May Day celebration in New York's Grand Central Palace, lectured at Carnegie Hall, and addressed protest rallies, meetings, and dinners in Boston, Chicago, New York, and Philadelphia, his audiences were limited largely to loyal socialists supplemented by enthusiastic Russians and interested unideological writers. His efforts evoked material support for the Russian Social Democrats, but they also stimulated some domestic interest about American Socialism. Still, this was a far more limited response than had been expected. Hillquit, though sympathetic to the Russians, observed, "Rarely did a man have greater opportunities to advance his cause, and rarely were they so utterly wasted and spoiled."[34]

By the summer of 1906, the interest of the American socialists in the Russian revolution had declined perceptibly. Some locals still urged that mass meetings be called "about the situation in Russia when the occasion arises," but few occasions arose. Matters moved in different channels. A certain ambivalence developed among American socialists. Priorities were blurred between all-out aid to Russia's revolutionaries and victims of oppression, or concentration on domestic wants and opportunities. Some leading socialists, Victor Berger among them, were reluctant to divert too much of their already limited resources to so vast a venture as Russia represented, especially when home demands were so urgent. Here, Progressive reform was in the air. Possibilities were great for improvements, and so were the dangers. For example, at the first meeting of the New York Socialist Party's General Committee after the proclamation of the October Manifesto, not a word was devoted to that milestone. Instead, the basic concern was about the mayoralty election and those comrades who strayed from the fold by voting for Hearst rather than for Algernon Lee. Debs was no exception. His interest was focused on Russian unions and strikes, not on the Manifesto and the Duma.[35]

There were Americans who threw themselves wholeheartedly into the Russian fray. For Jack London, these were the years of his "greatest activity for the socialist movement." John Spargo saw the revolution as the dethronement of the brute-god Mammon and the enthronement of humanity. Emma Goldman passionately wanted the end of Czarism and barbarism. George Herron was doing what he could to help the Russian workers "in their fateful struggle"; Meyer London, at the call of the Bund, "dropped everything, closed his office, bade farewell to his clients and plunged into the work of the Russian revolution." But these were exceptions. Again and again Algernon Lee reminded his friends that the Russian people required arms, ammunition, and "outspoken sympathy backed by material aid," not warnings and counsel. Isador Ladoff repeatedly criticized his fellow socialists for not really having done anything. He accused them of being caught up in local petty politics, personal jealousies, and pharisaic self-admiration so that they had lost sight of socialism as a world movement.[36]

The 1905–1906 Russian revolution contributed more to the growth of the American socialists than the socialists contributed to the revolution. Events in Russia during these two years bolstered domestic party membership. Party leaders tried to attract more radically-oriented labor, as well as interested ethnic and religious groups from eastern Europe. Seek to enlarge the socialist vote, *The Worker* editorialized: "If Russian workingmen are willing to 'throw their lives away' for the cause of freedom, American workers ought to be willing patiently to 'throw their votes away' for a few years more."

Even though the Russian revolution created temporary agreements among American socialists, ironically enough, it also produced centrifugal effects which tended more than ever to polarize the socialists. The result was a growing cleavage between the more dogmatic, organizational, Marxian, proletarian-oriented socialists, and the more humanistic, independent, non-Marxian, progressive-oriented groups. In short, 1905–1906 helped to fix attitudes and animosities which later fragmented the American socialist movement.[37]

If many Americans reacted adversely to the Russian revolutionary forces, many Russians reacted similarly to Progressive America. Leaders of the more radical Russian parties had come to America for money, material, and moral support. Their receptions had not been as enthusiastic or as productive as they had anticipated.

Many of them left disappointed and bitter. They took back with them the hard-set view of American socialists, who had failed to perceive real differences between Czarist Russia and post-Gilded-Age America. Russian visitors picked up the rhetoric of the literary Progressives, but the foreign commentators failed to understand what Ray Stannard Baker stated years later, "We 'muckraked' not because we hated our world but because we loved it. We were not hopeless, we were not cynical, we were not bitter."[38] Thus, the Russian revolution of 1905 not only contributed to the bifurcation of American socialism, but it also witnessed the beginning of the twentieth-century rejection of the United States as the international symbol of revolution.

SAUL BENISON

🙟🙠

The Enigma of Poliomyelitis: 1910

IN 1894, DR. CHARLES S. CAVERLY, the President of the
Vermont State Board of Health, reported an epidemic of poliomyelitis in some of the villages and towns of Otter Creek Valley
in Vermont.[1] This epidemic was not the first visitation of polio-
myclitis in the United States. As early as 1841, Dr. George Colmer, a Southern country doctor, observed sporadic cases of the
disease among children in West Feliciana Parish, Louisiana.[2] In
the half-century that followed, other physicians in various parts of
the country made similar observations.[3] Dr. Caverly, however, was
the first to observe and recognize epidemic poliomyelitis as such
in the nation. Following the Vermont outbreak, other epidemics
were reported. It has been estimated that between 1894 and 1906
seventeen poliomyelitis epidemics of varying degrees of severity
occurred. They seemed to follow no geographic pattern. No one,
of course, could predict where or when the next would occur.[4] In
spite of the increasing frequency of these outbreaks, and the record
of similar epidemics in Europe, neither the public nor physicians
in the United States paid much attention to the disease. Indeed,
in no state during this period was poliomyelitis even made a reportable disease.[5]

In 1907 a poliomyelitis epidemic of uncommon severity struck
the northeastern part of the United States. In Massachusetts the
State Board of Health, which had previously noted sporadic instances of the disease, reported 234 cases of paralysis throughout
the state.[6] In Pennsylvania 343 cases were recorded.[7] The epidemic, however, struck with greatest force at New York City and

228

its immediate suburbs. Here in a little less than a year 2,500 victims of paralysis were reported.[8] The poliomyelitis epidemic of 1907 was the largest outbreak of its kind to that date in the United States. If the epidemic produced a wide variety of melancholy statistics, it by the same token also created an atmosphere which made it difficult to disregard the threat of the disease any longer.

In the fall of 1907 the Massachusetts State Legislature authorized an inquiry into the occurrence of poliomyelitis with special reference to seeking out its cause.[9] In New York City that same autumn the New York Academy of Medicine, together with the New York Neurological Society, recruited a group of medical experts to investigate "the epidemiology, symptomatology, pathology, and treatment of poliomyelitis."[10] Later efforts of two members of this group, Dr. Simon Flexner of the Rockefeller Institute, and Dr. Israel Strauss of the Cornell Medical School, to delineate the pathology of poliomyelitis also marked the first attempts in this country to work experimentally with the disease. These experiments, essentially efforts to cultivate the incitant cause of poliomyelitis on artificial media, unfortunately failed.[11] The setbacks, however, were only temporary.

In October of 1908, during a severe outbreak of poliomyelitis in Vienna, Dr. Karl Landsteiner, then Proscktor at the Wilhelminen Spital, succeeded in passing the disease from a young polio victim to two experimental monkeys.[12] Although Dr. Landsteiner's achievement was an exceptional one, it was only a partial success, for later, when he tried to pass the disease from monkey to monkey, he failed. Other investigators, both in Europe and America, who subsequently attempted to extend Dr. Landsteiner's experiments, also failed.[13] Late in September of 1909, Dr. Simon Flexner, at the Rockefeller Institute, using basically the same techniques developed earlier by Dr. Landsteiner, succeeded. He not only transmitted poliomyelitis from a human being to monkeys, he passed the disease from monkey to monkey as well.[14] The importance of Dr. Flexner's exploit cannot be overemphasized, for in extending Dr. Landsteiner's findings he was able to establish what physicians had long suspected but could never prove, namely, that poliomyelitis was an infectious disease.

Immediately following this success Dr. Flexner devised a new series of experiments to learn more about the nature of poliomyelitis in laboratory animals. In a period of little more than a month he learned a number of new things about poliomyelitis. First, he discovered that the technique he used in inoculating his experimental monkeys was not actually necessary for passing the disease from animal to animal as he previously thought. Thus, no matter how he transmitted poliomyelitis to his animals, whether through intracerebral inoculation or intraperitoneal inoculation, or by inoculation into the sheath of the sciatic nerve, he found that the disease invariably established itself in the spinal cord and medulla of its victim. Further, he discovered that although the monkey was naturally refractory to poliomyelitis, the disease, once induced, was far more severe than in man.[15] His most notable achievement at this time was his ability to establish that poliomyelitis was not caused by a bacterium or a protozoan, as many bacteriologists then believed, but rather that the disease was caused by a virus.[16]

So rapid was the pace of poliomyelitis research in the autumn and winter of 1909 that Dr. Flexner's findings were independently and almost simultaneously discovered in a number of laboratories in Europe.[17] To many these successes presaged a rapid solution to the problem of poliomyelitis. Few examined closely the vast terra incognita that Dr. Landsteiner's and Dr. Flexner's research had actually opened. In 1909 no one knew what a virus was, save that it was ultramicroscopic and passed through all filters then used in laboratories. The nature of the specific virus that caused poliomyelitis was an even greater mystery. Many questions remained to be answered. Could it be cultivated in the laboratory? Could it withstand heat or cold? What was its incubation period? How was it transmitted? Could it be transmitted to other laboratory animals besides monkeys? Was it contagious? What were the forms of its immunity? How many types existed? In spite of these and other unknowns, the year 1909 ended on a promising note. Research had created an environment of hope. But even in this environment, the true dimensions of the poliomyelitis problem were not immediately perceived.

The success of Dr. Landsteiner's and Dr. Flexner's polio investigations in 1909 not only relieved some of the growing public fears of polio, it also served to bolster public confidence in medical research. In 1909 not everyone in the United States thought well of medical research. Indeed, from the turn of the twentieth century, organized groups of antivivisectionists continually agitated for legislation to deny the right of scientists to engage in animal experimentation. Although distinguished physicians and researchers such as William H. Welch, William W. Keen, and Walter B. Cannon succeeded from time to time in persuading various legislative committees to discard suggested antivivisection bills, their victories were ephemeral.[18] With every advance of experimental medicine, antivivisectionist harassment of medical researchers increased. During the spring and summer of 1910, Dr. Flexner took the opportunity on more than one occasion to remind the public of the importance of animal experimentation in the fight against polio. "The disease has a curious history," he told an audience at the annual meeting of the Medical Society of the State of New York on July 8, 1910.

Its appearance has been very mysterious in the past and it has usually had its own way. Now, it is to be hoped that we have entered upon an era of knowledge respecting the disease; and it is well to emphasize here in this city, the capital of the State, where the lawmakers of the State assemble every year, that whatever knowledge we have now secured and are promised in future grows out of the fact that animals have been used for experimental purposes for the benefit of the human race in the investigation of this disease.[19]

Dr. Flexner's defense of animal experimentation was not a pose taken in deference to an issue of great moment to medical research. It was, on the contrary, a deeply felt expression of faith which he reiterated time and again both publicly and privately. When Dr. Constantin Levaditi early in 1910 sent him articles embodying the results of the polio research carried on under the auspices of the Pasteur Institute in Paris, Dr. Flexner exuberantly replied, ". . . I am greatly interested in your work with Landsteiner on poliomyelitis and await eagerly your new developments. Is it not splendid that this terrible disease promises to yield to the experimental method of study?"[20]

There was ample reason for Dr. Flexner's enthusiasm. In spite of the fact that his laboratory at the beginning of 1910 was one of three[21] in the United States engaged in experimental polio research, in the weeks following his initial discoveries it seemed that he had but to ask a question in order to find new features of the nature and activity of polio virus. On January 1, 1910, Dr. Flexner reported that experiments that he had designed to test the resistance of polio virus to cold and drying showed virus which had been kept constantly frozen at from — 2°C. to — 4°C. for a period of forty days, and at +4°C. for a period of fifty days had retained its virulence. Similarly he discovered that polio virus suspended in a desiccator over caustic potash for seven days retained its virulence as well. These findings not only attested to the hardiness of the newly discovered virus, they also broke down any notion that the reduction in the number of polio cases with the onset of cold weather reflected actual destruction of the virus. In another series of experiments carried on simultaneously, Dr. Flexner also succeeded in establishing that if monkeys recovered from an attack of polio they could resist experimentally induced infections —an early experimental indication that an attack of polio might afford subsequent immunity.[22]

Unfortunately, not all of Dr. Flexner's wide-ranging investigations ended in discovery. A number, including his attempts to cultivate polio virus on artificial media, and to transmit polio to animals other than monkeys, failed. But these setbacks were not particularly disheartening. Other bacteriologists had long encountered difficulties in cultivating certain varieties of protozoa on artificial media.[23] While it is true that the failure to transmit polio to laboratory animals other than monkeys initially restricted the number of laboratories engaged in polio research, that failure did not hamper Dr. Flexner in his investigations. The Rockefeller Institute, which he directed, was one of the few institutions at that time in the United States which could afford to foster research which depended on such an expensive experimental animal. In another place, faced by the need for monkeys, Dr. Flexner's research might well have come to a stop; at the Institute it continued, its momentum undisturbed.

During the spring of 1910 Dr. Flexner reported still another series of rich new findings. In one experiment he discovered that if he removed the cerebrospinal fluid of a monkey 24 to 48 hours after an experimental infection, it contained enough distinct features to differentiate it from the cerebrospinal fluid of a monkey removed after the onset of paralysis.[24] The discovery was not only an important addition to the then existing pathological knowledge of polio, it had an immediate practical application as well. In effect it provided physicians with a diagnostic tool with which to distinguish between polio and other infections that presented similar clinical symptoms. Also it was a technique to discover inapparent or abortive cases of polio.[25]

In another experiment Dr. Flexner found that if he excised the nasal mucosa of an experimentally infected monkey, ground it, and passed it through a filter, he could with such an emulsion later bring down another monkey with polio, thereby proving that the nasal mucous membrane contained polio virus.[26] This discovery had a stunning import because it suggested that the portal of entry and elimination of polio virus in human infection was through the nose and that it therefore might be possible to control poliomyelitis by disinfecting the buccal and nasal discharges of polio victims. To many it appeared that Dr. Flexner had taken a major step toward solving the problem of the transmission of polio.[27]

So heartening was the early process of discovery that Dr. Flexner, in reviewing the various worldwide contributions of experimental to human poliomyelitis, told the Association of American Physicians in May of 1910 that so many important facts about the nature of polio virus and the spontaneous disease in man had been discovered that it was possible to say that a basis had been established "on which to develop measures of prevention and on which to build hopes for the working out of a specific method of treatment."[28] Yet even as Dr. Flexner announced his discoveries and voiced his hopes, disquieting evidence of a new rapid proliferation of poliomyelitis in the United States began to accumulate, overshadowing the substantive contributions which had been made in the laboratory to an understanding of the nature and activity of polio virus.

On March 10, 1910, Dr. Jocelyn Manning, who had made one of the early epidemiological studies of the polio outbreak in Wisconsin in 1908,[29] wrote to Dr. Flexner:

Do you not consider that anterior poliomyelitis is now prevalent throughout the country? I have requests for reprints (of my articles) from Oregon, Arizona, the East, and all points in the Middle West. Is it not true that the high mortality rate and the still higher percentage of permanent disabilities among children and adults is as sad a menace as that of those more dramatic infections which stand in the limelight?[30]

There was much substance to Dr. Manning's observations. Reports from various state boards of health revealed that in 1909 approximately 4,000 new cases of poliomyelitis had occurred in the United States, a figure well over twice the number of cases officially noted in 1908.[31] Nor was this the only alarming statistic. Equally troubling and bewildering, to physicians and public health officials, were the wide fluctuations of the incidence of the disease in states that had previously passed through an epidemic. Massachusetts, which had reported 136 cases in 1908, announced a new high of 923 cases in 1909.[32] New York, which had escaped an epidemic in 1908, reported approximately 175 cases in a series of outbreaks in such widely dispersed places as Brooklyn, Poughkeepsie, and Ogdensburg.[33] Minnesota, which had noted 160 polio victims in 1908, reported approximately 1,100 new cases at the end of 1909.[34] This widely fluctuating incidence of cases was not solely restricted to states which had previously passed through epidemics, there were equally sharp differences among some of the newly affected states as well. While some states like Maryland, Kansas, North Dakota, Montana, Oregon, and California noted an incidence ranging from "a few patients" to 100 cases, other states, like Nebraska, reported over 1,000 cases.[35]

Although poliomyelitis cut a wide swath across the American landscape in 1909, many public health officials comforted themselves with the assumption that this disease had only a local significance. Still, to those who looked, there was not only evidence that it was rapidly becoming a national problem, there were indications that it might become a continental problem as well. In 1909 both Cuba[36] and Canada reported sharp outbreaks of the disease. In Canada the appearance of poliomyelitis caused so much public apprehension in the western provinces that Canadian political authorities directed Dr. Charles T. Hodgetts, the medical adviser of the Commission on Conservation, to conduct a full-scale investigation of the disease.[37]

The polio epidemics which began in 1909 continued unabated throughout 1910. In August, 1911, Dr. Robert Lovett of the Harvard University Medical School informed readers of the *American*

Journal of Diseases of Children that the reported incidence of poliomyelitis in the United States in the year that had passed had risen to a new high of 8,700 cases. Of these, 1,459 had died—a figure almost three times the number of deaths due to poliomyelistic reported in 1909.[38] Even more ominous was the proliferation of the disease. Whereas in 1909 only 14 states reported cases of poliomyelitis, the following year 36 states noted its existence within their borders. In incidence and geographical distribution there could no longer be any doubt that poliomyelitis had become a national problem.[39]

In the process a new dimension was added to the struggle against the disease. No longer was poliomyelitis a disease which primarily engaged the interest and attention of a relatively small number of medical researchers and public health officials, its rapid proliferation had now made it the concern of medical practitioners throughout the country. Their training, their knowledge of the disease, their ability to make diagnosis, became immediate and overriding factors in the struggle against polio.

In 1910 the American physician did not inspire confidence. He simply was poorly educated. Although it is true that from the end of the nineteenth century increasing numbers of American physicians supplemented their education in European medical schools and hospitals, and while it is equally true that a number of medical schools in the United States during this same period were engaged in raising standards for medical education and practice, the norm of American medical education was shoddy. In 1910, Dr. Abraham Flexner, in a report for the Carnegie Foundation, bluntly informed the nation that from 1885 medical schools in the United States, in absolute disregard of public welfare, had engaged in an enormous overproduction of ill-educated and ill-trained physicians. He told his contemporaries:

Society reaps at this moment but a small fraction of the advantage which current knowledge has the power to confer. That sick man is relatively rare for whom all is done that is humanly feasible, as feasible in the small hamlet as in the large city, in the public hospital as in the private sanatorium. We have indeed in America medical practitioners not inferior to the best elsewhere, but there is probably no other country in the world in which there is so great a distance between the best, the average and the worst.[40]

Perhaps the best measure of the enormities and deficiencies that Dr. Flexner discovered in American medical education in 1910 was his suggestion that 120 out of 155 medical schools then operating in the United States either be closed or consolidated with stronger institutions.[41]

The Flexner report was not the first to suggest the necessity of a reform of American medical education. During the first decade of the twentieth century the American Medical Association, through its Council on Education, prepared similar reports.[42] In one sense, therefore, the Flexner report was part and parcel of a broad ongoing campaign of medical reform. It differed from reports that had gone before by virtue of the fact that it was prepared by a layman for the general public, and hence was not marred by the necessity of salving professional pride. As a critique, the Flexner report was savage. Yet in spirit, its analysis of existing medical school assets and liabilities was closer to a report by Dun and Bradstreet than to a muckraker's polemics. A generation that had difficulties in dealing with problems of good and evil, even when instructed and cajoled by such critics as Lincoln Steffens, Jacob Riis, and Upton Sinclair, might have had trouble taking the first steps to reform if Abraham Flexner had defined the problems of medical education simply in moral terms. Bankruptcy, on the other hand, was a fact whose consequences everyone understood. In the decade that followed the publication of the Flexner report 75 medical schools closed their doors, while the remainder made extensive reforms of curricula, staff, and facilities.[43] It must be remembered that the American physician called upon to minister to polio patients in 1910 was largely educated and trained in a medical school of the sort that Abraham Flexner either helped to destroy or to reform. His behavior toward such patients varied in considerable degree.

It must be said at the outset that many physicians were solicitous of, and devoted to, the needs of their polio patients, and made special efforts to bring to bear the best of existing medical techniques in coping with the disease. One such physician was Dr. George P. Shidler of York, Nebraska. Early in 1910, writing of his experiences in treating patients during the polio epidemics in eastern Nebraska the previous autumn, he observed:

I might say that all treatment from any standpoint was unavailable. Every form was tried—allopath, homeopath, eclectic, osteopath, Ridpath, and cowpath. About the only thing I really found of any moment was lumbar puncture for the excruciating pain in the back which only morphine in large doses succeeded in allaying. At first I thought the fluid pressure might have some influence on motor paralysis by pressure but after sufficient trials I had to desert that. . . . The little bacteriological work that I performed, and I blush to think that I did not make more of an effort to have some capable man sent here, was done at the bedside. I would take my scope, hand centrifuge, stains, and slides right with me. I regret that I did not try cultures. Next year I shall do this. . . .[44]

Dr. Shidler's concern for his patients did not end at the bedside. Following the epidemic he privately undertook an epidemiological analysis of the outbreak in York, Nebraska, and later published the results of his inquiry in the *Journal of the American Medical Association.* His report was among the first in the United States to point to personal contact as a key factor in the dissemination of poliomyelitis.[45]

On September 24, 1910, Dr. Michael Hoke, a young surgeon in Atlanta, Georgia, wrote to Dr. Simon Flexner at the Rockefeller Institute:

There are more cases of infantile paralysis in this state of recent occurrence than formerly. I want you to let me know if there are any facts upon which it can be decided how long these patients should be isolated after the acute symptoms have passed. They are beginning to come in here to me from the surrounding towns and states for orthopedic attention. I would like to have some standard lapse of time from the beginning of the disease to the beginning of treatment at which time all liability of conveying the disease will have passed.[46]

Dr. Hoke's concern for polio victims as well as the health of his other patients and neighbors was not a temporary one. A quarter of a century later, the interest of this orthopedic surgeon in problems of poliomyelitis led to an appointment as medical director at Georgia Warm Springs, where he helped established standards of care and treatment of polio patients that made that institution one of the most preeminent in the nation.[47]

Unfortunately, not all physicians were cast in the mold of Dr.

Shidler or Dr. Hoke. All too often requests for help and advice carried inflections that were alien to the spirit of the Hippocratic oath. When poliomyelitis appeared in Wisconsin in the autumn of 1910 a physician from Lake Geneva queried Dr. Flexner:

Have you arrived at any conclusion in regard to the length of time after a child has had poliomyelitis anterior that the disease can be transmitted? The possibility has come up of a patient coming to me, a child of two years, having had an attack four weeks ago, leaving paralysis of one leg. I should not attempt the care of him if there was any possibility of the disease being communicated.

It is not known whether Dr. Flexner's assurances that no physician to his knowledge ever contracted the disease from his patients allayed the fears of this particular practitioner. What is important is the fact that the fear existed.[48] If it revealed a defect in character it should be kept in mind that it was a defect that was nurtured by a poor professional education and, above all, a lack of knowledge of poliomyelitis as a disease. In truth, the latter was a bond that linked the majority of physicians in the United States in 1910—the well educated and the poorly educated, the brave and the cowardly.

In one sense it is a paradox to speak of a lack of knowledge of poliomyelitis in 1910. From 1890, well over 1,500 articles appeared in various medical journals in Europe and the United States which added substantially to new existing clinical, epidemiological, and experimental knowledge of poliomyelitis. Unfortunately, because of a variety of circumstances, much of this literature did not prove to be as useful to the general practitioner in the United States as it might have been. For example, much of the important work on poliomyelitis by such European authorities as Otto Medin, Ivar Wickman, Francis Harbitz, Olaf Scheel, Karl Landsteiner, Paul Römer, and Constantin Levaditi, although widely published in European medical periodicals, remained unavailable to a majority of monolingual American physicians by virtue of the fact that it was published in either French or German.[49] This linguistic difficulty was well understood by contemporary medical leaders in the United States. Following the epidemics of 1909 special efforts were made by such people as Bernard Sachs and Simon Flexner to obtain the translation of the most significant European literature on poliomyelitis.[50] It wasn't until 1913, however, that an English edition of Paul Römer's useful textbook on poliomyelitis was prepared for American physicians, and an edited translation of Ivar Wickman's classic work on epidemic poliomyelitis was published as a special monograph of the *Journal of Nervous and Mental Diseases*.[51] Many articles published in medical periodicals in the United States, like their European counterparts, also remained unavailable to the general practitioner. Some, because they appeared in journals of local medical societies and state health departments, which had a limited circulation; and others because they appeared in periodicals like the *Journal of Experimental Medicine*, which at that time had a very limited appeal.

In 1910 the general practitioner in large measure depended on medical textbooks for his information about poliomyelitis, and these unfortunately contained insufficient data on the disease. There were reasons for this deficiency. First, poliomyelitis in epidemic form was a relatively new phenomenon in the United States in 1910 and had at that time only recently captured the attention of general medical practitioners and medical teachers. Second, and perhaps more important, the results of the latest European and American medical research on poliomyelitis which was available in various medical journals had not yet been thoroughly integrated into textbook analyses. The latter phenomenon was not merely a condition of ordinary or run-of-the-mill textbooks, it was characteristic of excellent textbooks as well. Sir William Osler's *The Principles and Practice of Medicine*, one of the leading medical textbooks in the United States, devoted but four pages to poliomyelitis in its 7th edition, which appeared in 1910. Of these, approximately half a page was devoted to definition and etiology, half a page to diagnosis and prognosis, a page and a half to morbid anatomy and symptomatology, a page to treatment and a half-page to the appearance of the disease in adults.

The general character of Dr. Osler's treatment of poliomyelitis is perhaps best revealed by a portion of his discussion of etiology.

The cause is unknown. It has been attributed to cold, overexertion, and to falls. From the days of Mephibosheth infantile paralysis has been attributed to the carelessness of nurses in letting children fall. In young persons overexertion may have an influence. I saw one case which followed unusual effort in a football match. In the recent epidemics the bacteriology of the disease has been studied, but without definite results.[52]

Many physicians, when faced with poliomyelitis in 1910, complained bitterly over the lack of adequate information about the disease in their textbooks. "We are having an epidemic of acute poliomyelitis here in Hamilton [Ontario] and your reprints are a great source of pleasure to me," Dr. Theodore Coleman, a general practitioner, wrote to Dr. Flexner on August 1, 1910. "In your opinion I would gather that Landry's multiple and anterior polio are all gathered under acute poliomyelitis. We have at present 40 or 50 cases here to about 60,000 to 70,000 people. The clinical picture in the authorities, Hall, etc. are in my worthy opinion very rotten."[53] An editorial in the September, 1910, issue of the Bulletin of the Illinois State Board of Health, discussing the crisis of information on poliomyelitis, slyly suggested, ". . . someone has said that the textbooks on Acute Poliomyelitis written before 1907 should be burned."[54]

Such criticisms about the quality of textbook literature on poliomyelitis were by no means unique; other practitioners voiced similar complaints. The nub of their complaints was perhaps best expressed by the pediatrician Harry M. McClanahan of Omaha, Nebraska, in an address to a special symposium on poliomyelitis organized by the Nebraska Medical Association in May of 1910:

My conception of poliomyelitis previous to the New York epidemic was so at variance with the facts as determined by reading and clinical experience, that a review of the facts in view of our increased knowledge is necessary to a right understanding of the disease. Personal interviews with many physicians in the state have convinced me that they, like myself, did not appreciate its nature. During all my professional life I have seen occasional cases of infantile paralysis, frequently the true nature not being recognized until paralysis appeared, but until the epidemic of 1909, I had never seen a fatal case. . . . The articles in our standard textbooks certainly give us no description of the disease as it has occurred to us in actual practice.[55]

Those physicians in 1910 who knew of Simon Flexner's experimental work on polio turned to him for information about the nature of the disease. "A polio epidemic has just begun in Carthage, South Dakota," Dr. Ulysses Moore, a general practitioner, wrote Dr. Flexner on August 9, 1910. "If you have a monograph on its cause and treatment I should be pleased to receive same."[56] Although many requests to Dr. Flexner for information and advice came from physicians in the hinterlands of the Midwest and South, such requests were by no means restricted to physicians in these areas.[57] When poliomyelitis appeared in Bridgeport and New Haven, Connecticut, during the late summer of 1910, Dr. Virgil Gibney, director of the orthopedic service at the Hospital for the Ruptured and Crippled in New York, then on vacation, made a special trip to the Rockefeller Institute to learn from Dr. Flexner the latest information about poliomyelitis.[58]

Public health officials, long in the forefront in the struggle against epidemic disease, petitioned Dr. Flexner for information as well. On September 18, 1910, Dr. Herbert W. Conn, director of the laboratories of the Connecticut State Department of Health and one of the founders of the Society of American Bacteriologists, addressed the following note to Dr. Flexner:

I am writing to ask you if you will put me in the way of getting all possible information concerning present knowledge of infantile paralysis. . . . The disease has appeared here and I am constantly being asked for information. I know something of your work on the matter, and have hope that you can give me any papers that you may have published, or tell me where they can be found, and that you will also be kind enough to refer me to publications that will give me as full a knowledge on the subject as possible. I shall greatly appreciate any assistance that you will give me towards getting myself properly posted in regard to the disease.[59]

Given this lack of knowledge of poliomyelitis, it is important to ask whether physicians were capable of making a diagnosis of the disease—that basic skill that all practitioners need if they rationally hope to prevent or cure anything.

In 1910, and indeed for a good many years thereafter, patients could not count on physicians making a correct diagnosis of poliomyelitis. There were, to be sure, a number of physicians who had no difficulty in making such a diagnosis. When a polio epidemic occurred in the vicinity of Lake Placid in the summer of 1910, Dr. Malcolm Goodridge, the professor of therapeutics at the Cornell University Medical School, and Dr. Theodore Janeway, the professor of medicine at the College of Physicians and Surgeons at Columbia University, made the diagnosis of their polio patients swiftly and surely. Their major problem, it later turned out, was not in making a diagnosis but in establishing a focus of the epidemic and learning of the period of incubation of polio virus so that they could institute a reasonable period of isolation for their patients.[60] Dr. Paul Adin Lewis, Dr. Simon Flexner's assistant at the Rockefeller Institute, was so adept in making diagnosis of polio that when an epidemic broke out in Bethlehem, Pennsylvania, in 1910, the Rockefeller Institute sent him to that city to aid local physicians in making diagnosis, particularly of abortive cases.[61] Dr. Haven Emerson, then at the outset of his distinguished career in public health, was particularly sought out by physicians in the Metropolitan area of New York for his ability to diagnose polio.[62] There were others. The vast majority of physicians, however, had no such skills, and many were only too painfully aware of their inadequacy in this respect. The difficulties they faced were perhaps best expressed by Dr. W. B. Hambidge in a letter to Dr. Simon Flexner on the occasion of a strange outbreak in Ogdensburg, New York, in the autumn of 1909.

DEAR DR. FLEXNER,

I hope you will pardon me writing you, but I know that you are interested in anything relating to medicine.

I have recently seen three fatal cases—death occurring on the 3rd or 4th day—that present a clinical picture that I have never seen before, and I may say that other physicians who have seen them express that same opinion. I have also heard of a few more cases in our county [St. Lawrence]. One child was four, another about two and a half years, the third nine. First day there was fever but no chill and children not very sick, second day temperature about 104, pulse rapid, and facial appearance of profound toxaemia. Respiration accentuated, dullness and diminished breathing over one lobe of lung. The characteristic symptom was a rattling in larynx and accumulation of white stringy mucous in throat and no cough or effort to clear throat. The two younger children died on the 4th day with some motor paralysis. The nine-year-old child on the third day with convulsions. They suffer little or no pain, but were restless, nothing abnormal about pupils or reflexes, no retraction of head.

In the four-year-old child there may have been some paralysis of palate as the mother said the night she died, although she was not comatose she did not swallow and liquids came out of the nose. Please don't think there was diphtheria because the throat did not seem inflamed even. I fear I have not given you a vivid clinical picture, but if you could see those children, not comatose, with a profound secretion of mucous in throat and no effort to expel it, facies profoundly toxic, you would not soon forget it. The second and third cases I recognized at once when I entered the sick room as being of the same nature. Of course I know the textbooks describe cerebral pneumonia but I have failed to notice the throat symptoms in any of the literature at my disposal. One physician for whose opinion I have great respect believes it to be a new infection and that the lung changes are secondary and is an oedema. At death of first child I supposed I had a severe pneumococcus infection, but three deaths in quick succession and hearing of a few other cases has caused me to doubt my diagnosis. Any information you can give me will be much appreciated.

P.S. Since writing the above I have heard of several more deaths throughout the county. We are having in Northern New York quite a number of cases of anterior poliomyelitis. Is it that infection causing lesions in the basal ganglia?[63]

In reply Dr. Flexner told Dr. Hambidge that he had no doubt that the patients he saw had poliomyelitis.

The cases you describe are probably the type in which the lesions are in the medulla and brain rather than in the spinal cord. I am very interested in the disease and am studying it at present at the Rockefeller Institute. Its cause and mode of prevention are unknown and no specific treatment is known for it. If you could get permission to do an autopsy on a fatal case I would be willing to come and do it. There would be no fee charged and I would pay even the railroad fares. In this way the diagnosis could be established and you could help me in investigating the disease with a view to ascertaining its cause and mode of prevention.[64]

Not all difficulties in diagnosis occurred because of a lack of information about poliomyelitis. Some physicians, even those who were well informed, had difficulties because the early symptoms of polio, before the onset of paralysis, often simulated the symptoms of other diseases and in particular those of cerebrospinal meningitis. The difficulty in differentiating these two infections was a medical problem of long standing. In 1907, when Dr. Ivar Wickman published his classical monograph on poliomyelitis, *Beitrage zur Kenntnis der Heine–Medinschen Krankheit*, he took particu-

lar pains to point out that in the early stages of an attack of polio
it was frequently necessary for the physician to distinguish between meningitis and poliomyelitis.

The signs of meningeal irritation which can often be observed in
Heine–Medin's Disease [poliomyelitis] may under certain conditions
attain such prominence as convincingly to resemble some form of
meningitis. Vomiting, headache, pain and rigidity in the neck and
back, opisthotonus, Kernig's sign, tonic and clonic spasms, strabismus,
coma etc., all the symptoms of an acute meningitis in all degrees and
in all possible combinations may be added to the picture of the disease. Only in the chronic stage does the course differ from that of a
meningitis.[65]

Many early American commentators made a special point of including these particular observations of Dr. Wickman's in their
discussions of the symptomatology of poliomyelitis.[66] In spite of
the availability of such information, physicians continued to con-
fuse the two infections. The experience of Dr. Henry Elsner of
Syracuse, New York, is a case in point.

During the late summer of 1909 an epidemic of poliomyelitis
broke out in Syracuse, New York. In the beginning, the real nature of the epidemic was unknown. Indeed, a number of local
physicians were so confused by the varied symptoms presented by
their patients that they called on Henry Elsner, known locally
for his clinical ability, to help them diagnose in such cases. Although Dr. Elsner suspected that some of the patients he saw
might have poliomyelitis, the symptoms he observed caused enough
doubt in his mind for him to send on the case histories to Dr.
Simon Flexner at the Rockefeller Institute for further diagnosis:

The behavior of the cases is peculiar. The very severe lumbar and
cervical pains during the early stage of the disease, their relief with the
onset of paralysis and the return of severe pains on the sixth or seventh
day in many cases argues in favor of more or less invasion of the meninges. Would not the clinical history justify the diagnosis of meningo-
myelitis with greater involvement of the anterior horns rather than
simple uncomplicated poliomyelitis. This is the point upon which I
seek information from you at the present time.[67]

Dr. Flexner had no doubts. He replied:

I wish to draw your attention to the fact that it is not an uncommon
history for the cases of anterior poliomyelitis to be mistaken in the

first period for meningitis, on account of the striking symptoms referable to the meninges that sometimes overshadow the more characteristic symptoms due to poliomyelitis. The explanation for this is found in the fact that the meninges of fatal cases not infrequently show considerable cellular invasions, particularly about the blood vessels. I take it that Dr. Todd's patient belongs in this class and hardly justifies the diagnosis of meningo-myelitis more than many cases of poliomyelitis generally speaking.[68]

Dr. Elsner's confusions were not unique. Time and time again, general practitioners, as well as public health officials, were similarly perplexed. Early in September of 1910, Dr. C. F. Williams, the secretary of the South Carolina State Board of Health, petitioned the Rockefeller Institute for antimeningitis serum to help combat an incipient epidemic in Columbia, South Carolina. Some weeks later when Dr. Flexner inquired as to the condition of the patients who had received the antiserum, Dr. Williams sheepishly admitted that the antiserum was not used because subsequent examination revealed that one of the patients, suspected of having meningitis, actually had a meningeal form of infantile paralysis. "We have had two other cases of meningitis reported," Dr. Williams told Dr. Flexner, "but both like Dr. Watson's case proved to be poliomyelitis."[69]

Logically, in 1909 and in 1910, physicians should have had little difficulty in distinguishing between poliomyelitis and cerebrospinal meningitis. By 1909 it was common knowledge that a diagnosis of meningitis could be established by a laboratory determination of the existence of diplococcus intercellularis in the cerebrospinal fluid of suspected patients.[70] By the spring of 1910, Dr. Flexner, as previously pointed out, had established a series of new signs in the cerebrospinal fluid of polio infected patients which could further help differentiate poliomyelitis from meningitis.[71] The laboratory techniques to establish either diagnosis certainly existed by 1910. The difficulty that physicians had in differentiating the two infections was, however, less a demonstration of a lack of bacteriological knowledge among general practitioners than an indication that bacteriological and other procedures which might have been helpful in making a diagnosis of polio were either not used, or infrequently used, in daily medical practice in 1910.

The reasons were various. Some physicians were afraid to do lumbar punctures. Others either did not have the laboratory facilities to do a bacteriological examination of cerebrospinal fluid or did not know how to make such an analysis. "The lumbar puncture would be fine," Dr. Theodore Coleman told Dr. Flexner at the onset of the polio epidemic in Hamilton, Ontario, in 1910. "But with no facilities and perhaps no one who could tell the difference between a lymphocyte and a polymorphoneuclear leucocyte it makes it look like cruelty to the kid."[72] In the autumn of 1910, Dr. C. I. Redfield, a physician in Middletown, New York, resolved a personal dilemma in bacteriological analysis by sending the spinal fluid of a suspected case of poliomyelitis directly to the Rockefeller Institute. "My provisional diagnosis has been sporadic meningitis due to injury," he wrote. "Kindly examine the fluid and let me know at the earliest possible date what are the findings."[73]

Many physicians followed in Dr. Redfield's footsteps. The reason is not hard to find. It is written in a complaint made by Dr. Henry Powers at the beginning of the 1910 polio epidemic in Spokane, Washington.

The position in the community in respect to the cases of the disease in question is unchanged. There are undoubtedly some cases of Anterior Poliomyelitis present, and in so far as clinical diagnosis goes some cases of acute cerebral spinal meningitis, but the greater part of local MDs do not deal in bacteriological examinations and the two recent cases I have seen show no typical cocci.[74]

Throughout the epidemic summer of 1910, Dr. Flexner sought to persuade physicians of the necessity of doing lumbar punctures and examinations of the cerebrospinal fluid as a way of establishing a positive diagnosis of poliomyelitis before the onset of paralysis.[75] In spite of Dr. Flexner's persistence and zeal, many physicians remained unconvinced. Some even began to attack his views publicly. One such opponent was Dr. Edward Mayer, a highly respected general practitioner in Pittsburgh, Pennsylvania. The basis of his opposition is to be found in a letter he addressed to the *Journal of the American Medical Association* on September 24, 1910.

"Until we have a definite serum to use," he wrote, "I see no value in determining by examination of the cerebrospinal fluid the presence of a slight lymphocytosis, especially since if done before paralysis has occurred, it may be blamed by the relatives for the succeeding paralysis." In truth, Dr. Mayer was not convinced that Dr. Flexner's description of the altered nature of the cerebrospinal fluid before the onset of paralysis was a useful diagnostic sign.

Is this slight lymphocytosis with subsequent clearing of the fluid and constant increase of polymorphonuclear leucocytes characteristic of poliomyelitis only? I cannot see in what way it makes the diagnosis any more definite than excessive perspiration, the irregular tremor, the irritability and extreme prostration, the frequent urine suppression, etc., which mark the disease before paralysis. . . . Without any basis for my belief except personal convictions, I do not believe even an innocuous procedure as lumbar puncture advisable in these extremely prostrated subjects with their infiltrative edema and hemorrhage of the cord and meninges.[76]

There can be little doubt that Dr. Mayer's letter voiced many of the uncertainties that other physicians felt about doing lumbar puncture for diagnosing poliomyelitis. Dr. George H. Simmons, then the editor of the *Journal of the American Association,* deemed an answer to Dr. Mayer's letter so vital that he sent it to Dr. Flexner for immediate reply.[77] It is noteworthy that Dr. Flexner took great pains to answer both Dr. Mayer's direct and implied questions.

I do not believe that it is necessary or desirable to defer employing lumbar puncture until a specific form of treatment is discovered. It would seem necessary merely to recall the great value of lumbar puncture as an aid to diagnosis of tubercular and some other forms of meningitis for which there is at present no specific remedy to justify the employment of the procedure.

Although Dr. Flexner agreed with Dr. Mayer that it was necessary to exercise caution so that a misunderstanding did not arise in which a family might attribute the development of paralysis to lumbar puncture, he pointed out that the implied fear that lumbar puncture might be abused in the hands of the unskilled or inexperienced practitioner was not warranted. He continued:

Our experience with antimengingitis serum leads me to think that it will rarely happen that those unskilled or inexperienced will undertake to employ the puncture. . . . It should furthermore be noted that in

order to arrive at a diagnosis by this means laboratory knowledge is
required, since the fluid secured must be submitted to microscopical
and chemical examination, a fact which, in itself, introduces a limitation that would tend also to confine the method to the skillful.[78]

The heart of Dr. Flexner's rejoinder lay in his explicit reasons
for recommending lumbar puncture, for it was here that he basically differed with Dr. Mayer. The latter as a general practitioner
was unwilling to use a procedure that in any way might discomfit
his patient or jeopardize his relation with the patient or his family.[79] Dr. Flexner, although interested in the individual patient,
had none of the immediate concerns of the practitioner. As a
pathologist engaged in research, his immediate problem was to
understand the nature of the disease process. The medical issues
which engaged his attention were not those of the individual patient but those of preventive medicine. He told Dr. Mayer:

We are still very ignorant of the real extent of the epidemics of poliomyelitis and are, therefore, prevented from exercising due caution in
limiting its spread. We need especially to learn the frequency with
which cases of poliomyelitis that do not develop paralysis occur, and
what the leading symptoms are in these instances, since the so-called
abortive cases may be found to be the insidious means of the transmission of the infection. I am of the opinion that lumbar puncture
provides the one clinical method at present known for clearing up the
diagnosis of atypical cases of poliomyelitis or for determining the nature of the typical affection prior to the appearance of paralysis.[80]

Dr. Flexner's exchange with Dr. Mayer was not without result.
In the weeks and months that followed, physicians, as well as hospitals, increasingly began to examine the cerebrospinal fluid as a
way of diagnosing suspected cases of poliomyelitis. On March 4,
1911, Dr. Lewis Frissell, a young instructor in medicine at College
of Physicians and Surgeons at Columbia University, published a
case history in the *Journal of the American Medical Association* in
which lumbar puncture was successfully used to diagnose a case of
preparalytic poliomyelitis. Dr. Frissell's case history was not only
important in itself, it had another import as well. Dr. Flexner's
observations on the usefulness of lumbar puncture in diagnosing
cases of preparalytic polio were based on experimental evidence
supplied by monkeys. Dr. Frissell's report was the first in which

the corresponding reactions had been found in a human case of poliomyelitis.[81]

Dr. Flexner was not the only one in 1910 who sought to instruct physicians in the United States about the nature of polio. Nor was the educative process solely rooted in the laboratory. Under the impact of the epidemics of 1909 and 1910 a number of professional medical organizations and state boards of health began to tutor physicians on how to recognize and cope with poliomyelitis as well. Early in the spring of 1910 The American Pediatric Society and the American Orthopedic Association organized a special national symposium devoted to poliomyelitis in Washington, D.C. For a period of two days, from May 3 to May 5, a procession of experts lectured on various aspects of the symptomatology, epidemiology, and pathology of polio to an audience of the nation's pediatricians and orthopedists, the two groups most frequently called upon to treat polio cases. For many of those present the symposium served as introduction to the latest scientific information on polio. Later some would write of their gratitude for instruction received at this meeting.[82]

The educational efforts of state boards of health varied, frequently in relation to the severity of epidemics. Thus in Nebraska, which passed through a severe epidemic in the fall of 1909, the State Board of Health not only organized a special statewide polio symposium, it also delegated Dr. Frank Coulter, Professor of Nervous Diseases at Creighton University, to make a survey of the most recent clinical and experimental polio literature. Later Dr. Coulter's survey and the original articles prepared for the symposium were published in the *Western Medical Review* for the benefit and instruction of Nebraska physicians.[83]

In Massachusetts Dr. Robert Lovett, on behalf of the State Board of Health, took the occasion of the 1909 epidemic to approach the Massachusetts State Legislature for an appropriation of $10,000 to renew statewide epidemiological studies of polio. Although the Legislature pared down the amount to a final appropriation of $5,000, the sum enabled the board of health to employ Dr. Philip A. E. Sheppard and Dr. Thomas P. Hennelly to make epidemiological studies of the outbreaks in Fall River and Springfield, thus giving continuity to the epidemiological work on poliomyelitis carried on in Massachusetts since 1907. Such studies and their subsequent publication in monthly bulletins of the State Board of Health made Massachusetts physicians among the best-informed doctors in the country on polio.[84]

Although a number of state boards of health subsequently patterned their educational efforts after those organized in Nebraska and Massachusetts,[85] others contented themselves with less formal programs. In Illinois, for example, the State Board of Health obtained the August, 1910, issue of *Pediatrics*, which was devoted to a retrospect of the then current articles on polio, and reprinted it the following month in a special edition of its own monthly bulletin for the benefit of Illinois physicians.[86] In other states, boards of health simply issued special leaflets instructing physicians how to diagnose polio or else published accounts of state epidemics.[87] There can be no doubt, however, that no matter what the design or intensity of these educational programs, each gave impetus and sustenance to a growing public health attack against polio.

The impact of Dr. Flexner's educational activities, although equally profound, was largely in another direction. By his advice and continued assistance to physicians, he in effect established an extraordinary dialogue between the research laboratory and the practicing physician on problems of poliomyelitis. Each physician's request for help or information became the occasion for a counter-request by Dr. Flexner for case histories, epidemiological reports, and material from autopsies of polio victims.[88] In the course of this give and take, many physicians acquired an enhanced interest in poliomyelitis, a factor which later led to increased recognition of the disease, while others became increasingly aware of the needs of those who worked on the disease in the laboratory. Indeed, many physicians became unofficial collaborators with Dr. Flexner in his polio research and took an ardent interest in helping him.[89] In the course of these collaborations not only were the bonds between clinical medicine and medical research strengthened; important contributions to an understanding of the nature of polio were made as well. Events in Philadelphia, Pennsylvania, and Morehouse County, Louisiana, in 1910 and 1911, respectively, illustrate the substance of some of these developments.

Soon after the results of Dr. Flexner's early polio research were published in 1909, Dr. William Coplin, the medical director of the Jefferson Hospital, and Dr. Warfield Longcope, Professor of Medicine at the University of Pennsylvania Medical School in Philadelphia, asked Dr. Flexner for some pathological polio specimens from his experimental monkeys in order that they might instruct their students and colleagues on the nature of polio. The material was sent as asked.[90]

Early in March, 1910, Dr. Allan Marcy and Dr. Frank Hodge, two internes on Dr. Longcope's service, primed by their lectures on the pathology of polio, became suspicious that one of their young charges might have the disease. Although the clinical symptoms did not immediately suggest polio the doctors persisted in their suspicions, and when the child later died, received permission from Dr. Longcope to send specimens from the autopsy to Dr. Flexner for further examination. Among the specimens sent were a portion of the spinal cord and a mesenteric lymph node. Upon receipt of this material Dr. Flexner dutifully made separate suspensions of both the spinal cord and the mesenteric lymph node and inoculated two experimental monkeys with these materials. Within 10 days both monkeys began to show signs of paralysis. When they were later sacrificed it was discovered that the spinal cord of each monkey had the characteristic lesions of poliomyelitis. It was the first indication that polio virus was not only contained in the nervous system but might be present in other human organs as well.[91]

The nature of the collaboration in Louisiana was far different, but its results were no less significant. On March 7, 1911, W. J. Everett, city editor of the *Monroe News Star* in Monroe, Louisiana, addressed the following telegram to the Rockefeller Institute.

GENTLEMEN: There is an outbreak of infantile paralysis at Bastrop twenty miles north of Monroe and in the country between this city and that town. This city, noted through this section as having more children than any other city of its size in the country, is threatened with this dread disease. The doctors here say they are helpless as there is no cure for infantile paralysis. I have read in the press dispatches about experiments your institute has been making with this disease and I am going to ask you on behalf of the thousands of children in this section who are threatened to give us something about your experience. Is there a cure? If so, can you tell us something about the treatment? How the disease spreads? How it can be prevented?[92]

Mr. Everett's telegram was not the first indication that Dr. Flexner had received of this epidemic. Several days before, similar telegrams had arrived from Dr. William W. Butterworth of the Department of Pediatrics at Tulane University and Dr. David Hirsch, a practicing physician in Monroe, Louisiana. Characteristically, Dr. Flexner immediately sent the latest polio literature at hand to Dr. Butterworth and Dr. Hirsch and requested them in turn to send him portions of the spinal cord and nasal mucosa from any fatal cases that might be autopsied as well as epidemiological reports on the progress of the epidemic. In addition, he alerted Dr. Charles Duval, Chairman of the Pathology Department at Tulane, and an old acquaintance, to aid Dr. Butterworth in his search for pathological material.[93] Although a number of polio cases continued to be reported in the weeks that followed, Dr. Duval, then in the midst of his own work on leprosy, remained unimpressed with the outbreak. "The epidemic of poliomyelitis turned out to be little or nothing," he wrote Dr. Flexner on March 20. "It was chiefly a scare—no fatal cases and those afflicted, if poliomyelitic, were very mild indeed. However, Dr. Butterworth is on the look out for the disease and will let me know if anything turns up."[94]

Unlike Dr. Duval, both Dr. Butterworth and Dr. Hirsch continued to be interested in the outbreak and, although they had no opportunity to collect pathological material, they diligently traced the possible relationships of all reported cases.[95] On March 24, 1911, Dr. Butterworth summarized the course of the epidemic to that date for Dr. Flexner:

No new cases have developed. The facts in regard to this outbreak are these: It is quite probable that the first case was an abortive one, and not recognized as infantile paralysis. The first positive case was a child four or five years of age. A medical man with his wife and two children visited friends living in an adjoining house to the first positive case, and four days after their arrival one of his children went down with the same disease, two days later his second daughter became ill. Two days after his last mentioned child was taken ill, a child residing about a mile from this place developed poliomyelitis, and the fact is brought out that the doctor's family and the last mentioned patient's family had the same washwoman, who in all probability conveyed the infection. Later two cases developed about 15 miles from this point, which has been traced to a person who had been in contact with one of the previously mentioned infected cases. The two last mentioned cases developed after her arrival.[96]

Dr. Butterworth's letter was the first of several reports to Dr. Flexner which pointed to the contagious nature of poliomyelitis—a point which was not accepted by all physicians and bacteriologists in 1911.[97] There is no evidence that either Dr. Butterworth or Dr. Hirsch concerned themselves with the polio epidemic in Louisiana after March 24. However, the example of the usefulness of their cooperation with Dr. Flexner remained. When polio cases began to appear in Bonita, Louisiana, the following month, Dr. W. R. Knoepfel, a physician in Bonita, and Dr. O. M. Patterson, a local health officer in Bastrop, Louisiana, took up a new epidemiological investigation of poliomyelitis with Dr. Flexner's encouragement.[98] On May 19, 1911, Dr. Patterson sent an analysis of the outbreak to Dr. Flexner. Its significance is found in Dr. Flexner's reply:

I am greatly indebted to you for your very interesting report on the epidemic of poliomyelitis at Bastrop. The connection between the cases is so striking that I believe it important to publish the report, and I would also like to suggest that the publication be made in the *Journal of the American Medical Association*. Possibly you can secure still more data for inclusion. If you would like me to do so, I would be glad to prepare what I should regard as a suitable report on the basis of your report to me and any other data you could supply. I know of no series of cases that show the contagious nature of epidemic poliomyelitis better than the series studied by you.

I have one request to make; if any more cases arise to trace them carefully, and if any deaths occur to secure two or three inches of the affected portion of the spinal cord for me to be sent in pure glycerine. I would be greatly indebted to you.[99]

Dr. Patterson's reply to Dr. Flexner is missing. It is known, however, that in one respect he did not follow all of Dr. Flexner's suggestions. In 1912 Dr. Patterson's account of the polio epidemic in Morehouse County appeared in the *New Orleans Medical and Surgical Journal*.[100]

By 1910, research on poliomyelitis was guided by the independent logic of experiments conducted in the laboratory. It is clear from the foregoing, however, that the internal development of research was in part also based on the clinical observations, epidemiological investigations, and autopsy materials supplied by general practitioners who were called upon to cope with the disease at the bedside. Although many of these physicians were ignorant of the nature of poliomyelitis, the importance of the assistance they rendered cannot be overemphasized. It was their problems as well as their aid which helped those who worked in the laboratory to pose the questions and devise the experiments which led to an extension of poliomyelitis research. The pace of that research after 1910 was faltering and slow. Dr. Thomas Rivers, the dean of American virologists, once complained, "Progress in poliomyelitis research has not been continuous. In fact, at times we have gone backward instead of forward, and when we have gone forward, it has been by fits and starts instead of in a smooth, steady manner. At the roots of progress in poliomyelitis research, as in all research, lie proper concepts and adequate techniques."[101] In the end one had to wait for the development of virology as an independent biomedical discipline—or more than 40 years—before those concepts and techniques appeared. Today when we enjoy the fruits of the solution of the enigma of poliomyelitis, it would serve us well to remember the pain and the ignorance of the beginning.

CHARLES E. LARSEN

Ben Lindsey: Symbol of Radicalism in the 1920's

FEW MEN AROUSED MORE CONTROVERSY in the United States in the 1920's than Judge Ben B. Lindsey. To admirers he was a foremost exponent of reforms that would free the human spirit from centuries-old bonds of ignorance and bigotry. Lincoln Steffens, Clarence Darrow, Upton Sinclair, William Allen White, and David Starr Jordan gave him support. Thousands of ordinary citizens wrote to him, many seeking his advice, others expressing gratitude for his work. Lindsey was the symbol of rebellion against conventional standards. Spokesmen of "the old order," as H. G. Wells described Lindsey's critics, thought his ideas "atheistic," "bolshevistic," "anarchistic."[1] Worst of all, declared Billy Sunday in 1928, the Denver jurist would destroy the American home by encouraging the younger generation to practice what the evangelist called "barnyard marriage." Lindsey's opposition made him an object of "honorable enmity," said Thomas Mann, for demonstrating a "healthy, courageous and pure love for humanity."[2]

Conflict with the old order was not a new experience for Ben Lindsey. Before the First World War he was known throughout the United States, and even in Europe and Asia, as "the Kids' Judge" of Denver, the leading advocate of the burgeoning juvenile court movement. Although his early efforts to bring about a more humane treatment of youthful offenders were approved by the leaders of Denver, their attitude changed when Lindsey began to delve into matters they considered none of his business.[3] The

255

judge became convinced by experience in his own courtroom that betterment in the position of children required many changes in social and economic conditions.[4] Acting on this conviction, he began to explore "the swamp lands of politics and economic conditions that made for poverty and pain, discord and crime."[5] His discoveries stirred him to combat specific evils such as child labor, the lack of employers' liability laws, and special privileges enjoyed by Colorado corporations. When his attacks on the public utilities companies of Denver provoked them into declaring political war on him, Lindsey replied by writing such a detailed account of their activities that Walter Lippmann called it "the most convincing piece of muckraking ever done." *The Beast*, as Lindsey called his exposé, made enmities that lasted for more than two decades.[6]

Hostility to Lindsey was not confined to the interests, even in the prewar years. His attacks on a wide range of the old orthodoxies, both in the realm of ideas and in institutional practices, offended many whose dogmas were threatened. In his varied roles as judge, writer, and lecturer, Lindsey's questioning attitudes about the prevailing mores, eternal verities, and the positions of church and school challenged conservators of the nation's established social institutions.

Lindsey's attitudes reflected his experiences. During his childhood, his parents became converts to Roman Catholicism, causing a rift between his mother and her staunch Presbyterian father for whom Ben felt a deep affection.[7] Poor health of Ben's father in addition to financial problems forced the family to separate temporarily. Ben spent much of his adolescence with his maternal aunt and her strong-minded husband. Uncle Bates, as he was affectionately called, was very anti-Catholic but also very fond of young Ben.[8] Prior to his stay with his aunt's family, Ben had been a devout pupil in the preparatory school of Notre Dame University. Subsequently, he enrolled at Southwestern Baptist University in Tennessee.[9] Ben had a friendly and outgoing personality, even in his youth, and developed several warm and lasting friendships among teachers and students at both schools. On the intellectual level, however, the cumulative effect was to develop in him a distaste for all theology and a belief that religion must be judged by the results it produced in individuals and societies.

In his mature years, Lindsey sympathized with the Social Gospel movement, praised the writings of Walter Rauschenbusch and E. A. Ross, and criticized the churches when they adopted an attitude of lethargy or animosity toward social reform.[10] His pragmatic approach to religion and lack of concern with doctrine were apparent in a letter of advice to a beginning Sunday School teacher: "In my talks to the boys in Sunday school, I deal with everyday experiences and everyday affairs, and only dwell enough upon the lesson to keep them in touch with it."[11] He later commented on the irony of the fact that religion, which "was supposed to promote happiness," sometimes produced the opposite result.[12] His estimate of the ardor of some of the churches for promoting happiness was revealed in a letter soliciting funds for a recreation building with baths and a swimming pool for Denver's needy children: "I know it would do more good than a great many churches," he candidly observed to a wealthy donor.[13]

Lindsey fully subscribed to the liberal tenet that poverty and ignorance are the chief causes of crime and vice. While he felt that it was sometimes possible to reform wrongdoers by an ethical or religious approach, the most promising method in the long run was to change the environment.[14] "The kingdom of God on earth must come," he wrote to William Allen White, "but I do not believe it ever can come until we deal not only with the hearts of men, but those conditions under which men live and which are more or less responsible for the kinds of hearts they have and the response that comes from the heart."[15] Lindsey's greatest satisfaction, he confided to E. W. Scripps, lay in advocating measures that would alleviate "the sufferings and misfortunes of the oppressed."[16] He rejected the implicit assumption of the criminal law that the proper function of the courts was simply to act as "the punishment machine" of the State.[17] Even those whom society regarded as the most vicious criminals should be treated with altruism and compassion since the world was barely out of the Dark Ages in its knowledge of human motivation.[18] Here, then, was a potential antagonist of all traditionalists who confidently asserted either that man was innately wicked or that the social order must rest uncompromisingly upon the premises of free will and individual responsibility.

Lindsey made no effort to conceal his skepticism regarding conventional wisdom on crime and delinquency. Never one to put belief and practice into separate compartments, the judge occasionally came into open conflict with the community—or at least with some of its more vocal representatives. The Juvenile Court of Denver afforded him unique opportunities to act upon his convictions. It was grounded upon chancery principles which gave him a wider latitude than the ordinary criminal courts enjoyed in handling contributory delinquency cases. In election campaigns, the charge that the judge was too lenient in "sex cases" was a hardy perennial. Circulars were printed giving statistics which purportedly proved that most sex offenders who came before his court were released or given light sentences.[19] The popular image that the authors of the circulars sought to create was clear enough—Ben Lindsey was a muddle-headed do-gooder whose softness would convince the most depraved criminals that they could debauch youth with impunity.

Lindsey's defense against these charges was characteristically simple and direct. The fault did not lie with the juvenile court. It was the law that was unrealistic. He produced his own statistics to show that convictions for the same charges in the criminal courts, where concurrent jurisdiction existed, occurred in a small percentage of the complaints and indictments. This conviction rate did not reflect discredit upon the wisdom or integrity of judges or juries. Often it was the result of their unwillingness to enforce the harsh and foolish provisions of the law regarding statutory rape. The sole element required for conviction was that the girl's age be under eighteen. Evidence that the "victim" had given her consent—or, indeed, was the aggressor—or that she had a bad reputation was inadmissible. Since the penalty was severe, the defendant was often exonerated, particularly when he was in approximately the same age group as the girl or when the jury suspected that moral responsibility was divided about evenly between the parties, a condition which Lindsey believed was present in about ninety percent of the cases.[20] In defending his own court, Lindsey pointed out that it had certain advantages over the criminal courts. The flexibility and informality of its procedures permitted a more careful consideration of the human factors in each case. Also, his court did not have to face the dilemma of punishing the offender excessively or letting him go scot-free. The remedy could fit the situation. If payments were appropriate in order to meet medical expenses or provide support for a child, the continuing equitable jurisdiction of the court gave reasonable assurance that they would be made. A mandatory prison sentence, by contrast, usually had no effect other than to destroy the offender's earning power, thus punishing the innocent as well as the guilty.[21]

Lindsey's reply to his critics made sense to most citizens of Denver. He was reelected time after time from 1901 to 1924, often by a wider margin than candidates for any other office, in spite of his enemies' attempts to discredit him by accusations that covered the gamut from malingering to sexual misconduct.[22] The reasons for his popularity are not hard to fathom. As young Walter Lippmann admiringly wrote, Lindsey had captured the imagination of the whole country by his campaign for a decent and humane treatment of juvenile offenders.[23] Even the leading women of Denver supported him in this cause, although their husbands opposed their participating actively in the judge's election campaigns. Furthermore, Denverites knew that the little judge, whom Theodore Roosevelt affectionately dubbed "the Bull Mouse," was better known in the great world than any of his detractors.[24] They knew that Lindsey had addressed legislatures in a score of states and that he had appeared before a joint session of the Canadian Parliament to speak on children's legislation.[25] Visitors from Europe and Asia came to Denver to observe his methods. The argument carried conviction that Denver needed Lindsey more than Lindsey needed Denver. Finally, in an era of emergent progressivism, Lindsey was its most articulate Colorado representative.[26]

The campaigns in which Lindsey struggled to establish juvenile courts, to adopt woman suffrage, to reform the worst abuses of prisons, and to enact a number of electoral reforms in Colorado were largely or completely won by the end of the First World War. As the twenties began, he became increasingly concerned with new issues. By mid-decade, he found himself in the national limelight as the leading spokesman of the "revolution in manners and morals" so widely publicized in the press, popular magazines, and the movies.[27]

There were several reasons why Lindsey was able to assume this role. Already a national celebrity, his fame was based on solid achievements in numerous good causes. Lincoln Steffens had cele-

brated his work in a series of articles for *McClure's*.[28] *The Beast*
had been serialized in *Everybody's*.[29] Perhaps the largest number
of Americans recalled Lindsey most vividly as a public speaker.
His nationwide popularity as a lecturer prompted the Redpath
Lyceum Bureau to offer him a long-term contract at more than
five times his salary as a judge.[30] The same qualities that attracted
such large audiences in the prewar years—sincerity, intensity, em-
pathy, and an unfailing ability to dramatize an issue—were used
by Lindsey in the twenties in his efforts to bring about more
realistic attitudes toward sexual conduct.

Lindsey's views on the sexual mores of American society were
most fully developed in two books, *The Revolt of Modern Youth*
and *The Companionate Marriage*, published in 1925 and 1927.
The two volumes complemented each other. In *The Revolt of
Modern Youth* he emphasized the changes in attitudes among
younger people toward sexual questions and explored the reasons
for the new outlook. In *The Companionate Marriage* he proposed
a minimal program to deal with some of the most glaring defects
in legislation on the subject. Lindsey drew heavily from his own
experiences as a judge to support his conclusions, using assumed
names to cover the identities of the many adolescents and adults
whose attitudes and conduct he treated sympathetically, if not
always approvingly. Since Lindsey's reputation as a radical in the
twenties was based in large measure on the views he espoused—or
was said to have espoused—in these books, his comments on the
canons of "formal morality," to use Max Lerner's term, deserve
to be examined closely.[31]

Perhaps the most shocking aspect of Lindsey's writings, as far as
traditionalists were concerned, was his pervasive theme that there
was nothing sacrosanct about the prevailing moral code. It must
be judged, he averred, by its success or failure in meeting human
needs.

Our present marriage customs [he wrote,] are just as much a matter of
expediency as was bundling. They have the same degree of divine sanction, and like bundling they may be expected to last so long as they
work. When they fail to work a few rebels will start changing them, as
they are now doing; then the crowd will follow this lead; and God,
somewhat belatedly, will be found by His interpreters to have changed
His mind. The new custom will then be "the will of God"—so long

as it works. This epitomizes the whole process by which customs come into existence and then give way to other customs. We should do well to rationalize the process. By so doing we might spare ourselves a great deal of needless crime, tragedy and unhappiness.[32]

The judge believed that the formal moral code failed the pragmatic test. He documented its bankruptcy from cases of young girls who came or were brought to his court because they had premarital sexual relations. Lindsey's procedure, as he described it, was based on a number of pragmatic assumptions. The successful counselor first needed to win the confidence of the young person by convincing her that he was not passing a moral judgment on her and that his principal concern was to help her.[33] His sympathy had to be based on genuine conviction. Some people insisted on interpreting the sexual delicts of young people as "badness." "I call them mistakes," Lindsey declared. "And I deny that the children who make them are 'immoral.' I leave the charge of 'immorality' to those painfully moral persons who find their own record so clear that they can follow the bidding of the Master, and, without hesitation, cast the first stone."[34] After the girl's confidence had been won, the next step depended on the facts of the case. The objective was the least amount of anguish and suffering possible for all parties concerned. If pregnancy or venereal disease were present, every effort was made to handle the situation quietly and confidentially. Private charitable and religious institutions frequently cooperated in arranging adoptions for unwanted children. If the case did not involve disease or pregnancy, the girl was placed on probation or simply dismissed.

Lindsey contrasted this method with the traditionalist approach —the "vindictive morality" approach, as his friend Bertrand Russell called it.[35] Sometimes the state callously participated in the process, particularly through school administrators who were given wide discretion in deciding whether to disgrace a girl by expelling her from school. Society was usually the principal culprit, however. Lindsey singled out for denunciation as a vicious myth the Victorian notion that any girl who had sexual relations outside of marriage was ruined.[36] He cited numerous cases which revealed how girls were crushed by the social ostracism that followed exposure. When he encountered such cruelty, Lindsey found "restraint difficult and moderation of statement nearly impossible."[37]

Ruined they were indeed, he observed, but only because they were discovered. The fault lay in a violation of a social convention, "not in a mysterious 'defilement' conjured up by our tribal superstition."[38] Yet the punishment was often more lasting than it was for "much more anti-social conduct" such as slander, theft, or even assault. The examples Lindsey gave of girls whose secrets his court kept and who later became wives and mothers in stable family relationships lent credence to his view that in many instances "ruination" was an artificially created state of mind.[39] His description of a happy occasion when he and Mrs. Lindsey were visited by ten young matrons who had "gone wrong" in their high school days and who now proudly brought their babies to be introduced no doubt infuriated those moralists who insisted that the wages of sin must include hell on earth as well as in the hereafter.[40]

Lindsey's secular and pragmatic attitude toward adultery and divorce also challenged the conventional morality. Although he constantly reiterated that monogamous marriage was the ideal and attainable relationship for the vast majority of people, as well as the one which he found personally satisfying, he insisted on treating adultery and divorce as problems rather than crimes or sins.[41] His unwillingness to be shocked by the unconventional relationships which he described in his writings led his enemies to accuse him of advocating promiscuity.

Lindsey did not advocate promiscuity.[42] For those who insisted that monogamous marriage was a moral absolute, however, his views were indeed heretical. The judge's support of monogamy on the basis that it was the most practical institution for meeting human needs in an industrial society did not satisfy those who insisted that, without exceptions, monogamy rested upon immutable moral or natural laws. Lindsey pointed out that some people found monogamy unsatisfactory. In the case of freely consenting adults, whose actions did not hurt third parties, he felt that the law should not interfere.[43] He warned against the personal and social consequences of illicit sexual conduct, but tried to avoid coercion or exposure in dealing with people who confided in him.[44] There were situations in marriages, he found, in which a triangular relationship was a passing phase and the marriages were salvable when the monogamous partner showed forbearance.[45] Paradoxically, the law, which placed so many obstacles in the path of divorce supposedly in order to protect the family, was willing to forget this principle very quickly if either husband or wife committed adultery. Lindsey believed that the state had a moral obligation to make an effort to save marriages, particularly when children were involved. The social utility of preserving a family was of far greater importance than a single act of infidelity.[46] Undoubtedly, Lindsey's forthright presentation of the details of particular cases in support of his views intensified the shocked reaction of some of his readers.[47]

The term "companionate marriage," the title of Lindsey's second book dealing with the revolution in morals, eventually became the shorthand expression to embrace all of the judge's ideas on sexual topics. Actually, Lindsey's concept of companionate marriage was simpler than popular usage sometimes suggested.[48] "Companionate marriage," he stated, "is legal marriage, with legalized birth control, and with the right to divorce by mutual consent for childless couples, usually without payment of alimony."[49] A corollary was public education "of youth and married couples in the art of love, the laws of sex and life, better to equip them for their serious duties of marriage and parenthood."[50]

What was the rationale of Lindsey's proposals? Certain features of American law and society worked a serious hardship upon young people—and sometimes those not so young—in regard to marriage. Among the chief difficulties were the inability to support a family during the early years of marriage, the problem of obtaining the best information available about contraception, the harsh divorce laws of some states, and the inequities often associated with alimony payments.[51] The first two problems were usually interrelated. Young couples often had more children than they could support because they did not have access to reliable information about birth control. Lindsey placed the blame for this situation on federal legislation which forbade using the mails to provide such information and on state laws which imposed similar restrictions on licensed physicians. He proposed not merely that these laws be repealed but that it be a minimal function of states to provide instruction in contraceptive techniques for all who wanted it.[52]

Reforms in alimony and divorce legislation were also badly needed. Lindsey feared that the rigidity of existing divorce laws might sometimes discourage marriage itself. Some people would be deterred by the prospect of a costly and time-consuming adversary action if a mistake were made in the choice of a spouse. In one state, divorce was still not allowed for any cause.[53] In some states, notably New York, collusion was virtually required in order to obtain a divorce.[54] It was the supreme anomaly of the law of divorce in many states, Lindsey declared, that the one unmentionable ground for divorce was the fact that two adults agreed that they did not wish to remain married to each other.[55] When children were not involved, and the couple had failed in an honest effort to make the marriage work, Lindsey could see no justification for the law to impose such a rule. Further, he believed that alimony payments, especially in the case of childless couples, were often unfair and even against the public interest when they made it difficult for a man to re-marry and support a family.[56] Finally, Lindsey maintained that alimony was contrary to the principle of equal rights for women when the divorcée was young, childless, and able to work.[57]

Contraception and divorce by collusion were, of course, already widely accepted practices in the United States, at least among large segments of the middle and upper classes. In this respect, Lindsey emphasized, his proposals were really quite conservative.[58] He merely insisted on the need to codify existing customs. In regard to contraception, the codification was necessary because those who needed the information most desperately often could not obtain it.[59] In the matter of divorce, even the middle class sometimes suffered under the rules and had to pay too high a price to dissolve their marriages.[60]

It was hardly surprising that representatives of various orthodoxies who considered Lindsey's proposals radical felt obligated to dissent. Roman Catholic prelates necessarily balked at the entire scheme, since birth control and divorce were its essential ingredients. Other clergymen objected that the sacramental nature of matrimony was lightly regarded. Undoubtedly a suspicion that easily dissoluble marriages would be contracted insincerely, perhaps especially by young men, underlay some of the hostility to Lindsey's proposals. Some critics claimed that the program put too much stress on the hedonistic element in marriage. The Episcopal Bishop of New York, William Manning, professed to speak for them and many others when he replied to Lindsey's offer to debate the merits of companionate marriage:

In reply to your telegram I beg to say that for Christians the moral standards given to the world by Christ are not open to debate in spite of your assertions to the contrary. The temporary so-called companionate marriage advocated by yourself and others is not marriage but only another name for free love. Your teachings would not lead forward but backward to those conditions which destroyed the old pagan world. In your writings you reject and hold up to contempt the Christian ideal of morality and purity. Such teaching is a sin against God, an insult to the womanhood and manhood of our land, and should be condemned by all good citizens.[61]

Bishop Manning's confident assurance that he could interpret "the moral standards given to the world by Christ" was not shared by all Christians, nor was his personal attack on Lindsey approved in all clerical quarters. Some ministers wrote privately to Lindsey that they did not find his views irreconcilable with Christianity.[62] Some laymen had reservations about the psychological soundness of Lindsey's plan—chiefly, the wisdom of entering marriage with an explicit agreement that it could be dissolved by mutual consent if the parties decided they were incompatible—but managed to state their doubts without resorting to emotional attacks on Lindsey's integrity.[63] Winfred Ernest Garrison, reviewing Lindsey's book in *The Christian Century*, disagreed with Lindsey's proposals but held that they sprang from the judge's own deep interest in morality and deserved serious consideration. He doubted that many of Lindsey's more outspoken clerical critics had even read the book. The charge that the most beloved champion of children's rights in America had suddenly become "a deliberate and dangerous corrupter of youth" was not "a very intelligent estimate of the case," according to Garrison.[64] Nevertheless, temperate discussion of Lindsey's ideas often seemed to be the exception, not the rule.

The temptation was irresistible to ballyhoo companionate marriage. Sunday supplements and popular magazines, always eager to keep the twenties roaring, were soon calling it "pal marriage," "contract marriage," "jazz marriage," "free love," and—somewhat more sedately, perhaps—"trial marriage."[65] When two West Coast music teachers announced that they considered their marriage a companionate type, the Los Angeles *Examiner* photographed them sitting in their apartment and carried the headline, "Companionate Pair Just Like All Newlyweds." The story that followed contained the *non sequitur* that "they enjoy some domesticity, Judge Ben Lindsey notwithstanding, when they are through teaching for the day."[66] When the judge suggested, on a lecture tour, that the term "sanctity of the home" was sometimes used as a shibboleth by opponents of "honest marriages and scientific divorces," the San Francisco *Call-Bulletin* ran the headline, "Sanctity of Home Bunk."[67] James M. Allison, a syndicated columnist, wrote, "Judge Ben B. Lindsey of Denver is coming to New York. Report has it that he has run out of nut ideas and is coming here to get some new ones from the Greenwich Village Progressives."[68] An anonymous editorial writer in the Springfield (Mass.) *Daily News* doubted "that this nation will ever so degrade itself as to Russianize the marriage relation or to legalize the iniquitous birth-control measure advocated by Lindsey and his supporters."[69] Readers of the St. Louis *Star* were informed, "Lindsey's Trial Marriage Idea Bolshevistic, Says Divorce Judge."[70] A contemporary cartoon irrelevantly showed black and white children marching out of a foundling asylum. Each child bore a tag with the name Lindsey on it. The caption was "Companionate."[71] Perhaps Will Rogers was right when he punned, "Judge Lindsey and I went up together [in a Goodyear blimp] and discussed companionate marriage—which was over the heads of most people."[72]

The press did not have to manufacture news stories reflecting hostility to Lindsey. In 1928, a Unitarian minister felt it necessary to defend the judge against "the Blue Menace," as he called the spirit of bigotry and intolerance which claimed the right to censor everybody's ideas and regarded itself as enjoying a monopoly of patriotism.[73] The "pestiferous bug" was especially active in Boston where *The Revolt of Modern Youth* had recently been banned along with *Elmer Gantry* and *An American Tragedy*.[74] Apparently conditions in parts of the South were worse. Lindsey described his reception in the "Bible Belt" where he lectured in the presence of members of the Ku Klux Klan. In Birmingham, he wrote to H. G. Wells:

My lecture date was cancelled at a public indignation meeting of citizens who insisted that my advocacy of Companionate Marriage was advocacy of "free love," as they term it. The official organization in question is known as the Parent-Teacher Association. They were backed by the local Ministerial Association. A group of newspapermen, however, took over the engagement and under a terrific public protest of the fundamentalist clergy and a public parade of the Ku Klux Klan through the streets of Birmingham and about the auditorium where I was to speak, and with one of their officers with uplifted sword in the front of the hall to protest against my appearance, about four thousand people crowded into the hall and I delivered my address under police protection. I was escorted back to my hotel in the car of the Chief of Police with three plain clothes men. It may have been an exaggeration, but I was assured by one of the local committee that there was considerable fear for my safety and that the Chief of Police had informed him that one of his men had perhaps—without my knowing it—prevented an assault on me.[75]

The National Defense Committee criticized the Lewis and Clark Chapter of the Daughters of the American Revolution for "allowing" Lindsey to speak in Eugene, Oregon.[76] The international menace of "Lindseyism" received recognition when the Rev. Victor Capesius, President of the Evangelical Church of Austria, linked the judge and Bolshevism as "two destructive forces threatening to destroy . . . European civilization."[77] A Seattle minister exemplified the sillier side of threats of violence against the judge when he told a local Lions Club, "If Lindsey or any other moral degenerate made such a proposition to a daughter or sister of mine, I'd wring his dirty neck."[78]

Lindsey's image as a radical in the twenties was not exclusively the result of his outspoken views on sexual questions. The judge was adept at using pungent language to fire broadsides at various foibles of the times and freely used his talents. Among his targets were Prohibition, censorship, super-patriotism, Fundamentalism, and, finally and consistently, the Ku Klux Klan.

A genuine intellectual conversion explained Lindsey's opposition to Prohibition. His first experiences with young offenders and some of their parents had persuaded him that smoking and drinking were often associated with truancy and the worst aspects of juvenile gangs. In an early crusade, he campaigned against the "wine rooms" of Denver where minors were illegally served.[79] For a number of years he was Vice-President of the American Anti-Cigarette League. He accepted the endorsement of the Prohibition party in several elections and favored the Eighteenth Amendment when it was adopted. Within a few years, however, he concluded that Prohibition "has proved a poor way to obtain a desirable end."[80] Like many Americans, Lindsey was disturbed by the by-products, bootlegging and gangsterism.[81] Also, he became convinced that Prohibition was, in effect, class legislation, since well-to-do citizens could evade the law with relative ease and safety.[82] His third objection, however, was more fundamental in that it reflected a basic tenet of his evolving social philosophy. By the late twenties Lindsey had come to believe that higher standards of personal conduct in all spheres of life could be achieved only in a free environment that encouraged the development of voluntary moderation and restraint. "Your attitude toward Prohibition," he wrote, "is based on whether you believe human beings can be educated to decency and to voluntary restraint in the indulgence of an appetite, or that they must be restrained by force and law."[83] In retrospect, he felt that the nation had stood a better chance of evolving an ideal of temperance during the prewar years. But, he asserted in quasi-Menckenesque language, "it was . . . far too slow for the busybodies who think that people can be legislated into heaven. They instituted a form of direct action and bourgeois syndicalism which killed and aborted the delicate moral organism that was gestating in the spirit of this nation."[84]

Lindsey's position on censorship of books, plays, and movies was also an outgrowth of his belief that the process of maturing, both for societies and individuals, was largely a matter of learning to make one's choices freely and to live with the results. "The damnable and destructive thing about . . . these varied censorships . . . is that it removes from individuals all real responsibility for their own conduct. . . . It is like putting a man's arm in a sling and expecting it to be strong."[85] He insisted that "there is *nothing in the world* that is not a legitimate subject for honest discussion —yes, even for dishonest discussion."[86] He had faith that in a free society the truth "would survive by its own strength."[87] His essentially moderate libertarian stand was illustrated by his willingness to accept special rules for literature "not intended for immature minds" yet the value of which to society was undeniable.[88] Similarly, he accepted the need for restraints on "evident pornography which neither enlightens nor educates."[89] As always, the difficulty lay not in stating general propositions but in deciding concrete cases. Here Lindsey was usually not on the side of the censors. When the New York Society for the Suppression of Vice seized copies of *Madeleine*,[90] a rather pallid contemporary memoir of a woman of pleasure, he responded to a request for public support from the publishers with the statement, "To suppress such a book as *Madeleine* is to promote vice by hiding the truth, and those fostering it only brand themselves as dangerous cranks who deserve to be suppressed."[91] The judge also saw danger in the power of state and local movie censors.[92] At the time a national motion picture censorship law was under consideration, he feared that its administration would be controlled by "extreme Fundamentalist influences" and publicly testified against the proposed Upshaw bill.[93]

Everything in Lindsey's background made him a natural foe of those super-patriots of the twenties who identified their prejudices and self-interest with "Americanism." Even before the war his own election campaigns helped pave the way for his hatred of nativism in all its forms. He had always been a strong candidate in the Russian-Jewish and Italian precincts of Denver, where he was loved for his humanitarian and pro-labor sympathies. He had become accustomed to hearing his supporters called "foreigners" by enemies on Capitol Hill, some of whom vowed that they would never be ruled "by cattle like that."[94] He witnessed the sanctimonious use of the issue of patriotism by persons whose only real concern was to throttle the labor movement in its attempts to organize. Exasperated by Colorado Progressives who refused to go along with him in supporting the coal miners in the great strike of 1914, he found some solace in writing to William Allen White:

Most of the . . . crowd have deserted us for "law and order," that in this state is simply Dr. Johnson's "Patriotism is the refuge of scoundrels." When I see the infamous crooks wearing an American flag on the lapel of their coats—men who know no law and order, except for the other fellow—and observe the success with which they are capitalizing the very flag itself in behalf of their tyranny and oppression, it makes me boil with indignation. I tell our fellows that we should not let them get away with that, but we should wear flags ourselves and have it out as to what that flag really represents.[95]

Those authoritarian personalities who equated pacifism or suspicion of the military with doubtful patriotism no doubt considered Lindsey off base on this score, too. His attitude toward pacifism was the same as his attitude toward socialism.[96] Both movements, in his view, were legitimate criticisms of grave social evils. Both were often attacked by hypocrites whose patriotism was merely ill-clothed self-interest. The spirit of militarism was uncongenial to democratic institutions and should not be encouraged in the schools, Lindsey warned.[97] These views, however, did not lead him to see the spectre of militarism behind every bush. In response to the disapproval of some friends to his serving on the National Council of the Boy Scouts on the ground that the organization was, as Lindsey facetiously observed, "a military affair and a terrible conspiracy of the aristocrats to raise up the children to shoot down the proletariat," he asked Julia Lathrop for advice, since Hull House had a Boy Scouts patrol.[98] Miss Lathrop and Jane Addams, in separate replies, denied the charge, Miss Addams commenting, "if I thought it was at all military I would not have it for a minute."[99] Lindsey acknowledged that he agreed with the ladies on the main point but also remarked that he could understand his friends' suspicions when they saw "exploiting businessmen" serving on local councils and piously preaching platitudes to the boys. "It appears very absurd," he wrote, "to some of our friends among the Socialists and the labor people who have a very keen knowledge of fundamental justice."[100]

Although Lindsey sympathetically associated with pacifists and looked forward to the day when all battleships would be "junked or sunk," he never actually joined the ranks of pacifism.[101] In 1914, he was at first inclined to think that America should stay out of the war. However, the arguments for "Preparedness" appealed to his practical nature.[102] When a manifesto condemning President Wilson's December, 1915, statement on Preparedness became the major divisive issue among the passengers on Henry Ford's "peace ship," the judge was the most prominent spokesman for those who stood with Wilson.[103] After the United States became a belligerent, Lindsey fully supported the war effort but expressed regret that "so many of our former allies in the political and economic struggle in this country" remained unconvinced. He wrote to E. W. Scripps a hope that they would all be together again after the war "for the real constructive work in turning civilization right side up after it has been turned upside down."[104]

Lindsey's distrust of nationalism, and his abhorrence of its excesses, permeated his writings in the twenties. He deplored the censorship of "school histories that tell the truth about the American Revolution" and he castigated the " '200 percent Americanism' attitude toward Roman Catholics—not to mention, Jews, Negroes, and aliens" as a "yellow streak in our national life, a streak so yellow that a sane yellow dog would be ashamed to own it."[105] Having in mind the connotation that the words "one hundred percent American" had acquired, he declared on another occasion, "I'd walk around the world to avoid having that label pinned on me."[106] The pragmatic judge was annoyed whenever he heard the argument that new policies must be rejected if they were contrary to the wisdom of the Founding Fathers. A strong internationalist and supporter of the League of Nations, Lindsey sarcastically stated:

I have often wondered that our national sense of humor should have been so dormant that it kept right on sleeping while Henry Cabot Lodge and his cohorts were presenting . . . the fact that *Washington* had warned us against entangling alliances. And yet Henry Cabot Lodge was, in what seemed to me an evil way, intelligent. Perhaps that was why he used such an argument.[107]

In Fundamentalism Lindsey found a set of attitudes in total conflict with his own values. A clash was inevitable, for Fundamentalism in the twenties encompassed much more than a literal belief in the Bible. Richard Hofstadter has appropriately labeled it "the revolt against modernity."[108] Its spokesmen found no difficulty in recognizing as their implacable enemy the chief protagonist of "the revolt of modern youth." The recognition was mutual, and Lindsey knew that no compromise was possible.

I have been reading a good many letters of late, [he wrote] asking me how I reconcile some of the views I am expressing in this book with the Bible. I have one short and conclusive answer to that question. I don't reconcile it with the Bible. Moreover, I don't see why I should. Those of my views which are in accord with Holy Writ speak for themselves. Those which are not have to be classed with evolution, the roundness of the earth, and other matters which were not factors in the speculative thought of the ancient Jews. To say that modern sociology must deal with modern facts is not to flout or discount the Bible. It is to interpret that book in the corrective light of changing conditions.[109]

Lindsey adhered to this theme in his speeches, books, and private correspondence. His quarrel, he repeated frequently, was not with "religion" or even with the Church.[110] Rather, it was with that type of "Bible-olaters" who believed in an anthropomorphic God, the Seven Day creation, and who, "if the record had said that Jonah swallowed the whale, would have believed that."[111] Such true believers would not be dangerous, Lindsey asserted, if they confined themselves to holding these views as their private convictions. Unfortunately, a compulsion to make the whole society conform to its own rigid code seemed to be an integral part of the Fundamentalist syndrome. Hence, Fundamentalists foisted their ideas on everybody in the form of Prohibition, strict divorce laws, Comstock laws, and statutes forbidding the teaching of evolution.[112] When Lindsey heard of Billy Sunday's invectives against him, he commented, "He would be burning witches and heretics if he had his way."[113]

It was fitting that Judge Lindsey spent his final years in Denver engaged in a bitter struggle with the Ku Klux Klan. His open disdain for nativism, his denunciation of bigotry, and his jibes at Fundamentalism antagonized those who helped to make Colorado a bastion of Klan influence in the middle twenties.[114] To advocate reforms in the regulation of sexual conduct was a challenge to the Klan's role as self-appointed guardian of morality against the putative wave of licentiousness. As early as 1922, the Klan began a campaign to "put a clean man on the Juvenile Court," in the words of the Kligrapp of Denver Klan Number One.[115] Lindsey, an old campaigner who loved a good fight, denounced the Klan as "vicious and venomous."[116] When various proposals to condemn it in national party platforms were made in 1924, the judge relished the idea and stated:

As a Democrat, I heartily endorse the plank. The time has come when both parties must be frank with the people and courageously take a stand . . . for the open, free administration of government by all the people, or confess themselves on the side of hypocrisy and cowardice and privilege, for kliques, klans and klasses, working under cover in the interest of a government that is invisible and not . . . as the Constitution and law of the land intended it should be.[117]

In Colorado, 1924 was the apogee of Klan success at the polls.[118] Nevertheless, Lindsey won the largest number of votes in the Juvenile Court race, defeating his Klan-supported opponent, Royal C. Graham. The Klan-dominated Assembly soon introduced legislation to abolish the Court.[119] Graham also announced that he would contest the election. After two years of litigation, a hostile state supreme court reversed the decision of the trial court and disallowed all the ballots cast in the preponderantly Jewish precinct where Lindsey had received his strongest support.[120] Graham, however, never occupied Judge Lindsey's bench because he had committed suicide a few months earlier rather than face charges of gross financial irregularities while holding another public office.[121] The Board of County Commissioners chose Lindsey's successor. After helping the judge and Mrs. Lindsey destroy the notes that dealt with the confidences that scores of young people had given over the years in the privacy of the judge's chambers, the principal officers of the Court resigned.[122] The judge and his family eventually moved to California.

Ben Lindsey remains an appropriate symbol for the "radicalism" of the twenties. Although his economic and political beliefs were entirely in the mainstream of American constitutional democracy, his zeal for reform, his enthusiasm for experimentation, his identification in the public media with all that was considered avant-garde justify the characterization. Nor would Judge Lindsey have disclaimed it. Writing in 1925, he reflected:

I have tried to be honest, and yet to present the truth of recorded fact in a way that would not be needlessly shocking to persons who find such departures from their routine way of thought disturbing; who think there is comfort and security in Habit, safety in Conservative Tradition, and nothing but an unreasonable, foolish, and fruitless peril in the Radicalism that, true to its name, digs and explores amid the Roots of Things. In Life as in Mathematics, a Radical is the Root. From it springs other Life, luxuriant, spawning rankly abundant in the sun. Yet while it spawns it dreams—and dreams—and dreams of those illimitable things toward which it so awfully and mysteriously reaches. To me the whole meaning of Radicalism is these first and last things;

and the notion that it is merely a superficial and reckless extremism is itself a superficial reasoning that is unfortunately peculiar to most conservative thought. For conservative thought deals with the surfaces of things, not with their insides. It is interested in preserving the World As Is.[123]

In a decade of "tired radicals" Ben Lindsey showed no signs of fatigue. At the beginning of the decade, he was serving as chairman of a committee of judges to codify the laws of Colorado relating to women and children and launching a successful campaign to have legislation enacted for maternal assistance that went beyond the modest provisions of the federal Sheppard-Towner Act.[124] At the end of the decade, he was alternately fighting the forces of reaction in Colorado and addressing audiences in different parts of the country on the need for changes in the law of marriage and divorce. An admiring Fredric C. Howe wrote to him in 1931, when the personal fortunes of the judge, as well as those of the nation, seemed to be reaching their lowest ebb:

I used to wonder how you kept going so very much alone out in Colorado, for it was hard enough in Cleveland, but we had a bunch with a host in Tom Johnson who protected us as you were not protected. Also, we were merely lieutenants and you were the whole battalion. I have been going over the list of those battlers for freedom in your generation and mine and as I think them all over it is my opinion that you and Senator LaFollette were the loneliest fighters of the bunch. And it is more than doubly heroic to fight alone. And, in addition, you have never laid down on the contest; you, almost alone of the prewar radicals, are still on the firing line. I feel ashamed when I think how much you have been left to keep the fires burning when the rest of us threw up the sponge. . . . About the only thing I can do is to reach my hand across the Continent and send you and Mrs. Lindsey my love and gratitude. I have an appreciation for what she has gone through, too. Do keep your health and cheer. I have a belief that the sun is coming up over the edge of the horizon. Our New York Roosevelt is saying and understanding the things you write about. And there are others at the top who see them, too. It may be that we will have a chance to cheer after all.[125]

After two lean years in private practice in California and a brief service in the N.I.R.A. as Deputy Administrator for the Motion Picture Code, Lindsey was elected to the Superior Court of Los

Angeles County by the largest majority ever won by a candidate for judicial office in the state. Reelected in 1940, he continued to serve until his death. His breadth of interests and his unflagging ardor for reform were displayed in two episodes in his seventy-fourth year. On February 4, 1943, he wrote to Mayor LaGuardia suggesting the formation of a group interested in counteracting the type of journalism represented by Westbrook Pegler in order to prevent another loss of the peace.[126] On March 24, 1943, he wrote to a state senator about the urgency of adopting legislation which he had recently drafted for the protection of children. He mentioned that his wife and physician were afraid that a trip to Sacramento would tax his strength, but added, "It may be possible, however, that I could prevail upon them to let me go if you think there is a fairly good chance of getting the legislation through."[127] He died of a heart attack the following day.

WILLIAM E. LEUCHTENBURG

The Case of the Contentious Commissioner:
Humphreys' Executor v. U.S.

OF THE MANY CASES which come before the United States
Supreme Court, some are born to fame and some to obscurity.
On Black Monday, May 27, 1935, the Supreme Court delivered an
opinion about some sick chickens which won immediate acclaim
as one of the most significant decisions since the Dred Scott case.[1]
A few minutes earlier, the Court had ruled on a suit filed by the
estate of one William E. Humphrey, late of the Federal Trade
Commission. The Humphrey decision was overshadowed by the
Schechter opinion at the time, and only a few commentators have
accorded it the attention it deserves since. Poor Humphrey, so jeal-
ous of his reputation, has had the unhappy fate of having gone
down in more than one work of history, when history noticed him
at all, as "Humphries."[2] Yet the case of *Humphrey's Executor v.
U.S.* raised important questions about the prerogatives of the President and the doctrine of separation of powers, and it had consequences more far-reaching than its humble reputation would suggest.[3]

Born on March 31, 1862, on a farm near Alamo, Indiana, William Ewart Humphrey was destined to carry into the era of the
New Deal the values and aspirations of a Hoosier farmboy. After
attending Wabash College, Humphrey began law practice in the
college town of Crawfordsville. When the Panic of 1893 struck,
he decided to seek his fortune in the Pacific Northwest. In Seattle,

he rose quickly in the ranks of the Republican Party; by 1898 he was corporation counsel of the city. Four years later, he won election to the U.S. House of Representatives.

From 1903 to 1917 Humphrey faithfully represented the economic interests of his state. In these years, no more ardent member of the Republican Old Guard could be found anywhere in the country. He was a shrill standpatter and a fierce partisan. "If a Democrat is elected," he warned in 1912, "a panic will commence in this country within twenty-four hours after that news is flashed throughout the world."[4] Instead of the good-natured guile thought essential for a successful politician, Humphrey's manner was outspoken to the point of rudeness. He wrote one constituent:

I am in receipt of your letter in regard to the establishment of an office at Concrete. I will consider it a personal favor if you will write to the people who wrote to you concerning the matter and tell them that they are making a great nuisance of themselves and doing their cause no good by having people all over this state write me about this matter.[5]

In 1916 Humphrey made a bid for a U.S. Senate seat and met defeat. Never shy about demanding political favors as a matter of right, he now called on his former associates to find him a job as a lobbyist. Senator Wesley Jones actively solicited business interests in the Northwest to obtain remunerative employment for him.[6] To one such inquiry the shipping magnate, Robert Dollar, replied: "I feel confident that a fund will be raised immediately to employ Mr. Humphrey to look after the Pacific Coast Ship Owners interests."[7] But Humphrey's friends were embarrassed when the Tacoma *Times* learned of these overtures and published an account of them. Humphrey, the *Times* stated, had been "a noisy, ill-mannered, narrowly-partisan, always-carping critic of the Wilson administration. He was the pet G.O.P. baiter of Wilson, Wilson's policies, Wilson's appointees and Wilson's acts, in Congress and out. It became with him a mania."[8] Some of the groups Jones approached decided not to employ him, but Humphrey was too undeviating a supporter of business interests and had too much influence in Washington to be unconnected for long. Shortly after his term in Congress expired, he became a lobbyist for Northwestern lumber interests.

Humphrey, who always had his eye on the main chance, did not propose to spend the rest of his days as a lobbyist. He played an active role in national Republican politics; in the 1922 Congressional elections, he served as chairman of the Speakers Bureau of the Republican National Committee. He remained a forthright champion of the Grand Old Party and a vocal viewer-with-alarm. After the war, Humphrey had stated: "I think that our country today is facing a much more serious condition, so far as the perpetuity of our institutions is concerned, than it has at any time since the close of the Civil War."[9] His years in Washington, he said on another occasion, had given him "a profound distrust of the reformer."[10] Humphrey, in short, offered precisely that combination of economic orthodoxy and party loyalty that should have commended him to Republican administrations in Washington. Yet, for some years, although he was aggressive about calling attention to his services, he was passed by. Not until 1925 did his search for preferment end. That year, President Calvin Coolidge, who wanted just such a man as Humphrey, named him to the five-member Federal Trade Commission.

Coolidge's decision was a deliberate attempt to force this "independent" agency into line with the Administration's policies. The appointment of Humphrey proved to be the most important single event in the history of the FTC. By placing on the Commission an aggressive defender of business interests, it gave conservatives a 3-2 majority. Progressives were appalled. The effect of Humphrey's appointment, said Senator George Norris, was "to set the country back more than twenty-five years."[11]

Humphrey quickly transformed the FTC into an agency that served not as an overseer but a partner of business. Only three weeks after he took office, the Commission voted new rules of practice and procedure. Under the new rules, cases were settled informally with little investigation or publicity. As Humphrey explained: "So far as I can prevent it, the Federal Trade Commission is not going to be used as a publicity bureau to spread socialistic propaganda." *Outlook* observed: "Business has always hated and has steadily determined to throttle the Commission. Because of the change in control due to the appointment of Commissioner Humphrey, it is proceeding rapidly. . . ."[12]

Humphrey boasted of his own role in the alteration. "I certainly did make a revolutionary change in the method and policies of the commission," he was quoted as stating. "If it was going east before, it is going west now." Nor was he shy about admitting that he had stacked the FTC's board of review. "What of it?" he asked. "Do you think I would have a body of men working here under me that did not share my ideas about these matters? Not on your life. I would not hesitate a minute to cut their heads off if they disagreed with me. What in hell do you think I am here for?" Humphrey recognized that some disapproved of what he had done, but he dismissed these critics as "the vocal and beatific fringe, the pink edges that border both of the old parties." "No longer" would FTC serve "as a means of gratifying demagogues."[13]

A bald, round-faced man with a bushy mustache and beard, Humphrey was a pugnacious autocrat who seemed to be forever embroiled in controversy. He quarreled not only with his critics in Congress but with his fellow commissioners, Abram F. Myers and Charles W. Hunt. When Myers said that at some point a federal licensing law for corporations would be needed, Humphrey commented: "It would be hard to imagine a more socialistic proposal than this."[14] In the fall of 1927 Humphrey wrote President Coolidge to object to a statement by Myers and to state that he hoped the next appointment to the FTC would be one "in keeping with that of the rational and conservative business element in this country."[15]

Humphrey's solicitousness toward the "conservative business element" brought him into some steamy brawls with progressives of both parties. Early in 1928 Gifford Pinchot wrote him that he thought it was "hopeless" to expect an adequate investigation by the FTC of abuses in the utilities industry, "because of long personal experience with you as a bitter enemy of the Roosevelt Conservation policy, an opponent of Federal action and a lobbyist of lumbermen." Humphrey replied: "Your letter of regurgitated filth received. For your own famished sake, and for the infinite relief of the country, have your keeper lead you to a thistle patch." Then, characteristically, Humphrey released both letters to the press.[16]

Under Humphrey, the functions of the FTC atrophied, in part as a consequence of court decisions, but also because of Humphrey's policies.[17] Early in 1928 he wrote Senator Arthur Robinson that he objected to "fantastic fishing expeditions" by the Commission which were "doing the administration great harm with the business interests."[18] Subsequently, he opposed appropriations for FTC investigations of unfair business practices in a number of industries. Disgusted by the way in which Humphrey was frustrating the original intent of Congress in creating the Commission, Senators in both parties proposed to abolish the FTC. When President Herbert Hoover nominated Humphrey for another six-year term in 1931, the new Senator from Louisiana, Huey Long, made his maiden speech in opposition to confirmation, and twenty-eight Senators voted not to confirm. By the time Franklin D. Roosevelt had won election in 1932, Humphrey had become a symbol of all that progressives abhorred in the Old Order. In January, 1933, Congressman Wright Patman of Texas sounded a popular note when he voiced the hope that when Roosevelt entered the White House he would "certainly change the policy of the Federal Trade Commission and put it back to its original function or intent."[19]

As soon as the Hundred Days Congress concluded its historic session, President Roosevelt turned toward the task of manning the agencies that had been created that spring or which had had new assignments bestowed on them. The Federal Trade Commission had been designated by the National Industrial Recovery Act as a court of appeals in trade practices litigation. Even more important, the draftsmen of the Securities Act of 1933 had decided, surprisingly, to vest authority for administering the new law in the FTC. As James M. Landis, one of the draftsmen, later explained: "Its reputation as an effective regulatory agency during the Harding–Coolidge–Hoover era had admittedly not been of the highest, but we understood that the administration intended to restaff and reinvigorate it."[20]

As he thought about the new role of the FTC, Roosevelt scrawled his ideas about personnel on a White House pad:

Fed. Trade Comm	10,000
Humphrey—out	F. Murphy?
	La Follette?
March, Minn. ok	

McCulloch—dead   Perk?
Fergusson   ok
Hunt   retired[21]

Of the five positions on the Commission, two were vacant. Not only Edward A. McCulloch, a Democrat, but the Republican, Charles W. Hunt, listed by Roosevelt as "retired," had died recently. To these vacancies Roosevelt decided to name Erwin L. Davis of Tennessee and Raymond B. Stevens of New Hampshire, one of the authors of the original FTC Act of 1914 and a former special counsel to the Commission. The three remaining members were Humphrey, whose term would expire in 1937; C. H. March, a liberal Republican from Minnesota whose term ran until 1936; and Garland S. Ferguson, a North Carolina Democrat whose term was about to run out. Roosevelt resolved to reappoint Ferguson, to leave March undisturbed, but, as his note on the memo pad indicated, to oust Humphrey and to name someone like Detroit's Democratic mayor, Frank Murphy, or Philip La Follette, the progressive Republican from Wisconsin, in his place.

Toward the end of the second week in July, 1933, rumors began to circulate about the President's intentions. By July 13, they had reached as far as Myrtle Beach, South Carolina, where Senator E. D. "Cotton Ed" Smith wrote Roosevelt to ask him to defer action until they could confer.[22] Sometime in the next few days, Will Humphrey got wind of the disturbing news. On July 19, he wrote the President:

Information comes to me that you are going to ask my resignation. For what reason I do not know.

Senator Dill, who is more responsible for my being in this position and more interested personally and politically in my retaining it, is away and cannot be reached. His return is expected within a few days.

If final action cannot be delayed until his return, then in behalf of the Senator as well as myself, I feel that I should ask for a personal interview. If I have neglected any duty, done anything dishonorable, or discreditable; or have been guilty of disloyalty, it is not necessary for you to ask my resignation. Certainly it seems to me that it is not necessary to involve mutual friends in this matter.

For the greater part of forty years, I have been in the public service. I am not aware of anything discreditable in my record, or of any act that I would blot out. If that long service is ended by forced resignation, it would be to some extent a reflection on my career and would greatly injure me in my profession if I should again take up the practice of law.[23]

For half a century Humphrey had been playing the political game of favors and rewards. In his memory, he kept a ledger of good turns he had done for which he expected payment in full.[24] On July 25, he sent a typically blunt letter to Senator C. C. Dill, a Democrat from his own state of Washington:

I was amazed and shocked at what you said yesterday. If I had known what you told me a few weeks ago, it would have been entirely different, and I could easily have made other satisfactory arrangements.

Naturally, after I left you I got in touch with several of my friends, including Senators and other prominent people, who know about affairs of this kind. Each one said that the President would do whatever you desired in the matter, that he would not ask my resignation unless you acquiesced. This opinion I could not and cannot change. They did not think it advisable for them to attempt to do anything further, as they had been depending on your active assistance. . . .

I cannot believe, as I have been informed, and as you seem to believe, that the President is going to ask my resignation without giving me an opportunity to be heard. If it is done in this manner, as you well know, it will smirch my record and greatly handicap me in my profession. I think if he contemplates this, I have the right to insist that you protest such action and that you will arrange an interview with you and myself. . . .

I shall only add that I have carefully reviewed our many years of friendship, extending from the time you left the House of Representatives—a friendship of which I have been proud—and in all of those years I remember gratefully the many favors that I have received. Of those given, I shall not mention—only to say that they were given gladly, either when they were political or personal, without regard to the effect on me, and I have found nothing in all those years which I feel does not justify me in thinking I have the right to expect that you will be pleased to comply with the request I have made—and that you will do everything in your power to carry it out. And so I do believe. Nothing but your failure to do so will ever make me believe that you will not.[25]

Dill, who may already have interceded for Humphrey, was quick to oblige the Commissioner. On July 28 he wrote Roosevelt that he had heard a rumor, he hoped unfounded, that the President was planning to replace Humphrey with a "Progressive Republican." He pointed out that he had served in Congress with Humphrey; both had been members of the Committee on Rivers and Harbors. He reminded Roosevelt that when the IWW had incited hostile response to Secretary Josephus Daniels during World War I, Humphrey had leapt to Daniels' defense, and that Humphrey had displayed "disinterested kindness" to one of the President's wartime subordinates. "While Bill Humphrey is an ardent partisan in politics," Dill wrote, "I believe he has been equally as loyal in his public service to you as he was to your predecessors."[26]

Even before Dill wrote, Roosevelt had informed Humphrey that he would not grant him an interview. He continued:

Without any reflection at all upon you personally or upon the service you have rendered in your present capacity, I find it necessary to ask for your resignation as a member of the Federal Trade Commission. I do this because I feel that the aims and purpose of the Administration with respect to the work of the Commission can be carried out most effectively with personnel of my own selection.

May I take this opportunity to tell you that at the earnest request of Senator Dill, I have been withholding this action for some time but have now reached a definite decision to proceed along the lines I have in mind.[27]

By August 1 Humphrey had resigned himself to the fact that he was about to be fired, and he apparently planned no further overtures to persuade the President to reverse his decision. All he asked was a temporary reprieve. He wrote Roosevelt:

While I had heard that you intended to ask my resignation, I did not believe it until I received your letter. Naturally, I was somewhat disturbed and shocked on its receipt. If I could have had a personal interview with you before you made the request, the matter might have been arranged satisfactorily to all parties concerned. But it is not profitable to discuss the question now.

As you well understand, I have lost all professional and business connections after being out of practice for nine years. Naturally, I should like to consult my friends as to my future actions.

Humphrey, it appeared, desired only enough time to confer with friends in Seattle about returning to private practice.[28] On August 4, Roosevelt wired Humphrey that he appreciated his desire for time to make arrangements. Consequently, he was accepting the Commissioner's resignation but not to take effect until August 15.[29]

It was altogether out of character for so combative a man as Humphrey to accept being driven out of office this meekly. Sometime in the first two weeks of August, he sought legal advice; he was told that there were strong grounds for doubting that the President had the authority to remove him. As he later explained: "While I started out with the belief that the President had the power to remove for any cause he saw fit, fuller examination of the authorities convinces me beyond reasonable doubt that he can remove me only for the reasons specified in the statute, and after hearing." He had employed "two of the best Democratic lawyers," and they had confirmed the opinions of counsel he had consulted earlier.[30]

On August 11 Humphrey, in a letter to Roosevelt, denied that he had tendered his resignation. Nor, indeed, did he intend to resign. To do so would be interpreted as an admission that he was guilty of one or more of the failings that would, by statute, justify the President in removing him: "inefficiency, neglect of duty, or malfeasance in office." Moreover, if he were to quit in order to permit the President to have his way, the independence of all regulatory commissions would be placed in jeopardy. He concluded:

I am fully aware of the great power of the President, and of the dangerous consequences that may follow a refusal of his request, still—

> "I had as lief not be, as live to be
> In awe of such a thing as I myself."[31]

A week later Humphrey once more turned to Dill for help, this time stating his demand even more cavalierly. "I have reason to believe that things are in such shape that if you would send a telegram to the President, urging him—not only on political grounds, but on personal friendship, to stop the whole affair, that it would be done." He went on:

You will remember when certain parties were insisting upon your being indicted in the matter of the Colville Indian claims, and it accidentally came to my knowledge. While the parties argued that it was impossible for you to escape conviction and that the only course would be to throw yourself upon the mercy of the Court, I argued with them that even if this were true, that such action on your part carried no moral turpitude and that you were innocent of any intentional wrong doing; that you were a young man and it would tend largely to discredit you and would be a disgrace through life—and that I would not consent to it. Just recently I have seen one of the men who attended that conference, and without any prompting from me, when I mentioned the subject, he stated . . . he thought that this plea stopped further proceedings.

He further told the Senator of how he had saved him from "certain unfortunate real estate transactions" and of the political favors he had done for him. "Under the circumstances," Humphrey argued, "I feel fully justified in asking you to send the telegram."[32]

On August 21 from Spokane, Dill replied that he was "deeply grateful" for past favors from Humphrey but pointed out that Humphrey would not have been confirmed on either occasion when he had been nominated to the FTC save for Dill's intervention. Moreover, the Senator noted, he had twice asked Roosevelt not to remove Humphrey. "I did all I could for you this time when I was there, but after all the President is boss and I can't control his appointments," Dill wrote. "I think I have exhausted whatever influence I had in this particular matter." But the very next day Dill thought better of it. From a hotel in Ellensburg, Washington, he scribbled a note to Humphrey assuring him that he had not exhausted his influence, and that he was writing the President once more.[33]

Somewhat mollified by Dill's last note, Humphrey nonetheless assumed his familiar role of Republican partisan and threatened the Democratic Senator with reprisals for his party. He thought that there might be a collapse before the end of the year that would mean "complete defeat" for the Administration at the next election; certainly, the chances of the Democrats holding the House in the next election were no better than even. He could not understand why the President would run such a risk as to fire him. Humphrey warned Dill: "I am convinced that I can bring this case into Court at any time within the next five years, and if it is made a party issue my party will expect that it will be brought up at a time and in a manner when it will be most to their political advantage."[34]

Humphrey, who seems to have been genuinely surprised that a New Deal President might want to remove him, added:

I know that you have heard the charge that I am in favor of the "big interests." So far as this has any foundation in fact, it may grow out of cases wherein I have opposed issuing certain orders. But I have been sustained by the lower courts and by the Supreme Court in my dissents in these cases almost one hundred percent. Nothing further need be said to any lawyer in this connection. What is the use of spending money and time issuing orders that the courts will not sustain?

After observing that he had also been charged with opposing investigations, he observed: "I am and always have been opposed to investigations to be made by the Economic Division of an industry, to see whether—according to the Division—such industry was conducting its business in an economic way." He denied, however, that he had opposed appropriations for the FTC.[35]

If there had ever been a time when Dill might have dissuaded Roosevelt from acting—and that is highly improbable—that time had now passed.[36] As soon as Roosevelt had received Humphrey's letter of August 11, he had recognized that the Commissioner might refuse to resign, and he had initiated steps to build a case against him. On August 14 he sent a confidential memorandum to Attorney General Homer Cummings requesting him to look into the allegation that Humphrey had favored a cut in funds for the FTC's investigation of utilities in 1932. He also asked his new commissioner, Raymond Stevens, to examine a charge by Samuel I. Rosenman, one of the original Brain Trusters, that Humphrey had acted improperly in a rayon trust case. On August 17 Roosevelt received word that Stevens had reported that the "matter you asked him to investigate has reached a very critical stage. Anxious to talk with you as soon as possible."[37]

In the last two weeks in August reports reached the White House from the Department of Justice and from Stevens, who took advantage of his official position to comb the FTC files for evidence of wrongdoing by Humphrey. Some of the leads failed to prove out. It developed that Humphrey had not advocated a cut in FTC appropriations for the utilities probe, and his relation to the rayon affair was not clear-cut. Yet there was ample evidence that he had opposed FTC investigations, that he had belittled the work of the Commission, and that he had been guilty of using "intemperate and abusive language."[38]

Bolstered by the reports he had received from Stevens and others, the President was now ready to move once more. On August 31 Roosevelt, in a firm but tactful manner, requested Humphrey's resignation and asked that he have it in the next week. He stated: "You will, I know, realize that I do not feel that your mind and my mind go along together on either the policies or the administering of the Federal Trade Commission, and frankly, I think it is best for the people of this country that I should have full confidence."[39]

Even the unmistakably final tone of this letter did not convince Humphrey that Roosevelt truly meant to fire him. Once again he badgered Dill to wire the President to undertake an investigation. He stated "without reservation" that it was untrue that his mind and Roosevelt's did not go along together. "As I told you before, somebody has been lying to him," Humphrey asserted.[40] Nine days later Humphrey sent a lengthy letter to the President saying that Roosevelt's note of August 31 had gratified him, because for the first time he had been given a reason for his proposed removal. But he immediately added: "You are entirely mistaken as to the facts." He challenged Roosevelt to show where they differed on policies, and contended, strangely, that the FTC had been undivided, and hence that to criticize him was to censure the entire Commission. He was sure that the President had been victimized by "whisperings," "misrepresentations," and "insinuations," some of which may have been the result of "some sinister motive." He asked only for a fair hearing, and, identifying himself with St. Paul, asked: "Is it lawful to scourge a man, an American citizen, and uncondemned?"[41]

The President refused to see Humphrey, but he did ask Charles H. McCarthy, who had served as Roosevelt's secretary during his tenure as Assistant Secretary of the Navy, to telephone Humphrey. McCarthy explained that the President did not believe that Humphrey agreed with him either on FTC policy or on administration of the Securities Act, and that he wished to name a securities expert to the FTC. Quite apart from "the legal aspect of the matter," Humphrey would be well-advised to resign and avoid being humiliated, McCarthy said.[42] That very day Associated Press tickers reported news of the impending ouster. The A.P. story, Humphrey wrote Roosevelt ten days later, had confirmed him in his determination not to resign.[43]

Once Roosevelt accepted the fact that he could not persuade Humphrey to resign, he proceeded with plans to fire him and to appoint a successor. Since Philip La Follette either was unavailable or seemed an inadvisable choice, the President began negotiations with another progressive Republican from Wisconsin, George Mathews, formerly Wisconsin Public Utilities Commissioner and currently a rate expert for the receivers of the Insull empire. Mathews first sought assurance that he would not be involved in litigation with Humphrey. His fears were assuaged, and on October 3 the President learned that Mathews would accept an appointment to succeed Humphrey, if such an offer were made.[44] The White House then arranged to have a wire appointing Mathews sent on the same day, October 7, 1933, that a brisk note was delivered to Humphrey, stating: "Effective as of this date you are hereby removed from the office of Commissioner of the Federal Trade Commission."[45]

For Humphrey, the long struggle to win the President over had ended, and he made no attempt to disguise his fury. He wrote Roosevelt:

For weeks I have known that certain insurgent Republican Senators were demanding my removal, and that you desired my resignation because of reasons assigned by them but concealed from me. . . . I must presume that the charges made were given to you under seal of secrecy and that you feel you are in honor bound to regard them as such. I cannot think of any other justification for your refusal to give me an opportunity to meet these charges. These certain insurgents are cowards. They will not fight like men. . . . They destroy any who trust them. They betrayed the Republican Party. They will destroy the Democratic Party. They will betray you the moment it is to their interest so to do. They are character assassins. They stab only in the back and in the dark. This same collection of political hypocrites tried twice to prevent my confirmation but were defeated each time by a large majority, composed of Democrats and Republicans. These insurgents were too cowardly and dishonest to accept the verdict of an open and honorable fight, and now to accomplish their purpose, they come with slanderous and polluted lips and spew their putrid filth upon you under the pledge of secrecy. The history of American politics does not furnish a more infamous transaction.

These sanctified experts of expediency, who use a party name simply to be elected, are mental perverts who glorify treachery and intellectual dishonesty. . . .[46]

Humphrey was too much of a scrapper to give up the fight now. He retained William J. Donovan, former assistant to the Attorney General, as his lawyer, and carried his battle into the courts. On advice of counsel, he acted out a charade of pretending still to be the Commissioner.[47] On October 9 he wrote Mathews:

You are hereby notified that your appointment as Federal Trade Commissioner is invalid, because there was no vacancy to which you could be appointed, and you are notified that I am still a Member of the Federal Trade Commission, filling the term for which you are supposed to be appointed, and that I claim and shall claim the emoluments of the said office to the expiration of my present term.[48]

That same day, when the FTC held its regularly scheduled meeting, Humphrey turned up to hand the Commission a statement disputing the validity of his removal and to sit in silence for two hours while the commission conducted its business. The commissioners, however, voted to accept the validity of Humphrey's removal and of Mathews' appointment.[49] Humphrey also filed periodic claims for back pay with the disbursing officer of the FTC, but these claims were turned down, and the Acting Comptroller General ruled that Mathews' appointment was valid.[50]

The legal niceties having been attended to, Humphrey was ready to press his case. On October 20, he wrote Colonel Donovan that he thought "action should be taken soon." Predictably, he disagreed with his attorney's interpretation of legal precedents in the case.[51] On December 28, Humphrey filed suit in the U.S. Court of Claims contesting his removal and demanding $1,251.39 in back salary. (Eventually, the sum was raised to $3,043.06 with interest.)

Since Humphrey had been confirmed by the Senate for a full six-year term, he believed that Congress would resent Roosevelt's actions as an infringement on its prerogatives and that he could count on aid from that quarter. On January 18, 1934, Humphrey, once more exploiting his influence with Dill, secured an invitation to appear before the Senate Interstate Commerce Committee, of which Dill was chairman, to challenge the confirmation of Mathews. The Committee even postponed the hearing in order to accommodate Humphrey, who had been ill. Yet Humphrey expressed disappointment about one matter. "I doubt if we are going to have any Senator make a speech on our side of the case when the matter of Mr. Mathews' confirmation comes up for consideration," he wrote Colonel Donovan.[52] Silence in the Senate, Humphrey feared, would give the Court the impression that Congress was willing to waive its rights.

Humphrey's concern proved generally well-founded. The Senate, after brief speeches criticizing the President's action by two Old Guard Republicans, Simeon Fess of Ohio and Daniel O. Hastings of Delaware, confirmed the nomination of George C. Mathews unanimously.[53] In the House, only one voice was raised in protest, and even Representative Joseph L. Hooper, a Michigan Republican, conceded that it was not absolutely clear that Roosevelt did not have the legal right to remove Humphrey. Hooper rested much of his case on the argument that the President was not playing the game of party politics squarely. Since the law stipulated that no more than three of the five commissioners could be members of the same political party, Hooper reasoned not only that the other two places were reserved for Republicans but for bona fide, card-carrying Republicans at that. If Roosevelt had gone through with his reported intention to replace Humphrey with Philip La Follette, said Hooper, "it would be as though a Republican President had nominated Norman Thomas to the Trade Commission on the theory that he was a Democrat." Furthermore, Hooper warned, there were no limits to how far Roosevelt might go. He might, for example, remove a federal district judge; if he did, it would be "little more violent" an infringement than his ouster of Humphrey. "The law must be the law for magistrate and citizen alike or we are no longer a Republic," he declared. "Those who believe in arbitrary power may take comfort, perhaps, from incidents such as these; but they are big with disaster to democratic ideals and traditions and government."[54]

On February 14, 1934, four weeks after his testimony before Dill's committee, Humphrey suffered a stroke and died at the age of seventy-one. Yet this did not terminate his suit. The executor of Humphrey's estate, Samuel Rathbun, assumed the role of plaintiff, and the case henceforth bore two names: Rathbun v. U.S., and Humphrey's Executor v. U.S.[55] So the struggle went on. A bare-fisted brawler all his life, Humphrey continued to provide the occasion for a fight even after his death.

Early in 1935, President Roosevelt named Stanley Reed the new Solicitor General. When Reed took office, Attorney General Cummings called him in and solicitously suggested that he pick out a certain victory for the first case he would argue before the U.S. Supreme Court. Reed looked over the list of pending litigation with this in mind, and hit upon a sure winner: the Humphrey case.[56]

Reed's confidence stemmed from an opinion delivered by the Supreme Court in response to a suit filed by another federal official; like Humphrey, he was from the Pacific Northwest, quarrelsome, and had died before the Court ruled. The postmaster of Portland, Oregon, Frank S. Myers, appointed by President Woodrow Wilson to a four-year term with the advice and consent of the Senate, had been removed by Wilson in February, 1920, without the consent of the Senate, before his term had expired. He filed suit in the Court of Claims for back salary on the grounds that the President needed Senate consent to fire him, since an act of 1876 had stipulated: "Postmasters of the first, second and third classes shall be appointed and may be removed by the President by and with the advice and consent of the Senate, and may hold their offices for four years unless sooner removed or suspended according to law."[57] The Court of Claims ruled against Myers, and the case was appealed to the Supreme Court by Myers' widow.

Until the Myers case reached it, the Supreme Court had been circumspect about ruling on the President's removal power. The Court appeared to be willing to accept the precedent set by the so-called "Legislative Decision of 1789," when the First Congress, somewhat ambiguously, had recognized the right of the President to remove the Secretary of Foreign Affairs without its consent. Moreover, it was understandably reluctant to meddle in so "political" a question. On the few occasions the Court had spoken, it had construed liberally the President's removal power. In the

Shurtleff case, in upholding President William McKinley's ouster of a minor official, the Court had stated: "The right of removal would exist if the statute had not contained a word upon the subject. It does not exist by virtue of the grant, but it inheres in the right to appoint, unless limited by Constitution or statute." Yet the Shurtleff opinion was open to more than one interpretation, and the Court had still not defined the exact scope of the removal power.[58]

The Myers case, however, came to a court led by William Howard Taft, a Chief Justice who had no hesitation about intervening in matters that some previous courts would have shied away from. Stung by the many barbs flung at him by insurgent Congressmen during his term as president, Taft seized on this suit as a way to strike a blow for the authority of the Chief Executive. He quickly found that a majority of the justices shared his belief that Myers' ouster was a legitimate exercise of the President's power. But he was not content to confine himself to the issue at hand; he wished to define the widest possible latitude for the removal power. To this end, he called a rump meeting of the justices who supported him, and, to meet their objections, worked and reworked the draft of his opinion.[59] Not until a year and a half after arguments had been completed was Taft ready with his opinion. "I agree with you that we have not had a case in two generations of more importance," he told Justice Harlan Fiske Stone.[60]

On October 25, 1926, almost seven years after Myers had been ousted, the Court finally ruled on *Myers v. United States*. For a Court divided 6–3, Taft, in a sixty-one page opinion, sustained the decision of the Court of Claims. He ruled that the section of the act of 1876 requiring Senate concurrence in the removal of a postmaster was unconstitutional. Devoting almost half of his opinion to the "Legislative Decision of 1789," the Chief Justice claimed that there was ample historical precedent to support the view that the President's removal power was illimitable. Furthermore, he stated that the President's exclusive power of removal derived from his power to appoint and his obligation to execute the laws. Even more far-reaching was Taft's contention that this power was an inherent part of the executive power granted by Article II of the Constitution, and could not be circumscribed by Congress. All "executive officers of the United States" were subject to removal by the President at will.

Not content with enunciating this sweeping doctrine, the Chief Justice went out of his way to offer a brief obiter dictum which claimed that the President's removal power extended even to members of independent regulatory commissions. Taft stated:

There may be duties of a quasi-judicial character imposed on executive officers and members of executive tribunals whose decisions after hearing affect interests of individuals, the discharge of which the President can not in a particular case properly influence or control. But even in such a case, he may consider the decision after its rendition as a reason for removing the officer, on the ground that the discretion regularly entrusted to that officer by statute has not been on the whole intelligently or wisely exercised. Otherwise, he does not discharge his own constitutional duty of seeing that the laws be faithfully executed.[61]

Taft, who prided himself on his ability to mass the Court, suffered the embarrassment of three separate dissents. Justice Oliver Wendell Holmes required only three paragraphs to state his disapproval of the "spiders' webs" the Chief Justice had woven. Affirming his belief in the authority of Congress, Holmes stated: "We have to deal with an office that owes its existence to Congress and that Congress may abolish tomorrow. Its duration and the pay attached to it while it lasts depend on Congress alone. . . ."[62]

The irascible Justice James C. McReynolds prepared a dissent which ran to sixty-two pages. Instead of reading it, he delivered an acrid extemporaneous speech from the bench as he was later to do in the gold clause cases.[63] As Mark Sullivan of the New York *Herald Tribune* caught his remarks, McReynolds said: "The decision of the majority of the court is revolutionary, and the sooner the thinking people of the country understand it the better. Yesterday we supposed we had a government of definitely limited and specified powers. Today no one knows what those powers are."[64]

The most powerful dissent came from Justice Louis D. Brandeis. James M. Landis, who was Brandeis's law clerk at the time, later called the dissent "as thorough a piece of historical research as you would find in the Supreme Court reports anywhere." Landis explained:

It started out with a page and a half. It ended up with, oh, I should say approximately 35 pages. Months were spent on that. . . . I paged, literally paged, every one of the Senate journals from the time of the passage of the Tenure of Office Act. . . . Just in order to determine what the practice was. After all, practice is the important thing in determining constitutional law.

But Brandeis's point was not that under the Constitution the Senate had the power to join in dealing with the removal of an individual who had been appointed by and with the advice and consent of the Senate, which was the theory of the Tenure of Office Act. His point was that Congress, if it chose, as a whole, could place limitations on removal of officials that it created.[65]

A detailed, learned statement of his objections to Taft's arguments, Brandeis' dissenting opinion ran fifty-six pages. Embarrassed by its length, Brandeis offered to pay the cost of printing it, but Taft would not hear of it, although he deeply resented the opinion.[66] In his dissent, Brandeis disputed Taft's claim that the removal power was an inherent aspect of the authority of the Executive. Such power, he argued, came from Congress, and the Founding Fathers had opposed granting the President unlimited removal power. "The conviction prevailed then that the people must look to representative assemblies for protection of their liberties," Brandeis asserted. "And protection of the individual, even if he be an official, from arbitrary or capricious exercise of power was then believed to be an essential of free government." Moreover, he pointed out, the principle of separation of powers had been adopted "not to promote efficiency, but to preclude the exercise of arbitrary power. The purpose was, not to avoid friction, but, by means of the inevitable friction incident to the distribution of the governmental powers among three departments, to save the people from autocracy."[67]

The Myers decision stirred up a storm. For the first time since the Insular Cases a quarter of a century earlier, a Supreme Court decision won front page coverage in the morning newspapers. Taft's opinion met a volley of criticism in the law reviews and from a political spectrum ranging from liberals like Robert M. La Follette, Jr., to conservatives such as George Wharton Pepper. Thomas Reed Powell found the logic "lame," the language "inconclusive," the history "far from compelling." Senator Hiram Johnson declared that the opinion gratified those who thought the country needed a Mussolini.[68]

So disturbed was the National Municipal League by the possible consequences of the Myers decision for local as well as national officials that it invited Edward S. Corwin, McCormick Professor of Jurisprudence at Princeton University, to write an analysis. Corwin's monograph, published in 1927, assailed Taft's logic and his handling of historical data. The Chief Justice's opinion, Corwin protested, "permits congress to vest duties in executive officers in the performance of which they are to exercise their own independent judgment; then it permits the president to guillotine such officers for exercising the very discretion which congress has the right to require of them!" The power of removal, Corwin concluded, should vary with the nature of the office.[69]

Such widespread criticism of the Myers opinion should have made Roosevelt more hesitant about ousting Humphrey. Apparently, Roosevelt never thought to get a legal opinion from Cummings. Yet it is also true that Cummings raised no objections. Moreover, Stevens, who had known the FTC from its infancy, advised that, on the basis of the Shurtleff and Myers opinions, Roosevelt could remove Humphrey for whatever reason he wished. He suggested to the President that, in removing Humphrey, he adopt the very language of McKinley's order dismissing Shurtleff, and the President's final order did follow closely the form of McKinley's edict.[70]

There appeared to be good reason for Roosevelt, and for lieutenants like Stevens and Reed, to feel sanguine. If Taft's opinion had been raked over, it had also elicited considerable support.[71] Not only commentators who approved the opinion but some who deplored it stated that it was now the law of the land that FTC Commissioners were removable by the President at will.[72] A Chicago attorney, writing in the *American Political Science Review*, applauded the fact that the Court had recognized "the untrammeled control by the President of his subordinates, including . . . the Federal Trade Commission."[73] Furthermore, no amount of adverse commentary meant as much as the fact that only seven years had passed since a Chief Justice, supported by a majority of the justices, had offered such a drastic interpretation of the President's power and had, albeit in an obiter dictum, applied it to the specific problem at hand.

There was one final reason for optimism. The White House had consulted James M. Landis, and Landis, although sympathetic to the Brandeis dissent, had assured the President of his authority to remove Humphrey. Landis later told an interviewer:

I'm not sure who asked me, but I was asked by someone in very close connection with the White House as to what I thought about the President's power to remove a member of the Federal Trade Commission. I said I doubt whether there is anybody in the United States that can answer that question better than I can, because I went through the whole Myers controversy, and I know how insistent the Chief Justice (that was Taft) and the majority of the Court was, in placing in that opinion, even though it dealt with a fourth-class post-master . . . , statements to the effect that the President's power of removal extended to members of various independent commissions. I said, "That was deliberately put there. If that had not been put in there, I doubt whether some of the dissents would have been as bitter as they were."

So indirectly I advised Mr. Roosevelt that there was no question about his power to remove Humphrey.[74]

On May 1, 1935, Solicitor General Reed and Colonel Donovan came before the Supreme Court to argue the matter of Humphrey's claim. The case had been certified to the Supreme Court by the Court of Claims, which, instead of ruling, had posed two questions. Both centered on the provision of the FTC statute of 1914 which stipulated: "Any commissioner may be removed by the President for inefficiency, neglect of duty, or malfeasance in office."[75] The Court of Claims asked: Did this section limit the President's power to remove commissioners to one of these specific causes? If so, was such a limitation on the President's removal power constitutional?

The joust between Reed and Donovan took a predictable form. Reed claimed that the Myers and Shurtleff decisions offered sufficient precedent for the President's action. More than this, he reasoned that the duty to carry out faithfully such novel legislation as the Securities Act of 1933 "may presuppose wholehearted sympathy with the purposes and policy of the law, and energy and resourcefulness beyond that of the ordinarily efficient public servant. The President should be free to judge in what measure these qualities are possessed and to act upon that judgment." Donovan countered that *Shurtleff* was not relevant because it dealt with an official whose tenure had not been stipulated by statute, and that *Myers* was inapplicable because a postmaster belonged to a different category from a member of a regulatory commission, a type of agency whose independence must be safeguarded from executive domination.[76]

On May 27, 1935, less than a month after argument, the Supreme Court gathered for the next to the last time in the old Senate chamber. That October it would reconvene in the marble edifice across the Capitol Plaza. Shortly after noon the nine black-robed justices filed in. Six of the nine judges who had taken part in the Myers case marched in the procession; in the interim, Charles Evans Hughes had replaced Chief Justice Taft; Owen Roberts had succeeded Edward Sanford; and Holmes's berth had been filled by Benjamin Cardozo. Without ceremony, they proceeded to read the day's decisions. First came Pierce Butler's opinion for the Court in an insignificant life insurance suit; as Butler read, spectators in the crowded courtroom squirmed in their seats. They had come expecting more momentous events, and their boredom with this first opinion was unconcealed.[77]

Attention quickened as the Chief Justice nodded to Justice Sutherland, and Sutherland, in an indistinct murmur, began to read his fourteen-page opinion in the case of Humphrey's Executor v. U.S. For some minutes, as Sutherland recited the terms of the Federal Trade Commission Act, the thrust of his opinion was not apparent. In an orderly fashion, he dealt in turn with each of the questions posed by the Court of Claims. Did the FTC act restrict the power of a president to remove a commissioner except for cause? Of this, there could be little doubt. Nor was there any question at all that Roosevelt had not removed Humphrey for cause; instead of charging him with some dereliction like malfeasance, he had indiscreetly written that their minds had not gone along together.

The crucial question was the second one asked of the Court: Was the restriction on the President's removal power set forth in the FTC law valid? Here the Court came squarely up against the

Myers precedent. Although Sutherland had joined in Taft's opinion, he now denied its relevance to the Humphrey matter. All that the Myers decision had settled, he said, was that a president could dismiss a postmaster, but "the office of a postmaster is so essentially unlike the office now involved that the decision in the Myers case cannot be accepted as controlling." But had not the Chief Justice said a good deal more than that in the Myers case? Sutherland stated blandly: "In the course of the opinion of the court, expressions occur which tend to sustain the government's contention, but these are beyond the point involved, and therefore, do not come within the rule of stare decisis. In so far as they are out of harmony with the views here set forth, these expressions are disapproved." Without ever joining issue with Taft directly, Sutherland noted that "dicta . . . may be followed if sufficiently persuasive but . . . are not controlling."

Sutherland then sought to explain how the office of a federal trade commissioner differed from that of a first-class postmaster. "A postmaster is an executive officer restricted to the performance of executive functions," Sutherland stated. "He is charged with no duty at all related to either legislative or judicial power." The Myers decision, he insisted, applied to "purely executive officers," not to "an officer who occupies no place in the executive department and who exercises no part of the executive power vested by the Constitution in the President."

Sutherland continued:

The Federal Trade Commission is an administrative body created by Congress to carry into effect legislative policies. . . . Such a body cannot in any proper sense be characterized as an arm or eye of the executive. Its duties are performed without executive leave and . . . must be free from executive control. In administering the provisions of the statute . . . the commission acts in part quasi-legislatively and in part quasi-judicially. . . . To the extent that it exercises any executive function—as distinguished from executive power in the constitutional sense—it does so in the discharge and effectuation of its quasi-legislative or quasi-judicial powers, or as an agency of the legislative or judicial departments of the government.

After noting that if the President were conceded unlimited power to remove members of the FTC he would, in principle, be able to remove at will almost all civil officers, including judges of the Court of Claims, Sutherland declared:

We think it plain under the Constitution that illimitable power of removal is not possessed by the President in respect of officers of the character of those just named. The authority of Congress, in creating quasi-legislative or quasi-judicial agencies, to require them to act in discharge of their duties independently of executive control, cannot well be doubted; and that authority includes, as an appropriate incident, power to fix the period during which they shall continue, and to forbid their removal except for cause in the meantime.

The doctrine of illimitable power of removal, Sutherland contended, did violence to the principle of the separation of powers. "Its coercive influence," he observed, "threatens the independence of a commission, which is not only wholly disconnected from the executive department, but which . . . was created by Congress as a means of carrying into operation legislative and judicial powers, and as an agency of the legislative and judicial departments."

The President's power to remove, Sutherland concluded, hinged on the character of the office. The Myers decision, he reiterated, had been confined to "purely executive officers"; the decision in the pending case made clear that the President did not have unlimited power of removal over an officer like an FTC commissioner. He conceded that the Court might be leaving a "field of doubt" between the two rulings, but he added: "We leave such cases as may fall within it for future consideration and determination as they arise."[78]

Only when Sutherland ended his reading and no dissents were announced did the full import of the Court's decision become clear. By a unanimous 9–0 verdict, the Court had ruled that Roosevelt had exceeded his authority, and, by implication, it had instructed the Court of Claims to award Humphrey back pay. Sutherland had adroitly put together an opinion which caused a minimum of embarrassment for the Court, whatever other failings it might have had. There was not a suggestion in Sutherland's opinion that he, as well as three of his brethren—Van Devanter, Butler, and Stone—had gone along with Taft's sweeping opinion in the Myers case or that the President had grounds for believing that the Myers opinion represented the Court's view of the scope of his powers in 1933.[79] For Franklin Roosevelt, it was but the first of the rebuffs he would receive that afternoon. For Will Humphrey it was a posthumous triumph, the final victory the old warrior would ever win.

The "field of doubt" the Court had left was far more extensive than Sutherland suggested; no one has yet measured its metes and bounds. Even commentators who approved of the Humphrey decision found Sutherland's discussion of executive power confusing. Analysts familiar with the operation of the Federal Trade Commission were startled by his contention that an FTC Commissioner occupied "no place in the executive department." Nor could commissions like the FTC be categorized as "arms of Congress" in any meaningful sense, since they performed executive and judicial functions which Congress could not perform constitutionally. Moreover, as Robert E. Cushman has noted, "No task has been given to an independent regulatory commission which could not, with equal constitutional propriety, be given to an executive officer."[80]

E. S. Corwin, while generally in accord with the Humphrey verdict, has observed:

The truth is that some of Justice Sutherland's dicta are quite as extreme in one direction as some of Chief Justice Taft's dicta were in the opposite direction; and especially does he provoke wonderment by his assertion that a member of the Federal Trade Commission "*occupies no place in the executive department.*" . . . The dictum seems to have been the product of hasty composition, for certainly it is not to be squared by any verbal legerdemain with more deliberate utterances of the same Justice. . . . Moreover, if a Federal Trade Commissioner is not in the executive department, where is he? In the legislative department; or is he, forsooth, in the uncomfortable halfway situation of Mahomet's coffin, suspended " 'twixt Heaven and Earth?" . . . Nor is Justice Sutherland's endeavor to make out that [Federal Trade Commissioners] are any more "agents of Congress" than is a postmaster at all persuasive. Both officials get their powers—such as they are—from an exercise by Congress of its constitutionally delegated powers; there is no other possible source.[81]

Sutherland's implication that the FTC was in the legislative branch had first been enunciated during the debates on the FTC bill in 1914. Most lawmakers expressed no interest in the question whether the new commission was a direct agent of Congress, but when the measure was amended to expand the agency's powers, Senator Albert Cummins explained: "The trade commission that we here proposed to establish is purely an executive or administrative tribunal. It exercises no legislative function whatever." Alone of all the Senators, Sutherland persisted in describing the proposed agency as a "legislative commission." Strangely, in the light of the Humphrey opinion, it was Senator Sutherland who delivered the main argument against the constitutionality of the FTC bill; in particular, he objected that the new commission was being vested with judicial powers.[82] As Cushman has observed drily, in 1914 Sutherland had not yet "discovered the possibilities of the terms quasi-legislative and quasi-judicial."[83]

In 1937, a colloquy took place which raised doubts about whether Mr. Justice Sutherland understood the implications of his opinion in the Humphrey case. During oral argument, James W. Ryan, an attorney for a shipping company, stated that the Shipping Board was not in the executive branch. Cushman has described what ensued, as reported to him by someone who had observed the proceedings:

Justice Sutherland, who had been sitting back in his chair and asking occasional questions during the course of the argument, leaned forward quickly when he heard this.

"Did you say that the Shipping Board was not in the executive branch of the government?" He spoke as though he did not believe he had heard correctly, and several other Justices smiled condescendingly at counsel as though he were making a far-fetched proposition.

"Yes, your Honor," Mr. Ryan replied.

"What makes you think that? Where do you find any legal basis for such a conclusion?" the Justice wished to know.

"Why in your Honor's opinion in the Humphrey case, this Court held that the Federal Trade Commission and similar regulatory agencies were not in the executive branch of the government. The Shipping Board fell within the same general category as the Federal Trade Commission and the Interstate Commerce Commission." Mr. Ryan then proceeded to read certain portions of that opinion.

"What branch of the Government do you think the Shipping Board was in, if it was not in the executive branch?" the Justice wanted to know.

"In the legislative branch, your Honor."

Justice Sutherland shook his head, as though he disagreed, and seemed to be thinking the question over as the discussion went on to other points.[84]

Subsequent decisions by the Court have failed to clarify Sutherland's distinction between an "executive officer" and one exercising "legislative or judicial power."[85] When, in 1938, Roosevelt fired Arthur E. Morgan, chairman of the Tennessee Valley Authority, the President was charged with exceeding his authority, since it was said that the TVA was not in the executive department.[86] The Circuit Court of Appeals, however, sustained the President in an opinion which held that the TVA was primarily an arm of the executive branch. The Supreme Court declined to hear the case.[87] On the other hand, when President Dwight D. Eisenhower removed a Truman appointee from the War Claims Commission, the Supreme Court ruled against the President and awarded back salary. It held that a president could not remove a member of a quasi-judicial agency without cause, even if Congress had not stipulated grounds for removal.[88]

The actual effect of the Humphrey doctrine has been much less than some commentators have implied. Although the Court has twice ordered restitution of back pay, it has never restored a man to his job. To attempt to do so might carry the Court farther into the "political" forest than it would like to venture.[89] Nor has the Court ever had occasion to inquire whether a president had sufficient grounds for removing a commissioner "for cause." What would happen if a president decided to get rid of a member of the FTC and, to avert another Humphrey decision, trumped up a cause of removal stipulated by statute? One commentator has stated that it was "almost certain" that the courts would not challenge a president's discretion in assigning causes of removal.[90] Another has agreed that terms like "inefficiency" were so vague that courts would acknowledge that a president had "considerable, if not complete" discretionary authority.[91] Should a president, in the future, decide to fire a commissioner, he will no doubt have learned from the Humphrey decision that he should be more subtle than Roosevelt was in going about it.

In ruling out any kind of role for the President in the functioning of independent commissions, Sutherland never troubled to look at the actual history of the FTC and similar tribunals. One would not gather from the Court's opinion that any of Roosevelt's predecessors had ever tried to influence the commissions. Yet Wilson had secured inclusion in the FTC law of a clause authorizing the President to direct the Trade Commission to make investigations, and he had used this power frequently. As "weak" a president as Calvin Coolidge had made clear that he viewed these commissions as subordinate to the will of the Chief Executive. Coolidge, indeed, had gone far beyond anything Roosevelt later did in the Humphrey affair when, in offering an appointment on the Tariff Commission to David J. Lewis, he stipulated that Lewis submit an undated resignation which Coolidge could use at any time he saw fit.[92] Ironically, nothing demonstrated the determination of the administration in power to use the FTC as an instrument of its economic policy so well as Humphrey's own behavior under both Coolidge and Hoover. Pendleton Herring has noted:

There is more than a touch of irony in Humphrey's appeal to the court and the ground upon which he was sustained. Here was the most partisan-minded member of the Commission upheld in his position by the courts on the ground that the President had no right to intervene in the affairs of a quasi-judicial agency.[93]

Although Sutherland insisted that the FTC was a creature of Congress and must be kept independent of the Executive, Congress had, on more than one occasion, indicated its belief that the President had various kinds of authority over the commissions, and it had even scolded the President for their shortcomings. "In short," Cushman has written, "the commission was very definitely an agent of the executive branch and was recognized by Congress as being so." He summed up the situation at the time Roosevelt took office: "Throughout the discussions of this whole period there runs an underlying assumption that the commission's policy, if not actually directed from the White House, at least conforms to the President's wishes, that the President cannot escape responsibility for the commission's policy, and that an incoming President objecting to such policy should change it, if not by the actual issuance of orders to the commission, at least by the making of suitable appointments." In removing Humphrey, Cushman concluded, "the President was apparently doing in this situation what Congress assumed that he would and should do."[94]

Although Congress was perceived to be one of the beneficiaries of the Humphrey ruling, it found the implications of the opinion perplexing. In 1938, when Congress faced the question of drafting legislation to regulate the aviation industry, Representative Clarence Lea explained the measure that he was sponsoring: "It is the belief of the committee that we have written a bill in harmony with the Humphrey decision. We limit the power of the President to remove the members of the authority. We leave him unlimited authority to remove the members of the safety board and the administrator, because those officers are manifestly executive officers, concerning whom the President has the right of removal." The new bill created within a single authority two executive agencies whose officers were subject to discretionary removal by the President while the authority itself remained independent of presidential control, although it could delegate some of its jurisdiction to an officer under presidential control. In this fashion, Congress believed it was abiding by Sutherland's distinctions. Yet, the matter remained confusing:

> MR. BOREN. Under the Humphrey decision, the Federal Trade Commission is made an orphan child, so far as the three constitutional branches of the Government are concerned?
> MR. HESTER. That is correct.[95]

Sutherland's conception of the separation of powers was mechanistic. He failed to recognize that there was no way in which the fused functions of the independent tribunals may easily be reconciled with the doctrine of the separation of powers. The Interstate Commerce Commission, for example, has been variously described as "an executive body," "wholly legislative," and "in essence a judicial tribunal."[96] Sutherland's opinion gave most comfort to those who thought of the three branches as warring sovereignties and who aligned themselves with Congress against the President. The Detroit *Free Press*, in criticizing the removal of Humphrey, had referred to Congress and "the rival establishment centered in the White House."[97] At no point did the Court consider how the branches actually work together to enable the government to function.

For those who believed that the commissions must be kept independent of "political control," the Humphrey decision was a thrilling triumph. One authority on the FTC wrote afterwards: "This signal victory brought incalculable prestige to the Commission."[98] In a confidential interview a month after the decision, Brandeis, pleased by the outcome, warned that if such commissions could not exercise independent judgment, the country would be, in effect, a dictatorship. "What would happen to us if Huey Long were President and such a doctrine prevailed?" he asked.[99] "The real significance of the Humphrey doctrine," noted James M. Landis approvingly, lay "in its endorsement of administrative freedom of movement."[100] Yet others, equally devoted to democratic ideals, were dismayed by the decision. For those who wished modern government to be both effective and democratic, the clashing claims on behalf of independence on the one hand and party government and presidential leadership on the other raised some hard questions. It was these hard questions which Justice Sutherland and the Court never tried to answer.

Of the many misconceptions surrounding the Humphrey case, none is so striking as the misunderstanding of Franklin Roosevelt's aims. Many criticized the ouster as an attempt by the President to create another opportunity for patronage. Humphrey himself wrote Senator Dill: "The truth about it is that the action of the President is about the boldest act to restore the spoils system that has occurred since the days of Andrew Jackson."[101] Several weeks later, he protested to Senator Norris: "When I remember that during all the time I have been in this office, I have not written a political letter, or made a political speech, or made a political contribution . . . I feel exasperated that I should be removed for purely political reasons."[102] Humphrey's defenders repeatedly castigated Roosevelt for trying to "Tammanyize" the national government. "The deduction is a simple one, that Mr. Humphrey being a real Republican was therefore objectionable to the President," asserted Congressman Hooper. "If Mr. Hoover had removed a Democrat for *purely political reasons* from an office such as this, the country would have rung with denunciations."[103]

Those who attributed Roosevelt's removal of Humphrey to "political" motivations quite missed the point; the President fired

Humphrey not because he was a Republican but because the obstreperous Commissioner might disrupt an important phase of the New Deal recovery program. At first glance, it appears surprising that Roosevelt would run the risk of ousting Humphrey when he already had enough vacancies on the FTC to control the agency. Yet Humphrey was an adamant conservative. When a friend, in jest, called him a "standpatter," he replied: "When I think of the 'brain trust,' the progressives and the other fanatics and reformers, I think the word 'standpatter' is a badge of distinction and honor."[104] It seemed highly likely that Humphrey, as the senior member of a commission which now had added duties under the National Industrial Recovery Act and the Securities Act, would create dissension within the government. To be sure, any new administration must tolerate the presence of holdovers in such tribunals. But Roosevelt's coming to power in the crisis of March, 1933, was no ordinary changing of the guard; if the New Deal did not mark a "revolution" in American government, it did represent, in areas like regulation of Wall Street, a significant new departure. Roosevelt was unwilling to leave a man of the old order in charge of administering the legislation of the new order.

When the new President sought to rebuild the government to enable it to cope with the enormity of the Great Depression, he quickly recognized that the Federal Trade Commission cried for attention. If his administration was to have coherence, he could not permit the FTC to move in opposite directions from the National Recovery Administration in policies toward business. Furthermore, although it was no doubt a mistake to turn the administration of the Securities Act over to the FTC, once this had been done Roosevelt could not afford to maintain the fiction that the Commission was a tribunal which should be altogether "independent" of executive influence.

The FTC demanded executive leadership for other reasons as well. Born of high hopes, the Trade Commission had proven a painful disappointment.[105] A former commissioner remarked that the chief function of the FTC had come to be "preventing false and misleading advertising in reference to hair restorers, anti-fat remedies, etc.—a somewhat inglorious end to a noble experiment."[106] Called on to carry out a policy on the trusts on which no one could agree, the FTC had not only been hampered by the courts but assaulted by interest groups speaking through Congressmen. Commissioner Abram F. Myers recalled: "Senators who would not think of seeking to influence a court in the decision of a case pending before it have no compunction about stalking the halls of the Commission and offering ex parte arguments and representations concerning cases pending before it."[107] If the FTC was to maintain its independence against the claims of such interests, it needed strong backing from an administration which would take responsibility for its actions. Roosevelt believed, not unreasonably, that he could give that kind of support only if he had personnel sympathetic to his program. As early as 1926, Senator Norris had stated: "It seems to me that if the Commission is to function, if it is to continue to perform the work that the law designed it to perform, its personnel must be of men who believe in that kind of law."[108]

The removal of Humphrey should be seen not as an isolated episode but as one encounter in Roosevelt's campaign to reshape the national government. When the President took office he found most of the commissions manned by men hostile to the New Deal. "We stood in the city of Washington on March 4th," Raymond Moley recalled, "like a handful of marauders in a hostile territory."[109] Pendleton Herring has explained:

When President Franklin D. Roosevelt embarked upon his plans for national recovery, he gathered into his hands every strand of authority that might lead toward his objectives. At the level of the presidential office, a greater degree of integration was introduced into the federal administrative organization than has ever been witnessed in peacetime experience. And the reach of the President did not falter before the independent commissions. The problems of these bodies were regarded as presidential responsibilities as well. The tasks of the Federal Trade Commission, the Tariff Commission, or the Interstate Commerce Commission could not be separated from the rehabilitation of trade and industry. Yet how could these establishments participate in a national recovery program and still remain administrative agencies? The President got around this difficulty in his characteristically adroit fashion. Placing his key men in the departments was a simple matter, but bringing the independent establishment within his control required more ingenuity. The judicial calm of the Interstate Commerce Commission was left undisturbed, but the most able and aggressive commissioner was created federal coordinator of transportation. The Tariff Commission was reduced to a harmless position through the passage of the reciprocal tariff act. The Radio Commission was abolished outright and a New Deal commission took its place. The President secured the resignation of Hoover's chairman of the Power Commission and added two appointees of his own.[110]

The ouster of Humphrey represented only one step in this march of events.

For the rest of the decade, Roosevelt persisted in his determination to bring the independent regulatory tribunals under his control. As early as 1933, he had told Secretary of Commerce Daniel Roper: "I'd like to see all the independent commissions brought under the general supervision of Cabinet officers."[111] The multiplication of independent commissions, the Administration feared, would cripple the office of the president and seriously threaten the social objectives of the New Deal by making it harder to implement national policies. To deal with such problems, the President, early in 1936, set up a Committee on Administrative Management to prepare a plan for overhauling the machinery of the federal government. When it reported back Roosevelt expressed enthusiasm about most of its recommendations, but when he found that there was no concrete plan for the independent commissions, he inquired sourly: "Is that all you can say?"[112]

A month later he read a new draft, and this time he said, "I think that is grand."[113] In its report the Committee described tribunals like the FTC as constituting "a headless 'fourth branch' of the government, a haphazard deposit of irresponsible agencies and uncoordinated powers" which obstructed "effective over-all management of national administration." Noting the rapid proliferation of independent commissions, the Committee stated: "Every bit of executive and administrative authority which they enjoy means a relative weakening of the President, in whom, according to the Constitution, 'the executive Power shall be vested.' As they grow in number his stature is bound to diminish." To forestall this development the Committee proposed: "Any program to restore our constitutional idea of a fully coordinated Executive Branch responsible to the President must bring within the reach of that responsible control all work done by these independent commissions which is not judicial in nature."[114]

When the reorganization bill was introduced in Congress in 1937, it contained drastic provisions on the independent commissions. The measure authorized the President either to place these tribunals in a department or to abolish them outright. But Roosevelt's bill went down to defeat, in part because the independent commissions, as rival power centers, were able to rally opposition to it. The chairman of the Federal Trade Commission, for one, spoke out against permitting the President "to impair or thwart the functions of the Commission—perhaps even to render the Commission helpless."[115]

At the very same time that Roosevelt was attempting to push the reorganization bill through Congress in 1937, he was engaged in a not dissimilar struggle to win approval for his plan to "pack" the Supreme Court, a plan born in part out of his resentment at the Humphrey opinion.[116] Not only had the Court upheld the claim of Humphrey's estate for back pay, Rexford Tugwell has noted, but it "also—and this was the irritant—forbade future dismissals of the duly appointed and confirmed members of such commissions. It seemed vital to Franklin that the executive powers extensively employed by these 'semi-judicial' agencies should not remain beyond presidential control."[117]

Roosevelt and his lieutenants believed that Sutherland had gone out of his way to chastise Roosevelt unfairly. Had the Court admitted that it was modifying the Myers opinion, and had it conceded that the President might have been acting in good faith in justifying his action by that earlier opinion, the Court's ruling in the Humphrey case would not have aroused so much animosity. Robert H. Jackson has written:

Within the Administration there was a profound feeling that the opinion of the Court was written with a design to give the impression that the President had flouted the Constitution, rather than that the Court had simply changed its mind within the past ten years. The decision could easily have forestalled this by recognizing the President's reliance on an opinion of Chief Justice Taft. But the decision contained no such gracious acknowledgment. What the Court had before declared to be a constitutional duty of the President had become in Mr. Roosevelt a constitutional offense.

The Roosevelt circle thought that "the Court was applying to

President Roosevelt rules different from those it had applied to his predecessors" and that there was a "touch of malice" in Sutherland's opinion.[118]

Of Roosevelt's anger at the opinion there could be no doubt. Secretary of the Interior Harold Ickes reported on the Cabinet meeting of June 4, 1935: "The President said he had made a mistake in not preferring charges. He had actual proof of malfeasance in office, but he didn't want to file such charges against Humphreys, believing as he did that he could get rid of him by milder methods."[119] Sutherland's objection to presidential supremacy in 1935 when he had accepted Taft's opinion in 1926 raised the suspicion that the main difference in the two cases lay less in their nature than in the fact that FDR was now in the White House. The Humphrey case helped persuade the President that, sooner or later, he would have to take bold action against a Court which, out of personal animus toward him, was determined to embarrass him and to destroy his program.[120] Jackson commented later: "I really think the decision that made Roosevelt madder at the Court than any other decision was that damn little case of *Humphrey's Executor* v. *United States*. The President thought they went out of their way to spite him personally and they were giving him a different kind of deal than they were giving Taft."[121]

Tugwell has suggested not only that Roosevelt's decision to curb the Court may have come from irritation at the Humphrey decision, but that it was Roosevelt's anger at that opinion which determined the character of the particular plan he submitted, a plan doomed to defeat. Tugwell observed:

If Franklin, who not only had a vivid sense of presidential prerogatives but who by election and reelection was the chosen leader of the American people, felt that the obstructions of the Court constituted an impertinent denial of his right to act as leader, there was certainly justification. It has been suggested that the Humphries case constituted an affront to the presidency. It may very well have been that case, even more than the other decisions of 1935, which provided the motive for the post-election attempt to humiliate the Court in turn; for of all the ways open to him, Franklin does seem to have chosen the one most upsetting to judicial dignity. And it was this more than anything else—more even than the attempt to reduce the judicial power—which created reaction of a violence he hardly anticipated. Most of those who wanted to eliminate the interferences of the Court with progress still had a deep concern for its dignity. Senators who were lawyers, particularly, found that in the end they could not condone such an affront as was proposed.[122]

Joseph Alsop and Turner Catledge, authors of the standard account of the Supreme Court fight, have offered a similar interpretation. They wrote:

The President's character was the deciding element in the struggle. . . . Essentially the fight's course was decided by the fact that the Court had wantonly offended every strongest trait in the President.
Perhaps the most immediate of the Court's offenses was its denial of satisfaction to the President's taste for power. The President regards great powers as his prerogative. . . . It is significant that those close to him have said that he was most angered by the decision in the comparatively trivial Humphries case. . . . The President saw in the decision the most direct of all possible trespasses on his powers as Chief Executive; he was completely infuriated.[123]

When on February 5, 1937, Roosevelt precipitated the historic controversy over his plan to "pack" the Supreme Court, a number of his opponents traced the conflict back to the Humphrey decision. On the very next day, Representative Earl C. Michener, Michigan Republican, commented on Roosevelt's message:

The President used a lot of words and indulged in a lot of argument to tell Congress something the Congress already knew, to wit, that the President is convinced that if the mind of the Supreme Court, the mind of the Federal Trade Commission, as in the Humphrey case, or the mind of any other government agency does not run along with the President's mind, then the agency should be changed.[124]

The following month Ray Lyman Wilbur, who had been Hoover's Secretary of the Interior, wrote a friend: "In my judgment you are quite right in going back to the Humphrey decision. That was the first knock-out blow from the Court and no doubt was an offense to the idea that the Tammany system could be made national."[125] To an audience in Washington that same month, Dr. Edmund A. Walsh, S.J., Vice-President of Georgetown University, stated that future historians would trace the controversy between Roosevelt and the Court to the summary removal of Commissioner Humphrey. It was more important in triggering the dispute, he asserted, than the Schechter decision.[126]

Roosevelt, who had been frustrated by the Court in the Humphrey case and was to be rebuffed by Congress on the reorganization bill, met defeat on the Supreme Court measure, too. One reason for the setback was that many liberals who shared Roosevelt's annoyance at a Court which had invalidated so much social legislation did not agree with the President's conception of executive power, and as a consequence, they parted company with him in the Court fight. Tugwell has written:

They feared an indefinitely strengthened executive. They were highly sensitized to dictatorship by Hitler and Mussolini; and Franklin had shown signs, they thought, of suggestive impatience. Nevertheless, they . . . wanted . . . freedom for the legislative branch to regulate business in the interest of public welfare. They felt the same frustration that Franklin felt about the no man's land in which neither the federal nor the state governments could touch business enterprise. But they did not want, as Franklin did, to reconstitute the Court so that on no issue could it oppose the other branches. Decidedly, this was too much. They felt, for instance, that the Court was right in the matter of Humphries, which had so incensed Franklin.[127]

From his first communication to Humphrey, Roosevelt had displayed that indifference to public sensitivity about unchecked presidential power that was to cause him so much grief in the court-packing scheme. If the President's critics were sanctimonious, Roosevelt himself was careless about quieting uneasiness about the vast power concentrated in his hands. The President's action in removing Humphrey was not an arbitrary deed but a rational attempt to enable the presidency to emerge as the central institution to cope with the problems of the twentieth-century world. But it did not seem to be—and that made all the difference.

Notes

Preface

1. Inadequacies in reporting media make it impossible to recapture all of his production as represented in book reviews, newspaper and periodical essays, special lectures, pamphlets, reports, etc. Mr. Stephen Carson, a graduate student in history at the University of Illinois, struggled manfully against this insuperable difficulty, and, in concert with the cooperative University Library staff, assembled the bibliography reproduced below. The editors are in their debt. They have omitted book reviews from the Bibliography.

2. Henry Steele Commager, comp. and ed., *Freedom and Order: A Commentary on the American Political Scene* (New York: Braziller, 1966), vii–viii.

3. *Ibid.*, ix–x.

Accusatorial and Inquisitorial Systems of Criminal Procedure: The Beginnings

1. "The Answers of John Lambert to the Forty-five Articles," in John Foxe, *The Acts and Monuments of John Foxe: A New and Complete Edition*, ed. Rev. Stephen Reed Cattley (8 vols., London, 1837–41), V, 184. The principal documents on the Lambert case cover pp. 181–250.

2. *Ibid.*, V, 221.

3. William Stubbs, *The Constitutional History of England in Its Origin and Development* (3 vols., 2nd ed., Oxford, 1875), I, 90, 96, 101–103; James Bradley Thayer, *A Preliminary Treatise on Evidence at the Common Law* (Boston, 1898), 8–9; Sir Frederick Pollock and Frederic William Maitland, *The History of English Law before the Time of Edward I* (2 vols., 2nd ed., Cambridge, Eng., 1899), II, 598–603; and R. C. Van Caenegem, *Royal Writs in England from the Conquest to Glanvill* (London, 1959), Publications of the Selden Society, LXXVII, 16–17.

4. Thayer, 24–34. For a history of proof by oath and compurgation, also called "wager of law," see Homer C. Lea, *Superstition and Force* (3rd ed., Philadelphia, 1878), 22–99; see also Eugene James Moriarty, *Oaths in Ecclesiastical Courts* (Washington, 1937), Catholic University of America Canon Law Studies, CX, 12–22.

5. On ordeals, see Lea, 249–428, and Thayer, 34–39. For Anglo-Saxon documents on oaths, ordeals, and criminal procedure, see Carl Stephenson and Frederick G. Marcham, eds., *Sources of English Constitutional History*. A

Selection of Documents from A.D. 600 to the Present (New York, 1937), 2–25.

6. On trial by battle, see Lea, 101–247; Sir James Fitzjames Stephen, *A History of the Criminal Law of England* (London, 1883, 3 vols.), I, 245–246; and Sir William Holdsworth, *A History of English Law* (16 vols. [vols. individually rev.], London and Boston, 1903–1966), I (6th ed., rev.), 320; II (4th ed.), 197–198 and 360–364; III (6th ed., rev.), 609.

7. Thayer, 41–60; Pollock and Maitland, I, 137–142; Holdsworth, I, 312–313; and Charles Homer Haskins, *Norman Institutions* (Cambridge, Mass., 1925), 196–238. Some historians, returning to a view once popular in the nineteenth century, hold that the origins of the jury are to be found in Anglo-Saxon institutions. See Naomi D. Hurnard, "The Jury of Presentment and the Assize of Clarendon," *English Historical Review*, LVI (July, 1941), 377–410; Van Caenegem, op. cit., Chap. 4, "The Recognitions," 51–103; H. G. Richardson and G. O. Sayles, *The Governance of Medieval England from the Conquest to Magna Carta* (Edinburgh, 1963), 205–208; Doris M. Stenton, *English Justice between the Norman Conquest and the Great Charter, 1066–1215* (Philadelphia, 1964), 15–17. Van Caenegem, whose work is preeminent, distinguished between the inquest, which he associated with royal rights, chiefly fiscal, and recognitions, which he associated with judicial procedures of a "popular" origin before the Conquest. He concluded that "the older English historians were right. The jury was not some alien importation" (p. 103). The evidence for this thesis seems slim and supposititious. Van Caenegem does not, however, reject the view that the jury owed much to the Norman inquest: "We maintain that the common law recognitions were the outcome of two traditions . . ." (p. 60). Some historians evasively straddle the issue. See, e.g., Sir Frank Stenton, *Anglo-Saxon England* (2nd ed., Oxford, 1947), 643. The single outstanding fact is that until Henry II's time, the dominating modes of proof were compurgation, ordeal, and battle; that is, even a century after the Conquest, recognition and inquest were very weak and irregular institutions. Trial by jury developed because of the reforms of Henry II. V. H. Galbraith, *The Making of Domesday Book* (Oxford, 1961), disputes the old thesis that the main object of the Domesday census was to reassess taxes. He asserts, moreover, that the testimony of tenants as well as returns from the hundred provided the data for the making of the book. Although the Norman kings used the inquest mainly for administrative and financial inquiries until Henry II's time, they used it also, and very early, in land disputes. See the documents on inquests at Ely in 1080 and 1082, in Stephenson and Marcham, 39–40.

8. Van Caenegem, 61–68; F. W. Maitland, *Domesday Book and Beyond* (Cambridge, Eng., 1897); Holdsworth, I, 49–51, 264–273, 316, and II, 155–165; Pollock and Maitland, I, 150–152, 154–156; and Stephen, I, 101–102, 253. The quotation from Stephen is at p. 102.

9. Lea, 67–72, 84–87, and 179–198.

10. For an English translation of the Constitutions of Clarendon, see Stephenson and Marcham, 73–76, or George Burton Adams and H. Morse Stephens, eds., *Select Documents of English Constitutional History* (New York, 1929), 11–14. Articles 6 and 9 are relevant. See also Pollock and Maitland, I, 145; Holdsworth, I, 329 and III, 25; and Van Caenegem, 86–87.

11. The Assizes of Clarendon and Northampton are in Stephenson and Marcham, 76–82, and Adams and Stephens, 14–18, 20–23. See also Pollock and Maitland, I, 152 and II, 641; Holdsworth, I, 77; and Van Caenegem,

28–30. Cf. Richardson and Sayles on the rise of the eyre and for criticism of the stress conventionally placed on the Assize of Clarendon which they regard as apocryphal, pp. 173–215, 438–449. The Assizes in time filled the forests with outlaws, those who refused to show up for the ordeal or who failed it and fled to the forest rather than go into banishment. See Morris Keane, *The Outlaws of England* (Toronto, 1961).

12. Max Radin, *Handbook of Anglo-American Legal History* (St. Paul, 1936), 209–211; William Sharp McKechnie, *Magna Carta, A Commentary on the Great Charter of King John* (2nd ed., Glasgow, 1914), 359–367; Thayer, 68; Holdsworth, I, 57; and Pollock and Maitland, II, 587–588.

13. Van Caenegem, 55–56, 82–96, 260–335; Pollock and Maitland, I, 145–149.

14. Pollock and Maitland, I, 146–147, 149, and II, 621; Holdsworth, I, 327–328; Thayer, 61–63; Van Caenegem, 87–91; and, for the quotation from Glanville, *circa* 1187, Stephen, I, 256.

15. McKechnie, 369–393; Pollock and Maitland, I, 173; Thayer, 65.

16. Henry Charles Lea, *A History of the Inquisition of the Middle Ages* (3 vols., New York, 1955), I, 306, 320; Lea, *Superstition and Force*, 418–420; Pollock and Maitland, II, 599.

17. Stephen, I, 254, and for the quotation from Glanville, *ibid.*, I, 256; Pollock and Maitland, II, 599.

18. Quoted in Theodore F. T. Plucknett, *A Concise History of the Common Law* (5th ed., Boston, 1956), 119.

19. Pollock and Maitland, II, 644–649; Holdsworth, I, 324–325; and Thayer, 81–86.

20. Holdsworth, I, 326–327; Thayer, 71; and Pollock and Maitland, II, 650.

21. Pollock and Maitland, II, 619; Thayer, 74; and Plucknett, 126, for the quotation from the Statute of Westminster, I, Chap. 12 (1275).

22. Thayer, 75–80, and Stephen, I, 298–300.

23. Stephen, I, 257–259 and 297–298; Holdsworth, I, 276, 318, 322, and 325; Plucknett, 126–127; Pollock and Maitland, II, 648–649; and Thayer, 81–83.

24. Sir John Fortescue, *De Laudibus Legum Angliae*, trans. by A. Amos (Cambridge, Eng., 1825), 92–93, 100–101; Stephen, I, 263–264; Holdsworth, I, 332–335; Pollock and Maitland, II, 627–629.

25. For the quotation on Innocent III, John H. Wigmore, *A Panorama of the World's Legal Systems* (Washington, 1936), 953. See also Wigmore, *A Treatise on the Anglo-American System of Evidence in Trials at Common Law* (10 vols., 3rd ed., Boston, 1940), VIII (rev. 1961 by John T. McNaughton), Chap. 80, "Privilege Against Self-Incrimination," sect. 2250, 273–274; Lea, *Inquisition*, I, 320. On Innocent III and Magna Carta, see J. C. Holt, *Magna Carta* (Cambridge, Eng., 1965), 101, 139–148, 170. For the canon law code of criminal procedure and for Innocent III's contributions, see Aemilius Friedberg, ed., *Corpus Juris Canonici* (2 vols., Leipzig, 1879–1881), Vol. II, Book II, Title VII, *de juramento calumniae*, Chap. 6, 267–269; Book V, Title I, *de accusationibus, inquisitionibus, et denunciationibus*, Chaps. 1–27, 735–748; Book V, Title XXXIV, *de purgationem*, Chap. X, 872–873.

26. Wigmore, *Evidence*, VIII, 275, n. 28; A. Esmein, *A History of Continental Criminal Procedure, with Special Reference to France* (London, 1914), trans. by John Simpson, 80 and 91; A. Esmein, *Le Serment des In-*

culpés en Droit Canonique (Paris, 1896), 234–235, a pamphlet offprint of the essay of the same title published in Bibliotheque de L'École des Hautes Etudes–Sciences Religieuses, VII (1896), 231–248; Lea, Inquisition, I, 214; Lea, Superstition, 513. See also St. Augustine, The City of God (New York, 1950, 2 vols.), II, Book XIX, Chap. 6, 242. The quotation from Chrysostom is from The Homilies of S. John Chrysostom, Archbishop of Constantinople, on the Epistle of S. Paul the Apostle to the Hebrews, ed. P. E. Pusey (London, 1883), 362–363. The translation of the same passage, originally in Greek, by the Fathers of the English Dominican Province, is, "I do not say that you should lay bare your guilt publicly, nor accuse yourself before others." See The "Summa Theologica" of St. Thomas Aquinas (21 vols., London, 1929), X, 255 (Question LXIX, 1st Art., Obj. 1). See also Gratian, Decreti, Part II, Causa XXXIII, Quest. III, Chap. 87, in Friedberg, ed., Corpus Juris Canonici, I, 1184–1185.

27. Lea, Inquisition, I, 228, 229, 338, 372–373, 421, and 502. For a different view, see A. C. Shannon, The Popes and Heresy in the Thirteenth Century (Villanova, Pennsylvania, 1949) and Norman F. Cantor, Medieval History (New York, 1963), 491–492. Aquinas stated and rejected the dictum from Chrysostom. "Whatever is opposed to the glory of God is a mortal sin. . . . Now it is to the glory of God that the accused confess that which is alleged against him. . . . Therefore it is a mortal sin to lie in order to cover one's guilt." Aquinas also argued that a man must obey his superiors, including his judges. "Therefore the accused is in duty bound to tell the judge the truth which the latter exacts from him according to the form of law. . . . When a man is examined by the judge according to the order of justice, he does not lay bare his own guilt, but his guilt is unmasked by another, since the obligation of answering is imposed on him by one whom he is bound to obey." In effect what emerged from Aquinas is a rule that no man is bound to come forward and reveal his own guilt if it is unknown, or unsuspected, but once suspected or infamed, he must answer an incriminating question; the judge decided whether the question is legitimate, under the circumstances, and whether answer is required. Summa Theologica, X, 255–258 (Quest. LXIX, 1st Art. and 2nd Art., replies to objections). Later canonists such as Durantis, Gandinus, and Panormitanus followed Aquinas. See Esmein, Le Serment des Inculpés, 233–240. Certain speculative moral theologians of the sixteenth and seventeenth centuries "allowed a defendant in a criminal case where there was liability to a very severe penalty to evade a direct question regarding guilt." John R. Connery, S.J., "The Right to Silence," Marquette Law Review, XXXIX (Winter, 1955–56), 184. Father Connery wrote, "Should one be tempted to pass a rather harsh judgment on the theologians and jurists of the scholastic age who imposed on a criminal the obligation to confess his crime when legitimately questioned, it might be well to mention a few mitigating circumstances," chief among which was the theory of legal proofs. Ibid., 182. On legal proofs, see below, note 35.

28. Esmein, Criminal Procedure, 66–67, for the quotation. See also, ibid., 79–84, and Lea, Inquisition, I, 310–312. Van Caenegem observed that in the old trial by witnesses, where the parties brought witnesses, who supposedly knew the facts, to testify in their behalf, the ecclesiastical judge gathered the materials for his decision from their testimony; interrogating the witnesses was an obvious and easy step in this procedure. By contrast, under the English system the jurors were a neutral body from the neighborhood who knew

or could find the facts and found their own verdict, binding on the judge. Van Caenegem, 54. See also on this point, Pollock and Maitland, II, 658.

29. Lea, *Inquisition*, I, 310; Esmein, *Criminal Procedure*, 84–89; Friedberg, ed., *Corpus Juris Canonici*, Vol. II, Book V, Title I, *de accusat.*, Chap. 24, 745–747.

30. Esmein, *Criminal Procedure*, 82; Esmein, *Serment*, 231, 243; Helen Silving, "The Oath: I," *Yale Law Journal*, LXVIII (June, 1959), 1345.

31. Silving, "The Oath," 1346–1347; Moriarty, 33.

32. Wigmore, *Evidence*, 274; Esmein, *Criminal Procedure*, 87–89; and Lea, I, *Inquisition*, 401.

33. Esmein, *Criminal Procedure*, 92; Lea, *Inquisition*, I, 437–447.

34. Lea, *Inquisition*, I, 400–401.

35. A. Lawrence Lowell, "The Judicial Use of Torture," Part I, *Harvard Law Review*, XI (1897–98), 224–225; Lea, *Inquisition*, 416, 433–434; and, especially, Esmein, *Criminal Procedure*, 133, 251–275, and 622–626.

36. Lea, *Inquisition*, I, 337–338 and 421–422; the quotation from Gui is in *ibid.*, 431.

37. Lea, *Inquisition*, I, 421–428.

38. *Ibid.*, 407–421, 431, 434, and 440; Esmein, *Criminal Procedure*, 104–179, 288–321.

39. Holdsworth, I, 294 and III, 600–601; Stephen, I, 493; the quotation from Smith appears in Holdsworth, IX, 225 and Stephen, I, 347. For the original see Sir Thomas Smith, *De Republica Anglorum*, ed. L. Alston (Cambridge, Eng., 1906), 99.

40. Holdsworth, I, 319–320, and III, 609, 615–620; Stephen, I, 245–246; Pollock and Maitland, II, 658–659; and R. F. Hunnisett, *The Medieval Coroner* (Cambridge, Eng., 1961), 55.

41. Stephen, I, 355; Lea, *Inquisition*, I, 401; Thayer, 157; Fortescue, 93; Holdsworth, V (2nd ed.), 196, citing John Hawarde, *Les Reportes del Cases in Camera Stellata, 1593–1609*, ed. W. P. Baildon (London, 1894), 320.

42. Fortescue, 70–71.

43. Charles Austin Beard, *The Office of Justice of the Peace in England* (New York, 1904), 72–74; Holdsworth, V, 165, 185–186, 191; James Fosdick Baldwin, *The King's Council in England during the Middle Ages* (Oxford, 1913), 298; Lea, *Superstition*, 563–571; Lowell, Part II of "The Judicial Use of Torture," 290–297; and especially David Jardine, *A Reading on the Use of Torture in the Criminal Law of England* (London, 1837), 7–25; 59–63. The quotation from Smith, *De Republica*, is in the Alston ed., 105.

44. Beard, 72; Holdsworth, IV (2nd ed.), 528–530; Stephen, I, 219–220, 237–238.

45. Holdsworth, I, 294–297; III, 600–601, 622–623; V, 156, 191, 195; and IX, 224–225, 229; Stephen, I, 225.

46. Thayer, 158–159. See Jay A. Sigler, "A History of Double Jeopardy," *The American Journal of Legal History*, VII (Oct. 1963), 283–309.

47. *Ibid.*, 86–88; Holdsworth, I, 318; Stephen, I, 304; and Pollock and Maitland, II, 626–627.

48. Thayer, 137–155; Holdsworth, I, 337–342; and for Throckmorton's trial, see T. B. Howell, comp., *A Complete Collection of State Trials and Proceedings for High Treason and Other Crimes and Misdemeanors from the Earliest Period to the Year 1783* (21 vols., London, 1816), I, 869. Henceforth this source will be cited as *State Trials*.

49. Holdsworth, IX, 228, 233, 235; Stephen, I, 350, 416; and Throckmorton's trial in *State Trials*, I, 884–885, 886, 897, and 898.

50. *State Trials*, I, 901–902, and for Bushell's case, *ibid.*, VI, 999. The quotation from Smith, *De Republica*, appears in Thayer, 163, and Stephen, I, 306.

51. Pollock and Maitland, II, 658, and I, 138; Holdsworth, I, 318.

52. Maitland, "A Prologue to a History of English Law," in *Select Essays in Anglo-American Legal History*, comp. and ed. by a Committee of the Association of American Law Schools (3 vols., Boston, 1907), I, 7.

The Writ of Habeas Corpus: Early American Origins and Development

1. Quoted in George A. Billias, ed., *Law and Authority in Colonial America* (Barre, Mass., 1965), xi.

2. George Haskins, "Reception of the Common Law in Seventeenth-Century Massachusetts: A Case Study," in *ibid.*, 17.

3. Julius Goebel and T. Raymond Naughton, *Law Enforcement in Colonial New York* (New York, 1944), xxxv.

4. Paul Reinsch, "English Common Law in the Early American Colonies," in *Select Essays in Anglo-American Legal History* (Boston, 1907), I; William Hamersley, "Connecticut—The Origins of Her Courts and Laws," in William T. Davis, ed., *The New England States* (Boston, 1897), I.

5. Francis Aumann, *The Changing American Legal System: Some Selected Phases* (Columbus, 1940); Charles Hilkey, "Legal Development in Colonial Massachusetts," *Columbia University Studies in History, Economics, and Public Law*, XXXVII (1910); John T. Farrell, "The Administration of Justice in Connecticut About the Middle of the Eighteenth Century" (Ph.D. thesis, Yale, 1937); Herbert Pope, "The English Common Law in the United States," *Harvard Law Review*, 24 (1910–11); Goebel and Naughton, *op. cit.*

6. W. F. Bailey, *A Treatise on the Law of Habeas Corpus and Special Remedies* (St. Louis, 1926), 2.

7. William Blackstone, *Commentaries on the Laws of England* (Oxford, 1769), III, 131. For the origins of his use of the term, see Edward Jenks, "The Prerogative Writ in English Law," *Yale Law Journal*, XXXII (1923), 523, 533. Marshall has also called habeas corpus "a high prerogative writ." *Ex parte* Watkins 23 U.S. (3 Peters), 193, 201 (1830).

8. Roscoe Pound, "Interest of Personality," *Harvard Law Review*, XXVIII (1915), 343, 345. See also Julius Stone, *The Province and Function of Law* (Cambridge, 1950), 507 ff.; Eugene Ehrlich, *Fundamental Principles of the Sociology of Law* (Cambridge, 1936), 360–362.

9. T. V. Smith and Edward Lindeman, *Democratic Way of Life* (New York, 1951), 44.

10. Blackstone, *op. cit.* See also "Some Remarks on the Writ of Habeas Corpus Ad Subjiciendum," *Law Magazine*, LIV (1855), 280. The writ of habeas corpus assumes a number of functions and, consonant with them, takes varying forms. *Habeas corpus ad deliberandum et recipiendum* is substantively similar to *habeas corpus ad prosequendum*, though their literal meanings differ. Both are used to remove a prisoner to the jurisdiction wherein the offense was committed. *Habeas corpus ad respondendum* means literally,

"you have the body to answer," and is used to remove a prisoner from the jurisdiction of an inferior court, in order to charge him with an action in a higher court. It is similar to *habeas corpus ad faciendum et recipiendum*. This form itself has been found identical with *habeas corpus cum causa* (James Scott and Charles Roe, *The Law of Habeas Corpus* [Chicago, 1923], 9); but such a claim is doubtful. *Habeas corpus cum causa*, or more properly *cum causa et detentionis*, first made its appearance in fourteenth-century England in response to the changing legal and social order. Becoming the regnant form of habeas corpus, *cum causa* required the appearance of the prisoner in court, accompanied with an explanation of the cause of commitment. It was, therefore, a device by which the courts asked for the cause of detention, thereby subjecting detention to judicial scrutiny. Significantly, *cum causa* appeared at the time that the equity powers were taking shape and, while used by Chancery to correct unjust decisions of inferior courts, it was also a device whereby Chancery powers were enlarged at the expense of local tribunals. *Cum causa* was the major form of the writ used in England in the 1600's and 1700's at the time of settlement overseas and, very likely, given the hardly over scrupulous character of its colonial practitioners, was employed in lieu of *ad subjiciendum*, which is the major form of habeas corpus in use in the United States. (Its nearest contender may be *habeas corpus ad testificandum*, which is used to bring the prisoner into court so that he may testify in a cause in which he is not a party, unlike *ad subjiciendum*.)

11. Elvin Overton and J. S. Waterman, "Federal Habeas Corpus Statutes and Moore v. Dempsey," in *Selected Essays on Constitutional Law* (Chicago, 1938), II, 1479.

12. Ronald Sokol, *A Handbook of Federal Habeas Corpus* (Charlottesville, 1965), 3. See also Forrest G. Ferris and Forrest G. Ferris, Jr., *The Law of Extraordinary Legal Remedies* (St. Louis, 1926).

13. Ex parte Craig, 282 Fed. 138 (1922).

14. William Holdsworth, *A History of English Law* (London, 1909), II, 1. On Magna Carta as the source of habeas corpus, see Edward Ingersoll, *The Writ of Habeas Corpus* (Philadelphia, 1849), 11; Henry Hallam, *The Constitutional History of England* (Boston, 1829), I, 523; Edward Coke, *The Second Part of the Institutes of the Laws of England* (6th ed.; London, 1681), 55; "Some Remarks," in op. cit., 278; James Mackintosh, *The History of England* (London), I, 220.

15. Ferris, op. cit., 20–23.

16. On Coke's "complete misunderstanding of Magna Carta," see Max Radin, *Handbook of Anglo-American Legal History* (St. Paul, 1936), 286. One of the earliest expressions of confidence in the substantive relationship of Magna Carta and habeas corpus is to be found in a Commons bill, "Confirminge a branche of Magna Carta," introduced by James Morice, a prominent Puritan. Faith Thompson, *Magna Carta, Its Role in the Making of the English Constitution, 1300–1629* (Minneapolis, 1948), App. G, 394. Daniel Meador has a succinct commentary on Coke's misreading of the Great Charter, in *Habeas Corpus and Magna Carta* (Charlottesville, 1966), 22–23.

17. Meador, op. cit., 5.

18. Frederick Pollock & Frederick Maitland, *The History of English Law Before the Time of Edward I* (2nd ed.; London, 1898), II, 586–7. See also Maxwell Cohen, "Some Considerations on the Origins of Habeas Corpus," *Canadian Bar Review*, XVI (1938), 105.

19. Prior of Saint Fredericks case (1199) and Adam de Cardvil's case (1199), in Francis Palgrave, ed., *Rotuli Curiae Regis* (London, 1835), II, 178.

20. Robert S. Walker, *The Constitutional and Legal Development of Habeas Corpus as the Writ of Liberty* (Stillwater, 1960), 13. See also Cohen, *op. cit.*, 109.

21. Walker, *op. cit.*, 13–15.

22. Theodore F. T. Plucknett, *A Concise History of the Common Law* (London, 1936), 156.

23. Zechariah Chafee, "The Most Important Human Right in the Constitution," *Boston University Law Review*, XXXII (1952), 143.

24. George Chalmers, *Political Annals of the Present United Colonies, from their Settlement to the Peace of 1763* (London, 1780), I, 74. A. H. Carpenter, "Habeas Corpus in the Colonies," *American Historical Review*, VIII (1902–03), 18–27; Rollin C. Hurd, *A Treatise on the Right of Personal Liberty and on the Writ of Habeas Corpus* (Albany, 1858), 109. See also William S. Church, *A Treatise on the Writ of Habeas Corpus* (San Francisco, 1884), Chap. 1, Part 5.

25. Hilkey, *op. cit.*, 93–111. Thomas Lechford, *Plain-Dealing, Or Newes from New England* (1642), in Massachusetts Historical Society, *Collections*, III, 3rd ser. (1833), 83–87; Susie Ames, ed., *County Court Records of Accomack-Northampton, Virginia, 1632–1640* (Washington, 1954), xviii–xix.

26. Joseph H. Smith and Philip A. Crowl, eds., *Court Records of Prince Georges County, Maryland, 1696–1699* (Washington, 1964), xviii.

27. Article 26 of the Bay Colony's Body of Liberties, for instance, prohibited any man from giving a reward to another to represent him in court. George Haskins, *Law and Authority in Early Massachusetts* (New York, 1960), 186–187.

28. William R. Smith, *South Carolina as a Royal Province* (New York, 1903), 120.

29. Joseph H. Smith, ed., *Colonial Justice in Western Massachusetts* (1639–1702), *The Pynchon Court Record* (Cambridge, 1961), 19, 157–158. See also Michael Dalton, *The Countrey Justice, Containing the Practice of Justices of the Peace* (London, 1630), 311. Dalton's work barely mentions habeas corpus, and only in terms of its use with *certiorari* as a writ of error. For legal texts used by Massachusetts lawyers in the 1770's, see Emory Washburn, *Sketches of the Judicial History of Massachusetts* (Boston, 1840), 196–197.

30. Banishment and/or outlawry was the customary practice in early colonial history. It was even used by the Dutch in New Netherlands who, in many other respects, were more humane and progressive than the English. See A. J. F. Van Laer, ed., *Minutes of the Court of Rensselaerswyck, 1648–1652* (Albany, 1822), 120.

31. Essex County Court records indicate that the court, over a forty-seven-year span, imprisoned only eighty-seven times. George Dow, ed., *Records and Files of the Quarterly Courts of Essex County Massachusetts, 1636–1638*, 8 vols. (Salem, 1911–1921), *passim*. See also Zechariah Chafee, ed., *Records of the Suffolk County Court, 1671–1680*, in Colonial Society of Massachusetts, *Publications*, 2 vols. (Boston, 1933), *passim*; "Proceedings of the Provincial Court of Maryland," *Archives of Maryland, Proceedings and Acts of the General Assembly of Maryland* IV, 1637–1650; X, 1649/50–57; XLI, 1670–1/75; LXVI, 1675–7; "Proceedings of the General Court of Assizes held in the City of New York, October 6, 1680 to October 6, 1682," in

New-York Historical Society, *Collections, 1912* (New York, 1913), *passim.*
Bail, it might be added, was generally liberal in the colonies: see "Liberty
No. 18 of the Massachusetts Body of Liberties," and the articles entitled
"Clerkes of the writts" and "Suretyes, and goods attached" in the law of
1641, in William H. Whitmore, *Colonial Laws of Massachusetts* (Boston,
1887), 29, and Goebel and Naughton, *op. cit.,* Chap. 7.

32. Quoted in Daniel Boorstin, *The Americans,* Vol. I: *The Colonial Experience* (New York, 1958), 21. See also Samuel E. Morison, *Builders of the
Bay Colony* (sentry ed.; Boston, 1958), 226.

33. *The Colonial Laws of New York from the Year 1664 to the Revolution* . . . (Albany, 1894), I, 111–116. See also David Lovejoy, "Equality
and Empire The New York Charter of Libertyes, 1683," *William and Mary
Quarterly,* XXI (1964), 505.

34. Bernard C. Steiner, "Beginnings of Maryland," in *Johns Hopkins University Studies in History and Political Science,* Series XXI, No. 8 (Baltimore,
1903), 109. See also Mary P. Clarke, *Parliamentary Privilege in the American Colonies* (New Haven, 1943), 64, and H. D. Hazeltine, "The Influence
of Magna Carta on American Constitutional Development," in Henry E.
Malden, ed., *Magna Carta Commemoration Essays* (London, 1917), 180–194.

35. Washburn, *op. cit.,* 105 ff.

36. *Ibid.,* 106.

37. *Virginia Magazine of History and Biography,* I (1894), 109–113; Arthur
P. Scott, *Criminal Law in Colonial Virginia* (Chicago, 1930), 58 ff.

38. Hurd, *op. cit.,* 111. Lovejoy's careful study finds that the charter was
not disallowed until 1686; and by James II in instructions to Governor Don-
gan (*op. cit.,* 514).

39. Meador, *op. cit.,* 30. In Pennsylvania, the legislators made repeated
provision for the issuing of writs of habeas corpus in their various judiciary
laws, and these were repeatedly disallowed. Carpenter, *op. cit.,* 23. Massachusetts and South Carolina passed habeas corpus acts in 1692. The Carolina
law was disallowed by the proprietors (also in 1692) on the grounds that it
was unnecessary since the laws of England applied to the colony. Edward
McCrady, *The History of South Carolina Under the Proprietary Government,
1670–1719* (New York, 1897), 247–248, 517. The theory was abandoned in
1733, when a habeas corpus law was passed. W. R. Smith, *op. cit.,* 43–44.

40. Quoted in Leonard W. Labaree, ed., *Royal Instructions to British
Colonial Governors 1670–1776* (New York, 1935), I, 141.

41. Carpenter notes that the habeas corpus act "seems to have been enforced despite the decision of the proprietors, for we find that the act of 1712
repealed in so many words that of 1692"; and he attributed the discrepancy
between the revocations of the Massachusetts and South Carolina acts (of
1692) to the possibility that the latter was not submitted to England (*op.
cit.,* 23). Conceivably, the disallowance of the Massachusetts measure in 1695
was due to the more direct relationship between this colony and royal authority in England.

42. Review by George E. Woodbine, in *Yale Law Journal,* XLIII (1934),
1036.

43. Ellis Ames, ed., *The Acts and Resolves, Public and Private, of the
Province of the Massachusetts Bay* (Boston, 1902), IX (1708–1719), 33;
Washburn, *op. cit.,* 90.

44. Washburn, *op. cit.,* 152. The Massachusetts act was disallowed because

"the privilege has not as yet been granted in any of His Ma[jes]ty's Plantations" (*Acts and Resolves*, I, 95, 99) and never re-enacted.

45. *Archives of Maryland*, XLIX, 548; LVII, 16, 66, 80, 486; Washburn, *op. cit.*, 90.

46. Goebel & Naughton, *op. cit.*, 503.

47. See Burrough's case (1694), in Carroll T. Bond, ed., *Proceedings of the Maryland Court of Appeals, 1695–1729* (Washington, 1933), 46, 394; Smith, *Court Records of Prince Georges County*, cx–cxi.

48. Quoted in Meador, *op. cit.*, 30.

49. Hurd, *op. cit.*, 113; Scott, *op. cit.*, 58–69. The entire transcript, dated October, 1710, set forth in the form of a proclamation from Spotswood, is in Carpenter, *op. cit.*, 24–25. If a copy of the commitment was "denyd the Prisoner or any person requiring the same in his behalf," this should be grounds for demanding a writ of habeas corpus.

50. Washburn, *op. cit.*, 196; *Acts and Resolves*, IX, 33.

51. Goebel and Naughton, *op. cit.*, 155, n. 71.

52. *Ibid.*, 156, n. 71, on *King v. John Johnson* (1701).

53. Test of the warrant is in Hurd, *op. cit.*, 115.

54. The prisoners were released on bail after the second warrant. Meador, *op. cit.*, 31.

55. Labaree, *op. cit.*, I, 334–338. "The new law of 1712 in South Carolina provided that any two of the lords proprietors deputies, or the chief justice of the province, or any one of the lords proprietors deputies and one of the justices of the peace, or any two of the justices of the peace could put in execution the Habeas Corpus Act as 'fully, effectually and lawfully as any Lord Chancellor, Lord Keeper, or any of Her Majestie's Justices. . . .'" Quoted in Carpenter, *op. cit.*, 23. The 1712 act was basically the English Habeas Corpus Act. Chafee, *op. cit.*, 146, n. 14.

56. For complete descriptions of South Carolina events see W. R. Smith, *op. cit.*, 42–48, and Clarke, *op. cit.*, 248–251. Asserting that habeas corpus did not apply to those it took into custody, the House supported this claim by resolving, "his Majesty does allow the . . . same Privileges as The House of Commons doth enjoy in England." Quoted in M. E. Sirmans, *Colonial South Carolina* (Chapel Hill, 1966), 181.

57. Jack P. Greene, *The Quest for Power* (Chapel Hill, 1963), 55, 336. Mary Clarke has written about the issue of prerogative (which was raised in a number of prominent court cases in the colonies): "It took much clarifying of English political thought to arrive at the conclusion that prerogative was not superior to the common law; and it took much clarifying of thought in both England and America to come to a corresponding conclusion with regard to privilege." Clarke, *op. cit.*, 130.

58. W. R. Smith, *op. cit.*, 247–252. Landgrave Smith, in a memorial to the Assembly, included among his charges against the Chief Justice "that he was apprehended and carried before the Chief Justice, who signed a mittimus charging him with high treason; that he had applied for a habeas corpus, which had been denied him" and he prayed "that he might be declared within the benefit of the habeas corpus act. . . ." Edward McCrady, *The History of South Carolina Under the Royal Government, 1719–1776* (New York, 1899), 83.

59. *Trial of John Peter Zenger* (London, 1765), 13. See Leonard W. Levy, "Did the Zenger Case Really Matter? Freedom of the Press in Colonial New York," *William and Mary Quarterly*, XVII (1960), 3rd ser., 35–50.

60. Goebel and Naughton, *op. cit.*, 505.

61. *Acts and Resolves*, IV, 32.

62. On the conflict between Parliament and/or assemblies and the judiciary, see Clarke, *op. cit.*, 236.

63. Significantly, nothing appears in the official records about the writ. Goebel & Naughton, *op. cit.*, 506.

64. For a detailed account of the case, and events surrounding it, see "Votes and Proceedings of the House of Representatives of the Province of Pennsylvania (1682–1776)," in Gertrude MacKinney and Charles F. Hoban, eds., *Pennsylvania Archives* (October 14, 1756 to January 3, 1764), VI, 8th Ser. (1935), 4677–4716.

65. *Ibid.*, 4689. For a perceptive and scrupulously accurate study of the case and its implications for freedom of speech, see Leonard W. Levy's invaluable *Legacy of Suppression* (Cambridge, 1960), 51–61.

66. The outcome of this very complicated case, which was a victory for petitioners owing to the Privy Council's intervention and ruling, need not detain us here. Nor is it appropriate to comment on the implications for personal freedom when provincial legislatures insisted upon unrestrained prerogative. See Levy, *op. cit.*, 60–61. For a careful exposition of the case, see Clarke, *op. cit.*, 240–246.

67. Mathew Hale, *The History and Analysis of the Common Law of England* (London, 1713), 188.

68. Until 1784, when Virginia enacted its own Habeas Corpus Act (*Acts Passed at a General Assembly of the Commonwealth of Virginia* [Richmond, 1784], Chap. XXXV, 19), habeas corpus rested on Spotswood's Proclamation. South Carolina's writ was based upon the 1712 crown instruction and legislation. Sometime before the Revolution (the precise date is not known), Georgia also passed such a measure, which was identical to the English Habeas Corpus Act (Robert & George Watkins, *Digest of the Laws of the State of Georgia* [Philadelphia, 1800], 18). For Pennsylvania's law of 1785, see *Laws of the Commonwealth of Pennsylvania, 1781–1790* (Philadelphia, 1793), 241. New York's law was passed in 1787: see *Laws of the State of New York* (New York, 1789), I, 77.

69. Benjamin P. Poore, ed., *The Federal and State Constitutions* (Washington, 1877), I, 972. The constitutions of Georgia, New Hampshire, Delaware, and Pennsylvania all took cognizance of the privilege of habeas corpus by 1790. *Ibid.*, I, 279, 383; II, 1307, 1555.

70. Chafee, *op. cit.*, 146.

71. Jonathan Elliot, ed., *Debates in the Several State Conventions on the Adoption of the Federal Constitution . . . Together with the Journal of the Federal Convention* (2nd ed.; Philadelphia, 1845), V, 484.

72. *Ibid.* For observations on the federal suspension clause in the Massachusetts ratifying convention, see *ibid.*, II, 108. Robert Lansing, at the Poughkeepsie convention, moved that the federal clause be amended to prohibit suspension for more than six months. *Ibid.*, II, 407.

73. "It seems to have been assumed," a recent commentator has stated, "either that the right to the writ was conferred by implication in the antisuspension provision or that it existed under the common law in force in the several states." Dallin H. Oaks, "Habeas Corpus in the States—1776–1865," *University of Chicago Law Review*, XXXII (1964–1965), 248–249.

74. *Ibid.* Any number of state constitutions suggest that the prevailing view of the writ was that, being of fundamental importance, it need not be spelled

out in an explicit constitutional guarantee. E.g., the constitutions of Georgia from 1777–1793, the first assuming that the English Habeas Corpus Act was operative and the third merely including a non-suspension clause. Poore, op. cit., I, 383, 386, 395.

75. Meador, op. cit., 33. See also Charles Warren, "Federal and State Court Interference," Harvard Law Review, XLIII (1930), 345.

76. Oaks, op. cit., 249.

77. 1 U.S. Statutes-at-Large, 81 (1789).

78. For the argument that the right of individual liberty was sufficiently protected under state law, and that the right of a federal court to issue the writ would create jurisdictional difficulties, see Annals of Congress (Washington, 1834), I, 828.

79. 1 U.S. Statutes-at-Large, 81–2 (1789).

80. Ex parte Bollman, 8 U.S. (4 Cranch), 94–95 (1807).

John Locke in the Great Unitarian Controversy

1. Professor Curti's essay first appeared in the Huntington Library Bulletin, No. 11 (April, 1937), 207–251. It is reprinted in his Probing Our Past (New York, 1955), 69–118.

2. Louis Hartz, The Liberal Tradition in America: An Interpretation of American Political Thought Since the Revolution (New York, 1955).

3. This problem is best identified in Herbert Schneider, A History of American Philosophy (2nd ed.; New York, 1963), Chaps. 22, 36; Joseph L. Blau, Men and Movements in American Philosophy (New York, 1952), Chaps. 3, 6; and in Octavius B. Frothingham, Transcendentalism in New England, A History (New York, 1886).

4. To find the chronology of Locke's Essay in nineteenth-century American classrooms, one can begin with a survey of ten colleges made by C. Emory Aldrich that appeared in his "Report to the Council" in Proceedings of the American Antiquarian Association (April, 1879), 22–39. The use of Locke at Harvard is traced in Benjamin Rand, "Philosophical Instruction in Harvard University from 1636 to 1900," The Harvard Graduates' Magazine, XXXVII (1928–29), 29–47, 188–200.

5. One might begin here with two of the "Classics in Education" series under the general editorship of Lawrence A. Cremin: Peter Gay's edition of Locke's Some Thoughts Concerning Education (New York, 1964), and Francis W. Garforth's edition of Locke's Of the Conduct of the Understanding (New York, 1966). The educational influence of Locke outside the schoolroom, which is perhaps an even more important theme, is discussed in an unpublished paper by Daniel Calhoun, "Repression: The Lockean Tradition in American Child-Rearing" (December, 1966).

6. A good brief introduction to Lockian political and constitutional thought on this problem is found in Alpheus Thomas Mason and Richard H. Leach, In Quest of Freedom (Englewood Cliffs, N.J., 1959), 9–19. See also Benjamin F. Wright, American Interpretations of Natural Law: A Study in the History of Natural Law (Cambridge, 1931), passim; and Edward S. Corwin, The "Higher Law" Background of American Constitutional Law (Ithaca, N.Y., 1955).

7. Lockian sensational psychology has not, of course, been the major theme in the development of American academic psychology. But much needed is a study of the history of academic psychology in the United States that would

be similar to L. S. Hearnshaw's *A Short History of British Psychology, 1840–1940* (London, 1964), which picks up the Lockian theme where it is relevant. *Cf.* Erwin A. Esper, *A History of Psychology* (Philadelphia, 1964), 170–179. The influence of the Scottish common-sense school in academic psychology, built partly upon Lockian sensationalism, is traced in Frank M. Albrecht, "The New Psychology in America, 1880–1895" (unpublished Ph.D. dissertation, The Johns Hopkins University, 1960).

8. Vernon Louis Parrington, *The Romantic Revolution in America, 1800–1860* (New York, 1927, and later editions); Henry Steele Commager, *Theodore Parker* (Boston, 1936, and later editions).

9. Conrad Wright, *The Beginnings of Unitarianism in America* (Boston, 1955); William W. Fenn, "The Unitarians," in *The Religious History of New England: King's Chapel Lectures* (Cambridge, 1917); George W. Cooke, *Unitarianism in America: A History of Its Origin and Development* (Boston, 1902).

10. Schneider, *op. cit.*, 200–201; Williston Walker, *A History of the Congregational Churches in the United States* (New York, 1907), 349–353.

11. Samuel Spring, *Two Discourses on Christ's Selfexistence, Addressed to the Second Congregational Society in Newburyport, March 3, 1805* (Newburyport, Mass., 1805), 45–46, 51–52.

12. *The Works of Leonard Woods, D.D.* (5 vols.; Boston, 1851), IV, *passim*; Henry Ware, Sr., *Letters to Trinitarians and Calvinists* (Cambridge, 1820); Earl Morse Wilbur, *A History of Unitarianism in Transylvania, England and America* (2 vols.; Cambridge, 1952), II, 430.

13. The group of forty-four Massachusetts ministers and laymen who met on January 27, 1825, to consider forming a Unitarian association was divided in its opinion. Consequently, it was a smaller group of the younger men favorable to an association who, by May 25, 1825, carried through their plan and the next day persuaded the Berry Street Conference of ministers in Boston to form the American Unitarian Association. James Walker's illuminating minutes of the January meeting are printed in David B. Parke, *The Epic of Unitarianism* (Boston, 1960), 100–104.

14. Quoted in Paul Revere Frothingham, *Edward Everett* (Boston, 1925), 13.

15. Rand, *op. cit.*, 36.

16. [Andrews Norton], "A Defense of Liberal Christianity," *General Repository and Review*, I (January, 1812), 21.

17. *Loc. cit.*

18. *Ibid.*, 9.

19. *Ibid.*, 10.

20. *Ibid.*, 24.

21. [Andrews Norton], "Letter to Dr. Holmes," *General Repository and Review*, III (April, 1813), 299–323.

22. [Norton], "Defense," 25, 11; "A Contrast between Calvinism and Hopkinsianism," *General Repository and Review*, III (April, 1813), 377–378; "Pamphlets of N. and T. Worcester," *ibid.*, II (July, 1812), 180.

23. Wright, *op. cit.*, 158–159 and *passim*. Another Unitarian journal, *The Christian Disciple*, was founded in 1813. Since it was the forerunner of *The Christian Examiner*, which became the official journal of Unitarianism from the 1820's through the 1860's, it may have some claim to being the first institutional journal of American Unitarianism. However, it was unpolemical in theology and devoted mainly to the cause of peace and to giving employ-

ment to Noah Worcester. I think Norton's *Review* clearly supersedes it in institutional importance.

24. *A Sermon, Preached in The First Presbyterian Church, in the City of Baltimore, October 19, 1820; At the Ordination and Installation of The Reverend William Nevins, as Pastor of Said Church. By Samuel Miller, D.D.* (Baltimore, 1820). Jared Sparks heard Miller deliver this sermon. In 1823, when the controversy had been concluded and each man had given the other a personal copy of his published *Letters*, the two men corresponded and agreed politely to disagree in their opinions, but protested their respect for one another. Miller claimed that his Baltimore sermon was one he had earlier delivered *verbatim* in Princeton and that, since he did not know Sparks was in the congregation, he never preached *ad hominem*. Surely, however, he must have anticipated having some Unitarians in the audience when the occasion obviously called for a formal orthodox reply to Channing. Sparks to Miller, Baltimore, September 18, 1823; Miller to Sparks, October 27, 1823. Miller Correspondence, Box IV, Princeton University Library.

25. Miller, *A Sermon* . . . , 10.

26. *Ibid.*, 17, 22.

27. *Ibid.*, 20.

28. *Ibid.*, 19–20.

29. *Ibid.*, 20–21. In correspondence later with the famous annalist of the American pulpit, William B. Sprague, Miller privately reiterated his assessment of Baltimore Unitarians. Sprague had complimented Miller on the handsome appearance of his collected *Letters on Unitarianism*. Miller replied: "I was induced to print the first edition in the handsome & expensive manner which you speak of, in order to catch the attention, & excite, if possible, the respect, of the gay, fashionable, & wealthy people of Baltimore." Miller to Sprague, Princeton, May 4, 1822. Miller Correspondence, Box IV, Princeton University Library.

30. A Unitarian of Baltimore [Jared Sparks], "Letter to the Rev. Dr. Miller, on the Charges Against Unitarians contained in his late Ordination Sermon in Baltimore," *The Unitarian Miscellany and Christian Monitor*, I (March, 1821), 138. All of Sparks's letters in *The Unitarian Miscellany* were later published as one volume: *An Inquiry into the Comparative Moral Tendency of Trinitarian and Unitarian Doctrines; In a Series of Letters to the Rev. Dr. Miller, of Princeton* (Boston, 1823).

31. Miller, *A Sermon* . . . , 14–15.

32. Samuel Miller, *Letters on Unitarianism; Addressed to the Members of the First Presbyterian Church, in the City of Baltimore* (Trenton, 1821), 197 ff., 272 ff. Miller's eight letters, or replies, to Sparks in this volume were first published as separate pamphlets in Baltimore.

33. *Ibid.*, 107 ff.

34. Leslie Stephen, *History of English Thought in the Eighteenth Century* (third edition; New York, 1949), II, 386. Cf. Roland N. Stromberg, *Religious Liberalism in Eighteenth-Century England* (London, 1954), 10–11.

35. [James Renwick Willson], *Dr. Watts, An Anti-Trinitarian; Demonstrated in a Review of Dr. Miller's Letter to the Editor of the Unitarian Miscellany* (Philadelphia, 1821). Willson claimed that Miller was merely unfamiliar with Watts's heresies. It was conceivable to Willson, however, that Watts had been an Arian who possibly would receive salvation, whereas Locke had been a Socinian with no hope of salvation.

36. Miller, *Letters on Unitarianism*, 109–110.

37. *Ibid.*, 108.
38. [Jared Sparks], "Third Letter to the Rev. Dr. Miller, on his Charges against Unitarians," *The Unitarian Miscellany*, I (June, 1821), 274–275.
39. [Jared Sparks], "Ninth Letter to the Rev. Dr. Miller. On the Theological Sentiments of Newton, Locke, and Watts," *Unitarian Miscellany*, II (March, 1822), 274.
40. *Ibid.*, 276, 281.
41. Miller, *Letters on Unitarianism*, 232.
42. *Ibid.*, 63–65, 287–298.
43. In later years their quarrel was patched up when Sparks asked Miller to write the life of Jonathan Edwards for Sparks's "American Biography" series. Miller complied, expressing some astonishment at the request from his former opponent. When Sparks received Miller's completed manuscript on Edwards, for which Miller was later paid one dollar a printed page, Sparks indicated that perhaps both of them had improved as historians. He wrote to Miller that he had read the manuscript with "lively interest," and he added: "It is certain that some of the *opinions* do not agree with mine, but they are such as I expected in a Life of Edwards, and especially from your pen. In a biography it seems to me, that a man's *sentiments*, as well as his character and acts, should be set forth; so far at least as to state what they are, with proper explanations. This should be done rather historically, than by a direct attempt to enforce them. I think you have preserved the right medium." Sparks to Miller, Cambridge, February 14, October 11, 1837. Miller Correspondence, Box IV, Princeton University Library. See also Herbert B. Adams, *The Life and Writings of Jared Sparks* (Boston, 1893), I, 176–202.
44. The relevance of Locke to the Transcendentalist movement was clearly and charmingly described many years ago in the work of Octavius Brooks Frothingham, *op. cit.* A recent analysis is Cameron Thompson, "John Locke and New England Transcendentalism," *The New England Quarterly*, XXXV (December, 1962), 435–457. That transcendentalism was at heart a *religious* movement is pithily expressed in Perry Miller's Introduction to his collection, *The Transcendentalists* (Cambridge, 1950).
45. [Alexander Hill Everett], "History of Intellectual Philosophy," *North American Review*, XXIX (July, 1829), 67–123, especially 79, 120–123; [James Walker], "Unitarianism Vindicated against the Charge of Skeptical and Infidel Tendencies," *Christian Examiner*, XI (November, 1831), 178–195; [W. B. O. Peabody], Review of "The Life of John Locke . . . By Lord King," *Christian Examiner*, XI (January, 1832), 380–403; [Francis Parkman], "Memoir of Roger Williams . . . By James D. Knowles," *Christian Examiner*, XVI (March, 1834), 72–97, especially 89–90; [Francis Bowen], "Locke and the Transcendentalists," *Christian Examiner*, XXIII (November, 1837), 170–194.
46. Walker, "Unitarianism Vindicated Against the Charge of Skeptical and Infidel Tendencies," 178.
47. *Ibid.*, 183, 187.
48. *Ibid.*, 188.
49. Cooke, *op. cit.*, 5.
50. [Sparks], "On the Theological Sentiments of Newton, Locke, and Watts," 276.
51. Herbert Schneider, "The Intellectual Background of William Ellery Channing," *Church History*, VII (March, 1938), 3–23; Adams, *op. cit.*, I,

138–145; Arthur W. Brown, *Always Young for Liberty* (Syracuse, 1956), Chap. 10.

52. Adams, *op. cit.*, I, 125–126, 138, 169, 197–198; Clarence Gohdes, "Some Notes on the Unitarian Church in the Ante-Bellum South: A Contribution to the History of Southern Liberalism," in D. K. Jackson, ed., *American Studies in Honor of William Kenneth Boyd, by Members of the Americana Club of Duke University* (Durham, N.C., 1940), 327–366.

53. The modern reader of Miller's *Letters on Unitarianism* might prefer to characterize him as intolerant, especially after perusing Miller's final pages (286–298) on the meaning of Presbyterian "toleration."

54. [Sparks], "On the Theological Sentiments of Newton, Locke, and Watts," 274–281.

55. Francis Bowen was one of the few Unitarians to recognize Locke as an empiricist in the Baconian tradition. See his article on Newton and Locke in *The Knickerbocker*, VI (November, 1835), 415–419, which I read as a clearer statement on this aspect of Locke than Bowen's famous article two years later on "Locke and the Transcendentalists." It remained, however, for an anonymous reviewer on the orthodox side to put Locke squarely in the Baconian tradition of inductive method. "Psychology," *Princeton Review*, XV (April, 1843), 227–250, especially 238 ff.

56. William B. Sprague, "Samuel Miller," in *Annals of the American Pulpit* (New York, 1858), III, 602–603.

57. [Orestes Brownson], "Philosophy and Common Sense," *Boston Quarterly Review*, I (January, 1838), 83–106; quoted at 97–101. This article was a reply to Francis Bowen's essay on "Locke and the Transcendentalists."

58. [Orestes Brownson], Review of "*The Evidences of the Genuineness of the Four Gospels*, By Andrews Norton . . . ," *Boston Quarterly Review*, II (January, 1839), 86–113; quoted at 110–112.

59. [Orestes Brownson], Review of "*Unitarianism Vindicated Against the Charge of Skeptical Tendencies*, By James Walker . . . ," *Boston Quarterly Review*, II (July, 1839), 378–385; quoted at 382–383.

60. *Loc. cit.*

61. Wilson Smith, *Professors & Public Ethics: Studies of Northern Moral Philosophers Before the Civil War* (Ithaca, N.Y., 1956), Chaps. 2–3, 9.

62. Adams, *op. cit.*, Chaps. 6–7; Samuel Eliot Morison, "Jared Sparks," in the *Dictionary of American Biography*.

Libertarianism's Loss: The Case of Horace Holley and Transylvania University

1. Richard Hofstadter and Walter Metzger, *The Development of Academic Freedom in the United States* (New York, 1955), 247.

2. *Ibid.*, 61–63, 115.

3. *Ibid.*, 90–91, 114, 125.

4. William Hening, *The Statutes at Large*, X, 287–288.

5. There are two histories of Transylvania covering the antebellum period. The older and better organized is Robert Peter's *Transylvania University, Its Origin, Rise, Decline, and Fall* (Louisville, Ky., 1896). The more recent account is Walter Jennings, *Transylvania: Pioneer University of the West* (New York, 1955).

6. Hofstadter and Metzger, *op. cit.*, 143. Also, George P. Schmidt, *The Old Time College President* (New York, 1930), 27.

7. John Pope, W. T. Barry, James Prentiss, J. Cabell Breckinridge to Holley, November 18, 1817. Holley Papers, Transylvania College.

8. Following biographical data excerpted from Charles Caldwell, *A Discourse on the Genius and Character of the Rev. Horace Holley* (Boston, 1828), 100–140.

9. Rebecca Smith Lee, *Mary Austin Holley* (Austin, Texas, 1962), 55–65.

10. Caldwell, *op. cit.*, 138, states that Loring in his *The Hundred Boston Orators* judged Stillman and Holley to be the most eloquent pastors ever to stand in Boston pulpits.

11. Holley to John Tyler, July 18, 1819. L. Gay Papers, Mass. Hist. Soc.

12. Holley to Mary Holley, May 27, 1818, in Caldwell, *op. cit.*, 162.

13. *Ibid.*, 152.

14. *Ibid.*, 153.

15. *Ibid.*, 157.

16. James F. Hopkins, ed., *The Papers of Henry Clay* (Lexington, Ky., 1961), II, 613. ". . . you have come among us not in the character of a Reformer, but to place yourself at the head of an institution of learning; that your object is not to propagate religious truth, but to capacitate the mind for the acquisition of truth of all kinds."

17. Schmid, *op. cit.*, 69.

18. Niels Sonne, *Liberal Kentucky, 1780–1828* (New York, 1939), Chap. 1. Also, Clement Eaton, *Freedom of Thought in the Old South* (Durham, N.C., 1940), Chap. 1.

19. Sonne, *op. cit.*, 9.

20. Ernest T. Thompson, *Presbyterians in the South*, Vol. I (Richmond, Va., 1963), 266–267.

21. Hofstadter and Metzger, *op. cit.*, 244.

22. *Ibid.*, 239.

23. Sonne, *op. cit.*, 108–110.

24. This material on Kentucky Governors and their relation to education is derived from an interesting study by Edsel T. Godbey, *The Governors of Kentucky and Education, 1780–1852* in the *Bulletin of the Bureau of School Service*, XXXII (June, 1960). It fills the entire issue.

25. *Ibid.*, 41–46.

26. Thomas D. Clark, *A History of Kentucky* (New York, 1937), Chap. 60; also, Godbey, *op. cit.*, 30–33.

27. Glyndon Van Deusen, *The Life of Henry Clay* (Boston, 1937), 194–195.

28. Caldwell, *op. cit.*, 199.

29. Benjamin Silliman to Holley, July 27, 1819; Edward Livingston to Holley, Sept. 12, 1825; Dr. John C. Warren to Holley, July 31, 1824. Holley Papers, Transylvania.

30. Robert and Johanna Peter, *History of the Medical Department of Transylvania University* (Louisville, 1905), *passim*.

31. John Rowan to Holley, Nov. 11, 1819. Holley Papers, Transylvania College.

32. Richard E. Call, *The Life and Writings of Rafinesque* (Louisville, 1895), 15.

33. Rebecca Smith Lee, *op. cit.*, 127.

34. Holley to Jefferson, October 10, 1821. Jefferson Papers, Mass. Hist. Soc. Jared Sparks to Holley, September 14, 1825; Benjamin Silliman to Holley, July 27, 1819; John Adams to Holley, December 25, 1818; George Ticknor to Holley, May 5, 1825; Joseph Story to Holley, March 4, 1819. Holley Papers, Transylvania College.

35. Caldwell, op. cit., 51.

36. Ibid., 56–58.

37. See the excellent study of this relationship in Richard C. Wade, *The Urban Frontier: The Rise of the Western Cities, 1790–1830* (Cambridge, 1959), 233–239, 331–334.

38. Reprinted in Caldwell, op. cit., 262–264.

39. Richard Hofstadter and Wilson Smith, eds., *American Higher Education: A Documentary History* (Chicago, 1961), I, 255.

40. See Jennings, op. cit., Chap. 6: also, Sonne, op. cit., Chap. 6.

41. Rev. Robert Davidson, D.D., *The History of the Presbyterian Church in the State of Kentucky* (New York, 1847), 298.

42. Hofstadter and Smith, op. cit., I, 170–171.

43. Hofstadter and Metzger, op. cit., 32.

44. Sonne, op. cit., 187–190.

45. Rebecca Smith Lee, op. cit., 125.

46. Horace Holley, *A Discourse on the Death of Col. Morrison* (Lexington, 1823), 19.

47. Holley to John Tyler, July 18, 1819. L. Gay Papers, Massachusetts Historical Society. "Observation, common sense, reason, pure morals, our natural and irradicable affections when cultivated and sanctified by intelligence and benevolence, the social virtues, a catholic temper; patience under the contemplation of the follies, and prejudices of society, at the same time a love of truth and a judicious zeal for its defence and propagation . . . such a mode of Christian faith as makes it harmonise with the words and providence of God, such an interpretation of the Bible as does not institute war between the revelation by book and that by nature . . . are the elements of a wise, religious, and truly orthodox man. . . ."

48. Sonne, op. cit., 196–199.

49. S. V. Marshall to Robert Marshall, May 23, 1823. Marshall Papers, Shane Collection, Presbyterian Historical Society, Philadelphia.

50. Holley to Willard Phillips, March 26, 1820. Willard Phillips Papers, Massachusetts Historical Society.

51. Rebecca Smith Lee, op. cit., 123–124.

52. Asa Earl Martin, *The Anti-Slavery Movement in Kentucky Prior to 1850* (Louisville, 1918), Chaps. 1–3.

53. Holley to Willard Phillips, March 26, 1820, op. cit.

54. Sonne, op. cit., 242–247.

55. Ibid., 248–249.

56. Godbey, op. cit., Chap. 4.

57. Caldwell, op. cit., 237; Rebecca Smith Lee, op. cit., 166.

58. Sonne, op. cit., 252–253.

59. Jennings, op. cit., 150.

60. Henry Clay to Holley, February 21, 1826. Holley Papers, Transylvania.

61. Sonne, op. cit., 226–227.

62. Ibid., 215–218.

63. Caldwell, op. cit., 225–226.

64. *Ibid.*, 72.
65. Rebecca Smith Lee, *op. cit.*, 166.
66. Caldwell, *op. cit.*, 214.

Frederick Douglass' Vision for America: A Case Study in Nineteenth-Century Negro Protest

1. See the two biographies, Philip S. Foner, *Frederick Douglass: A Biography* (New York, 1964), and especially Benjamin Quarles, *Frederick Douglass* (Washington, 1948).
2. On Negro thought in the nineteenth century see especially Carter G. Woodson, ed., *The Negro Mind as Reflected in Letters Written During the Crisis, 1800–1860* (Washington, 1926); Howard H. Bell, "A Survey of the Negro Convention Movement, 1830–1861" (Unpublished doctoral dissertation, Northwestern University, 1953); August Meier, *Negro Thought in America, 1880–1915*, Chaps. 1 to 7.
3. Quarles, *Frederick Douglass*, Chaps. 1–5, 7–9; Foner, *Frederick Douglass*, Parts I and II; Quarles, "Abolition's Different Drummer: Frederick Douglass," in Martin Duberman, ed., *The Antislavery Vanguard: New Essays on the Abolitionists* (Princeton, 1965), 123–34.
4. Douglass, "The Claims of Our Common Cause," Address to the 1853 Colored National Convention, in *Proceedings of the Colored National Convention . . . 1853* (Rochester, 1853), 19.
5. Douglass, "The Right to Criticize American Institutions," Speech before the American Anti-Slavery Society, May 11, 1847, reprinted in Foner, ed., *The Life and Writings of Frederick Douglass* (4 vols., New York, 1950–1955), I, 236.
6. *North Star*, Nov. 9, 1849.
7. Douglass to Sidney Howard Gay, Sept. 17, 1847, in Foner, *Life and Writings*, I, 265.
8. *Douglass' Monthly*, October, 1860.
9. Douglass, *Life and Times of Frederick Douglass* (Hartford, 1882), 250–51.
10. *Ibid.*, 298–99; Quarles, *Frederick Douglass*, 108.
11. Quarles, *Frederick Douglass*, 101–102.
12. *Ibid.*, p. 219; Foner, *Frederick Douglass*, 231–32; Douglass, *Life and Times*, 402–404.
13. *North Star*, January 19, 1849.
14. *Ibid.*, July 14, 1848.
15. *Ibid.*, June 13, 1850.
16. *Frederick Douglass' Paper*, March 4, 1853. See also Douglass and others, Address to the Colored People of the United States of the colored national convention of 1848, *North Star*, September 29, 1848; and *Proceedings of the National Convention of Colored People . . . 1847* (Troy, N.Y., 1847), 37–38.
17. *Frederick Douglass' Paper*, March 11, 1853.
18. Douglass to Harriet Beecher Stowe, March 8, 1853, in *Proceedings of the Colored National Convention, 1853*, 33–38.
19. *Ibid.*, 22–40. On the 1853–1855 movement for industrial education generally, see Bell, "Survey of the Negro Convention Movement," 171–75.

20. *Frederick Douglass' Paper*, October 5, 1855.
21. *North Star*, December 3, 1847.
22. Address to the Colored People of the United States, 1848 national convention, in *North Star*, September 29, 1848.
23. *Ibid.*, July 14, 1848.
24. *Ibid.*, January 19, 1849.
25. Douglass, "The Present Condition and Future Prospects of the Negro People," Speech at annual meeting of the American and Foreign Anti-Slavery Society, New York, May, 1853, reprinted in Foner, *Life and Writings*, II, 243, 246.
26. *North Star*, August 10 and October 29, 1849.
27. *Ibid.*, December 14, 1849; *Frederick Douglass' Paper*, April 13, 1855.
28. Bell, "Survey of the Negro Convention Movement," *passim*.
29. *North Star*, January 19, 1848.
30. *Ibid.*, November 16, 1849.
31. *Douglass' Monthly*, February, 1859.
32. *Ibid.*, April, 1861.
33. *Ibid.*, May, 1861.
34. Douglass, "The Mission of the War," 1863, MS, Frederick Douglass Papers at the Frederick Douglass Home, Washington, D.C.; available on microfilm at the Schomburg Collection, New York Public Library, Reel 13.
35. Quarles, *Frederick Douglass*, Chaps. 11 and 12; Foner, *Frederick Douglass*, Part III; James M. McPherson, *The Negro's Civil War* (New York, 1965), 17–18, 37–40, 161–63.
36. Douglass, "Our Work is Not Done," Speech delivered at the Annual Meeting of the American Anti-Slavery Society, Philadelphia, December 3–4, 1863, reprinted in Foner, *Life and Writings*, III, 381. See also Quarles, *Frederick Douglass*, 214–15; Douglass, *Life and Times*, 418.
37. *Douglass' Monthly*, June, 1863.
38. Douglass, "A Composite Nation," Lecture, 1867, MS, Douglass Papers, Microfilm Reel 13.
39. Douglass, "What the Black Man Wants," in William D. Kelley, Wendell Phillips, and Frederick Douglass, *The Equality of All Men Before the Law* (Boston, 1865), 36–37; *New National Era*, August 24, 1871.
40. *Proceedings of the National Convention of Colored Men . . . 1864* (Boston, 1864), 13–14; Douglass, "Address to the People of the United States," Delivered at National Convention of Colored Men, Louisville, 1883, in *Three Addresses on the Relations Subsisting Between the White and Colored People of the United States* (Washington, 1886), 4–6.
41. *The New Era*, January 27, 1870; Douglass to Gerrit Smith, September 26, 1873, cited in Quarles, *Frederick Douglass*, 110.
42. *Proceedings of the National Convention of Colored Men, 1864*, 5; Appendix to Douglass, *Life and Times*, 561–62.
43. *New National Era*, April 20, 1871.
44. *Ibid.*, February 2, 1871.
45. Douglass, "Address to the People of the United States," Louisville Convention, 1883, in *Three Addresses*, 12–13.
46. Douglass, "The Color Line," *North American Review*, CXXXII (June, 1881), 568–75; *Proceedings of the Civil Rights Mass-Meeting . . . Washington, October 22, 1883* (Washington, 1883), 5, 7, 8, 14; Douglass, "Address on American Civilization" (1884), MS, Douglass Papers, Microfilm Reel 13.

47. Hayes made Douglass Marshal of the District of Columbia; Garfield and Arthur appointed him Recorder of the Deeds of the District of Columbia; and Harrison made him minister to Haiti.

48. Alexandria, Va. *People's Advocate*, October 6, 1883; New York *Globe*, Sept. 29, 1883; Douglass, "The Future of the Race," *African Methodist Episcopal Church Review*, VI (October, 1889), 232–33; Douglass, *Life and Times* (Hartford, 1891 ed.), 559; Douglass, "The Cause of Republican Defeat" (1890), MS, Douglass Papers, Microfilm Reel 12.

49. Quarles, *Frederick Douglass*, 260.

50. Douglass to C. N. Bliss, October 5, 1887, Douglass Papers, Microfilm Reel 1.

51. Cleveland *Gazette*, October 30, 1886.

52. Douglass to D. A. Straker, August 2, 1888, Douglass Papers, Microfilm Reel 1.

53. Quarles, *Frederick Douglass*, 354.

54. For example, *New National Era*, September 27, 1870.

55. Douglass, *Address . . . on the Twenty-First Anniversary of Emancipation in the District of Columbia* (Washington, 1883), 16.

56. Francis J. Grimké, "The Second Marriage of Frederick Douglass," *Journal of Negro History*, XIX (July, 1934), 324–29; Douglass to George L. Ruffin, January 28 [1884], photostatic copy, Ruffin Papers, Howard University Library. Ruffin, a Massachusetts lawyer, was the first Negro appointed to a judgeship in the North.

57. Douglass, "The Future of the Colored Race," *North American Review*, CXLII (May, 1886), 438–39.

58. Douglass, "The Future of the Race," *AME Church Review*, op. cit., 225–36.

59. Samuel R. Spencer, Jr., *Booker T. Washington and the Negro's Place in American Life* (Boston, 1955), 108; Washington to Douglass, April 2, 1894, Douglass Papers, Microfilm Reel 7.

60. Douglass, "Oration" delivered at Manassas Industrial School, Virginia, September 3, 1894, MS, Douglass Papers, Microfilm Reel 13.

61. Douglass, "The Future of the Race," *AME Church Review*, op. cit., 225–26.

The Narrow Escape from a "Compromise of 1860": Secession and the Constitution

1. MS memorandum by John C. Ropes, Feb. 8, 1870, of conversation in September 1869 with Edwin M. Stanton, Horatio Woodman Papers, Massachusetts Historical Society.

2. *Ibid.* Differing interpretations on Buchanan are in Philip S. Klein, *President James Buchanan, A Biography* (University Park: Pennsylvania State University Press, 1962), and in Benjamin P. Thomas and Harold M. Hyman, *Stanton: The Life and Times of Lincoln's Secretary of War* (New York: Knopf, 1962), Chaps. 5–6.

3. As example, Buchanan paid respectful attention to his new Attorney General, Edwin M. Stanton, who he believed ". . . has not his superior as a lawyer in the United States." Buchanan to Harriet Lane, November 4, 1860, Buchanan-Johnston Papers, Library of Congress. The President and Stanton studied intensively a book just out on American constitutional law

and history: Nathaniel C. Towle's *A History and Analysis of the Constitution of the United States* (Boston: Little, Brown, 1860), underlining passages and adding many marginal comments. Buchanan heavily underscored this passage: "The Constitution of the United States was ordained and established not by the United States in their sovereign capacities, but, as the preamble declares, by the people of the United States. . . . The Constitution was not, therefore, carved out of existing State sovereignties, nor a surrender of powers already existing in the State governments. On the other hand, the sovereign powers, vested in the State governments by their respective constitutions, remained unaltered and unimpaired, except so far as they are granted to the government of the United States. . . . The United States *is* a *government*, and consequently, a body politic and corporate, capable of attaining the objects for which it was created, by the means which are necessary for their attainment" (pp. 39–40; copy owned by Mrs. E. K. Van Swearingen).

4. Holt to James O. Harrison, Jan. 14, 1861, Harrison Papers, Library of Congress.

5. Burgess, *The Civil War and the Constitution, 1859–1865* (New York: Scribner's, 1901), I, 80. By Burgess' analysis the secessionist argument, that leaned so heavily upon a tortured extrapolation from the Tenth Amendment, was a "mere jugglery of words." *Ibid.*, 76.

6. James D. Richardson, comp., *A Compilation of the Messages and Papers of the Presidents of the United States* (Washington: Government Printing Office, 1897), V, 626–637. Hereafter this collection is cited as Richardson, *M & P.*

7. See George Selden Henry, Jr., "Radical Republican Policy toward the Negro during Reconstruction, 1862–1872" (Ph.D. dissertation, Yale University, 1963), Chaps. 1–2; George M. Frederickson, *The Inner Civil War: Northern Intellectuals and the Crisis of the Union* (New York: Harper & Row, 1965), Chap. 4.

8. As example of sensitivity to the speech and its effects, see James Eliot Cabot, *Letter to the Governor of Massachusetts on the Occasion of his Late Proclamation of August 20, 1861* (Boston: Loring, 1861), p. 9, where, referring to December 1860, Cabot asked: "What is the 'organic principle' of the Republican party? What is it amid the heterogeneous elements wherefrom it is built, that each member of it acknowledged as his? Surely, every candid person, whether he voted with that party or not, will agree that its distinctive tenet, and accordingly the policy from which it could in no event depart, was opposition to the extension of slavery within the national territory. Its course, if not indeed like a Roman road straight over hill and dale to that mark, should at least be expected to keep the main direction, with only such deviations, if any, as should be plainly necessary to avoid worse."

9. Bellows, *The Advantage of Testing Our Principles, Compensatory of the Evils of Serious Times: A Discourse on Sunday Morning, Feb. 17, 1861, before the Second Unitarian Society of Philadelphia* (Philadelphia: Sherman, 1861). On equality, see Frederickson, *Inner Civil War*, passim, and Donald Dwight Braden, "The Concept of Equality in American Political Thought" (Ph.D. dissertation; University of Southern California, 1944), Chaps. 8–10.

10. December 31, 1860, to Charles Nordhoff, in *Letters of James Russell Lowell*, ed. Charles Eliot Norton (New York: Harpers, 1894), I, 308.

11. Frederickson, *The Inner Civil War*, 48–49; and see Robert Albrecht, "The Response of the Transcendentalists to the Civil War," *New England Quarterly*, XXXVIII (March, 1965), 21–34.

12. James McPherson, *The Struggle for Equality: Abolitionists and the Negro in the Civil War and Reconstruction* (Princeton: Princeton University Press, 1964); Frederickson, *The Inner Civil War*, Chaps. 4–5, errs on the war-intellectual interaction.

13. Fear existed that further secession in the North or invasion from the South would result in the loss of Washington before Lincoln was sworn in. As example, in January, 1861, Stanton told Senator Charles Sumner of Massachusetts that ". . . he does not think it probable, hardly possible, that we shall be here on the 4th March. . . . It is feared that the [federal] Departments will be seized and occupied [by secessionists] as forts." Sumner to Governor John A. Andrew, January 28, 1861, Andrew Papers, Massachusetts Historical Society.

14. *Congressional Globe* (hereafter cited as *CG*), 36 Cong., 2 sess., 99–104.

15. Charles Francis Adams, *The Constitutional Ethics of Secession* (Boston and New York: Houghton, Mifflin, 1903); Hermann E. Von Holst, *The Constitutional and Political History of the United States* (Chicago: Callaghan, 1876–92), VII, 377.

16. Burgess, *Civil War and the Constitution*, I, 96–97.

17. Crittenden hoped that northern states would repeal their personal liberty laws in anticipation of the ratification of his amendment; *CG*, 36 Cong., 2 sess., 114; Bestor, "The American Civil War as a Constitutional Crisis," *American Historical Review*, LXIX (January, 1964), 341, 343; and for a differing analysis, Albert K. Kirwan, *John J. Crittenden: The Struggle for the Union* (Lexington: University of Kentucky Press, 1962), 366–421.

18. In addition to Buchanan's constitutional constrictions, disbelief in the chance of violence kept the President from allowing anything approaching adequate preparations. See Stanton to Ohio Senator Salmon P. Chase, January 23, 1861, Chase Papers, Historical Society of Pennsylvania.

19. Stephen A. Douglas to C. H. Lanphier, December 25, 1860, George Fort Milton Papers, Library of Congress; Robert W. Johannsen, "The Douglas Democracy and the Crisis of Disunion," *Civil War History*, IX (September, 1963), 231.

20. Giddings, *History of the Rebellion: Its Causes and Cures* (New York: Follet, Foster, 1864), 455. Forty years later the historian Burgess, *Civil War and the Constitution*, I, 99, recalled that "The cardinal principle of the Republican creed was the arrest of the further extension of slavery. It was with them not simply a party platform, or a political policy, which might be sacrificed without the violation of any principle of justice or morality, but it was the fundamental ethical principle of their existence. To agree to Mr. Toombs's demands, or to Mr. Crittenden's propositions, would have been for the Republicans political and moral suicide."

21. Wilder Dwight to Horace Gray, February 27, 1861, Gray Papers, Library of Congress. A different judgment on the peace-effort is in Robert A. Gunderson, *Old Gentleman's Convention: The Washington Peace Conference of 1861* (Madison: University of Wisconsin Press, 1961).

22. The three quotations are respectively December 11 and 17, 1860, February 1, 1861, in Roy P. Basler *et al.*, eds., *The Collected Works of Abraham Lincoln* (New Brunswick: Rutgers University Press, 1953), IV, 150, 154, 183.

23. Lorraine A. Williams, "Northern Intellectual Attitudes toward Lincoln, 1860–1865," *Illinois State Historical Society Journal*, LVII (Autumn, 1964), 270–277.

24. A recent example of such an attempt is in Johannsen, "The Douglas

Democracy and the Crisis of Disunion," 232, where the suggestion is made that "At the time, party position seemed [to Lincoln] more important than the nation's problems."

25. CG, 36 Cong., 2 sess., 1284–1285, 1403. Note that the federal territories and the District of Columbia were not included in the terms of the proposal.

26. Lincoln, Works, IV, 270.

27. Herman V. Ames, "Proposed Amendments to the Constitution of the United States during the First Century of its History," American Historical Association, Annual Report (1896), II, 23–49.

28. Burgess, Civil War and the Constitution, I, 99–100.

29. Pollard, The Lost Cause (New York: Carleton, 1866), 43; Roy Franklin Nichols, Blueprints for Leviathan: American Style (New York: Atheneum, 1963), 134–143.

30. Kirwan, Crittenden, 392–394; CG, 36 Cong., 2 sess., 211, 237, 264–267, App., 38–42.

31. The Round Table, III (Boston, January 20, 1866), 40.

32. CG, 36 Cong., 2 sess., 341–346.

Some Catholic Churchmen as Americanizers

1. The American Mind: An Interpretation of American Thought and Character since the 1880's (New Haven, 1950), 193.

2. Milton M. Gordon, Assimilation in American Life: The Role of Race, Religion, and National Origins (New York, 1964), see pp. 6–8. Will Herberg, Protestant, Catholic, Jew: An Essay in American Religious Sociology (New York, 1960); John Higham, Strangers in the Land: Patterns of American Nativism, 1860–1925 (New York, 1963), Chap. 9. Nowhere does Higham exclude the possibility that other agencies were active participants in the Americanization process, but neither does he make any reference to the Commager thesis. Two studies by Joseph H. Fichter, S.J., delineate the internal structure and dynamics of Catholic community life in this country. See Social Relations in the Urban Parish (Chicago, 1954) and Southern Parish, Vol. 1, Dynamics of a City Church (Chicago, 1951).

3. Gordon, 60–68.

4. "Assimilation, social," in Encyclopedia of the Social Sciences, Edwin Seligman and Alvin Johnson, eds. (New York, 1930), II, 281. Cf. Gordon, 63.

5. Gordon, 85 ff.

6. J. Hector St. John Crèvecoeur, Letters from an American Farmer (New York, 1925), 54–5.

7. Gordon, 13, 115 ff.

8. Ibid., 109–110.

9. Ellis, American Catholicism (Chicago, 1956); Nathan Glazer and Daniel Moyninan, Beyond the Melting Pot: the Negroes, Puerto Ricans, Jews, Italians and Irish of New York City (Cambridge, 1963), 312.

10. Gordon, 98–99.

11. Howard C. Hill, "The Americanization Movement," American Journal of Sociology, XXIV (May, 1919), 629.

12. Ibid., 630.

13. James H. Moynihan, *The Life of Archbishop John Ireland: A Definitive Biography* (New York, 1953), 109.

14. Ellis, 51.

15. Gordon, 100.

16. Ellis, 58.

17. Alfonso Zaratti, O.C.D., *The Work of the Catholic Church in the United States of America* (Rome, 1956), 331–2.

18. Ellis, 57.

19. James P. Shannon, *Catholic Colonization on the Western Frontier* (New Haven, 1957), 267.

20. Moynihan, *Ireland*, 7.

21. *Ibid.*, 51–2.

22. *Ibid.*, 61–2; cf. *Northwestern Chronicle*, October 26, 1888.

23. *Ibid.*

24. John Ireland, *The Church in Modern Society* (2 vols., St. Paul, 1905), II, 247.

25. *Ibid.*, I, 180.

26. Robert Cross, *The Emergence of Liberal Catholicism in America* (Cambridge, 1958), 88.

27. Moynihan, *Ireland*, 45.

28. *Ibid.*, 58.

29. *Ibid.*, 106.

30. *Church in Modern Society*, I, 168.

31. *Ibid.*, 175–6.

32. *Ibid.*, 179–80. Ireland, in a recent election, had openly supported Father Sylvester Malone, successful candidate on the Republican ticket for the N.Y. State Board of Regents. The Democrats had nominated Bishop McQuaid of Rochester, who thought it unseemly to work publicly for his election. After this speech, Ireland gleefully reported to Cardinal Gibbons that "people were wicked enough to see in those words an allusion to His Lordship of Rochester." Moynihan, 263.

33. *Ibid.*, I, 188–9.

34. M. S. Pahorezki, *The Social and Political Activities of William J. Onahan* (Washington, D.C., 1942), 173–90. Cf. Cross, 100–1, who pointed out that the liberals, as bad as a purely Catholic party may have seemed to them, equally deplored the automatic identification of most Catholics with the Democratic party. This deprived Catholics of their rightful political influence on public affairs, an influence that the "real popularity of the Church in America made possible."

35. *Church in Modern Society*, I, 190.

36. *Ibid.*, 195.

37. Theodore Maynard, *The Story of American Catholicism* (New York, 1941), 223; Peter Guilday, *The Life and Times of John England, First Bishop of Charleston, 1786–1842* (2 vols., N.Y., 1927), I, 447.

38. Zaratti, *Work of the Catholic Church in U.S.*, 330–1.

39. Moynihan, *Ireland*, 62–3. The role of the "ethnic church" in maintaining the ethnic community as a cohesive social system has been well demonstrated in W. Lloyd Warner and Leo Srole, *The Social System of American Ethnic Groups* (New Haven, 1945). Certainly the policy of the Church subsequently was not to foster nationality communalism any longer than nec-

essary. Cf. C. J. Nuesse and Thomas J. Harte, C.SS.R., eds., *The Sociology of the Parish* (Milwaukee, 1951), 45–71, and Gordon, 196–200.

40. Moynihan, 63; Colman J. Barry, O.S.B., *The Catholic Church and German Americans* (Milwaukee, 1953), 101–2; Cross, *Emergence of Liberal Catholicism*, 89.

41. Cross, 89; "Irish Agitation in America," *Forum*, IV (December, 1887), 400–1.

42. Barry, 101–2.

43. Cross, 89.

44. *Ibid.*; see also L. R. Hubbard, "Nationality and Religion," *Catholic World*, 50 (December, 1889), 396–400; "The Church and Modern Society," *Catholic World*, 65 (May, 1897), 218; Higham, *Strangers in the Land*, 118; Robert Cross's review of David F. Sweeney's *Life of John Lancaster Spalding: First Bishop of Peoria, 1840–1916* (New York, 1965) in *American Historical Review*, XXI (July, 1966), 1457.

45. Ireland, *The Church and Modern Society*, I, 91, 206–7; Barry, 119; *Northwestern Chronicle*, August 10, 17, 1888.

46. Ireland, II, 226; Cross, 89.

47. Cross, 89–90.

48. John A. Hawgood, *The Tragedy of German-America* (New York, 1940), 39; Cross, 90; Barry, 212–13.

49. *Question of Nationality*, 39–46; Cross, 90.

50. "A Critic of the Great Republic," *Catholic World*, 40 (November, 1884), 247–9. As to Walburg's assertion that religion and national origins, while both cultural phenomena, are distinctly different institutions which do not necessarily vary concomitantly. See Gordon, 27.

51. *Question of Nationality*, 39–46; Cross, 90.

52. *Question of Nationality*, 57, 61. Michael Shaughnessy, *Has the Immigrant Kept the Faith?* (New York, 1925), 250 ff.

53. *Question of Nationality*, 26–7, 43–8; Cross, 25–6.

54. John Gilmary Shea, in the *Catholic News*, June 28, 1891; quoted in Barry, 151 n.

55. Cross, 92; Walburg, *Question of Nationality*, 31–2.

56. Cross, 88–9; Moynihan, *Ireland*, 64; Barry, 102; *Catholic World*, 50 (November, 1899), 246.

57. *New York Times*, October 2, 1892; Barry, 214 n.; Cross, 92.

58. Oscar Handlin, *The Uprooted: the Epic Story of the Great Migrations that Made the American People* (Boston, 1952), 133–5.

59. Cross, 91; Moynihan, *Ireland*, 60. Rome's answer also declared that the "Sacred Congregation of the Propaganda will never consider these petitions."

60. Barry, Appendix, IV, 313–5.

61. Moynihan, *Ireland*, 63–4; Cross, 93.

62. Moynihan, 64; *New York Herald*, June 1, 1891.

63. *Ibid.*, 64–5; St. Paul *Pioneer Press*, June 12, 1891.

64. Moynihan, *Ireland*, 65; Baltimore Cathedral Archives, Ireland to Gibbons, St. Paul, May 30, 1891.

65. Cross, 93–94.

66. The President's remarks, in Gibbons' version, appear in Barry, 156–7. They were forwarded in a letter to Monsignor Denis O'Connell from Cape May, dated July 12, 1891, which is in the Archives of the Diocese of Richmond. Cf. Cross, 93–4, and John Tracy Ellis, *The Life of James Cardinal*

Gibbons, Archbishop of Baltimore, 1834–1921 (2 vols., Milwaukee, 1952), I, 371–4.

67. The second memorial appears in Barry, Appendix V, 316; cf. Moynihan, *Ireland*, 66–8. The best treatment of Cahenslyism is found in Barry, *The Catholic Church and German Americans*. John Meng has written two useful articles, "Cahenslyism: The First Stage, 1883–1891," *Catholic Historical Review*, XXXI (January, 1946), 389–413, and "Cahenslyism: The Second Chapter," 32 (October, 1946), 302–40.

68. The pallium is the circular band of white wool worn on the shoulder of the pope and archbishops to symbolize the fullness of the episcopal power enjoyed by the pontiff and shared in by the archbishops. Formerly it was a part of the coat of arms of the see of Canterbury, and though an outward sign of the union with the Holy See, it is still used by Anglican Archbishops as well as Catholic. See Donald Atwater, ed., *A Catholic Dictionary* (3d ed. New York, 1958), 365.

69. Gibbons' speech is quoted *in extenso* in Barry, 162–3.

70. Cross, 93–4.

71. Quoted in the *St. Raphaels Blatt*, Barry, 166–7.

72. Gordon, 217. "The defeat of Cahenslyism saved the Catholic Church in this country from the kind of fragmentation along ethnic-cultural lines that American Protestantism has had to undergo. And it left the Irish . . . in an even stronger position . . ." in the Church. Herberg, *Protestant, Catholic, Jew*, 145.

73. John L. Thomas, S.J., "Nationalities and American Catholicism," in *Catholic Church, U.S.A.*, ed., Louis J. Putz (Chicago, 1956), 159.

74. See Gordon, 202 ff.

75. In the archdiocese of Chicago, for example, there were as late as 1960, 144 territorial parishes as compared to 140 national parishes. Thomas, "Nationalities and American Catholicism," *op. cit.*, 162. See also Gordon, 200–1. For a fuller discussion of the problem, see Thomas J. Harte, "Racial and National Parishes in the U.S.," in *The Sociology of the Parish*, 154–177.

76. Gordon, 199.

77. *Ibid.*, 217; Will Herberg, *Protestant, Catholic, Jew*, 149–153.

78. Herberg, 148. Everett C. Hughes is quoted as noting that in the past Catholics have looked for the definition of "good American" largely to non-Catholics. But as Catholics have increasingly moved into the managerial and professional classes, they have been able to influence the definition of "good American," and have taken the lead in the crusade against Communism, in defining the "bad American" as well. Herberg, n. 167; cf. David Riesman, *Individualism Reconsidered* (New York, 1954), 391.

79. *Sociology of the Parish*, 160.

80. *The Immigrant in American History* (Cambridge, 1948), 105.

81. Thomas, *Catholic Church, U.S.A.*, 160.

82. Gordon, 136–39.

83. Hecker is quoted in Walter J. Ong, S.J., *American Catholic Crossroads: Religious-Secular Encounters in the Modern World* (New York, 1959), 57.

American Socialists and the Russian Revolution of 1905–1906

1. The research for this article was substantially aided by a Summer Faculty Fellowship made available by the University of Florida.

2. For background see William Mailly, "The Socialist Party," in William D. P. Bliss, ed., *The New Encyclopedia of Social Reform* (New York, 1908), 1150–51; David Shannon, *The Socialist Party of America* (New York, 1955), 5; Ira Kipnis, *The American Socialist Movement, 1897–1912* (New York, 1952), 162–63; William J. Ghent in *The Worker* (New York), February 19, 1905; Upton Sinclair, "The Socialist Party," *World's Work*, XI (April, 1906), 7431–32. Data on organization are in John C. Chase, Letterbook: 1906–1907, Tamiment Institute Library, City of New York (hereinafter cited as TIL); Minutes of the Meetings of the General Committee of Local New York, Social Democratic Party (hereinafter SDP), 1904–1906; Minute Book, New York City Executive Committee, SDP, 1904–1905; Minutes of the 30th Assembly District, New York, SDP, 26–27, 52–53, February 8, October 25, 1905, all TIL; Ralph Chaplin, *Wobbly: The Rough-and-Tumble Story of an American Radical* (Chicago, 1948), 53.

3. Shannon, *Socialist Party of America*, 8, 8–19, 21, 53, 61; William Z. Foster, *From Bryan to Stalin* (1937), 29; E. H. Thomas to Morris Hillquit, Milwaukee, May 19, 1905, Hillquit Papers, State Historical Society of Wisconsin (hereinafter cited as SHSW). Times would change and Simons later joined Berger's *Milwaukee Leader*. See also George D. Herron, Florence, Italy, October 19, 1905; William Mailly to Morris Hillquit, Toledo, February 6, November 15, 1905; John C. Chase to Morris Hillquit, New York, January 10, 1905, Hillquit Papers, SHSW; William Mailly to Algernon Lee, Toledo, August 24, 1905, Algernon Lee Papers, TIL.

4. The *Chicago Socialist*, July 8, 1905, on accusations against DeLeon; Charles H. Kerr to Morris Hillquit, Chicago, October 4, 1905, Hillquit Papers, SHSW; *Wilshire's Magazine*, VI (September, 1904), 363; IX (June, 1905); William J. Ghent, "The Appeal and Its Influence," *Survey*, XXVI (April 1, 1911); *Social Democratic Herald*, August 13, 1904; *International Socialist Review*, V (September, 1904), 150–52. Shannon, *Socialist Party of America*, 21–22, has general data.

5. Eugene V. Debs, "The Russian Revolt No Surprise," *Miners Magazine*, VI (February 16, 1905), 9; *The Worker*, February 12, 1905; VI (February 23, 1905), 3; *The Daily People*, February 14, 1905 in DeLeon, *Russia in Revolution*, 20–22; *The Weekly People*, January and February, 1905; *The Chicago Socialist*, March 4, 1905.

6. *The Worker*, July 8, 15, 1905; *The Chicago Socialist*, June 3, July 15, 1905; *Wilshire's Magazine*, VIII (June, 1905), 8; (August, 1905), 8; William Mailly, ed., *National Convention of the Socialist Party held at Chicago, Illinois, May 1 to 6, 1904* (Chicago, 1904), 66, 169–70, 323; *Social Democratic Herald*, September 2, 1905; *Miners Magazine*, VI (January 19, 1905), 4; *The Weekly People*, July 1, 1905; Sen Katayama, "Attitude of Japanese Socialists Toward the Present War," *International Socialist Review*, IV (1903–04), 514; Hyman Kublin, *Asian Revolutionary: The Life of Sen Katayama* (Princeton, N.J., 1964), 167–68; Harvey Goldberg, *The Life of Jean Jaures* (Madison, Wisc., 1962), 324, 542.

7. *Miners Magazine*, VII (August 31, 1905), 3; *The Chicago Socialist*, August 12, 1905; *The Weekly People*, August and September, 1905; Emma Goldman, *Living My Life* (New York, 1934), 372; *Jewish Daily Forward* (New York), October 30, 31, 1906; Ernest Poole, *The Bridge: My Own Story* (New York, 1940), 168–69; and see the long page-one editorial by Victor Berger in the *Social Democratic Herald*, November 4, 1905.

8. *Wilshire's Magazine*, IX (December, 1905), 9; *Miners Magazine*, VII

(November 9, 1905), 3; *The Daily People*, October 28, 1905, in DeLeon, *Russia in Revolution*, 25–27; *The Weekly People*, November and December, 1905; *The Worker*, November 4, 11, December 30, 1905, February 10, 1906; *The Chicago Socialist*, December 30, 1905; *Social Democratic Herald*, January 6, 20, 1906.

9. *International Socialist Review*, VI (April, 1906), 626–27; *The Weekly People*, May 12, 1906; *Wilshire's Magazine*, X (June, 1906), 5; *The Worker*, May 5, 12, June 9, 1906.

10. *Industrial Worker*, July, 1906; *Wilshire's Magazine*, X (September, 1906), 6; (November, 1906), 8; *The Worker*, July 28, 1906, June 22, 1907; *The Daily People*, July 26, 1906, in DeLeon, *Russia in Revolution*, 38–39; *International Socialist Review*, VII (August, 1907), 114–15; *Social Democratic Herald*, July 28, 1906. During the two months following the dissolution of the Duma, there was a marked decline in Russian news coverage and a virtual disappearance of the subject from editorial columns for the remainder of the year. See also *Social Democratic Herald*, December 24, 1904, March 18, 1905, January 27, 1906; *The Chicago Socialist* (November 11, 1905); *The Weekly People*, December 2, 1905; Simon O. Pollock, "The Russian Bastile," *International Socialist Review*, VII (March, 1907), 533–45; *Miners Magazine*, VI (February 16, 1905), 3; (April 6, 1905), 9; VII (November 30, 1905), 10; (January 4, 1906), 3.

11. Debs, "The Russian Revolt No Surprise," p. 9; *Social Democratic Herald*, February 4, March 4, 1905; *The Weekly People*, February 11, 1905; *The Worker*, December 23, 1905; *The Daily People*, December 5, 1905, in DeLeon, *Russia in Revolution*, 27–29.

12. Minutes of Meetings of the General Committee of Local New York, SDP, November 25, 1905, TIL; *The Chicago Socialist*, November 18, December 16, 1905; "In the Land of Liberty," *Miners Magazine*, VII (October 19, 1905), 6; *Wilshire's Magazine*, X (July, 1906), 4; *The Chicago Socialist*, July 22, 1905; *The Weekly People*, October 21, 1905.

13. *The Chicago Socialist*, July 8, September 30, 1905; *The Weekly People*, October 21, December 23, 1905; *The Social Democratic Herald*, December 23, 1905; Social Democratic Party, Minute Book, New York State Committee, August 23, 1904–May 5, 1906 (TIL); Minutes of Meetings of the General Committee of Local New York, SDP, June 11, 1904–December 22, 1906 (TIL); *Socialist Party Weekly Bulletin*, 1904–07; *Socialist Party Official Bulletin*, 1904–07; *Jewish Exponent* (Philadelphia), September 29, 1905; *Jewish Comment* (Baltimore), October 6, 1905; Mordecai Soltes, *The Yiddish Press: An Americanizing Agency* (New York, 1950), 95; *The American Hebrew*, December 22, 1905; Harry H. Rogoff, *An East Side Epic: The Life and Work of Meyer London* (New York, 1930), 24; Moses Rischin, *The Promised City: New York's Jews, 1870–1914* (Cambridge, Mass., 1962), 163; Stuart E. Rosenberg, *The Jewish Community in Rochester, 1843–1925* (New York, 1954), 153; *Jewish Daily Forward*, November and December, 1905.

14. *The Chicago Socialist*, November 4, 18, December 9, 1905; "The Revolution in Russia," *Miners Magazine*, VI (April 6, 1905), 9–10; "The Socialists Lead in Russia," *ibid.*, VII (November 30, 1905), 13; *The Worker*, March 18, 1905, and November and December, 1905, *passim*; *International Socialist Review*, VII (July, 1906), 49–50; *Social Democratic Herald*, January 28, 1905.

15. O. Leonard, "Revolutionary Russia," *International Socialist Review*,

VI (July, 1905), 1–7; Guy E. Miller, "Russia," Miners Magazine, VII (February 8, 1906), 9–10. See also the survey in International Socialist Review, V (February, 1905), 495 (March, 1905), 561–63; Social Democratic Herald, December 31, 1904.

16. V. L. Berger, "Russian Revolution Impossible . . . ," Social Democratic Herald, February 4, 1905; ibid., January 28, April 15, December 16, 1905; "The Impossibility of a Russian Social Revolution," Wilshire's Magazine, VIII (August, 1905), 8. Also, see ibid., X (March, 1906), 7 (April, 1906), 6.

17. International Socialist Review, VI (November, 1905), 310–11; Algie M. Simons, "A World Revolution in Progress," The Chicago Socialist, December 16, 1905; The Chicago Tribune, December 20, 1905; The Chicago Socialist, November 11, 25, December 2, 23, 1905, January 27, 1906.

18. The Industrial Worker, February, 1906; Miners Magazine, VI (May 11, 1905), 13–14, (August 17, 1905), 11; VII (September 14, 1905), 8–9, (December 7, 1905), 8–9; Bill Haywood's Book: The Autobiography of William D. Haywood (New York, 929), 186–87; Ray Ginger, The Bending Cross: A Biography of Eugene Victor Debs (New Brunswick, N.J., 1949), 239; Paul F. Brissenden, Launching the IWW: A Study of American Syndicalism (New York, 1957), 17; Voice of Labor (Chicago), January, 1905; The Weekly People, February 25, July 8, December 2, 1905; Social Democratic Herald, March 4, 18, 1905; International Socialist Review, VI (February, 1906), 498–99.

19. Minute Book, New York City Executive Committee, SDP, October 16, 1905, TIL; The Chicago Socialists, January 6, 1906; Rogoff, An East Side Epic, 26–27; Letter, A. E. Briggs, Elk Grove, California, to the Sacramento Star, reprinted in the Miners Magazine, VI (June 29, 1905), 9–10, VIII (September 13, 1906), 15; Address of President David M. Parry in The Proceedings of the Tenth Annual Convention of the National Association of Manufacturers of the United States of America Held at Atlanta, Georgia, May 16, 17, 18, 1905 (New York, n.d.), 37–39; The Weekly People, January 27, 1906; The Daily People, January 29, 1905, in DeLeon, Russia in Revolution, 16–19.

20. Social Democratic Herald, August 19, 1905; The Chicago Socialist, February 4, May 6, September 16, December 30, 1905; Miners Magazine, VI (June 29, 1905), 3; VII (January 11, 1906), 7–8; VII (March 22, 1906), 15; Wilshire's Magazine, X (January, 1906), 8; X (February, 1906), 5; Chaplin, Wobbly, 79; The Weekly People, December 17, 1904, February 4, August 26, 1905.

21. Social Democratic Herald, August 6, 1904, January 28, 1905; "Russianism in Illinois," Miners Magazine, VI (April 20, 1905), 9; and see VII (March 22, 1906), 15. Max Hayes, "A Warning to the Enemy," ibid., VII (May 3, 1906), 8; and see also VIII (June 28, 1906), 3; "In Colorado's Siberia," ibid., VIII (August 30, 1906), 6; ibid., VI (February 9, 1905), 4 (February 16, 1905), 3 (May 25, 1905), 3–9, VII (December 21, 1905), 8–9 (April 19, 1906), 9 (May 10, 1906), 3 (May 24, 1906), 4, VIII (July 12, 1906), 9; Social Democratic Herald, January 28, 1905; The Chicago Socialist, January 6, 1906; Appeal to Reason, August 25, 1906; The Worker, June 30, 1906; Wilshire's Magazine, X (January, 1906), 8.

22. The Weekly People, February 18, July 1, 8, 28, November 18, 1905; The Worker, December 23, 1905; Address, W. E. Trautmann, July 7, 1905, Chicago, in Miners Magazine, VI (August 17, 1905), 11, and see ibid., VI

(February 16, 1905), 3–4; (April 20, 1905), 10; (June 29, 1905), 11; (August 24, 1905), 11; VII (January 4, 1906), 6; Address, Daniel DeLeon, July 10, 1905, in *ibid.*, VII (November 9, 1905), 9–11; *The Industrial Worker*, January, February, 1906; *Voice of Labor*, March, 1905; Algie M. Simons, "A World Revolution in Progress," *The Chicago Socialist*, December 16, 1905, and see *ibid.*, November 11, 1905.

23. *The Cleveland Citizen*, February 18, 1905; Cincinnati *Brauer-Zeitung*, February 4, 1905; *Appeal to Reason*, February 11, 1905; *Miners Magazine*, VII (November 16, 1905), 4 (December 7, 1905), 3; *The Chicago Socialist*, February 18, October 14, 1905; *The Worker*, February 5, 1905; it is exceedingly difficult to draw any kind of distinction here between the response of socialists and of Jews both to Bloody Sunday and to the events which followed. Many Russian-born Jews, albeit a minority, were also socialists or associated with the Bund. Much more important, however, was the fact that the overwhelming majority of American Jews, regardless of political outlook, hated the Russian government and rejoiced in a movement which promised some relief to their pogrom-stricken coreligionists and relatives.

24. *Jewish Daily Forward*, January 26, 28, 1905; *The Worker*, January 29, February 5, 12, 26, 1905; *The Chicago Socialists*, February 22, 1905; "Sympathy for Russian Revolutionists," *Miners Magazine*, VI (February 23, 1905), 5.

25. *The Worker*, March 12, 1905; New York *Evening Journal*, May 20, 1905. This figure of 30,000 can be misleading unless one recognizes that the mass meeting on Oct. 7 was a joint effort of some seventy-two organizations and that most of the participants were mourners from the "Yiddish-speaking section" of New York protesting against Russian brutality and tyranny. *Jewish Comment*, October 13, 1905; see also Minute Book, New York City Executive Committee, SDP, November 27, December 18, 1905, TIL; *Miners Magazine*, VII (January 11, 1906), 14; *The Chicago Socialist*, October 14, December 16, 23, 30, 1905, January 6, 1906; Minutes of the Meetings of the General Committee of Local New York, SDP, November 25, 1905, TIL.

26. James Joll, *The Second International, 1889–1914* (New York, 1956), 126; *The Worker*, November 25, 1905, January 13, 1906; *The Chicago Socialist*, December 30, 1905, January 6, 1906; *Social Democratic Herald*, January 13, 1906; *The Weekly People*, December 23, 1905; Minutes of the 30th Assembly District, New York, SDP, January 10, 1906, 60–61, TIL; Minute Book, New York State Committee, SDP, January 9, 1906, TIL.

27. *The Worker*, January 13, 27, 1906; Minute Book of the 6th and 10th Assembly Districts, New York, SDP, January 18, 1906, TIL; *The Weekly People*, January 27, 1906; *The Chicago Socialist*, January 13, 27, 1906; Chaplin, *Wobbly*, 93.

28. Letter, M. S. Hayes to M. Hillquit, Cleveland, February 4, 1905; W. Mailly to M. Hillquit, Toledo, February 6, 1905; W. J. Ghent to M. Hillquit, ca. April, 1905, Hillquit Papers, SHSW; *International Socialist Review*, V (February, 1905), 495; *The Worker*, February 19, November 18, 1905; Minute Book of the 6th and 10th Assembly Districts, New York, SDP, July 20, 1905, TIL; Minute Book, New York City Executive Committee, SDP, October 16, 1905, February 12, 1906, TIL; *Miners Magazine*, VII (November 30, 1905), 13 (January 4, 1906), 4.

29. *The Worker*, March 12, July 22, August 5, 1905, January 27, April 28, July 14, October 6, December 8, 1906; *The Socialist* (Toledo), March 3, 1906; *The Socialist Party Weekly Bulletin*, March 9, 1907; *Miners Magazine*,

VIII (June 28, 1906), 10; *The Weekly People*, April 29, 1905; *Wilshire's Magazine*, VII (March, 1905), 5; *The Chicago Socialist*, August 19, 1905.

30. Minutes of the Meetings of the General Committee of Local New York, SDP, January 28, July 22, 1905, TIL; Minutes of the 30th Assembly District, New York, SDP, March 14, 1906, p. 66, TIL; Minute Book, New York City Executive Committee, SDP, December 18, 1905, TIL. One author indicates that the national budget of the Socialist Party jumped from $17,000 in 1905 to $31,000 in 1906, but that half of this increase went for specific purposes such as aid to the Western Federation of Miners and Russian revolutionary relief; see Kipnis, *The American Socialist Movement*, 165. Obviously, a very small percentage of the funds collected filtered through the national organization. See also *Miners Magazine*, VI (June 1, 1905), 3; *Wilshire's Magazine*, VII (March, 1905), 5; *The Chicago Socialist*, August 19, 1905.

31. Letter, M. S. Hayes to M. Hillquit, Cleveland, February 4, 1905, Hillquit Papers, SHSW; Rogoff, *An East Side Epic*, 25–27; *The Weekly People*, May 19, 1906; Moses Rischin, "The Jewish Labor Movement in America: A Social Interpretation," *Labor History*, IV (Fall, 1963), 233. For a detailed account of the Russian visitors, see the author's "The Reception of Russian Revolutionary Leaders in America, 1904–1906," *American Quarterly*, XVIII (Fall, 1966), 452–476.

32. Alice Stone Blackwell, ed., *The Little Grandmother of the Russian Revolution: Reminiscences and Letters of Catherine Breshkovsky* (Boston, 1917), 111–25, 132; Emma Goldman, *Living My Life*, 362–64; *Social Democratic Herald*, December 10, 1904, February 11, 1905; Ernest Poole, "Katherine Breshkovsky: A Russian Revolutionist," *Outlook*, LXXIX (January 7, 1905), 78–88; Minutes of the Meetings of the General Committee of Local New York, SDP, March 24, 1906, TIL.

33. Thomas A. Bailey, *America Faces Russia* (Ithaca, N.Y., 1950), 187; *Social Democratic Herald*, March 11, 1905, July 14, 1906; *New York Times*, April 11, 1906; Ernest Poole, "Maxim Gorki in New York," *Slavonic and East European Review*, XXII (May, 1944), 78–83; Filia Holtzman, "A Mission That Failed: Gor'kij in America," *Slavic and East European Journal*, VII (Fall, 1962), 227–231. See also: Alexander Kaun, *Maxim Gorky and His Russia* (New York, 1931), 569–601 (Appendix I—"Maxim Gorky in the United States"). Other data are in *Wilshire's Magazine*, VII (March, 1905), 5; X (May, 1906), 1, 3, 10, 16–17; *Bill Haywood's Book*, 199–200; Upton Sinclair, *The Brass Check: A Study of American Journalism* (Pasadena, Cal., 1919), 59; *The Worker*, April 28, June 16, July 7, August 11, 1906; *Miners Magazine*, VII (April 26, 1906), 3 (May 10, 1906), 8; *Industrial Worker*, May, 1906.

34. Minutes of the Meetings of the General Committee of Local New York, SDP, April 14, 1906, TIL; *The Worker*, May 5, 19, August 4, 1906; *Appeal to Reason*, May 5, 1906; *Industrial Worker*, May, 1906; *Wilshire's Magazine*, X (August, 1906), 14; Holtzman, "A Mission That Failed . . . ," 233; Morris Hillquit, *Loose Leaves From a Busy Life* (New York, 1934), 110–13.

35. Minutes of the 22nd Assembly District, New York, Socialist Party, July 25, 1906, p. 76, TIL, on mass meetings quotation. See for other data *The Chicago Socialist*, March 25, 1905; Minutes of the Meetings of the General Committee of Local New York, SDP, November 11, 1905, TIL; Eugene V. Debs, "Miscellaneous Magazines, 1892–1909 Inclusive," Debs

Collection, TIL; Eugene V. Debs, Scrapbooks, vol. 7 (1904–07), TIL; personal interview with Mr. Norman Thomas, New York, August 6, 1962.

36. Philip S. Foner, *Jack London: American Rebel* (New York, 1947), 63; *The Chicago Socialist*, October 7, 1905; Emma Goldman, "The Blood-Freezing Callousness in the World," n.d., Emma Goldman Papers, 1906–1940, Manuscript Division, New York Public Library; Letter, George Herron to Morris Hillquit, Florence, Italy, March 18, June 21, 1905, Hillquit Papers, SHSW; Rogoff, *An East Side Epic*, 24–28; Algernon Lee, "Occasional Contributions and Communications," Letters to the *New York Times*, February 12, 1906, March 8, 1907; Isador Ladoff, "Russian Revolution and American Socialists," *Appeal to Reason*, January 20, 1905.

37. *The Worker*, February 3, 1906. The group referred to as humanistic, etc., constituted almost a separate breed of socialists. It included William English Walling, Charles Edward Russell, Ernest Poole, Kellogg Durland, Arthur Bullard, and James G. Phelps Stokes, who had come to socialism largely as a result of muckraking and settlement house activities. Many were wealthy and able to go to Russia as observers and magazine commentators. They tended to be less ideological, less committed to the Russian Social Democrats, and more sympathetic to the peasants and Social Revolutionaries. There was, too, more personal involvement in their response to the Russian Revolution and less interest in grinding the socialist ax at home. They were more emotionally aroused by the brutalities and pogroms and closer in spirit to the bulk of the muckrakers, social gospelers, and strong progressives. However, in order to keep the present article within proper limits and because of the far-ranging impact of these individuals on general American opinion, the author will treat this group in a separate work.

38. David Grayson, *American Chronicle: The Autobiography of Ray Stannard Baker* (New York, 1945), 226.

The Enigma of Poliomyelitis: 1910

1. C. S. Caverly, "Preliminary Report of an Epidemic of Paralytic Disease, Occurring in Vermont in the Summer of 1894," *Yale Medical Journal*, I (1894), 4; "Notes of an Epidemic of Acute Anterior Poliomyelitis," *Journal of the American Medical Association*, XXVI (1896), 1. See also *Argus and Patriot*, new series XLIV, No. 42 (September 5, 1894), 1.

2. G. Colmer, "Paralysis in Teething Children," *American Journal of Medical Science*, V (1843), 248. For an excellent account of Dr. Colmer's medical career see A. E. Casey and E. H. Hinden, "George Colmer and the Epidemiology of Poliomyelitis," *Southern Medical Journal*, XXXVII (1944), 471.

3. See especially C. F. Taylor, *Infantile Paralysis and Its Attendant Deformities* (Philadelphia, 1867); G. H. Taylor, *Paralysis and Other Affections of the Nerves, Their Cure by Vibratory and Special Movements* (New York, 1871); W. R. Birdsall, "Cases of Poliomyelitis Anterior in Which the Abdominal Muscles Were Affected," *Journal of Nervous and Mental Diseases*, VI (1881), 482; J. J. Putnam and E. M. Taylor, "Is Acute Poliomyelitis Unusually Prevalent This Season?" *Boston Medical and Surgical Journal*, CCXXIX (1893), 509.

4. L. E. Holt and F. H. Bartlett, "The Epidemiology of Acute Poliomyelitis, a Study of Thirty-five Epidemics," *American Journal of Medical Science*,

CXXXV (1908), 74. The chronological listing of epidemics contained at the end of the paper includes European epidemics as well. An excellent supplement to Dr. Holt's and Dr. Bartlett's listing is to be found in the appendiceal chronology accompanying A Monograph on the Epidemic of Poliomyelitis in New York City in 1916 (New York, 1917). For accounts of some epidemics in Alabama, Maine, and California before 1906 see E. D. Bondurant, "Acute Anterior Poliomyelitis," Medical News, LXXVII (1900), 245; J. M. Taylor, "An Epidemic of Poliomyelitis," Philadelphia Medical Journal, I (1898), 298; H. M. Sherman, "Cases of Poliomyelitis," Occidental Medical Times, XI (1897), 445; L. Newmark, "A Little Epidemic of Poliomyelitis," Medical News, LXXIV (1899), 101; A. Woods, "A Report of an Epidemic of Acute Anterior Poliomyelitis," Occidental Medical Times, XVII (1903), 77.

5. Poliomyelitis was first made a reportable disease by the state of Massachusetts in 1909. Although 24 states made poliomyelitis reportable in 1910, only three states, Massachusetts, Minnesota, and Pennsylvania, made such reporting mandatory by name. In other states it was reportable under the broad rubric of infectious and contagious diseases. In part, the problem of reporting poliomyelitis was related to the general neglect at that time in collecting morbidity statistics. See further, J. Collins, "The Epidemiology of Poliomyelitis, a Plea That It May Be Considered a Reportable Quarantinable Disease," Journal of American Medical Association, LIV (1910), 1925; J. W. Trask, "Morbidity Statistics in the United States," Transactions Eighth Annual Conference State and Territorial Health Officers (1910), 37–50.

6. R. W. Lovett, "The Occurrence of Infantile Paralysis in Massachusetts in 1907," Boston Medical and Surgical Journal, CLIX (1908), 131.

7. H. Fox, "Report on the Epidemic of Acute Poliomyelitis in Northwestern Pennsylvania During the Autumn of 1907," in Second Annual Report of the Commissioner of Health of the Commonwealth of Pennsylvania (Harrisburg, Pa., 1907); S. M. Free, "The Poliomyelitis Epidemic in the State of Pennsylvania," Journal of Nervous and Mental Diseases, XXXV (1908), 259.

8. The best analysis of the New York epidemic of 1907 is the Collective Investigation Committee, Epidemic Poliomyelitis: Report on the New York Epidemic of 1907 ("Nervous and Mental Disease Monograph Series," No. 6 [New York, 1910]).

9. For the development of the Massachusetts inquiry, see: R. Lovett and H. C. Emerson, "The Occurrence of Infantile Paralysis in Massachusetts in 1908," Boston Medical and Surgical Journal, CLXI (1909), 112; M. Richardson, "The Occurrence of Infantile Paralysis in Massachusetts, 1907–1912," in Transactions International Congress Hygiene and Demography, 1912, I (Washington, D.C., 1913), 615, n. 1.

10. The Collective Investigation Committee, op. cit., 4–9.

11. For an account of the pathological investigations conducted by Dr. Flexner and Dr. Strauss see Collective Investigation Committee, op. cit., 57–104. The early poliomyelitis research conducted at the Rockefeller Institute is best followed in S. Flexner and M. Wollstein, "Anterior Poliomyelitis Study," Report to the Board of Scientific Directors of the Rockefeller Institute (January 1, 1908); M. Wollstein, "A Biological Study of the Cerebrospinal Fluid in Anterior Poliomyelitis," Journal of Experimental Medicine, X (1908), 476; H. Noguchi, "Bacterial Investigation of the Intestinal Flora of Cases of Acute Poliomyelitis," Report to the Board of Scientific Directors of the Rockefeller Institute (April 15, 1908).

12. For the development of the 1908 poliomyelitis epidemic in Vienna, see

J. Zappert, "Die Poliomyelitis Erkrankungen in Wien und Nieder Osstreich in Jahre 1908," *Wiener Klinische Wochenschrift*, XXII (1909), 1661. The best brief biographical sketch of Dr. Landsteiner's career is P. F. Rous, "Karl Landsteiner, 1868–1943," *Obituary Notices of the Fellows of the Royal Society*, V (1947), 295. The first notice of Dr. Landsteiner's experimental work on poliomyelitis appeared as an untitled abstract in *Wiener Klinische Wochenschrift*, No. 52 (1908). Several months later Dr. Landsteiner published an extended paper on this work. See K. Landsteiner and E. Popper, "Uebertragung der Poliomyelitis Acuta auf Affen," *Zeitschrift fuer Immunitate forschung und Experimentelle Therapie*, II (1909–10), 377.

13. See especially, W. Knoepfelmacher, "Experimentelle Uebertragung der Poliomyelitis Acuta auf Affen," *Medizinische Klinik*, V (1909), 1671; and I. Strauss and F. M. Huntoon, "Experimental Studies on the Etiology of Acute Poliomyelitis," *New York Medical Journal*, XCI (1910), 64.

14. For the difficulties in the development in this research see Paul A. Lewis to Simon Flexner, September 7, 1909; September 12, 1909; September 15, 1909; and Simon Flexner to Helen Flexner, September 19, 1909, Simon Flexner Papers, the Library of the American Philosophical Society. The report of the successful experiment is to be found in S. Flexner and P. A. Lewis, "The Transmission of Acute Poliomyelitis to Monkeys," *Journal of American Medical Association*, LIII (1909), 1639.

15. S. Flexner and P. A. Lewis, "The Transmission of Epidemic Poliomyelitis to Monkeys, a Further Note," *Journal of the American Medical Association*, LIII (1909), 1913.

16. S. Flexner and P. A. Lewis, "The Nature of the Virus of Epidemic Poliomyelitis," *Journal of the American Medical Association*, LIII (1909), 2095. For a discussion of the development of the theories of the bacterial origin of poliomyelitis, see P. H. Römer, *Epidemic Infantile Paralysis* (New York, 1913), 24–25.

17. P. H. Römer, "Untersuchungen zur Aetiologie der epidemischen Kinderlähmung," *Muenchener Medizinische Wochenschrift*, No. 49 (1909); K. Landsteiner and C. Levaditi, "La transmission de la paralysie infantile aux singes," *Comptes Rendues Societé de Biologie à Paris*, LXVII (1909), 592; C. Leiner and R. V. Wiesner, "Experimentelle Untersuchungen über poliomyelitis acuta anterior," *Wiener Klinische Wochenschrift*, No. 49 (1909).

18. There is no adequate history of the anti-vivisection movement in the United States. The substance of the debate between the medical community and anti-vivisectionists at the beginning of the twentieth century can be followed in U. S. Senate: Committee of the District of Columbia, 56th Congress, 1st session, Hearing on Vivisection, Washington, D.C., 1900. See also S. Flexner and J. T. Flexner, *William H. Welch and the Heroic Age of American Medicine* (New York: Viking Press, 1941), 254–262; W. W. Keen, *Animal Experimentation and Medical Progress* (Boston: Houghton Mifflin Co., 1914); M. J. Rosenau, "The Role of Animal Experimentation in the Diagnosis of Disease," *Journal of the American Medical Association*, LIV (1910), 97.

19. S. Flexner, "Experimental Poliomyelitis," *New York State Journal of Medicine*, X (1910), 330.

20. S. Flexner, *Animal Experimentation and Infectious Diseases*, Pamphlet (New York, 1908), issued under auspices of the Committee on Experimental Medicine of the Medical Society of the State of New York; Simon Flexner to Constantin Levaditi, January 26, 1910, Simon Flexner Papers.

21. The other laboratories engaged in experimental poliomyelitis research at the beginning of 1910 were those of Dr. Israel Strauss at the Cornell Medical School and Dr. W. P. Lucas at the Harvard Medical School.

22. These experiments may be traced in S. Flexner and P. A. Lewis, "Epidemic Poliomyelitis in Monkeys," *Journal of the American Medical Association*, LIV (1910), 45; "Experimental Epidemic Poliomyelitis in Monkeys," *Journal of Experimental Medicine*, XII (1910), 227.

23. Much of the early research on poliomyelitis was modeled after research on syphilis and cerebrospinal meningitis. Dr. Karl Landsteiner's choice of the monkey as an experimental animal was dictated by his use of that animal in his previous investigations of syphilis. Dr. Flexner's choice of the monkey was likewise prompted by his successful use of that animal in his earlier research on cerebrospinal meningitis. The difficulties that some investigators had in cultivating the spirochete and the meningococcus on artificial media made it easier to accept similar difficulties in cultivating polio virus. No one, so far as is known, suspected that such difficulties existed because viruses differed from bacteria and protozoa. The idea that viruses were nothing more than very small bacteria persisted until the late nineteen twenties when Dr. Thomas Rivers of the Rockefeller Institute postulated that viruses were essentially obligate parasites that could only live and multiply in the presence of a living susceptible cell. See further T. M. Rivers, "Filterable Viruses," *Journal of Bacteriology*, XIV (1927), 217.

24. The cerebrospinal fluid at such time was opalescent, had an increase in protein, was rich in small cells, and was spontaneously coagulable.

25. S. Flexner and P. A. Lewis, "Experimental Epidemic Poliomyelitis in Monkeys: Sixth Note," *Journal of the American Medical Association*, LIV (1910), 140.

26. S. Flexner and P. A. Lewis, "Epidemic Poliomyelitis in Monkeys: A Mode of Spontaneous Infection," *Journal of the American Medical Association*, LIV (1910), 535.

27. The experiment was beautifully done and correct. The implication that Dr. Flexner drew from the experiment was wrong. The error persisted until the late 1930's when Dr. Charles Swan in Australia and Dr. Albert Sabin in the United States presented evidence that the olfactory pathway was not the usual portal of entry for polio virus in man. See further: C. Swan, "The Anatomical Distribution and Character of the Lesions of Poliomyelitis, *Australian Journal of Experimental Biology and Medical Science*, XVII (1939), 345; A. B. Sabin, "The Olfactory Bulbs in Human Poliomyelitis," *American Journal of Diseases of Children*, LX (1940), 1313.

28. S. Flexner, "The Contribution of the Experimental to Human Poliomyelitis," *Journal of the American Medical Association*, LV (1910), 1105.

29. J. V. Manning, "Report of the Recent Epidemic of Spinal Paralysis in Wisconsin," *Wisconsin Medical Journal*, VIII (1909), 308.

30. Jocelyn Manning to Simon Flexner, March 10, 1910, Simon Flexner Papers.

31. J. W. Sever, "Anterior Poliomyelitis: A Review of the Recent Literature in Regard to the Epidemiology, Etiology, Modes of Transmission, Bacteriology and Pathology; Its Clinical Manifestations and Its Treatment," *Inter-State Medical Journal*, XXI (1914), 595.

32. R. W. Lovett, "The Occurrence of Infantile Paralysis in Massachusetts in 1908," *Monthly Bulletin State Board of Health of Massachusetts*, IV

(1909), 139; "The Occurrence of Infantile Paralysis in Massachusetts in 1909," *Monthly Bulletin State Board of Health of Massachusetts,* V (1910), 175.

33. There are no adequate statistics for the New York epidemics of 1909. The number given above is gleaned from a series of letters from physicians in New York City and State reporting cases in their districts to Dr. Simon Flexner. See further, J. F. Terriberry to Simon Flexner, August 24, 1909; LeGrand Kerr to Simon Flexner, October 1, 1909 (53 cases reported in Brooklyn August 7 to September 4, 1909); A. H. Allen to Henry Elsner, October 14, 1909; Alex. O. Snowden to Simon Flexner, October 26, 1909; Simon Flexner to Alexander Snowden, October 27, 1909; W. H. Hambidge to Simon Flexner, October 28, 1909, Simon Flexner Papers.

34. H. W. Hill, "The Epidemiology of Anterior Poliomyelitis," *Journal of Minnesota Medical Association,* XXIX (1909), 369; "Epidemiologic Study of Anterior Poliomyelitis in Minnesota," *Transactions Section Preventive Medicine and Public Health, American Medical Association* (1910), 305–339; A. S. Hamilton, "Epidemic Poliomyelitis in Minnesota in 1908," *Journal of Minnesota Medical Association,* XXX (1910), 2.

35. See especially *Bulletin Kansas State Board of Health,* VI, No. 7 (1910); E. R. Kelly, W. Gellhorn, J. B. Manning, *Report of Infantile Paralysis in the State of Washington 1910* (Olympia, Washington; 1911), 6–8; F. F. Gundrum, "Acute Poliomyelitis in California," *Journal of the American Medical Association,* LVIII (1912), 254; F. E. Coulter, "Acute Anterior Poliomyelitis," *Western Medical Review,* XIV (1909), 408; H. M. McClanahan, "A Brief Report of the Nebraska Epidemic of Poliomyelitis," *Journal of American Medical Association,* LV (1910), 1160; *A Monograph on the Epidemic of Poliomyelitis in New York City in 1916,* Table I, "Epidemics of Poliomyelitis in the United States prior to 1916" (New York Department of Health, 1917), 353.

36. M. G. Lebredo and A. Recio, "Poliomyelitis Anterior Aguda Epidemica: Epidemia de Cuba 1909," *San. y benific. Bol. ofic., Habana,* III (1910), 170.

37. Charles T. Hodgetts to Simon Flexner, January 11, 1910, Simon Flexner Papers.

38. R. W. Lovett, "The Occurrence of Infantile Paralysis in the United States and Canada in 1910," *American Journal of Diseases of Children,* II (1911), 65.

39. *United States Public Health Reports,* XXVI (March 3, 1911), 242–243, is a detailed compilation of reported cases in 1910 by state.

40. A. Flexner, *Medical Education in the United States and Canada,* Bulletin No. 4, Carnegie Foundation (New York, 1910), 20.

41. A. Flexner, *An Autobiography* (New York, 1960), 73–88.

42. V. Johnson, "The Council on Medical Education and Hospitals," in M. Fishbein, *A History of the American Medical Association* (Philadelphia, 1947), 887–899.

43. Richard H. Shyrock, *American Medical Research* (New York, 1947), 119–120.

44. George P. Shidler to Simon Flexner, February 4, 1910, Simon Flexner Papers.

45. G. P. Shidler, "The Epidemic of Spinal Disease in Nebraska," *Journal of the American Medical Association,* LIV (1910), 277.

46. Michael Hoke to Simon Flexner, September 24, 1910; Simon Flexner to Michael Hoke, September 28, 1910, Simon Flexner Papers.

47. T. Walker, *Roosevelt and The Warm Springs Story* (New York, 1953), 197–201.

48. Harry Pogue to Simon Flexner, September 6, 1910; Simon Flexner to Harry Pogue, September 9, 1910, Simon Flexner Papers.

49. See further M. Fishbein, ed., *A Bibliography of Infantile Paralysis, 1789–1949* (2nd ed., Philadelphia, 1951). In 1907 a summary of F. Harbitz and O. Scheel, *Pathologisch-anatomische Untersuchungen über akute Poliomyelitis und verwandte Krankheiten* (Christiania, 1907) appeared in the *Journal of the American Medical Association* as a special article, F. Harbitz and O. Scheel, "Epidemic Acute Poliomyelitis in Norway in the Years 1903 to 1906," XLIX (1907), 1420.

50. For a discussion of this problem see E. B. Almgren to Simon Flexner, October 25, 1910; Simon Flexner to E. B. Almgren, October 27, 1910, Simon Flexner Papers.

51. P. H. Römer, *Epidemic Infantile Paralysis*, translated by H. R. Prentice (New York, 1913); I. Wickman, *Acute Poliomyelitis*, translated by W. J. M. A. Maloney, *Nervous and Mental Disease Monograph Series*, No. 16 (New York, 1913) is actually an edited version of Dr. Wickman's original volume. The first American textbook on poliomyelitis did not appear before 1914, H. W. Frauenthal and J. V. Manning, *A Manual of Infantile Paralysis* (Philadelphia, 1914).

52. W. Osler, *The Principles and Practice of Medicine* (7th ed., New York, 1910), 915.

53. Theodore Coleman to Simon Flexner, August 1, 1910; Simon Flexner Papers.

54. "Acute Poliomyelitis," editorial in *Bulletin of the Illinois State Board of Health*, VI, No. 9 (1910).

55. H. M. McClanahan, "Clinical Varieties of Poliomyelitis," *Western Medical Review*, XV (1910), 386.

56. Ulysses Moore to Simon Flexner, August 1, 1910, Simon Flexner Papers.

57. There are many such letters of inquiry about poliomyelitis from physicians throughout the United States in the Simon Flexner papers. The following are representative for the year 1910. G. M. McCaskey to Simon Flexner, November 9, 1910 (Ft. Wayne, Indiana); Harvey R. Sanborn to Simon Flexner, October 13, 1910 (Providence, R.I.); H. H. Donnelly to Simon Flexner, September 19, 1910 (Washington, D.C.); W. F. Batman to Simon Flexner, September 5, 1910 (Ladoga, Indiana); A. L. Skoog to Simon Flexner, September 16, 1910 (Kansas City, Missouri); Bernard Oettinger to Simon Flexner, July 11, 1910 (Denver, Colorado); J. B. Walker to Simon Flexner, November 18, 1910 (Effingham, Illinois). Simon Flexner Papers.

58. Virgil P. Gibney to Simon Flexner, August 15, 1910; Simon Flexner to Virgil P. Gibney, August 17, 1910. Simon Flexner Papers.

59. Herbert W. Conn to Simon Flexner, September 18, 1910, Simon Flexner Papers.

60. Malcolm Goodridge to Simon Flexner, July 26, 1910; Simon Flexner to Malcolm Goodridge, July 28, 1910; Malcolm Goodridge to Simon Flexner, July 30, 1910; Simon Flexner to Malcolm Goodridge, August 2, 1910; Malcolm Goodridge to Simon Flexner, August 11, 1910; Simon Flexner to Malcolm Goodridge, August 13, 1910; Theodore Janeway to Simon Flexner, August 25, 1910; Simon Flexner to Theodore Janeway, August 26, 1910;

Theodore Janeway to Simon Flexner, August 31, 1910; Simon Flexner to Theodore Janeway, September 1, 1910. Simon Flexner Papers.

61. Paul A. Lewis to Simon Flexner, July 16, 1910; July 18, 1910, Simon Flexner Papers.

62. Dr. Flexner frequently recommended Dr. Emerson for such tasks. A typical letter of thanks from Emerson to Flexner is found appended to a case record. "Through your reference I saw yesterday for Dr. E. K. Conrad of Hackensack, N.J., a case of acute poliomyelitis in a boy of 16½ and I will add a sketch of his case if it may interest you." Haven Emerson to Simon Flexner, August 24, 1911, Simon Flexner Papers.

63. W. B. Hambidge to Simon Flexner, October 15, 1909, Simon Flexner Papers.

64. Simon Flexner to W. B. Hambidge, October 19, 1909, Simon Flexner Papers.

65. I. Wickman, op. cit., 77.

66. E. R. Kelley, W. Gellhorn, J. B. Manning, op. cit., 20–28; R. L. Lovett and M. Richardson, "Infantile Paralysis with Especial Reference to Its Occurrence in Massachusetts 1907–1910" in Infantile Paralysis in Massachusetts During 1910 (Boston, 1911), 64.

67. Henry L. Elsner to Simon Flexner, October 26, 1909. The genesis of Dr. Elsner's poliomyelitis diagnostic activities can be traced in: Henry L. Elsner to Simon Flexner, October 13, 1909; October 20, 1909. Simon Flexner Papers.

68. Simon Flexner to Henry L. Elsner, October 27, 1909, Simon Flexner Papers.

69. C. F. Williams to Simon Flexner, September 15, 1910; Simon Flexner to C. F. Williams, September 19, 1910. Simon Flexner Papers.

70. S. Flexner and J. W. Jobling, "Serum Treatment of Epidemic Cerebro-Spinal Meningitis," Journal of Experimental Medicine, X (1908), 141. ("During the prevalence of epidemics of cerebro-spinal meningitis in America and Europe from 1904 to 1907 Diplococcus intracellularis, discovered by Weichselbaum in 1887, was established finally as the cause of epidemic meningitis.")

71. See note 24.

72. Theodore Coleman to Simon Flexner, August 23, 1910, Simon Flexner Papers.

73. C. I. Redfield to Simon Flexner, October 12, 1910, Simon Flexner Papers.

74. Henry Power to Simon Flexner, July 18, 1910, Simon Flexner Papers.

75. For a typical letter of advice on the need to examine cerebrospinal fluid, see Simon Flexner to Langley Porter, Aug. 17, 1910: "Indications are that an early diagnosis of suspected cases and a definite diagnosis of abortive cases may possibly be made by the early employment of lumbar puncture. The changes in the cerebrospinal fluid are quite definite, and should suffice for diagnosis. The only difficulty is of course the carrying out of the puncture in regions away from cities and physicians who have had experience in making such punctures, but an investigation such as you propose carrying out could be made to be of immense importance if the personnel of the committee of investigation could be so arranged that it could personally conduct such a method of investigation, even in places remote from cities where the epidemic is prevailing. I am sending you a set of reprints which we have issued, in one of which the changes in the spinal fluid are described especially, namely, the

reprint from the *Journal of Experimental Medicine*." Simon Flexner Papers. Dr. Langley Porter was President of the San Francisco County Medical Society.

76. Edward E. Mayer to George H. Simmons, September 24, 1910, Simon Flexner Papers.

77. George H. Simmons to Simon Flexner, September 26, 1910, Simon Flexner Papers.

78. Simon Flexner to George H. Simmons, October 1, 1910, Simon Flexner Papers.

79. Dr. Mayer's point was a good one. His clinical reasons for objecting to lumbar puncture were excellent and parents often did object to lumbar puncture as a procedure. Dr. F. W. Mohr, a practitioner in Ottawa, Canada, who tried to get some cerebrospinal fluid from a case of poliomyelitis for Dr. Flexner had to report, "I regret that I cannot get any fresh spinal fluid as the relatives object to further puncture." F. W. Mohr to Simon Flexner, August 17, 1910, Simon Flexner Papers.

80. Simon Flexner to George Simmons, October 1, 1910, Simon Flexner Papers.

81. Dr. Flexner played a decisive role in guiding Dr. Frissell's work and arranging for the publication of his paper. Simon Flexner to Lewis Frissell, January 12, 1911; Lewis Frissell to Simon Flexner, January 13, 1911; Simon Flexner to George H. Simmons, January 20, 1911. Simon Flexner Papers. See also, L. F. Frissell, "Report of a Case of Epidemic Anterior Poliomyelitis: Diagnosis in Preparalytic Stage by Lumbar Puncture," *Journal of the American Medical Association*, LVI (1911), 661.

82. "Report of a Symposium on Poliomyelitis Held by the American Pediatric Society, May 3–5, 1910," *Journal of the American Medical Association*, LIV (1910), 1888.

83. F. E. Coulter to Simon Flexner, April 5, 1910. "The eastern portion of Nebraska during this last autumn has suffered from a severe epidemic of poliomyelitis, and the subject will be up for an extensive discussion, at the coming meeting of our State Society. . . . You will please understand I do not wish in any way to seem to anticipate any of your most excellent work, but my desire is simply to get some of your conclusions that bear your stamp of approval, that I may in turn give them to the profession of Nebraska, fully accredited to you." See also *Western Medical Review*, XV (1910), 422–25, for a précis of the discussion at the symposium. The issue also contains several original articles on poliomyelitis.

84. Robert W. Lovett to Simon Flexner, October 15, 1910, Simon Flexner Papers; T. P. Hennelly, "An Investigation Concerning Infantile Paralysis as It Occurred in the City of Fall River in 1910," P. A. E. Sheppard, "A Study of an Epidemic of Infantile Paralysis in Springfield, Massachusetts in 1910," in *Infantile Paralysis in Massachusetts During 1910* (Boston, 1911), 36–54; 95–144.

85. New York State patterned its educational activities after those organized in Nebraska and Massachusetts, as did the State of Washington. See further N. Y. State Health Department news service report November 30, 1910, on a special appropriation for investigation of epidemic paralysis, and E. R. Kelley, Walter Gelhorn, John B. Manning, *op. cit.*, 3–4.

86. *Bulletin of the Illinois State Board of Health*, VI, No. 9 (September, 1910).

87. The circular issued by the Kansas State Department of Health on

poliomyelitis on July 13, 1910, is typical of these efforts: "To County and
Municipal Health Officers—It seems almost certain that we have had another epidemic of Anterior Poliomyelitis. Four cases have already occurred in
Phillips County, and one case reported this morning from Brown County,
with a newspaper report of a case in Kingman County. Flexner of the Rockefeller Institute has demonstrated that the infectious agent is eliminated through
the nasal and pharyngeal discharges and it is likely that the fecal discharges
are also infective, owing to the fact that young children usually swallow the
mucous secretions of the throat; the findings of Flexner, together with the
clinical history of the epidemic, proves it to be a disease of highly infectious
character; and it is therefore ordered that all cases be required to be rigidly
quarantined, in the usual way, separating as early as possible the sick from
the well children of the afflicted household, and seeing to it that the nasal,
pharyngeal and fecal discharges be properly and effectively sterilized. Individual drinking and eating utensils should be used, and the fly excluded from
the sick room to the greatest extent possible. Outside toilets should be made
fly-proof, and a general sanitary survey of the premises made, and insanitary
conditions promptly remedied. Thorough and effective disinfection must be
practiced after the termination of every case. The extent of this year's epidemic will, in a measure at least, be conditioned upon the vigilance and
energy of Health Officers in combatting the spread of the disease. We are,
therefore, counting on you to use prompt and energetic measures in every
case in your jurisdiction. Report of new cases should be made by wire to this
department. Very truly yours, S. J. Crumbine, M.D., Secretary."

88. Dr. Flexner's letter to Dr. Joseph A. Cooke of Meriden, Connecticut,
is typical. "I regret that the matter of a serum of poliomyelitis is still entirely in the experimental stage, so that I cannot offer you any for the treatment of the patients. I shall be interested in learning something about the
patients, namely, their age, extent of paralysis and the relation of the cases
to each other. Should, at any time, a case of poliomyelitis that you are treating terminate fatally, it would be a great help to us if we could secure a
small portion of the spinal cord preserved in pure glycerine." Simon Flexner
to Joseph A. Cooke, June 28, 1910, Simon Flexner Papers.

89. Most physicians, from the humblest practitioner in the Midwest to
those who were in the public eye in New York, eagerly supplied Dr. Flexner
with case records, cerebrospinal fluid, and autopsy material from polio cases
which ended fatally. Often there were difficulties in obtaining autopsy materials. One physician in Athens, Ohio, after getting the right to do an autopsy,
hurriedly performed the operation in a nearby barn at midnight lest the be-
reaved father change his mind and deprive Dr. Flexner of the spinal cord
he had promised. Bernard A. LeRoy to Simon Flexner, September 6, 1910.
See also, Harlow Brooks to Simon Flexner, November 3, 1910. "Should the
patient die, I think very likely that we can obtain an autopsy as the family
is one of intelligent people and we shall be delighted of course to give such
material to you as you desire, should he not live." Simon Flexner Papers.

90. W. H. C. Coplin to Simon Flexner, January 27, 1910; Simon Flexner
to W. H. C. Coplin, January 28, 1910; W. H. C. Coplin to Simon Flexner,
January 29, 1910; Simon Flexner to W. H. C. Coplin, January 31, 1910;
Simon Flexner to W. H. C. Coplin, February 25, 1910. Simon Flexner
Papers.

91. Warfield Longcope to Simon Flexner, March 8, 1910; Simon Flexner
to Warfield Longcope, March 9, 1910; Warfield Longcope to Simon Flexner,

March 11, 1910; Simon Flexner to Warfield Longcope, March 21, 1910; Warfield Longcope to Simon Flexner, March 21, 1910. Simon Flexner Papers. See also Simon Flexner and P. A. Lewis, "Experimental Epidemic Poliomyelitis in Monkeys," *Journal of the American Medical Association*, LIV (1910), 1140.

92. W. J. Everett to Simon Flexner, telegram, March 7, 1911, Simon Flexner Papers.

93. W. W. Butterworth to Simon Flexner, telegram, March 6, 1911; D. I. Hirsch to Simon Flexner, March 4, 1911; Simon Flexner to W. W. Butterworth, March 6, 1911; Simon Flexner to D. I. Hirsch, March 7, 1911; Simon Flexner to Charles Duval, March 6, 1911. Simon Flexner Papers. It is of interest that on March 1, 1911, Dr. J. H. Slaughter attracted by news reports of Dr. Robert Osgood's polio experiments at Harvard, sent Dr. Osgood an early report on the polio epidemic in Louisiana. Dr. Osgood promptly sent the information to Dr. Flexner for disposition. J. H. Slaughter to Robert Osgood, March 1, 1911; Robert Osgood to Simon Flexner, March 8, 1911. Simon Flexner Papers.

94. Charles Duval to Simon Flexner, March 20, 1911, Simon Flexner Papers.

95. D. I. Hirsch to Simon Flexner, March 11, 1911; Simon Flexner to D. I. Hirsch, March 18, 1911; D. I. Hirsch to Simon Flexner, March 22, 1911. Simon Flexner Papers.

96. W. W. Butterworth to Simon Flexner, March 24, 1911, Simon Flexner Papers.

97. Dr. H. W. Hill, epidemiologist of the Minnesota State Board of Health, was one of those who steadfastly opposed the notion that poliomyelitis was a contagious disease. See especially H. W. Hill, "The Contagiousness of Poliomyelitis," *Journal of the Minnesota State Medical Association and Northwestern Lancet*, XXX (1910), 111. Some of the early epidemiological reports from Massachusetts suggested that the disease was only mildly contagious. It wasn't until J. F. Anderson and W. H. Frost established the existence of abortive cases that the contagious nature of poliomyelitis became more apparent. See further H. C. Emerson, "An Epidemic of Infantile Paralysis in Western Massachusetts in 1908," *Monthly Bulletin of Massachusetts State Board of Health*, July, 1909, 25; J. F. Anderson and W. H. Frost, "The Diagnosis of Abortive Cases of Poliomyelitis by the Demonstration of Specific Antibodies," *Society of Experimental Biology and Medicine*, VIII (1911), 54.

98. W. R. Knoepfel to Simon Flexner, April 28, 1911; May 15, 1911; Simon Flexner to W. R. Knoepfel, May 18, 1911. Simon Flexner Papers.

99. Simon Flexner to O. M. Patterson, May 24, 1911, Simon Flexner Papers.

100. Dr. Flexner's correspondence with Dr. Patterson continued over a period of several months. Under Dr. Flexner's direction Dr. Patterson collected detailed case histories and constructed a map showing the location of each case in Morehouse County. The paper that Dr. Flexner originally envisaged, however, was not published in the *Journal of the American Medical Association*. C. N. Dalton to Simon Flexner, July 7, 1911; Simon Flexner to C. N. Dalton, July 11, 1911; Simon Flexner to O. M. Patterson, August 21, 1911; October 2, 1911, Simon Flexner Papers. See also O. M. Patterson, "My Experience with Poliomyelitis or Infantile Paralysis as Health Officer for the Parish of Morehouse During 1911," *New Orleans Medical and Surgical Journal*, LXV (1912–13), 812.

101. T. M. Rivers, "The Story of Research on Poliomyelitis," *Proceedings of American Philosophical Society*, XCVIII, No. 4 (1954), 254.

Ben Lindsey: Symbol of Radicalism in the 1920's

1. H. G. Wells to Lindsey, March 30, 1927, *Benjamin Barr Lindsey Collection*, Manuscripts Division, Library of Congress (cited hereafter as *BBLC*), Container 155. The only concise and comprehensive biographical sketch of Benjamin Barr Lindsey (1869–1943) appears in Vol. 32 *National Cyclopedia of American Biography* (New York: James T. White and Co., 1945), 486–487. Two brief but excellent treatments of Lindsey's early career and influence as a reformer in Denver are Louis Filler, *Crusaders for American Liberalism* (New York: Harcourt, Brace, 1939), 262–268, and Eric Goldman, *Rendezvous with Destiny* (New York: Alfred A. Knopf, 1953), 121–123. Two of Lindsey's closest friends reminisced about the early Denver days: Lincoln Steffens, *Autobiography* (New York: Harcourt, Brace, 1931), Part III, Chap. 23; George Creel, *Rebel at Large* (New York: G. P. Putnam's Sons, 1947), 119–124, *passim*. Two semi-autobiographical works by Lindsey are cited in Notes 3 and 6, *infra*. Two unpublished studies of his career before the 1920's are Peter Gregg Slater, "Judge Benjamin Barr Lindsey and the Denver Juvenile Court during the Progressive Era" (M.A. thesis, Brown University, 1962) and Frances Huber, *The Progressive Career of Ben B. Lindsey, 1900–1920* (Ann Arbor: University Microfilms, 1963). Scattered references in the secondary literature of the Progressive period add nothing significant to the treatments by Filler and Goldman. Textbooks have usually only made brief references to Lindsey's role as founder of the Juvenile Court of Denver or his advocacy of "companionate marriage" in the 1920's. The present writer is completing a biography of Lindsey.

2. Billy Sunday's comment appears in the San Francisco *News*, January 10, 1928. Thomas Mann's statement was quoted on a printed handbill advertising the Dutch edition of Lindsey's *The Companionate Marriage*, *BBLC*, Container 162.

3. Ben B. Lindsey and Rube Borough, *The Dangerous Life* (New York: Horace Liveright, 1931, cited hereafter by title only), 142–143.

4. Lindsey to Lincoln Steffens, March 16, 1914, *BBLC*, Container 45.

5. *The Dangerous Life*, 143.

6. Ben B. Lindsey and Harvey J. O'Higgins, *The Beast* (New York, 1910, cited hereafter by title only). Walter Lippmann, *A Preface to Politics* (New York, 1913), 253.

7. *The Dangerous Life*, 26.

8. C. T. Bates to Friend Lindsey (Ben's father, Landy Tunstall Lindsey), September 4, 1880; C. T. Bates to Ben B. Lindsey, April 10, 1890; *BBLC*, Container 79.

9. Lindsey later observed, "The schooling I received there would amount to about the first year in high school." Lindsey to Selena S. Martin, October 24, 1907, *BBLC*, Container 11.

10. Lindsey to Walter Rauschenbusch, April 10, 1911, *BBLC*, Container 32. Lindsey to H. W. Trimble, January 31, 1911, *ibid.*, Container 30.

11. Lindsey to unidentified Sunday school teacher, September 8, 1905, *BBLC*, Container 5.

12. *The Dangerous Life*, 26.

13. Lindsey to Walter S. Cheesman, May 2, 1905, *BBLC*, Container 3.

14. Lindsey to Lee S. Gray, Superintendent of Schools, Palmer, Massachusetts, October 28, 1907, *BBLC*, Container 11.

15. Lindsey to William Allen White, July 3, 1911, *BBLC*, Container 32.

16. Lindsey to E. W. Scripps, November 2, 1911, *BBLC*, Container 35. Lindsey was replying to Scripps, who had written to him about the trial of the McNamaras in Los Angeles for dynamiting the offices of the Los Angeles *Times*: "I do not believe that either Darrow or myself are aware of any altruistic sentiments. I think our motive is more of contempt and hatred for the sins of our class than pure love for their victims." E. W. Scripps to Lindsey, September 11, 1911, *BBLC*, Container 33.

17. *The Dangerous Life*, 282–307.

18. Lindsey to Kate Campbell Robertson, June 8, 1914, *BBLC*, Container 138.

19. Cf., collection of circulars published by "The Women's Protective League," *BBLC*, Container 289.

20. *The Dangerous Life*, 293.

21. *Ibid.*, 293–295.

22. For descriptions of tactics used by Lindsey's opposition, cf., *The Beast*, 119–121, 231–232, passim; Ben B. Lindsey, *A Secret Political League: Who and What It Is* (Denver, 1913).

23. Lippmann, *A Preface to Politics*, 253–254. Walter Lippmann to Lindsey, November 20, 1913, *BBLC*, Container 136.

24. A former resident of Denver and officer of Lindsey's court, Mrs. Richard Hogue, has suggested that the oft-expressed first wish of visiting celebrities in Denver "to see Judge Lindsey" added to the intense animosity felt toward him in Denver society. Interview with author, Remington, Virginia, December 29, 1965.

25. Lindsey to Manager, Associated Press, August 8, 1905; Lindsey to Edward Bok, January 23, 1907. *BBLC*, Containers 4, 9.

26. Among Lindsey's friends and correspondents, whose political campaigns he actively supported at various times, were Tom Johnson, Robert M. La-Follette, Francis Heney, Hiram Johnson, Brand Whitlock, Charles Evans Hughes, and Joseph Folk. Lindsey was a Democrat but temporarily quit the party to support the Progressive ticket in 1912. Theodore Roosevelt was a close personal friend and gave strong public support to Lindsey in his political fights in Denver.

27. Frederick Lewis Allen, *Only Yesterday* (New York: Harper and Brothers, 1931), 115–118. V. F. Calverton, *The Bankruptcy of Marriage* (New York: Macaulay, 1928) and Floyd Dell, *Love in the Machine Age* (New York: Farrar, 1931), both popular treatments of the sexual revolution of the twenties, drew heavily on Lindsey. Cf., Walter Lippmann, *A Preface to Morals* (New York: Macmillan, 1929), Chap. 14 ("Love in the Great Society"). According to Edgar Ansel Mowrer, *Die Kameradschaftsehe* (German translation of *The Companionate Marriage*) "was found a few months ago on nearly every parlor table in Berlin." Des Moines *Tribune*, February 11, 1929.

28. Lincoln Steffens, "Ben B. Lindsey: The Just Judge," *McClure's Magazine* (October–December, 1906), 27:563–581; 28:74–88, 162–176.

29. Ben B. Lindsey, "The Beast and the Jungle," *Everybody's Magazine* (October, 1909–May, 1910), 21:431–452, 579–598, 770–784; 22:41–53, 231–244, 391–406, 528–540, 632–644.

30. Several of Lindsey's friends, including Lincoln Steffens and Upton Sinclair, urged him to do so on the ground that Denver was too small an arena

for the judge's talents. Charles and Mary Beard advised him: "Judging from the splendid lecture we heard you give in New Milford, you could find all the platforms you wanted for an indefinite period and could help immensely not only the juvenile movement but the whole progressive movement as well." Charles and Mary Beard to Lindsey, June 15, 1915, BBLC, Container 50.

31. The "formal codes," according to Lerner, are the codes to which society pays lip-service as opposed to the "operative codes" by which it lives. Max Lerner, America as a Civilization (New York: Simon and Schuster, 1957), 672–675, passim.

32. Ben B. Lindsey and Wainwright Evans, The Companionate Marriage (New York: Boni and Liveright, 1927, cited hereafter by title only), 90.

33. Lindsey used the same basic method with boys. Cf., The Dangerous Life, Chap. 3, "The Artistry of Approach."

34. Ben B. Lindsey and Wainwright Evans, The Revolt of Modern Youth (New York: Boni and Liveright, 1925, cited hereafter by title only), 77.

35. Bertrand Russell to Lindsey, April 26, 1927, BBLC, Container 154.

36. The Revolt of Modern Youth, 185.

37. Ibid., 14–15.

38. Ibid., 118.

39. It was also an objective fact, as Lindsey pointed out, when a girl lost her job or had trouble finding a husband in the local community because of newspaper publicity. He campaigned successfully for legislation prohibiting the publication of girls' names in such cases. The Dangerous Life, 108, 293–295.

40. The Revolt of Modern Youth, 71–72.

41. The Companionate Marriage, 98.

42. He denied that the reforms he advocated in legislation on marriage, divorce, and birth control would encourage an increase in promiscuity. The Revolt of Modern Youth, 171.

43. The Companionate Marriage, 82.

44. A year after the publication of The Companionate Marriage he wrote to a young man who asked his advice: "I do not favor the relationships you refer to for young people except in marriage. Due to the fact that I have a great deal of charity for those who do not live up to this rule, and whom I have always been willing to help in their difficulties, a false impression has perhaps gone out as to my real views. I think it would be much better if you would try and avoid anything of the kind. It would seem to me that if you could confide in your parents on both sides they might help you in an early marriage, in which you could refrain from having children until you were ready and able to take care of them." Lindsey to X, August 22, 1928, BBLC, Container 161. A few months later, Lindsey warned a teen-age correspondent: "A girl cannot take the risk that boys take. . . . If either one of the boys in question had the real love for you that he ought to have, then you should get married; in the meantime, as to the thing you ask me about, my advice is, don't." Lindsey to X, October 17, 1928, BBLC, Container 162 (Lindsey's italics).

45. The Companionate Marriage, 98–99.

46. The duty of the state to make an earnest effort to save marriages, particularly when children were involved, was one of Lindsey's most fervid convictions. Cf., Ben B. Lindsey, "The House of Human Welfare," The Forum (December, 1927), 78:101–116. The principle was embodied in the Children's Court of Conciliation, established in California in 1939. Robert W.

Kenny, who introduced the legislation creating it when he was state senator from Los Angeles County, gives Lindsey full credit as originator of the court. Robert W. Kenny to author, February 19, 1965.

47. Cf., *The Revolt of Modern Youth*, 177–178, 239–243. *The Companionate Marriage*, 142–148.

48. It was also more complicated in the sense that the term was sometimes loosely equated with licentiousness. Cf., Note 61, *infra*.

49. *The Companionate Marriage*, Preface, v.

50. *The Dangerous Life*, 356–357.

51. Some of the same criticisms, particularly regarding alimony and divorce, were being made forty years later. Cf., Christopher Lasch, "Divorce American Style," *The New York Review of Books*, February 17, 1966, 2–3.

52. *The Companionate Marriage*, 150.

53. This situation lasted until 1948 when South Carolina adopted a moderately liberal divorce law.

54. The New York statute, which made adultery the only ground for divorce, was not liberalized until 1966.

55. *The Companionate Marriage*, 376.

56. *Ibid.*, 259.

57. *Ibid.*, 257–258.

58. *Ibid.*, 141.

59. Thousands of married people, chiefly but by no means entirely from rural areas, wrote to Lindsey following the publication of *The Companionate Marriage*, asking him how they could obtain information about contraception. *BBLC*, especially Containers 74–78.

60. *The Dangerous Life*, 303–304.

61. William T. Manning to Lindsey, February 8, 1927, *BBLC*, Container 154.

62. E.g., Lynn T. White, D.D., to Lindsey, January 4, 1927: "The better I understand your purpose and methods, the surer I am they approximate what Christ would do if He were incarnate again. It is inevitable that so fine a piece of human engineering should be sincerely misunderstood by some and deliberately misrepresented by others. However, please remember that a great host of people understand and cordially support your work." *BBLC*, Container 153.

63. E.g., Jane Addams to Lindsey, October 19, 1927; David Starr Jordan to Lindsey, November 3, 1927. *BBLC*, Containers 74, 75.

64. *The Christian Century* (November 10, 1927), 44:1328–1329.

65. Cf., *BBLC*, Scrapbook 29, which contains a large number of newspaper clippings dealing mostly with debates on companionate marriage. Lindsey had two objections to the term "trial marriage" as a synonym for his proposals. First, the word "trial" put the primary emphasis on the tentative, provisional, and experimental nature of the union. The psychological basis of a trial marriage was "a candid recognition that it will probably be a temporary episode." The assumption in companionate marriage was that the union would be permanent but, at least temporarily, childless. A second objection was the imprecision of the term "trial marriage" which sometimes led the public to associate it with "free love" or cohabitation without legal marriage. *The Companionate Marriage*, 139–141.

66. Los Angeles *Examiner*, May 13, 1928.

67. San Francisco *Call-Bulletin*, January 31, 1928.

68. Cincinnati *Times-Star*, November 24, 1927.

69. Springfield *Daily News*, March 8, 1928.

70. St. Louis *Star*, March 20, 1928.

71. The cartoon, which is not identified as to source, appears in *BBLC*, Scrapbook 29.

72. The comment appeared in Will Rogers' daily squib in more than fifty newspapers on March 30, 1928.

73. Springfield (Mass.) *Republican*, March 20, 1928. The Unitarian minister was the Rev. Vivian T. Pomeroy of Milton, Massachusetts, who was attacking the Massachusetts Public Interests League. The League was originally formed as an employers' organization to oppose ratification of the proposed child labor amendment. Norman Hapgood, ed., *Professional Patriots* (New York: Boni, 1928), 8–9.

74. New York *Telegram*, April 16, 1927.

75. Lindsey to H. G. Wells, May 14, 1927, *BBLC*, Container 156.

76. Portland *Journal*, April 28, 1928.

77. Chicago *Tribune* (European edition), July 1, 1929.

78. Seattle *Star*, March 9, 1927.

79. *The Beast*, 97–101.

80. *The Companionate Marriage*, 372.

81. For a discussion of the factors which led some prewar progressives who had supported Prohibition to change their minds, cf., Andrew Sinclair, *Prohibition: The Era of Excess* (Boston: Little, Brown, 1962), 311–312.

82. New York *Times*, October 10, 1921.

83. *The Companionate Marriage*, 320. "Your attitude toward the time-honored sex taboos is based on precisely the same choice," he added.

84. *Loc. cit.*

85. *The Revolt of Modern Youth*, 164.

86. *Ibid.*, 280 (Lindsey's italics).

87. *Loc. cit.*

88. *Ibid.*, 166–167.

89. *Loc. cit.*

90. (New York: Harper and Brothers, 1919). The author's name was not disclosed in the book.

91. Lindsey to Harper and Brothers, October 27, 1919, *BBLC*, Container 141.

92. New York *Daily News*, March 6, 1921; New York *Journal*, February 11, 1926.

93. Lindsey to E. Haldemann-Julius, April 18, 1926, *BBLC*, Container 153. Ruth Biery, "Judge Ben Lindsey Defends Flapper Movies," *Photoplay* (November, 1927), 29, 41.

94. *The Beast*, 281, passim. The term "Capitol Hill" refers here to Denver, not Washington, D.C.

95. Lindsey to William Allen White, June 19, 1914, *BBLC*, Container 138.

96. Lindsey to Anna Louise Strong, October 31, 1911, *BBLC*, Container 34.

97. Lindsey to Secretary, Department of Charities and Corrections, State of Oklahoma, February 13, 1908, *BBLC*, Container 14.

98. Lindsey to Julia Lathrop, October 24, 1912, *BBLC*, Container 131.

99. Julia Lathrop to Lindsey, October 27, 1912; Jane Addams to Lindsey, October 28, 1912. *BBLC*, Container 131.

100. Lindsey to Jane Addams, October 31, 1912, *BBLC*, Container 131.

101. *The Revolt of Modern Youth*, 348.

102. There was a continuity in his pragmatic approach to international affairs in the Thirties. Although he hoped for peace, he believed that the Nazi regime probably made the realization impossible. He led a public protest meeting in Los Angeles against Nazi persecution of the Jews in 1938 and condemned isolationism in 1940–1941. Lindsey to Earl Warren, November 30, 1938. Lindsey to Max Levand, November 7, 1941. *BBLC*, Containers 192, 195.

103. New York *American*, December 14, 1915.

104. Lindsey to E. W. Scripps, November 13, 1917, *BBLC*, Container 157.

105. *The Revolt of Modern Youth*, 166–167, 282.

106. *The Companionate Marriage*, 181.

107. *The Revolt of Modern Youth*, 293 (Lindsey's italics).

108. Richard Hofstadter, *Anti-Intellectualism in American Life* (New York: Knopf, 1964), Chap. 5. It had become, Hofstadter states, "a religious style shaped by a desire to strike back against everything modern—the higher criticism, evolutionism, the social gospel, rationalism of any kind." 121.

109. *The Companionate Marriage*, 223.

110. Lindsey to Albert Roden, January 17, 1928, *BBLC*, Container 76. Cf., *The Companionate Marriage*, 338–339.

111. *The Companionate Marriage*, 383.

112. *Ibid.*, p. 384. *The Revolt of Modern Youth*, 313.

113. San Francisco *News*, January 10, 1928.

114. James H. Davis, "Colorado under the Klan," *The Colorado Magazine* (Spring, 1965), 17:93–108.

115. R. E. Strickland to L. D. Wade, Imperial Kligrapp, Knights of the Ku Klux Klan, Atlanta, Georgia, January 25, 1922, *BBLC*, Container 151. Ben B. Lindsey, "My Fight with the Ku Klux Klan," *Survey Graphic* (June 1, 1925), 54:271–274, 319–321.

116. Los Angeles *Examiner*, January 21, 1923.

117. New York *World*, June 1, 1924.

118. Davis, "Colorado under the Klan," 93.

119. *Ibid.*, 94–95.

120. People *ex rel.* Graham *et al.* v. Lindsey, 80 Colorado 465 (1927). A good brief account of the litigation appears in the New York *Times*, January 25, 1927. *The Dangerous Life* treats the case at greater length, 393–395, *passim.*

121. *The Dangerous Life*, 395.

122. *Rocky Mountain News*, July 10, 1927; Denver *Post*, September 19, 1927.

123. *The Revolt of Modern Youth*, 363.

124. Lindsey to Governor-Elect William E. Sweet, November 13, 1922; Lindsey to Owen E. Lovejoy, March 19, 1923, *BBLC*, Containers 66, 67.

125. Fredric C. Howe to Lindsey, April 6, 1931, *BBLC*, Container 167.

126. Lindsey to Fiorello H. LaGuardia, February 4, 1943, *BBLC*, Container 196.

127. Lindsey to Jack B. Tenney, March 24, 1943, *BBLC*, Container 196.

The Case of the Contentious Commissioner: Humphrey's Executor v. U.S.

1. A. L. A. Schechter Poultry Corp. et al. v. United States, 295 U.S. 553; Dred Scott v. Sandford, 19 How. 393 (1857).
2. See, for example, C. Perry Patterson, *Presidential Government in the United States* (Chapel Hill: University of North Carolina Press, 1947), 153.
3. I am happy to acknowledge my indebtedness to an outstanding paper on the Humphrey and Myers cases, "Two Against the President," prepared for my graduate colloquium on the American political process by John W. Chambers.
4. W. E. Humphrey to C. B. Bagley, February 3, 1912, Bagley MSS, University of Washington Libraries, Seattle, Wash. The letters in these and other collections at the University of Washington were kindly made available to me on microfilm by Richard C. Berner and Robert E. Burke.
5. Humphrey to E. G. Eames [sic], October 29, 1906, Edwin G. Ames MSS, University of Washington.
6. See, for example, Jones to Joshua Green, April 10, 1917, Wesley Jones MSS, University of Washington.
7. Dollar to Jones, April 12, 1917, Jones MSS.
8. Tacoma *Times*, May 4, 1917, clipping, Jones MSS.
9. Humphrey to E. G. Ames, October 27, 1919, Ames MSS.
10. G. Cullom Davis, "The Transformation of the Federal Trade Commission, 1914–1929," *Mississippi Valley Historical Review*, XLIX (December, 1962), 447.
11. *Ibid.*, 447–48.
12. Thomas C. Blaisdell, Jr., *The Federal Trade Commission* (New York: Columbia University Press, 1932), 82.
13. G. Cullom Davis, "Transformation of FTC," 448–51.
14. Mimeographed statements, William E. Humphrey MSS, Library of Congress, Box 2.
15. Humphrey to Coolidge, October 10, 1927, Humphrey MSS, Box 1.
16. Pinchot to Humphrey, February 22, 1928; Humphrey to Pinchot, n.d., Humphrey MSS, Box 1.
17. For the role of the courts, see Myron W. Watkins, "An Appraisal of the Work of the Federal Trade Commission," *Columbia Law Review*, XXXII (February, 1932), 278.
18. Humphrey to Robinson, January 27, 1928, Humphrey MSS, Box 1.
19. Robert E. Cushman, *The Independent Regulatory Commissions* (New York: Oxford University Press, 1941), 226.
20. James M. Landis, "The Legislative History of the Securities Act of 1933," *George Washington Law Review*, XXVIII (October, 1959), 34.
21. Memorandum, Franklin D. Roosevelt Library, Hyde Park, N.Y. (henceforth FDRL), Official File (henceforth OF) 100, Box 1. Roosevelt misspelled Ferguson's name.
22. E. D. Smith to FDR, July 13, 1933, FDRL OF 100, Box 2.
23. Humphrey to FDR, July 19, 1933, FDRL OF 100, Box 2.
24. For Humphrey's conception of loyalty, see Pendleton Herring, "The Federal Trade Commissioners," *George Washington Law Review*, VIII (January–February, 1940), 353. As early as 1912 he had telegraphed: "In view of

attitude of Star and the rest of outfit of Anarchists can you not persuade Dovall to stop fighting me for judgeship. I feel that I have a right to ask my friends to protect my reputation." Humphrey to E. G. Ames, January 15, 1912, Ames MS.

25. Humphrey to Dill, July 25, 1933, Humphrey MSS, Box 1.

26. Dill to FDR, July 28, 1933, Humphrey MSS, Box 1.

27. FDR to Humphrey, July 25, 1933, FDRL OF 100, Box 2.

28. Humphrey to FDR, August 1, 1933, Humphrey MSS, Box 1.

29. FDR to Humphrey, August 4, 1933, Humphrey MSS, Box 1.

30. Humphrey to C. C. Dill, August 28, 1933, Humphrey MSS, Box 1.

31. Humphrey to FDR, August 11, 1933, Humphrey MSS, Box 1.

32. Humphrey to Dill, August 18, 1933, Humphrey MSS, Box 1.

33. Dill to Humphrey, August 21, August 22, 1933, Humphrey MSS, Box 1. Dill's second note addressed him as "Dear Humphreys."

34. Humphrey to C. C. Dill, August 28, 1933, Humphrey MSS, Box 1. Humphrey's hometown newspaper, the Seattle *Times*, which may have had access to confidential information, stated: "In the present instance he is acting under the advice of Republican Senate leaders." *Congressional Record*, 73rd Cong., 2nd Sess., p. 1682.

35. Humphrey to Dill, August 28, 1933, Humphrey MSS, Box 1.

36. Moreover, by now, Dill, understandably, was miffed. He replied to Humphrey: "I assure you I never for one moment thought our friendship was strained. I have done more for you than I ever did for any republican in this country." C. C. Dill to Humphrey, September 1, 1933, Humphrey MSS, Box 1.

37. FDR to Marvin H. McIntyre, August 18, 1933; Stephen T. Early to FDR, August 17, 1933, FDRL OF 100, Box 2.

38. William Stanley to Stephen T. Early, August 19, 1933; R.F. to Early, August 22, 1933; Raymond Stevens to FDR, August 26, 1933; Stevens to Cummings, August 26, 1933; Memorandum, probably from Stevens, n.d., FDRL OF 100, Box 2.

39. FDR to Humphrey, August 31, 1933, Humphrey MSS, Box 1.

40. Humphrey to C. C. Dill, September 2, 1933, Humphrey MSS, Box 1.

41. Humphrey to FDR, September 11, 1933, Humphrey MSS, Box 1.

42. Humphrey to McCarthy, September 17, 1933; McCarthy to FDR, September 18, 1933, FDRL OF 100, Box 2.

43. Omaha *World Herald*, n.d., clipping; Humphrey to FDR, September 27, 1933, Humphrey MSS, Box 1.

44. Mathews to M. J. McIntyre, October 3, 1933, and McIntyre's notations, FDRL OF 100, Box 2.

45. FDR to Mathews, October 7, 1933, FDRL OF 100, Box 1; FDR to Humphrey, October 7, 1933, Humphrey MSS, Box 1.

46. Humphrey to FDR, October 10, 1933, Humphrey MSS, Box 1. Humphrey added: "This letter will probably be withheld from you. If not, one of your secretaries will probably disclose to you the facts which have influenced him to join so persistently in the demand for my removal. He knows that he arranged over the White House telephone for a certain attorney to have a personal interview with me. In that interview, the attorney demanded that I in my official capacity, as a Member of the Federal Trade Commission, take certain action favorable to his clients in a private litigation which was then being prosecuted. I refused to accede to his demands, and I was sustained in this action by the unanimous vote of the Commission."

47. A memorandum from "M.B.H.," undated but penciled "September," stated: "I hope Mr. H. will preserve his inchoate right to accruing salary by appearing regularly at each regular session, even though it be but to acquiesce in the action of the Commission in excluding him and bowing himself out." Humphrey MSS, Box 1.

48. Humphrey to Mathews, October 9, 1933, Humphrey MSS, Box 1.

49. Humphrey to FTC, FTC to Humphrey, October 9, 1933; Press release, FTC, October 9, 1933, Humphrey MSS, Box 1; *New York Times*, October 10, 1933.

50. Humphrey to Rudolph Schwickardi, October 9, October 17, 1933; Humphrey to Otis Johnson, et al., November 2, 1933; R. L. Golze to R. B. Schwickardi, November 11, 1933, Humphrey MSS, Box 1.

51. Humphrey to Donovan, October 20, 1933, Humphrey MSS, Box 1.

52. Humphrey to Donovan, January 19, 1934, Humphrey MSS, Box 1.

53. *Congressional Record*, 73rd Cong., 2nd Sess., 1679–84.

54. *Ibid.*, 1289–91. Cushman overstated the matter in writing that Roosevelt's action "evoked no protest in either house of Congress and practically no comment." Cushman, *Independent Regulatory Commissions*, 226. In addition to these few protests in Congress, widespread criticism in newspaper editorials greeted news of the ouster.

55. The actual docket title was *Rathbun, Executor v. United States*. Some commentators refer to it as the Rathbun case, but it is more generally known as *Humphrey's Executor v. U.S.*

56. Wesley McCune, *The Nine Young Men* (New York: Harper, 1947), 61.

57. 19 Stat. 80, 81 (1876), U.S. Comp. Stat. (1916) 7190.

58. Shurtleff v. United States, 189 U.S. 311, 316–317 (1902). See, too, Ex parte Hennen, 13 Pet. 230, 258 (1839); Parsons v. U.S. 167 U.S. 324, 339 (1897); Carl Russell Fish, "Removal of Officials by the Presidents of the United States," *Annual Report of the American Historical Association: The Year 1899* (2 vols., Washington: Government Printing Office, 1900), I, 67–86.

59. Alpheus Thomas Mason, *Harlan Fiske Stone* (New York: Viking, 1956), 222–231; Mason, *William Howard Taft: Chief Justice* (New York: Simon and Schuster, 1965), 225–255; Henry F. Pringle, *The Life and Times of William Howard Taft* (2 vols., Hamden, Conn.: Archon Books, 1964), II, 1023–1027; Taft to Stone, n.d., Stone MSS, LC, Box 54.

60. Taft to Stone, December 26, 1925, Stone MSS, Box 54.

61. 272 U.S. 135 (1926). James M. Landis has noted: "Some efforts were made to remove this unnecessary dictum but Taft was adamant." Landis, "Mr. Justice Brandeis: A Law Clerk's View," *Publication of the American Jewish Historical Society*, XLVI (June, 1957), 472. Authorities differ on the number of pages consumed by each opinion; I have followed the pagination in the *U.S. Reports*.

62. 272 U.S. at 177.

63. Perry v. United States, 294 U.S. 330 and other cases; an annotated version of his dissent in the gold clause cases may be found in the James McReynolds MSS, Alderman Library, University of Virginia, Charlottesville, Va. Taft wrote of McReynolds' performance in the Myers case: "His exhibition in the Court room was such as to disgust Holmes." Mason, *Taft*, 227.

64. New York *Herald-Tribune*, October 26, 1926.

65. James M. Landis, Columbia Oral History Collection, 37–39.

66. Mason, *Taft*, 226. Taft observed: "Brandeis can not avoid writing an opinion in a way in which he wishes to spread himself, as if he were writing an article for the Harvard Law Review."

67. 272 U.S. 240–295, especially at 293–295. The dissents, Stone wrote Taft, "have rather assumed that the people speak only through legislation, forgetting for the moment that the people spoke through the Constitution and the legislative branch, as well as other branches of the government, have only such powers as were conferred upon it by the Constitution." Stone to Taft, March 29, 1926, Stone MSS, Box 54.

68. Powell, "Spinning Out the Executive Power," *New Republic*, XLVIII (November 17, 1926), 369; *New York Times*, November 7, 16, 1926; Morton Keller, *In Defense of Yesterday* (New York: Coward-McCann, 1958), 181; George B. Galloway, "The Consequences of the Myers Decision," *American Law Review*, LXI (July–August, 1927), 481–508; James Hart, "Tenure of Office under the Constitution," *Johns Hopkins University Studies in Historical and Political Science*, Extra Volumes, New Series, No. 9 (Baltimore: The Johns Hopkins Press, 1930); George Wharton Pepper, *Family Quarrels* (New York: Baker, Voorhis, 1931), 124; Wilson K. Doyle, *Independent Commissions in the Federal Government* (Chapel Hill: University of North Carolina Press, 1939), 23–24.

69. Corwin, *The President's Removal Power under the Constitution* (New York: National Municipal League, 1927), 3.

70. Stevens to FDR, August 26, 1933, FDRL OF 100, Box 2.

71. Doyle, *Independent Commissions*, 24; *Illinois Law Review*, XXI (March, 1927), 733–36; *Oregon Law Review*, VI (February, 1927), 165–171; *Virginia Law Review*, XIII (December, 1926), 122–27; *Michigan Law Review*, XXV (January, 1927), 280–87. However, most of the commentators ignored Taft's dictum, and the *Michigan Law Review*, while supporting the Chief Justice's opinion, denied that members of the Federal Trade Commission were now "subject to the President's pleasures or caprice." *Loc. cit.*, at 287.

72. *University of Cincinnati Law Review*, I (January, 1927), 74–79. Corwin, the chief critic of the decision, went so far as to state that laws like the FTC act were now "void." Corwin, *President's Removal Power*, 7. See, too, the discussion in Hart, "Tenure of Office," 369–373, taking off from Springer *et al.* v. Philippine Islands, 277 U.S. 189 (1928).

73. Albert Langeluttig, " 'The Bearing of Myers v. United States Upon the Independence of Federal Administrative Tribunals'—A Criticism," *American Political Science Review*, XXIV (February, 1950), 65.

74. J. M. Landis, Columbia Oral History Collection, 39–41. Landis added: "My own feelings were a little curious, because I'd been with Brandeis on the dissent in the Myers case, and if I had had an independent opportunity to look at the situation, I would have been on the side of Humphrey. But having the background that I did, I had a feeling that there was a certain amount of precedent that would govern here, and that the answer would be that." Myers, it should be noted, was a first-class, not a "fourth-class," postmaster.

75. Certificate from the Court of Claims, filed January 26, 1935, U.S. Briefs 1934, No. 405.

76. Both arguments are printed in 295 U.S. 604–618 (1935).

77. *Washington Post*, May 28, 1935.

78. Humphrey's Executor v. United States, 295 U.S. 602 (1935).

79. Joel Paschal, *Mr. Justice Sutherland* (Princeton: Princeton University

Press, 1951), 184–185. It is possible that more than one of these men may have tried to persuade Taft to modify his opinion. Yet their objections were not strong enough for them to have filed a concurring opinion, let alone a dissent. The Court, it should be added, did not embrace the extreme view that the President's illimitable removal power is restricted to purely executive officers. McReynolds, who apparently believed the Court had not gone far enough, concurred in the Sutherland opinion but noted tersely that his dissent in Myers had stated "his views concerning the power of the President to remove appointees." 295 U.S. at 632.

80. Cushman, *Independent Regulatory Commissions*, 450–451. See, too, *Columbia Law Review*, XXXV (June, 1935), 936–938; *Harvard Law Review*, XLIX (December, 1935), 330–331.

81. Edward S. Corwin, *The President: Office and Powers 1787–1957* (New York: New York University Press, 1957), 93.

82. Cushman, *Independent Regulatory Commissions*, 177–213.

83. *Ibid.*, 445–446.

84. *Ibid.*, 447–448.

85. Louis W. Koenig, *The Chief Executive* (New York: Harcourt, Brace & World, 1964), 159.

86. For a statement of this view see Arthur Larson, "Has the President an Inherent Power of Removal of His Non-Executive Appointments?" *Tennessee Law Review*, XVI (March, 1940), 259–290.

87. Morgan v. Tennessee Valley Authority, 115 F. 2d 990 (6th Circ. 1940); Cert. denied, 312 U.S. 701 (1941).

88. Wiener v. U.S., 357 U.S. 349 (1958); *George Washington Law Review*, XXVII (October, 1958), 129–132. The Court might have dealt with the removal power in the Lovett case, but it chose, instead, to invalidate the statute as a bill of attainder. U.S. v. Lovett, 328 U.S. 303 (1946). The Court has not yet found occasion to define the scope of the power of Congress to participate in removals, a matter that captured attention recently when some Congressmen threatened to compel Sargent Shriver to relinquish one of his two government posts.

89. Corwin, *The President: Office and Powers*, 85–86.

90. Patterson, *Presidential Government in the United States*, 153.

91. Doyle, *Independent Commissions*, 30–31.

92. Clippings, David J. Lewis ms., Duke University Library, Durham, North Carolina. Arthur R. Burns has pointed out: "The policies of the Federal Trade Commission have been molded by the careful selection of its personnel and by pressure from the executive arm of the state."

93. Herring, "Federal Trade Commissioners," 356.

94. Cushman, *Independent Regulatory Commissions*, 222–226.

95. *Ibid.*, 410–15. When the Humphrey opinion was delivered, Congress was in the process of enacting the Wagner labor bill. After the opinion, Congress modified the measure to stipulate that the National Labor Relations Board was to be an agent of Congress, not the President. *Ibid.*, 363–66.

96. *Ibid.*, 418.

97. *Congressional Record*, 73d Cong., 2d Sess., 1679.

98. S. Chesterfield Oppenheim, "Federal Trade Commission Silver Anniversary Issue: Foreword," *George Washington Law Review*, VIII (January–February, 1940), 253.

99. A. T. Mason, *Brandeis: A Free Man's Life* (New York: Viking, 1946), 619.

100. Landis, *The Administrative Process* (New Haven: Yale University Press, 1938), 115.

101. Humphrey to C. C. Dill, August 18, 1933, Humphrey MSS, Box 1.

102. Humphrey to Norris, October 4, 1933, *idem*.

103. *Congressional Record*, 73d Cong., 2nd Sess., 1290–1291. Emphasis added.

104. Humphrey to Jerry A. Mathews, September 22, 1933, Humphrey MSS, Box 1.

105. E. Pendleton Herring, "Politics, Personalities, and the Federal Trade Commission," *American Political Science Review*, XXVIII (December, 1934), 1020–1021.

106. *Ibid.*, 1021.

107. *Ibid.*

108. Herring, "Politics, Personalities, and the Federal Trade Commission: II," *American Political Science Review*, XXIX (February, 1935), 31.

109. Raymond Moley, *After Seven Years* (New York: Harper, 1939), 128.

110. Herring, "Politics, Personalities and the Federal Trade Commission: II," 32–33.

111. Richard Polenberg, *Reorganizing Roosevelt's Government* (Cambridge: Harvard University Press, 1966), 25.

112. *Ibid.*, 20–21. The Humphrey decision proved to be a stumbling block for the reorganization plan, both during the drafting stage and in its subsequent travail in Congress. See Robert E. Cushman, "Independent Boards and Commissions and their Relation to the President," typescript, Charles Merriam ms., University of Chicago Library, Chicago, Illinois, Box 260; Memorandum from H. G. Moulton to Louis Brownlow, March 24, 1937, *idem*.

113. *Ibid.*, 21.

114. Corwin, *The President: Office and Powers*, 96–97.

115. Polenberg, *Reorganizing Roosevelt's Government*, 44, 91. By 1938, the FTC was one of the agencies exempted from the provisions of the bill.

116. For the relation of the two controversies, see the perceptive comments in Barry Karl, *Executive Reorganization and Reform in the New Deal* (Cambridge: Harvard University Press, 1963), 247–48.

117. Rexford G. Tugwell, *The Democratic Roosevelt* (Garden City, New York: Doubleday, 1957), 393.

118. Robert H. Jackson, *The Struggle for Judicial Supremacy* (New York: Alfred A. Knopf, 1941), 108–09. Not until Justice Felix Frankfurter's opinion in the Wiener case in 1958 did the Court admit that Roosevelt's assertion of authority had a basis in Taft's opinion. Walter F. Murphy, *Congress and the Court* (Chicago: University of Chicago Press, 1962), 279, n. 107.

119. *The Secret Diary of Harold L. Ickes* (3 vols., New York: Simon and Schuster, 1954), I, 374. I have not attempted to correct the spelling of Humphrey's name in this and other quotations.

120. Moley, *After Seven Years*, 301. Landis later observed: "In those early days of the New Deal, there were some decisions of the Supreme Court of the United States whose sole purpose was to embarrass the President of the United States." Landis, COHC, 39–41.

121. Eugene C. Gerhart, *America's Advocate: Robert H. Jackson* (Indianapolis: Bobbs-Merrill, 1958), 99.

122. Tugwell, *The Democratic Roosevelt*, 392. For an early statement by a leading constitutional historian in defense of the Court as the guardian of liberty, because of its decision in the Humphrey case, see *Chicago Tribune*,

June 9, 1935, clipping, Andrews C. McLaughlin ms., University of Chicago.

123. Joseph Alsop and Turner Catledge, *The 168 Days* (Garden City, N.Y.: Doubleday, 1938), 13–14.

124. Flint (Mich.) *Journal*, February 7, 1937, clipping, Prentiss Brown Scrapbooks, St. Ignace, Michigan (privately held). I am indebted to Mr. Brown, formerly U.S. Senator from Michigan, for permitting me to borrow his scrapbooks and diaries.

125. Ray Lyman Wilbur to Dr. Arthur Hill Daniels, March 15, 1937, Wilbur MSS, Stanford University, Stanford, California.

126. Washington *Post*, March 6, 1937. One woman asked: "Is Mr. Roosevelt's venom due to the fact that the nine old men ruled against his injustice in dismissing William E. Humphrey?" Mrs. Barbour Walker to Hon. House of Congress, April 9, 1937, W. W. Ball ms., Duke University. See, too, Edward H. Neary to Josiah Bailey, n.d. [1937], Bailey ms., Supreme Court file, Duke University.

127. Tugwell, *Democratic Roosevelt*, 400.

Bibliography of Henry Steele Commager

DISSERTATION

"Struensee and the Reform Movement in Denmark." Unpublished Ph.D. dissertation, University of Chicago, 1928.

BOOKS

The Growth of the American Republic, with Samuel Eliot Morison. 2 vols. (Originally published in 1930; 5th ed., New York: Oxford University Press, 1962. Subsequent editions in 1937, 1942, 1950 [Chaps. 1–6 of Vol. II published separately, 1962, as *The Reconstruction* and *The Passage of the American Frontier*].)

Our Nation's Development, with William Edward Dodd and Eugene Campbell Barker. New York: Row, Peterson, 1934.

Theodore Parker: Yankee Crusader. Boston: Beacon Press, 1962. (Originally published Boston: Little, Brown, 1936. Subsequent editions, Beacon Press, 1947, 1960.)

The Building of Our Nation, with Eugene C. Barker and Walter P. Webb. Originally published New York: Row, Peterson, 1937, 1941, 1946.

Our Nation, with Eugene C. Barker. New York: Row, Peterson, 1941.

A Short History of the United States, with Allan Nevins. 5th ed., rev. and enl., New York: A. A. Knopf, 1966. (Originally titled *America: The Story of a Free People*. Boston: Little, Brown, 1942, 1943; and *The Pocket History of the United States*. New York: Pocket Books, 1943; rev. New York: Overseas editions, 1944; enl. New York: Modern Library, 1951, 1956.)

Majority Rule and Minority Rights. James W. Richards Lectures in History, University of Virginia. New York: Oxford University Press, 1943.

369

The American Mind: An Interpretation of American Thought and Character Since the 1800's. New Haven: Yale University Press, 1950.

America's Robert E. Lee, with Lynd Ward. Boston: Houghton Mifflin, 1951.

Europe and America Since 1492, with Geoffrey Bruun. Boston: Houghton Mifflin, 1954.

Freedom, Loyalty, Dissent. New York: Oxford University Press, 1954.

The First Book of American History. New York: Watts, 1957.

The Great Declaration: A Book for Young Americans. Indianapolis: Bobbs-Merrill, 1958.

The Great Proclamation: A Book for Young Americans. Indianapolis: Bobbs-Merrill, 1960.

The Great Constitution: A Book for Young Americans. Indianapolis: Bobbs-Merrill, 1961.

Crusaders for Freedom. New York: Doubleday, 1962.

The Nature and the Study of History. Columbus, Ohio: Merrill, 1965.

Freedom and Order: A Commentary on the American Political Scene. New York: Braziller, 1966.

The Search for a Usable Past. New York: Alfred A. Knopf, 1967.

COMPENDIA AND EDITED BOOKS

Documents of American History. 2 vols. 7th ed., New York: Appleton-Century-Crofts, 1963. (Originally published, F. S. Crofts, 1934, 1940, 1943; Appleton-Century-Crofts, 1948, 1949, 1958.)

The Heritage of America: Readings in American History, with Allan Nevins. Rev. ed., Boston: D. C. Heath, 1949. (Originally published in 1939.)

The Story of the Second World War. Boston: Little, Brown, 1945.

de Tocqueville, Alexis. Democracy in America. Tr. by Henry Reeve. An abridgement. New York: Oxford University Press, 1947.

American Perspective: The United States Through Foreign Eyes. New York: Random House, 1947–1962.

The St. Nicholas Anthology. New York: Random House, 1948.

Selections from the Federalist. New York: Appleton-Century-Crofts, 1949.

The Blue and The Gray. 2 vols. Indianapolis: Bobbs-Merrill Company, 1950.

Living Ideas in America. New York: Harper, 1951.

The Encyclopedia of American History, with Richard B. Morris. Rev. and enl., New York: Harper, 1961. (Originally published in 1953.)

Photographic History of the Civil War. 5 vols. New York: Yoseloff, 1957.

Official Atlas of the Civil War. New York: Yoseloff, 1958.

Picture History of the United States of America. New York: Watts, 1958.

The Spirit of Seventy-Six: The Story of the American Revolution as Told by Participants, with Richard B. Morris. 2 vols. Indianapolis: Bobbs-Merrill, 1958.

The Era of Reform 1830–1860. Princeton: Van Nostrand, 1960.

Theodore Parker: An Anthology. Boston: Beacon, 1960.

Webster, Noah. *American Spelling Book.* New York: Columbia Teachers College Press, 1963.

The Defeat of the Confederacy. Princeton: Van Nostrand, 1964.

Churchill's History of the English-Speaking Peoples. Arr. for one volume. New York: Dodd, Mead, 1965.

Fifty Basic Civil War Documents. Princeton: Van Nostrand, 1965.

Lester Ward and the Welfare State. Indianapolis: Bobbs Merrill, 1967.

The Struggle for Racial Equality. New York: Harper & Row, 1967.

Was America a Mistake? New York: Harper & Row, 1967.

ARTICLES, ESSAYS, REVIEW ESSAYS, SPECIAL SPEECHES AND ADDRESSES, TRANSLATIONS

"The Foundation's Foreign Service: History," *American Scandinavian Review,* XV (February, 1927), 107–108.

"England and the Oregon Treaty of 1846," *Oregon Historical Quarterly,* XXVIII (March, 1927), 18–38.

"Henry Adams," *South Atlantic Quarterly,* XXVI (July, 1927), 252–265.

Steen Steensen Blicher, "Gypsy Life," translation, *American Scandinavian Review,* XV (October, 1927), 602–606.

Herman Bang, "Pastor," translation, *American Scandinavian Review,* XV (December, 1927), 745–753.

"Literature of the Pioneer West," *Minnesota History,* VIII (December, 1927), 319–328.

Herman Bang, "Last Evening," translation, *American Scandinavian Review,* XVII (March, 1929), 168–171.

Astrid Ehrencron (Müller) Kidde, "Tragedy at Herrhult Station," translation, *American Scandinavian Review,* XVII (August, 1929), 484–493.

"Modern Studies of Washington," *Publisher's Weekly,* CXXI (January 30, 1932), 507–509.

"The Dilemma of Theodore Parker," *New England Quarterly,* VI (1933), 257–277.

"Tempest in a Boston Tea Cup," *New England Quarterly,* VI (1933), 651–675.

"Farewell to Laissez-faire," *Current History,* XXXVIII (August, 1933), 513–520.

"Theodore Parker, Intellectual Gourmand," *American Scholar*, III (Summer, 1934), 257–266.

"Regimentation: A New Bogey," *Current History*, XL (July, 1934), 385–391.

"The Blasphemy of Abner Kneeland," *New England Quarterly*, VIII (1935), 24–41.

"The Literature of American History, 1934," *Social Studies*, XXVI (April, 1935), 233–253.

"South Carolina Dictator," *Current History*, XLIII (March, 1936), 568–572.

"The Literature of American History, 1935," *Social Studies*, XXVII (April–May, 1936), 251–268.

"When 'We The People' Take Action," *New York Times Magazine*, April 4, 1937, 6 ff.

"Constitutional History and the Higher Law," in *The Constitution Reconsidered*, ed., Conyers Reed. New York: Columbia University Press, 1938, 225–246.

"Recent and Forthcoming Books on American History," *Publisher's Weekly*, CXXXIII (January 29, 1938), 462–465.

"Can Roosevelt Draw New Party Lines?" *New York Times Magazine*, September 4, 1938, 3 ff.

"Nation or the States: Which Shall Dominate?" *New York Times Magazine*, November 28, 1937, 4 ff.

"Our Commonwealth: Bryce's Prophetic Vision," *New York Times Magazine*, August 7, 1938, 6 ff.

"The New Year Puts a Challenge to Us," *New York Times Magazine*, January 1, 1939, 1 ff.

" 'To Secure the Blessings of Liberty,' " *New York Times Magazine*, April 9, 1939, 4 ff.

"Echoes of Marshall," *New York Times Magazine*, June 11, 1939, 10 ff.

"One-Two-Or Three Terms?" *New York Times Magazine*, July 23, 1939, 1 ff.

"Today's Events in the Light of History," *Scholastic*, XXXVI (February 5, 1940), 7.

"Highlights of Convention History," *Scholastic*, XXXVI (April 29, 1940), 9–10.

"Third-Term Tradition Meets Greatest Test," *New York Times, News of the Week in Review*. July 21, 1940, 7.

"Should the Powers of the Federal Government Be Increased?" *Congressional Digest*, XIX (August, 1940), 203–206.

"Party Strife: Signs of Health," *New York Times Magazine*, October 6, 1940, 3 ff.

"Far-reaching Distortions of History," *New York Times Magazine*, October 27, 1940, 5 ff.

"Keystones of Our National Unity," *New York Times Magazine*, November 10, 1940, 3 ff.

"Our Beginnings: A Lesson for Today," *New York Times Magazine*, January 26, 1941, 3 ff.

"Are We Creating a Dictator?" *New York Times Magazine*, March 2, 1941, 3 ff.

"Roaring Forties," *New York Times Magazine*, March 30, 1941, 14 ff.

"Still the Hope of the Human Race," *New York Times Magazine*, July 20, 1941, 4 ff.

"Heritage of America," *Scholastic*, XXXIX (September 15, 1941) to XL (May 25, 1942), *passim*.

"Will 1941 Repeat the History of 1917?" *New York Times Magazine*, September 28, 1941, 3 ff.

"War Powers of the President," *New York Times Magazine*, October 19, 1941, 18 ff.

"Charter of Our Way of Life," *New York Times Magazine*, December 14, 1941, 6 ff.

"John Fiske," *Massachusetts Historical Society Proceedings*, CXVI (1942), 332.

"The Last Best Hope of Earth," *Scholastic*, XXXIX (January 5, 1942), 13.

"Why the War Came," *Scholastic*, XL (February 2, 1942), 8 ff.

"Issues of the War," *Scholastic*, XL (March 9, 1942), 7 ff.

"Conduct of the War," *Scholastic*, XL (April 20, 1942), 6 ff.

"Bases of a Lasting Peace," *Scholastic*, XL (May 25, 1942), 6–7.

"We Hold These Truths—," *New York Times Magazine*, July 5, 1942, 5 ff.

"U-Boat Menace in Two Wars," *Scholastic*, XLI (September 14, 1942), 13.

"The Peoples' War," *Scholastic*, XLI (September 21, 1942), 7.

"It Has Happened Before," *Scholastic*, XLI (September 28, 1942), 9.

"Diplomatic Front," *Scholastic*, XLI (October 5, 1942), 13.

"450th Columbus Day," *Scholastic*, XLI (October 12, 1942), 6.

"How Public Opinion Affects the Conduct of the War," *Scholastic*, XLI (October 19, 1942), 12.

"Presidential Powers in War Time," *Scholastic*, XLI (October 26, 1942), 7.

"Propaganda in American History," *Scholastic*, XLI (November 2, 1942), 12.

"Woodrow Wilson as Propagandist," *Scholastic*, XLI (November 9, 1942), 9.

"Understanding Great Britain," *Scholastic*, XLI (November 16, 1942), 7.

"America Goes Back to England," *Scholastic*, XLI (December 7, 1942), 12.

"Bells of Old England," *Scholastic*, XLI (January 4, 1942), 9.

"Public Education in England," *Scholastic*, XLI (January 11, 1943), 10.

"College and University Education," *Scholastic*, XLI (January 18, 1943), 9.

"England Plans to Abolish Want," *Scholastic*, XLII (February 1, 1943), 11.

"British Fortitude," *Scholastic*, XLII (February 8, 1943), 11.

"Ireland and World War II," *Scholastic*, XLII (February 15, 1943), 9.

"Lessons from Britain," *Scholastic*, XLII (February 22, 1943), 9.

"Wartime Efficiency," *Scholastic*, XLII (March 1, 1943), 7.

"Challenge to Ireland's Neutrality," *New York Times Magazine*, March 7, 1943, 7 ff.

"Negroes and the War," *Scholastic*, XLII (March 8, 1943), 9.

"Up From Slavery," *Scholastic*, XLII (March 15, 1943), 7.

"Civil Liberties and Democracy," *Scholastic*, XLII (March 22, 1943), 13.

"Planning Is No Novelty," *Scholastic*, XLII (March 29, 1943), 7.

"Senators and the Peace," *Scholastic*, XLII (April 5, 1943), 9.

"Thomas Jefferson Still Survives," *Publisher's Weekly*, CXLIII (April 10, 1943), 1504–1506.

"Thomas Jefferson: 1743–1943," *Scholastic*, XLII (April 12, 1943), 3.

"They Had Meatless Days, Too," *Scholastic*, XLII (April 19, 1943), 9.

"Bugaboo of Bureaucracy," *Scholastic*, XLII (May 3, 1943), 7.

"Trade Pacts in U. S. History," *Scholastic*, XLII (May 17, 1943), 7.

"When Labor Challenged Government," *Scholastic*, XLII (May 24, 1943), 5.

"Judicial Review and Democracy," *Virginia Quarterly Review*, XIX (Summer, 1943), 417–428.

"Editorial," *American Scholar*, XII (July, 1943), 261–262.

"We Hold These Truths, Now as in 1776," *New York Times Magazine*, July 4, 1943, 6 ff.

"What Answer Will America Make?" *New York Times Magazine*, October 3, 1943, 5 ff.

"American Institutions," *Scholastic*, XLIII (September 13, 1943) to XLIV (May 22, 1944), *passim*.

"Theirs is to Reason Why, Says Britain," *New York Times Magazine*, February 27, 1944, 10 ff.

"He Opened All Eyes to the Rights of Man," *New York Times Magazine*, April 9, 1944, 18 ff.

"National Government and the States," *Scholastic*, XLV (September 11, 1944), 10.

"Federal-State Cooperation in Recent History," *Scholastic*, XLV (September 18, 1944), 9–10.

"The Race Problem in America," *Scholastic*, XLV (September 25, 1944), 9.

"Large States Versus Small," *American Mercury*, LIX (October, 1944), 495–500.

"Bureaucracy: Is Red Tape Necessary?" *Scholastic*, XLV (October 2, 1944), 8.

"Labor in U. S. Politics," *Scholastic*, XLV (October 9, 1944), 7.

"America Learns from History," *Scholastic*, XLV (October 16, 1944), 7.

"The Electoral College," *Scholastic*, XLV (October 23, 1944), 8.

"The Role of the Opposition," *Scholastic*, XLV (October 30, 1944), 7.

"United States Relations With Russia," *Scholastic*, XLV (November 6, 1944), 11.

"Philippines, A Pattern of Stewardship," *Scholastic*, XLV (November 13, 1944), 7.

"Saving Our Forests," *Scholastic*, XLV (November 27, 1944), 8.

"The Election Settled Old Issues," *Scholastic*, XLV (December 4, 1944), 5.

"War Criminals and the Right of Asylum," *Scholastic*, XLV (December 11, 1944), 9.

"Our Heritage from Britain," *Scholastic*, XLV (January 8, 1945), 9.

"The Presidency and Foreign Affairs," *Scholastic*, XLV (January 15, 1945), 7.

"Nisei: What Future for the Japanese-Americans?" *Scholastic*, XLV (January 22, 1945), 7.

"Argentina Walks Alone," *Scholastic*, XLVI (February 5, 1945), 7.

"Treaties of Alliance," *Scholastic*, XLVI (February 12, 1945), 7.

"The President's Cabinet," *Scholastic*, XLVI (February 19, 1945), 7.

"States and the Poll Tax," *Scholastic*, XLVI (February 26, 1945), 9.

"The History of Federal Aid to Education," *Scholastic*, XLVI (March 5, 1945), 7.

"Germany May Try It Again!" *Scholastic*, XLVI (March 12, 1945), 7.

"Pan-Americanism," *Scholastic*, XLVI (March 19, 1945), 7.

"When France Gave Us a Helping Hand," *Scholastic*, XLVI (March 26, 1945), 13.

"Women in War, 1861–1865," *Scholastic*, XLVI (April 2, 1945), 7.

"Wars are Won in History Books," *Scholastic*, XLVI (April 2, 1945), 3–4.

"Twelve Years of Roosevelt," *American Mercury*, LX (April, 1945), 391–401.

"Growing Pains of a Doctrine," *Scholastic*, XLVI (April 16, 1945), 9.

"Florida's 100th Birthday," *Scholastic*, XLVI (April 30, 1945), 7.

"Things of the Spirit," *Survey Graphic*, XXXIV (May, 1945), 237–240 ff.

"Roosevelt's Place in History," *Scholastic*, XLVI (May 7, 1945), 5–6.

"Good Neighbors," *Scholastic*, XLVI (May 14, 1945), 12.

"The Negro Problem in Our Democracy," *American Mercury*, LX (June, 1945), 751–756.

"What Makes for Presidential Greatness," *New York Times Magazine*, July 22, 1942, 13 ff.

"Winston Churchill: An Appreciation," *American Mercury*, LXI (August, 1945), 135–146.

"The Shift from War to Peace," *Scholastic,* XLVII (September 17, 1945), 9.

"No More War Debts," *Scholastic,* XLVII (September 24, 1945), 7.

"When Johnny Comes Marching Home," *Scholastic,* XLVII (October 1, 1945), 10.

"American Leadership in War and Peace," *Scholastic,* XLVII (October 8, 1945), 8.

"Our Non-Partisan Supreme Court," *Scholastic,* XLVII (October 15, 1945), 8.

"America Comes of Age," *Scholastic,* XLVII (October 22, 1945), 11.

"The Power of the President in Foreign Affairs," *Scholastic,* XLVII (October 29, 1945), 7.

"The Chief of Staff Reports," *Scholastic,* XLVII (November 12, 1945), 12; (November 19, 1945), 5.

"Great Mysteries of World War II," *New York Times Magazine,* November 25, 1945, 10 ff.

"The German Problem," *American Mercury,* LXI (December, 1945), 753–757.

"John Jay, Our First Chief Justice," *Scholastic,* XLVII (December 3, 1945), 5.

"Text Books and the Peace," *Scholastic,* XLVII (December 10, 1945), 5.

"State Planning and Freedom," *American Mercury,* LXII (January, 1946), 113–117.

"The Search for Peace," *New York Times Magazine,* January 13, 1946, 6 ff.

"War Surpluses for Scholarships," *Scholastic,* XLVII (January 21, 1946), 5.

"Where Are We Headed?" *American Mercury,* CLXXVII (February, 1946), 54–60.

"Strong Presidents and Willful Congresses," *Scholastic,* XLVIII (February 4, 1946), 10.

"This Occupation Is Different," *Scholastic,* XLVIII (February 11, 1946), 5.

"Choosing a Capital," *Scholastic,* XLVIII (February 25, 1946), 8.

"The Income Tax and How It Grew," *Scholastic,* XLVIII (March 4, 1946), 5.

"Money to Burn," *Scholastic,* XLVIII (March 11, 1946), 5.

"The President's Inner Circle," *Scholastic,* XLVIII (March 18, 1946), 11.

"The Right to Strike," *Scholastic,* XLVIII (March 25, 1946), 9.

"British-American Cooperation," *Scholastic,* XLVIII (April 1, 1946), 8.

"When Presidents Die," *Scholastic,* XLVIII (April 8, 1946), 7 ff.

"The United States and Mexico," *Scholastic,* XLVIII (April 15, 1946), 9.

"Don't Believe Anything You Read!" *Nation,* CLXII (April 20,

1946), 463–465. Reprinted as "So You Think It's All Propaganda," *SD*, XX (July, 1946), 21–24.

"The Melting Pot Cools," *Scholastic*, XLVIII (April 22, 1946), 9.

"Transportation Built an Empire," *Scholastic*, XLVIII (April 29, 1946), 9.

"Oregon Centenary," *Scholastic*, XLVIII (May 6, 1946), 6.

"Third Parties and the Party System," *Scholastic* (May 13, 1946), 20.

"World Power and American Ideals," *Scholastic*, XLVIII (May 20, 1946), 17.

"Peace-Making: 1919, 1946," *Scholastic*, XLIX (September 16, 1946), 7.

"The League That Failed," *Scholastic*, XLIX (September 23, 1946), 8.

"Play Ball!" *Scholastic*, XLIX (September 30, 1946), 8.

"The Eighteen-Nineties: A Watershed in American History," *New York Times Book Review*, October 6, 1946, 7 ff.

"Does the Klan Ride to its Death?" *Scholastic*, XLIX (October 7, 1946), 7.

"The Rise of the Social Service State," *Scholastic*, XLIX (October 14, 1946), 7.

"The Challenge to Labor's Political Role," *New York Times Magazine*, October 20, 1946, 17 ff.

"Family Squabble in the Cabinet," *Scholastic*, XLIX (October 21, 1946), 7.

"The Supreme Court and the Bill of Rights," *Scholastic*, XLIX (October 28, 1946), 7.

"This Year We Elect Congress," *Scholastic*, XLIX (November 4, 1946), 7.

"Armistice Day: Lest We Forget," *Scholastic*, XLIX (November 11, 1946), 8.

"Government by Generals," *Scholastic*, XLIX (November 18, 1946), 7.

"The Policy of the Good Neighbor," *Scholastic*, XLIX (November 25, 1946), 7.

"The Nineteenth-Century American," *Atlantic Monthly*, CLXXVIII (December, 1946), 71–78.

"The American Middle Way," *Scholastic*, XLIX (December 2, 1946), 11.

"1846, Year of Wonder," *Scholastic*, XLIX (December 9, 1946), 7.

"Swapping Horses in Midstream," *Scholastic*, XLIX (January 6, 1947), 10.

"Texas Centenary," *Scholastic*, XLIX (January 7, 1947), 8.

"Uncle Sam Says Don't," *Scholastic*, XLIX (January 13, 1947), 7.

"Zigzag of Tariffs," *Scholastic*, XLIX (January 20, 1947), 7.

"Two Terms for Presidents," *Scholastic*, L (February 3, 1947), 11.

"Edison: Typical American," *Scholastic*, L (February 10, 1947), 13.

"Uncle Sam's Good Deed," *Scholastic*, L (February 17, 1947), 8–9.

"Legislating Loyalty," *Scholastic*, L (February 24, 1947), 7.

"Generals in Politics," *Scholastic*, L (March 3, 1947), 7.

"America's Apple Man," *Scholastic*, L (March 10, 1947), 7.

"The Rise and Decline of the British Empire," *Scholastic*, L (March 24, 1947), 7.

"Presidential Succession," *Scholastic*, L (March 31, 1947), 7.

"Washington Witch-hunt," *Nation*, CLXIV (April 5, 1947), 385–388; also in *Freedom and Order* (see Book Section), 73–77.

"The Truman Doctrine," *Scholastic*, L (April 7, 1947), 7.

"Railroads: The Cement of America," *Scholastic*, L (April 14, 1947), 34.

"Only Two Terms for President?" *New York Times Magazine*, April 27, 1947, 13 ff.

"Mormons and the Founding of Utah," *Scholastic*, L (April 28, 1947), 11.

"The Changing American Family," *Scholastic*, L (May 5, 1947), 7.

"Turning Point for Labor," *Scholastic*, L (May 12, 1947), 7.

"What Is American?" *Scholastic*, L (May 19, 1947), 20.

"Memoirs: The Personal Touch," *New York Times Book Review*, August 3, 1947, 1 ff.

"Who Is Loyal to America?" *Harper's Magazine*, CLXLV (September, 1947), 193–199.

"Yardstick for a Presidential Candidate," *New York Times Magazine*, October 5, 1947, 7 ff.

"The American Religious Scene," *Nineteenth Century and After*, CXLIII (January, 1948), 13–20.

"America in World Affairs," *Scholastic*. 1947: LI (September 15), 7; (September 22), 10; (September 29), 7; (October 6), 7; (October 13), 10; (October 20), 9; (November 3), 7; (November 10), 9; (November 17), 7; (December 1), 9; (December 8), 16; (December 15), 10. 1948: LI (January 5), 9; (January 12), 16; (January 19), 9; LII (February 9), 9 ff.; (March 1), 9; (March 8), 9 ff.; (March 15), 9; (March 22), 9; (April 5), 10; (April 12), 10; (April 19), 8; (April 26), 9; (May 3), 10; (May 10), 18; (May 17), 9 ff.; (May 24), 12.

"The American Architect," *Nineteenth Century and After*, CXLIII (April, 1948), 212–221.

"Return to Howells," *Spectator*, CLXXX (May 28, 1948), 642.

"English Traits: One Hundred Years Later," *Nineteenth Century and After*, CXLIV (July, 1948), 1–10; Reprinted in *Atlantic Monthly*, CLXXXII (August, 1948), 61–65.

"Should We Outlaw the Communist Party?" *New York Times Magazine*, August 28, 1948, 7 ff.

"Super: This Must Go In! Editing the St. Nicholas Anthology," *Publisher's Weekly*, CLIV (October 30, 1948), 1874–1877.

"American Political Parties," *Parliamentary Affairs*, III (Winter, 1949), 214–225.

"Portrait of the American," in *Years of the Modern*, ed., John W. Chase, New York: Longmans, Green, 1949, 3–34.

"Analysis of the American Character," *New York Times Magazine*, January 2, 1949, 5 ff.

"My Country Store," *Scholastic*, LIV (March 16, 1949), 9.

"The American Character," *Nineteenth Century and After*, CXLV (April, 1949), 199–206.

"Appraisal of the Welfare State," *New York Times Magazine*, May 15, 1949, 10 ff.

"Children's Books Yesterday and Today," *Nation*, CLXVIII (May 21, 1949), 586–587.

"Further Word on the Filibuster," *Survey*, LXXXV (June, 1949), 319.

"Real Danger: Fear of Ideas," *New York Times Magazine*, June 26, 1949, 7 ff.

"Red-Baiting in the Colleges," *New Republic*, CXXI (July 25, 1949), 10–13; also in *Freedom and Order*, 78–85.

"American History in Literature," *Scholastic*, 1949: LV (September 21), 18–19; (November 9), 12–13; (November 30), 16–17.

"The Cult of the Irrational in American Literature," *Nineteenth Century and After*, CXLVI (October, 1949), 245–250.

"Traditionalism in American Literature," *Nineteenth Century and After*, CXLVI (November, 1949), 311–326.

"What Ideas Are Safe?" *Saturday Review of Literature*, XXXII (November 5, 1949), 20–21; also in *Freedom and Order*, 86–90.

"Yesterday's Youngsters—and Today's," *New York Times Book Review: Children's Section*, November 13, 1949, 4.

"1900–1950: From Victorian to Atomic Age," *New York Times Magazine*, December 25, 1949, 3–7 ff.

"Five Great Problems of the New Half-Century," *New York Times Magazine*, January 1, 1950, 3 ff.

"American History in Literature," *Scholastic*, 1950: LV (January 4), 14–15; LVI (February 1), 10–11; (February 22), 10–11; (March 22), 8–9; (April 19), 12–13; (May 10), 12–13; LVII (October 4), 16–17; (October 18), 16–17; (November 8), 14–15; (November 29), 12–13.

"What Is The Matter With America's Schools?" *Bulletin of America's Forum of the Air*, XIII (1950), 1–12.

"The American Political Party," *American Scholar*, XIX (Summer, 1950), 309–316.

"War and the United States People," *Américas*, II (October, 1950), 1 ff.

"Our Schools Have Kept Us Free," *Life*, XXIX (October 16, 1950), 46–47; abridged in *Journal of the National Education Association*, XL (January, 1951), 18–20; and *Reader's Digest*, LVIII (January, 1951), 119–123.

"The Challenge to the American Character," *New York Times Magazine*, November 26, 1950, 9 ff.

"The Pragmatic Necessity for Freedom," in *Civil Liberties Under Attack*, ed., Clair Wilcox, Philadelphia: University of Pennsylvania Press, 1951, 1–22.

"American History in Literature," *Scholastic*, 1951: LVII (January 3), 10–11; LVIII (February 7), 18–19; (February 28), 10–11; (March 14), 12–13; (April 25), 14–15; (May 16), 10–11.

"Presidential Power: The Issue Analyzed," *New York Times Magazine*, January 14, 1951, 11 ff.

"What the United States Must Do to Implement Current Policy," *Foreign Policy Bulletin*, XXX (January 26, 1951), 1–2.

"Inquiry Into 'Appeasement,'" *New York Times Magazine*, February 11, 1951, 8 ff.; also in *Freedom and Order*, 257–265.

"Does the President Have Too Much Power?" *New York Times Magazine*, April 1, 1951, 15 ff.

"The Acid Test for Our Character," *New York Times Magazine*, April 29, 1951, 12 ff.

"The Declaration Is for Today!" *New York Times Magazine*, July 1, 1951, 5 ff.

"The English Character: An Interpretation," *Saturday Review of Literature*, XXXIV (October 13, 1951), 20–21.

"Common Bonds," *Saturday Review of Literature*, XXXIV (October 13, 1951), 30.

"The Lessons of April 6, 1917," *New York Times Magazine*, April 6, 1952, 13 ff.

"Freedom is a Necessity," *Nation's Schools*, XLIX (June, 1952), 43–46.

"Heroes and Emotions," *United Nations World*, VI (July, 1952), 18–21.

"When Majors Wrote for Minors," *Saturday Review*, XXXV (May 10, 1952), 10–11 ff.

"Was Yalta a Calamity? A Debate," *New York Times Magazine*, August 3, 1952, 7 ff.; also in *Freedom and Order*, 266–275, under title "Yalta Reconsidered."

"Is It the Man or Is It the Issue?" *New York Times Magazine*, October 12, 1952, 13 ff.

"Is Freedom Really Necessary?" *Saturday Review*, XXXVI (February 21, 1953), 11–12 ff; also in *Freedom and Order*, 91–102.

"The Fighting Printer and a Free Press," *New York Times Magazine*, April 19, 1953, 13 ff.

"Yet The Nation Survived," *New York Times Magazine*, July 5, 1953, 5 ff; also in *Freedom and Order*, 178–184.

"Perilous Folly of Senator Bricker," *Reporter*, IX (October 13, 1953), 12–17.

"Joseph Story," in Gaspar G. Bacon Lectures on the Constitution of the United States, 1940–1950. Boston: Boston University Press, 1953, 33–94.

"Guilt and Innocence By Association," *New York Times Magazine*, November 8, 1953, 13 ff.; excerpt in *Bulletin of the Atomic Scientists*, X (March, 1954), 111.

"America's Not So Dubious Battle," *Reporter*, IX (November 24, 1953), 42 ff.

Ethics in Public Life, Felix Adler Lecture, 1954. New York: New York Society for Ethical Culture, 1954.

"The Nature of American Nationalism," The Gottesman Lectures, University of Uppsala, Sweden in Courtlandt Canby and Nancy E. Gross, eds., *The World of History*, New York: Mentor, 1954, 178–189.

"Maker of History, Writer of History," *Reporter*, X (January 19, 1954), 34–38.

"Ten Guideposts for Our Foreign Policy," *New York Times Magazine*, February 21, 1954, 7 ff.

"The Courage and Common Sense of Elmer Davis," *Reporter*, X (April 13, 1954), 44–45.

"The Open Mind and the Closed Border," *Reporter*, XI (July 6, 1954), 38–39.

"Our Schools and the Climate of Freedom," *National Parent-Teacher*, XLIX (September, 1954), 14–16 ff.

"Dangerous Myths in American Diplomacy," *Reporter*, XI (September 23, 1954), 54–55.

"Why Are We Mad at Teacher?" *Reporter*, XI (October 21, 1954), 39–41.

"States' Rights and Senator Newberger," *Reporter*, XI (December 2, 1954), 42–44.

"Education: For Whom and For What?" with D. W. Brogan, *Bulletin of America's Town Meeting of the Air*, XXI (1955), 1–12.

Federal Centralization and the Press, American Newspaper Guild, Twin Cities Chapter, Minn., Ninth Annual Memorial Lecture, 1955 (n.p.); also in *Freedom and Order*, 118–135.

"The Plight of the Liberals, L. F. Budenz," *American Mercury*, LXXX (April, 1955), 27–32.

"Agenda of Democracy," *Journal of Home Economics*, XLVII (September, 1955), 474–478.

"The Right of Dissent," *Current History*, XXIX (October, 1955), 197–203; also in *Freedom and Order*, 136–145.

"Tests of a Free Society," *Wisconsin Journal of Education*, LXXXVIII (October, 1955), 10–13; reprinted in *Midland Schools*, LXX (October, 1955), 10–11 ff.; *School and Community*, XLII (November, 1955), 14–17; *Kentucky School Journal*, XXXIV (December, 1955), 7–9 ff.; *Michigan Education Journal*, XXXIII (May, 1956), 422–425; excerpts printed in *Arizona Teacher*, XLIV (December, 1955), 12–13 ff.

"Perilous Delusions of Security," Reporter, XIII (November 3, 1955), 32–35.

"How It All Looked to Mr. Truman," Reporter, XIII (December 1, 1955), 42–45.

"Tom Paine Talks Back to Providence," Saturday Review, XXXVIII (December 24, 1955), 5–7 ff.; also in Freedom and Order, 103–109.

"The American Character," (London) Times Literary Supplement, XXVII–XXVIII (January 6, 1956), 2810.

"Franklin Still Speaks to Us," New York Times Magazine, January 15, 1956, 19 ff.

"The Problem Isn't Bricks, It's Brains," New York Times Magazine, January 29, 1956, 11 ff.

"Ideas, Ideas and Inspiration," Library Journal, LXXXI (February 1, 1956), 326–329.

"The American Tradition," Collier's, CXXXVII (April 27, 1956), 21.

"Why Almost Half of Us Don't Vote," New York Times Magazine, October 28, 1956, 14 ff.

"Should the United Nations Expel Aggressors?" Foreign Policy Bulletin, XXXVI (December 15, 1956), 49–50.

"The United States and the Integration of Europe," in European Integration, ed., Charles Grove Haines. Baltimore: Johns Hopkins University Press, 1957, 262–278; also in Freedom and Order, 53–69.

"If Only We Wouldn't Talk So Much!" Reporter, XVII (August 8, 1957), 52–54.

"Where Government May Not Trespass," New York Times Magazine, November 24, 1957, 30 ff.

"A Nation of Travelers: An Editorial," Saturday Review, XLI (January 11, 1958), 24 ff.

"A Historian Looks at the American High School," School Review, LXVI (Spring, 1958), 1–18.

"Victims of Success," Saturday Review, XLI (May 3, 1958), 12–14 ff.

"Jefferson and the Book-Burners," American Heritage, IX (August, 1958), 65–68.

"Noah Webster, 1758–1958," Saturday Review, XLI (October 18, 1958), 10–12 ff.

"The Constitution: Was It An Economic Document?" American Heritage, X (December, 1958), 58–61 ff.

"Telling the Story of the Revolution," (with Richard B. Morris), Saturday Review, XLI (December 27, 1958), 9–10 ff.

"Transition in Education," in Annual Schoolmen's Week Proceedings, Education in Transition, ed., Frederick C. Gruber, Philadelphia: University of Pennsylvania Press, 1959, 11–18.

"History Should Tell a Story," Senior Scholastic, LXXIV (March 13, 1959), 9–10.

"The United States in 1970, Three Forecasts," *New York Times Magazine*, May 17, 1959, 76.

"Brave World of the Year 2000," *New York Times Magazine*, November 1, 1959, 24 ff.

"Quantity and Quality in Higher Education," in *Education in Free Society*, Pitcairn-Crabbe Lecture, ser. 2, Vol. II, Pittsburgh: University of Pittsburgh Press, 1960, 1–26.

"Urgent Query: Why Do We Lack Statesmen?" *New York Times Magazine*, January 17, 1960, 21 ff.

"Is Ivy Necessary?" *Saturday Review*, XLIII (September 17, 1960), 69–70 ff.

"Big Lesson from a Small Nation," *New York Times Magazine*, October 2, 1960, 16–17 ff.

"Jefferson Was Only Thirty-three When—," *New York Times Magazine*, October 23, 1960, 18 ff.; also in *Freedom and Order*, 200–205, under title "Presidential Age—And Youth."

"Washington Would Have Lost A TV Debate," *New York Times Magazine*, October 30, 1960, 13 ff.; also in *Freedom and Order*, 194–199, under title "Television and the Elections."

"Jane Addams: 1860–1960," *Saturday Review*, XLIII (December 24, 1960), 26–27.

"The Study of Immigration," in *Immigration and American History Essays in Honor of Theodore C. Blegen*, Minneapolis: The University of Minnesota Press, 1961, 3–7.

"Wayfaring Scholars," *Saturday Review*, XLIV (February 18, 1961), 56–57.

"Cost of College, Who Should Pay?" *New York Times Magazine*, February 26, 1961, 11 ff.

"Give the Games Back to the Students," *New York Times Magazine*, April 16, 1961, 27 ff.

"We Have Changed, and Must," *New York Times Magazine*, April 30, 1961, 10 ff.; also in *Freedom and Order*, 238–245, under title "Change in History."

"Quarter Century: Its Advances," *Look*, XXV (June 6, 1961), 80.

"Our Declaration Is Still A Rallying Cry," *New York Times Magazine*, July 2, 1961, 5 ff.; also in *Freedom and Order*, 171–177.

"Do We Have A Class Society?" *Virginia Quarterly Review*, XXXVII (Fall, 1961), 548–557; also in *Freedom and Order*, 215–223.

"She Has Seen Dark Days Before," *New York Times Magazine*, October 8, 1961, 11; abridged under title "There Will Always Be An England," *Reader's Digest*, LXXX (January, 1962), 153–156.

Our Schools Have Kept Us Free (Washington: Music Educators National Conference [National Education Ass.]), 1962.

"Leadership in Eighteenth-Century America and Today," in *Excellence and Leadership in a Democracy*, eds., Stephen R. Graubard and Gerald Holton, New York: Columbia University Press, 1962, 25–46; also in *Freedom and Order*, 149–170.

"McGuffey and His Readers," *Saturday Review*, XLV (June 16, 1962), 50–51 ff.

"The Second War of American Independence," *New York Times Magazine*, June 17, 1962, 15–16 ff.

"Government and the Arts," *Freedom and Order*, 225–237.

"His Eye On The Eagle," *Saturday Review*, XLVI (January 19, 1963), 35–36.

"To Form a Much Less Perfect Union," *New York Times Magazine*, July 14, 1963, 5 ff.; also in *Freedom and Order*, 185–193.

"How the Lost Cause Was Lost," *New York Times Magazine*, August 4, 1963, 10–11 ff.

"Passport Barrier: It Must Come Down," *New York Times Magazine*, October 20, 1963, 12 ff.; also in *Freedom and Order*, 110–117, under title "Freedom and the Right to Travel."

"The Case Against the Republicans," *New York Times Magazine*, January 12, 1964, 9 ff.; also in *Freedom and Order*, 206–212, under title "The Republican Party Repudiates its History."

"The Ambiguous American," *New York Times Magazine*, May 3, 1964, 16 ff.; also in *Freedom and Order*, 246–254.

"Is Freedom an Academic Question?" *Saturday Review*, XLVII (June 20, 1964), 54–56.

"The Search for a Useable Past," *American Heritage*, XVI (February, 1965), 4–9 ff.

"Why History," *American Education*, I (June, 1965), 26–29.

"A Historian Looks at Our Political Morality," *Saturday Review*, XLVIII (July 10, 1965), 16–18; also in *Freedom and Order*, 279–285.

"Vietnam: A Debate. The Problem of Dissent," *Saturday Review*, XLVIII (December 18, 1965), 21–23, 81; in *Freedom and Order*, 286–294.

"Should the Historian Make Moral Judgments?" *American Heritage*, XVII (February, 1966), 26–27 ff.

"Should Historians Write Contemporary History?" *Saturday Review*, XLIX (February 12, 1966), 18–20 ff.

"Debate on Vietnam Policy," *Massachusetts Review*, VII (Spring, 1966), 412–419.

"Our Vietnamese Commitment," *Diplomat*, XVII (June, 1966), 23–24 ff.; also in *Freedom and Order*, 295–304.

"Television: The Medium in Search of Its Character," *TV Guide*, XIV (June 25, 1966), 6–10.

"The Nature of Academic Freedom," *Saturday Review*, XLIX (August 27, 1966), 13–15, 37.

"Can We Control the War in Vietnam?" *Saturday Review*, XLIX (September 17, 1966), 25–27.

INTRODUCTIONS

James Bryce. *Reflections on American Institutions*, selections from *The American Commonwealth*. Greenwich, Conn.: Fawcett, 1961.

Contemporary Civilization. Chicago: Scott, Foresman, 1961.

Chester Bowles. *Conscience of a Liberal*. Evanston, Ill.: Harper and Row, 1962.

William Dean Howells. *The Rise of Silas Lapham*. New York: Limited Editions Club, 1961.

Contributors

RICHARD B. MORRIS is Gouverneur Morris Professor of History, Columbia University

ALLAN NEVINS is De Witt Clinton Professor Emeritus of American History, Columbia University, and Senior Associate, The Huntington Library

LEONARD W. LEVY is Earl Warren Professor of Constitutional History, Brandeis University

MILTON CANTOR is Professor of History, University of Massachusetts

WILSON SMITH is Professor of History, University of California at Davis

JOHN D. WRIGHT, JR. is Professor of History, Transylvania College

AUGUST MEIER is Professor of History, Kent State University

HAROLD M. HYMAN is Professor of History, University of Illinois

MARIAN McKENNA is Professor of History, University of Calgary

ARTHUR W. THOMPSON (died 1965) was Professor of History, University of Florida

SAUL BENISON is Adjunct Professor of History, Brandeis University

CHARLES E. LARSEN is Professor of History, Mills College

WILLIAM E. LEUCHTENBURG is Professor of History, Columbia University

Index

400